SUBLIME
AND GROTESQUE

SUBLIME
AND GROTESQUE

a study of
FRENCH ROMANTIC DRAMA

W. D. HOWARTH
Professor of Classical French Literature
University of Bristol

HARRAP LONDON

First published in Great Britain 1975
by GEORGE G. HARRAP & CO. LTD.
182–184 High Holborn, London WC1V 7AX

© *W. D. Howarth* 1975

ISBN 0 245 52661 7

Printed in Great Britain by
Western Printing Services Ltd, Bristol

Contents

Contents

Appendix

Illustrations

Acknowledgements

MY principal debt is to those scholars whose works have been invaluable sources of factual information about the rich background of theatre history in the period under review. Maurice Descotes's *Le Drame romantique et ses grands créateurs* has been especially useful (and how very much more useful still it would have been if it had contained an Index!); and I have also found the late Robert Baldick's *Life and Times of Frédérick Lemaître*, M. Carlson's *Theatre of the French Revolution* and H. F. Collins's *Talma: a Biography of an Actor* extremely helpful. I should like to express my thanks to Mme Sylvie Chevalley for her kindness in answering queries about the repertory of the Comédie-Française; to the library staffs of the Taylorian Library, Oxford, and the Wills Memorial Library, Bristol; to Gordon Kelsey of the Arts Faculty Photographic Unit, University of Bristol; to Dorothy Bjørnerud, Joyce Ferrier, and Liliane Stunt for their willing and efficient typing assistance; and finally to my wife for her patient help with Appendices, Index, and proofs.

W.D.H.

Introduction

IT is not only outside France that French Romantic drama has suffered from academic neglect: French, as well as foreign, scholars have always been reluctant to take a serious interest in it, and in fact there exists no thorough and adequate critical study of the subject as a whole. Recent years have, it is true, brought monographs on limited aspects of Romantic drama, and studies of individual authors—though it is only Musset, among the playwrights of this generation, who seems to have received the serious attention befitting a major writer—and, of course, critical editions and *éditions scolaires* are available of a number of individual plays[1]. But although, to put it at its lowest level, this is regarded as a subject of some importance in both literary and theatrical history, even by those who would concede little intrinsic merit of a lasting nature to any of the plays concerned, nevertheless university and sixth-form teachers, in this country at any rate, have long been conscious that there is no really satisfactory 'étude d'ensemble' to which students can be referred. Of works published in the last twenty years Maurice Descotes's *Le Drame romantique et ses grands créateurs*[2], though an admirable work in its particular field—that of theatre history— does not pretend to offer a critical study of Romantic drama; Robert Baldick's *Life and Times of Frédérick Lemaître*[3], while giving a very lively and well-informed account of the Parisian theatrical scene, is essentially a literary biography; and A. Brun's *Deux Proses de théâtre*[4], which does provide a very perceptive critical study of dramatic works of the period, concentrates exclusively on a stylistic approach, and deals only with those plays written in prose; while of the latest works, *A Stage for Poets* by C. Affron[5] and *The French Stage in the Nineteenth Century* by Marvin Carlson[6], one limits its survey to a small selection of the works of Hugo and Musset, and the other again studies theatrical history, not dramatic literature.

To some extent, this academic neglect of the subject[7] matches the state of affairs existing within the theatre in France; though here again, Musset stands apart from his contemporaries. His one-act *proverbes* continue to be favourite curtain-raisers at the Comédie-Française; his more substantial comedies are regularly played; and there have even been distinguished productions of *Lorenzaccio*. But the fortunes of Hugo, Vigny and Dumas have been much less bright. Although certain plays like *Chatterton* and *Ruy Blas* have remained on the repertory and have been produced from time to time, one has the impression that this is more out of a spirit of piety towards literary 'classics' than from a real conviction of the permanent merits of these plays as living theatre[8]. Outside the national theatres, there was a very successful production of Dumas's *Kean* (in Sartre's adaptation, with Pierre Brasseur in the leading role) in Paris in the mid-1950s; *Marie Tudor* was performed by the Théâtre National Populaire in 1955; and one could count a handful of scattered provincial revivals of plays of the period. But it would hardly be an exaggeration to say that the drama of the quarter-century that we term the Romantic period is largely *terra incognita* even to those playgoers who are well versed in both the classical repertory and the works of the contemporary *avant-garde*[9].

This widespread neglect of the playwrights of the Romantic period, both by the academic world and by the professional theatre, is perhaps to be seen as resulting from the combination of two tendencies, neither of them very new, in the history of French cultural taste. The first, which seems to have become increasingly apparent in the post-war years, is a general lack of sympathy for the Romantic in literature on the part of the reading public. The taste of the mid-twentieth century runs to something subtler and yet more down-to-earth, something less ingenuous in its self-absorption, than is shown by the typical writing of the Romantic age, so that the lyric poetry of the period, as well as the *roman personnel*, have experienced the same sort of disfavour as has overtaken Romantic drama. Though it is true that academic fashion does not necessarily follow the tastes of a cultured reading public, it would seem that the naive introspection shown by the Lamartine of 'Le Lac', the Musset of 'Les Nuits' and the Vigny of 'La Maison du berger' is no more popular with present-day readers than are Romantic heroes like Chatterton, Didier or Antony with present-day playgoers and producers. Where authors of the period have retained, or regained, a wider appeal it is because, like Constant or Stendhal, they preserve a late-eighteenth-century astringency of style, or develop a subtlety in psychological analysis which looks forward beyond the Romantic period; or else because, like Nerval (and the *German* Romantics), they look forward to the much profounder and more rewarding soul-searchings of Baudelaire and later poets.

The second factor is that within the practical theatre, particularly the 'official' theatre represented by the Comédie-Française and (until quite recently) the Odéon, the dramatic works of the Romantic generation have shared in the disfavour traditionally shown to almost all the plays of the eighteenth and nineteenth centuries except for those of Marivaux and Beaumarchais. Only these two playwrights (and perhaps Musset, to the extent to which he is unrepresentative of 'Romantic' tendencies in the theatre) have remained on the repertory alongside the three giants of the seventeenth century. Otherwise, it is impossible to list more than a small handful of works (one thinks of *La Dame aux camélias*, or *Cyrano de Bergerac*; and there has recently been a distinct vogue for some of Feydeau's comedies) that can be regarded as permanent features of the active repertory—though they have now been joined there by the major works of Claudel, Giraudoux, Montherlant, and other modern dramatists. The 'polarization' of the reputation of the plays and playwrights of the past—the great on one side, the dead museum-pieces on the other—is a remarkable feature of French theatrical history: whatever its causes—the very real pre-eminence of Corneille, Molière and Racine, coupled with excessively conservative tendencies among management, actors and public at the Comédie-Française, where the classical has always been preferred to other forms of drama—the effect is that not only the Romantic dramatists, but also such important 'minor classics' among the playwrights of the past as Rotrou, Dancourt, and even Voltaire, have been consigned by the passage of time to a sort of limbo from which they are seldom if ever revived.

It would be easy to make an exaggerated claim for the merits of French Romantic drama. Obviously, a genuine masterpiece will succeed in imposing itself on a nation's repertory, in spite of the vagaries of literary fashions, and in spite of conservative tradition in the theatre; and none of these plays (apart perhaps from *Lorenzaccio*) is a masterpiece, judged by absolute standards. However, some plays of the period possess qualities that would justify at any rate the occasional revival: not necessarily those that were most successful at the time, since as M. Descotes has shown[10], the success or failure of particular plays in the 1830s was determined to a considerable extent by such factors as political censorship, hostile 'claques', and the author's personal relationships with managers, actors and actresses. My own predilections would be in favour of *Marion de Lorme* among Hugo's plays—not an outstanding success when it was first produced, by any means—and Dumas's *Antony*. Whatever faults these plays may embody—crudity of certain effects, a lack of subtlety all too common in the theatre of the period—both of them suggest to the reader a strong theatrical appeal, and the ability to express emotions through the medium of truly dramatic writing. It is true that the Romantic hero became a rather predictable stereotype, but among the embodiments of this type in the theatre, Didier and Antony stand out, for me at any rate, as both memorable and credible, and I should expect these two plays to be capable of producing a powerful effect in the theatre.

At the time when they were first produced, Hugo's plays shocked by their lack of unity of tone and their offences against 'good taste'; and much of the critical disfavour shown to them in academic circles surely derives from the pervasive influence of so-called 'Lansonian' positivism which placed far too much emphasis on the appeal to reason[11]. In most other fields, this excessively rationalistic attitude towards imaginative writing is now discredited, in favour of a critical approach which looks for evidence of an individual imagination at work, and is prepared to allow for touches of fantasy, however arbitrary; while in the theatre itself, an audience of the 1970s, attuned to the Theatre of Cruelty and the Theatre of the Absurd, would hardly cavil at some of the shocks and surprises which so disturbed contemporaries of Hugo and Dumas.

On the other hand, it has become fashionable in our own day to denigrate the purely literary attributes of drama, in favour of those non-literary factors which make for theatrical spectacle. While it is evident that no play can succeed on the stage without certain theatrical qualities, it is equally clear that pure spectacle is bound to be ephemeral, and that no play can either impose itself on the contemporary public, or retain an interest for posterity, if it lacks genuine literary qualities of content or style. Among the 8,000 or more plays produced during the period 1826–50, the vast majority represent merely the ephemeral 'journalism' of the theatre; but there were plays which stood out from this mass in the eyes of contemporaries. Whether because of their authors' literary ambitions, or because they were written in conformity with an explicit aesthetic credo; whether they brought to life in memorable artistic form a period of the past, or presented in a challenging manner some contemporary social issue, it is the plays with a recognizably 'literary' character which have retained an interest for posterity, and it is these plays which represent for us today the corpus of 'Romantic drama'. The present book attempts to show how the social and literary climate of the Romantic period, as well as material conditions in the theatres of the time, helped to create such plays, and to suggest why some of them were more successful than others. At the same time, it goes beyond this purely historical approach, and attempts a critical evaluation, giving due weight to considerations of a theatrical, as well as of a literary, order.

I am not arguing for the complete rehabilitation of the work of the Romantic playwrights; it is not a case of rescuing from undeserved neglect outstanding contributions to the world's stock of dramatic masterpieces. However, I believe that to apply to these authors and their plays the sort of critical approach that is now generally taken for granted in dealing with works of other periods should at least lead to a fuller understanding and a more equitable appreciation of the work of a group of young playwrights whose vigorous and controversial creative activity gives them a significant place in the history of French drama.

Notes to Introduction

1. The full-scale critical editions of *Chatterton* by L. Petroni (Bologna, 1962) and of *Ruy Blas* by A. Ubersfeld (Vol. I, Besançon and Paris, 1971) are in a class apart; but mention should also be made of P. Dimoff, *La Genèse de Lorenzaccio*,

Geneva, 1936, which contains a critical edition of Musset's play alongside the texts of its principal sources, as well as of a critical edition of Balzac's theatre by R. Guise (3 vols., Paris, 1969–71).

2. Paris, P.U.F., n.d. (1955).

3. London, 1959.

4. Gap, 1954.

5. Princeton, N.J., 1971.

6. Metuchen, N.J., 1972.

7. Among exceptions to this generalization, mention must be made of the issue of the periodical *Esprit Créateur* devoted to Romantic drama in 1965, which contains several interesting articles. Perhaps the most valuable general study is that by A. Nebout (*Le Drame romantique*, Paris, 1895); it has recently been reprinted (Geneva, 1970).

8. As far as Dumas is concerned, the contents of the special number of *Europe* (February-March 1970) which marked the centenary of his death make it clear that he is known today as a novelist rather than a dramatist. However, this issue does contain excellent articles on the playwright by Mmes Sylvie Chevalley and Annie Ubersfeld; while the 'fortunes' of Dumas at the Comédie-Française have more recently been recorded in *Alexandre Dumas père et la Comédie-Française* by S. Chevalley and F. Bassan (Paris, 1972).

9. For instance, a recent survey of the work of the French provincial drama companies, covering approximately the period 1969–70, shows that the 175 titles recorded (representing the classics of the French repertory, new plays, and translations of foreign works) include only two examples of Romantic drama: Hugo's *Angelo* and Musset's *Le Chandelier*; though two other Hugo titles (*Mangeront-ils?* and *Mille Francs de récompense*) illustrate the occasional (and surely rather perverse) attempt to generate interest in his later 'armchair theatre', while continuing to neglect earlier plays genuinely written for the stage.

10. *Op. cit., passim.*

11. Cf. the pages devoted to Hugo's drama in Lanson's *Histoire de la littérature française*, in which phrases like the following abound: "invraisemblances . . .; la maigreur psychologique de ses personnages . . .; d'une fausseté ridicule . . .; la plus complète inintelligence de la vérité et de la vie . . .; c'est véritablement manquer de sens commun . . .; nulle part l'action n'est vraie, directement tirée de la réalité commune" (Revised edition, Paris, Hachette, n.d., pp. 975ff.).

1   Eighteenth-century Signposts

(i) Sense and sensibility

TRADITIONAL literary history has often misrepresented the nature of the Romantic revolution in the theatre. According to the version put out by the Romantic publicists themselves, there was a sudden, dramatic explosion of new ideas both of form and content; and though there have been studies enough which have investigated the sources and antecedents of the *Préface de Cromwell* and *Hernani*, for instance, they have never quite dispelled certain misconceptions about the place of Romanticism in the history of French drama. The merits of the *Préface* of 1827, and the importance of *Hernani* as a play, as well as of the furore which it aroused, are indisputable; but rather than the beginning of a new era, these represent the culmination of a long and gradual process.

Nearly all of the features generally considered to be characteristic of Romantic drama can be seen to be well represented in the drama, as in other literary genres, of preceding generations. With Voltaire, tragedy had extended its range to include subjects from French national history[1]; in the hands of Voltaire, de Belloy and other eighteenth-century playwrights, it had been made to serve the purposes of patriotic, anti-clerical or democratic propaganda[2]; with Voltaire and his contemporaries, again, it had reflected the intellectual curiosity of the Enlightenment towards civilizations and cultures other than those of Western Europe[3]; while with Diderot and other exponents of 'le drame bourgeois', a serious attempt had been made to mirror the occupations and the preoccupations of the ordinary playgoer[4]. Above all, the 'Romantic sensibility' was not the peculiar prerogative of the playwrights of the 1830s, any more than of the poets of the 1820s. Not only Rousseau's Saint-Preux and Chateaubriand's René, but also the heroes of numerous

tragedies, 'drames' and 'comédies larmoyantes' going right back
to the first half of the eighteenth century, have a recognizable
affinity with Romantic heroes such as Hernani or Chatterton.
However, these eighteenth-century developments were seldom,
if ever, matched by a correspondingly fresh attitude towards
form and language, so that any survey of the drama of this
earlier period from a stylistic point of view must be a predominantly critical one. The sensibility of the eighteenth
century in many ways looks forward to and helps to prepare the
aesthetic and moral climate of the Romantic generation[5]: the
Man of Feeling had already come into being in the early
eighteenth century; but lack of inventiveness with regard to
dramatic forms and linguistic conventions meant that he was
still forced to express himself in a manner which inhibited the
spontaneous display of his feelings.

Eighteenth-century sensibility is a phenomenon which can
be recognized throughout the art and the literature of the age,
but which proves elusive when one tries to pin it down and
define it. It is not, of course, that the feelings of the eighteenth-
century Frenchman were essentially different from those of
his seventeenth-century counterpart, but there was a definite
reaction against the priorities, as it were, which education,
training and convention had imposed on the previous century:

Le xviie siècle ne vit guère par les sens ou, plus exactement,
sa littérature n'exprime pas la sensation directe, et, restant
intellectuelle, n'exprime pas l'art entier; elle distingue entre
les arts nés de la sensation et les arts nés des aspirations de
l'âme, et s'en tient aux seconds.[6]

Sensations exist, even in the context of seventeenth-century art
and literature, but they are not allowed any great value in
themselves: it is the task of the artist to subordinate to more
permanent truths of a moral or spiritual nature those spontaneous and ephemeral phenomena which Corneille's Pauline
calls "Ces surprises des sens que la raison surmonte"[7]. The
literature of the new century produced a reversal of these
priorities: spontaneous feeling acquired an importance in its
own right, sensations were self-consciously analysed, and if
needs be provoked, in order to provide material for such analysis.

It was not a purely French phenomenon, though the transition was more sudden and more pronounced in France than elsewhere. Trahard rejects Lanson's over-intellectual analysis of the causes, according to which "la vieille galanterie française, la philosophie sensualiste, l'esprit d'analyse scientifique, le scepticisme religieux et la corruption des mœurs" combined to produce "la sensibilité, sorte de mysticisme laïque à l'usage de mathématiciens libertins"[8]. He sees it rather as dependent on the relaxation of various repressive forces in society at the end of the reign of Louis XIV, which allowed a freer rein to something hitherto held in check[9]. Whatever the reasons, eighteenth-century Frenchmen soon came to expect a work of art to provide the sort of direct stimulus to sensual feeling that had been denied them by the literature and other art-forms of the previous fifty years or more. In the theatre, this change in public taste had a very pronounced effect: whereas in the case of more private kinds of writing the expression of feelings was on the whole more spontaneous, and therefore less contrived, and the reactions of the reader more sincere, the reactions of the spectator in the theatre were influenced by the pressure of fashion. The public display of emotion became the order of the day, and playwrights catered for this new taste by means that were inevitably calculated rather than restrained.

According to Trahard, it was not until 1730 or thereabouts that these new attitudes imposed themselves on the writers and artists of the time: ". . . le moment où l'abbé Prévost, Marivaux et Voltaire publient *Manon Lescaut, La Vie de Marianne* et *Zaïre*; alors, la sensibilité française, qui s'est éveillée dès 1720 avec les premières comédies de Marivaux, devient assez forte pour créer une forme d'art originale"[10]. However, this seems to be rather conservative dating: in tragedy, at least, 'originality' of this sort seems to have manifested itself a good deal earlier than the date (1732) of the example quoted, that of Voltaire's *Zaïre*. The simplest way of describing the kinds of tragedy written to cater for the taste of the new age is to say that in Aristotelian terms they cease to be tragic: the two ingredients of pity and fear no longer combine to produce Aristotle's finely balanced catharsis, but are separated and pushed to the extremes, respectively, of a much more superficial pathos and a much more arbitrary horror. Instead of the genuine tragic hero whose error or fault brings about his downfall in spite of his admirable qualities, we have something approaching the black-and-white characteriza-tion of melodrama. Like all generalizations, of course, this goes too far: a hero like Orosmane in *Zaïre*, modelled on Othello, remains very much in the Aristotelian mould. However, even in this play Zaïre herself more typically exemplifies the blame-less heroine, victim of the prejudices and passions of others.

It is the name of Crébillon which more than any other is identified with the 'blood-and-thunder' tendency in eighteenth-century tragedy. And from a very early date, too: his first play, *Idoménée*, of 1705, opens with a couplet which sets the tone of his most characteristic writing for the theatre:

> Où suis-je? Quelle horreur m'épouvante et me suit?
> Quel tremblement, o ciel! et quelle affreuse nuit!

Basically, shorn of some of Crébillon's own complications, the plot is that of the King of Crete who, to save his life in a storm, promises the gods to sacrifice the life of the first of his subjects he meets when he sets foot on dry land, and then finds that this is his son: a clear polarization of the two main characters into guilty agent and pathetic victim. The legend of Atreus and Thyestes provided an equally clear case, that of the man who avenges his brother's seduction of his wife by killing his brother's children and serving them up to him in a pie. Crébillon strength-ens our revulsion from Atrée by imagining a gap of twenty years between the offence and the act of vengeance; he also reduces the children to a single son, Plisthène, now a youth of twenty, who fills the role of innocent victim; he throws in the theme of threatened incest in order to add spice to the mixture; and he does not neglect the 'scène à faire', the recognition-scene between Plisthène (who has grown up thinking Atrée was his father) and his real father Thyeste. This is preceded by the 'cri du sang', which was to become a more or less obligatory prelude to any recognition-scene:

> De noirs pressentiments viennent m'épouvanter;
> Je sens à chaque instant que mes craintes redoublent;
> Que pour vous en secret mes entrailles se troublent:
> Je combats vainement de si vives douleurs:
> Un pouvoir inconnu me fait verser des pleurs. (IV, iii)

It seems that Plisthène is going to be forced to kill his own father; but this, like the threatened incest, is merely to titillate the audience's taste for strong sensation, and the proprieties must finally be observed at all costs:

> Tout semblait réserver dans un jour si funeste
> Ma main au parricide et mon cœur à l'inceste. (IV, iv)

Crébillon's most celebrated tragedy was *Rhadamiste et Zénobie* (1711), and it is this play which provides the best illustration of his cliché-like use of 'sensational' vocabulary. Moreover, whereas in an author like Racine the use of such emotively-charged words as *fureur, transport, horreur, cruel, affreux*, is almost always justified by their placing at an emotional climax, carefully prepared and standing out in intensity from the rest of the dialogue, matters are very different with Crébillon. The highest density in any single scene in *Rhadamiste* is in an expository scene—Act II, scene i—in which the hero appears for the first time and introduces himself to his confidant; this is his opening speech:

> Hiéron, plût aux dieux que la main ennemie
> Qui me ravit le sceptre eût terminé ma vie.
> Mais le ciel m'a laissé, pour prix de ma fureur,
> Des jours qu'il a tissus de tristesse et d'horreur.
> Loin de faire éclater ton zèle ni ta joie
> Pour un roi malheureux que le sort te renvoie,
> Ne me regarde plus que comme un furieux,
> Trop digne du courroux des hommes et des dieux;
> Qu'a proscrit dès longtemps la vengeance céleste;
> De crimes, de remords assemblage funeste;
> Indigne de la vie et de ton amitié;
> Objet digne d'horreur, mais digne de pitié;
> Traître envers la nature, envers l'amour perfide;
> Usurpateur ingrat, parjure, parricide.
> Sans les remords affreux qui déchirent mon cœur,
> Hiéron, j'oublierais qu'il est un ciel vengeur.

With such an extravagant and improvident attitude to language, the coinage soon becomes debased, and the climax is deprived of any force it might have had.

Crébillon was not alone in this fault of tending to rely on self-portraits: many of the authors of the imitative 'comédies de caractère' of the period portray their heroes in a similar way. The true dramatist works differently: he knows the value of the art of preparation, and learns how to make his characters reveal their true natures by their actions, not by a static self-portrait. The self-portrait smacks too much of the villain of melodrama letting the audience into his confidence, and is a poor substitute for really dramatic character-portrayal. *Rhadamiste* is in fact a frenzied melodrama, rather poorly versified; but it was evidently what the public wanted, for it not only had a good run of 33 performances in 1711, but remained on the repertory until 1829, achieving more performances in this period than *Cinna*, *Polyeucte* or *Mithridate*[11].

Houdard de la Motte showed himself very much in tune with the new mode of feeling when he wrote attacking the tiresome convention of the *récit*: "Combien d'actions que le spectateur voudrait voir, et qu'on lui dérobe sous prétexte de règle, pour ne les remplacer que par des récits insipides en comparaison des actions mêmes"[12]. With themes such as incest and the 'coupe ensanglantée', Crébillon of course had to fall back on the *récit*, in other words to rely on purely *literary* means to create the particular effects of fury and frenzy that he strove after. La Motte, however, and other dramatists who preferred to portray a more domesticated passion in an attempt to move their audience to tears rather than to terror, were much freer to introduce visual aids. Diderot was to advocate the sentimental *tableau* as a powerful aid to dramatic effect some forty years later; but the first sentimental *tableaux* occur in pathetic tragedies such as *Inès de Castro* and *Zaïre*. In the former play Don Pèdre, son of the King of Portugal, has contracted a clandestine marriage with Inès, a commoner. He is sentenced to death for his rebellious refusal to marry a princess of his father's choice; the fact of his love for Inès cannot move his father, nor can the disclosure of their marriage, but the King is persuaded by the appearance of their two small children, and by the touching spectacle of Inès as the mother of his own grandchildren (it is in fact too late: Inès has already been poisoned by the evil Queen, the princess's mother, and the play closes with her death—a powerful ending, but one which stamps *Inès de Castro* as pathetic rather than truly tragic). Again, in *Zaïre* we have the powerful *tableau*, well-loved by contemporary engravers, of the dying Lusignan, just released from half a lifetime of imprisonment by the Saracens, surrounded by his family, and with Zaïre herself, the long-lost daughter he had believed dead, newly restored to him but possibly lost to the true faith: "Mon Dieu qui me la rends, me la rends-tu chrétienne?" (II, iii) There is no doubt that the public was powerfully moved by spectacles such as these, and that they were capable of moving readers as well as spectators; but the Marquis d'Argenson sounds a warning note when he writes, à propos of *Inès de Castro*:

> Tout l'art de l'attendrissement est poussé à la perfection; on la relirait cent fois que c'est toujours avec effusion de larmes. Il faut donc pardonner à quelques faiblesses de poésie en faveur d'un sujet si bien traité: les succès de pièces dramatiques ne viennent pas de la seule versification.[13]

Inès de Castro and *Zaïre* have stood the test of time a good deal better than Crébillon's plays, but even so it is difficult to see in them much more than an interesting indication of the taste of their age: once 'effusion de larmes' had ceased to be quite so fashionable, their literary and dramaturgical merits were not such as to recommend them to new generations of playgoers.

The heroines of La Chaussée's 'comédies larmoyantes' make precisely the same appeal to our sympathy as do Inès and Zaïre: they represent persecuted innocence—though in 'comédie larmoyante' innocence tends to be persecuted by error and misunderstanding rather than by evil. This has one important consequence as regards construction, in that the dénouement can be brought about by conversion to a right way of thinking, by means of example or precept: the dramatist need not resort to the artificial scheming of a valet or the intervention of some *deus ex machina*. Thus in *Mélanide*, a plot of some degree of complication is resolved by a very simple and forceful dénouement. Mélanide, having contracted a 'secret hyménée' eighteen years earlier with the Comte d'Ormancé, had been separated from him at the instance of his family, and has brought up D'Arviane, the fruit of this union, in genteel poverty (he is ignorant of his birth, and thinks Mélanide is his aunt); they

have been befriended by the wealthy Dorisée, whose daughter
Rosalie D'Arviane loves. She returns this love, but her mother
wants to marry her to a far more eligible older suitor, the
Marquis d'Orvigny. The latter is none other than the Comte
d'Ormancé, now succeeded to his father's title; he has searched
for Mélanide for years, but now, thinking her dead, has
abandoned himself to his passion for Rosalie, so that the dis-
covery that Mélanide is alive, far from providing the solution,
only precipitates his moral crisis. The fiery D'Arviane, learning
in Act IV that Mélanide is his mother, guesses that D'Orvigny
is his father, provokes him, and in Act V confronts him with a
challenge; and it is this scene, rather than the more conventional recognition-scene between the boy and his mother, that
is the real 'scène à faire' of the play, providing a sentimental and
moral climax which arouses a genuine *pathétique*:

> ... J'ai cru de faux soupçons: ah! daignez m'excuser:
> Ils étaient trop flatteurs pour ne pas m'abuser.
> On m'avait mal instruit. Rentrons dans ma misère.
> Avant que de sortir de l'erreur la plus chère,
> Et de quitter un nom que j'avais usurpé,
> Vous-même montrez-moi que je m'étais trompé;
> Vous pouvez m'en donner la preuve la plus sûre;
> Je vous ai fait tantôt une assez grande injure;
> En rival furieux, je me suis égaré;
> Si vous ne m'êtes rien, je n'ai rien réparé.
> L'excuse n'a plus lieu. Votre honneur vous engage
> A laver dans mon sang un si sensible outrage.
> Osez donc me punir, puisque vous le devez.
> Vous allez m'arracher Rosalie; achevez,
> Prenez aussi ma vie, elle me désespère.
>
> — Malheureux! Qu'oses-tu proposer à ton père?

The father is converted by an appeal to his sensibility—as one
of the other characters had said earlier: "Il est trop vertueux
pour n'être pas fidèle"—and the play closes with the comforting
formula:

> O ciel! tu me fais voir, en comblant tous mes vœux,
> Que le devoir n'est fait que pour nous rendre heureux!

D'Orvigny is not the only character whose sensibility operates as a moral corrective. In the case of the young hero D'Arviane, it is this that keeps his impetuosity in check, and prevents it from developing into an anti-social individualism. For if his "Plus je sens vivement, plus je sens que je suis" (II, iv) can be seen as the rejoinder of the new Man of Feeling to the 'cogito ergo sum' of his Cartesian predecessors, the Rousseauistic undertones of this affirmation still at this point remain implicit. A century later, Romantic heroes without number, their eyes having been opened to the fact that we do not all feel in the same way, were to base a totally individualistic ethic on just such a proposition; for the time being, La Chaussée and his contemporaries have no difficulty in directing their characters' sensibility into socially acceptable channels—indeed, it is by their sensibility rather than by their rational faculties that they acknowledge the moral imperatives.

It would be wrong to exaggerate La Chaussée's originality. In spite of his obvious attempt, in a play like *Mélanide*, to break away from some of the limitations of traditional 'haute comédie' and to make the moral dilemmas of ordinary people the subject of a serious dramatic work, there is still a big gulf between 'comédie larmoyante' and at any rate the theoretical programme of Diderot's 'drame bourgeois'. Whereas Diderot, and the other writers of 'drames' like Sedaine and Beaumarchais, aimed to produce a detailed copy of the material setting of ordinary life— "transporter au théâtre le salon de Clairville comme il est"[14]— and an equally faithful copy of the speech, mannerisms and gestures of ordinary life, La Chaussée on the contrary is concerned only that the emotional reactions of his characters should resemble those of their real-life counterparts; the setting of his plays remains conventional and indeterminate, and—an even more fundamental difference—he retains the stylized and elevated diction which is so remote from everyday speech[15].

(*ii*) *Poetry and prose*

AS Auerbach has shown in *Mimesis*[16], the chief obstacle to the development of realism in the eighteenth-century French novel was the continued acceptance of the classical hierarchy of literary genres and styles; and the same observation would apply with equal force in the dramatic literature of the period.

Contemporary English authors knew no such inhibitions: Defoe is able to give a far more convincingly lifelike picture of the London of his day in *Moll Flanders* than Prévost can do with the Parisian scenes in *Manon Lescaut,* because he can draw on a wider vocabulary and is not forever striving after the stylistic effects of 'le style noble'. By the same token in the theatre, Lillo's *London Merchant* and Moore's *Gamester,* for all their overt moralizing and excess of sentiment, come much nearer than *Mélanide* to expressing the flavour of real speech. It is not that prose was unacceptable to audiences at the Théâtre-Français; nor is it merely the simple choice of verse rather than prose which matters: La Chaussée evidently not only valued the prestige of the five-act verse comedy, but also preferred the harmonious elegance of 'le style noble' to the less elevated diction of, say, Molière's verse comedies. Incapable of realizing, or reluctant to adopt, the sort of language that would have taken serious comedy a long way in the direction of 'drame bourgeois' by giving it a convincingly *domestic* flavour, he did, however, attempt to augment the *pathetic* appeal of his plays by a deliberate assimilation of some of the stylistic features normally associated with tragedy.

First of all the liberal use of the *sentence,* or moral maxim, that feature taken from Senecan tragedy in the first place, and used with varying degrees of discretion by most dramatists throughout the classical period, helps to give the scenes of discussion in which *Mélanide* abounds a character of sententious generalization; for example:

Répandre ses malheurs, c'est les multiplier...   (IV, i)

On ne hait pas toujours ceux qu'on rend malheureux...
   (V, ii)

On s'embellit encore en voyant ce qu'on aime...   (IV, ii)

or, most weighty of all, from the scene of moral crisis:

Le penchant doit finir où commence le crime. (III, vi)

As regards the general tone of La Chaussée's vocabulary, we have the standard 'noble' imagery of *fers* and *flammes, chaînes* and *feux*; *trépas* even makes its appearance for 'mort'; *le sort* is constantly appealed to; and at moments of crisis we run through the whole gamut of 'tragic' vocabulary:

> ...Dans ce doute affreux, tout se confond en moi,
> Haine, désir, terreur, espoir, amour, effroi.
> Je ne démêle rien dans ce trouble funeste:
> Qui m'en fera sortir? (IV, vi)

The dignified vocabulary of 'le style noble' is matched by a declamatory phrasing also borrowed from the tragic dramatists. Occasionally La Chaussée will experiment with a discreet approach to the 'style entrecoupé' affected by Diderot in his 'drames'; but generally he prefers the more formal effect produced by apostrophe and other rhetorical devices, without departing from a coherent grammatical structure:

> Ah! perfide, arrêtez; c'est l'arrêt de ma mort! (IV, i)

> Ah! Rosalie, hélas! dois-je vivre, ou mourir? (III, iv)

It would be quite wrong to disparage the dramatist's use of these devices. They enable him to achieve a truly pathetic quality, even in rare instances a suggestion of tragic force; what he does not even try to achieve, however, is the portrayal of ordinary people expressing themselves in everyday language. His characters might perhaps be accepted as representative, but when faced with their emotional or moral dilemmas they still express themselves in the same way as the Rodrigues or the Orestes of a century earlier: and this attempt to capture 'le sublime' was evidently more in keeping with contemporary sensibility than any attempt at down-to-earth realism.

It is ironical that Diderot, the champion of realism in the theatre, should make greater use of the convention of the soliloquy than Racine does in any of his tragedies (there are eleven in *Le Fils naturel* and eight in *Le Père de famille*, while none of Racine's plays contains more than seven). He comments that "le monologue est un moment de repos pour l'action, et de trouble pour le personnage"[17], and judged by this criterion the soliloquies in *Le Fils naturel* must show a very apt use of the convention, since they reveal Dorval (nearly all are spoken by him) in a state of prodigious agitation:

> Quel jour d'amertume et de trouble! Quelle variété de tour-ments! Il semble que d'épaisses ténèbres se forment autour de moi, et couvrent ce cœur accablé sous mille sentiments douloureux!... O Ciel, ne m'accorderas-tu pas un moment de repos!... Le mensonge, la dissimulation, me sont en horreur; et dans un instant j'en impose à mon ami, à sa sœur, à Rosalie... Que doit-elle penser de moi?... Que déciderai-je de son amant?... Quel parti prendre avec Constance?... Dorval, cesseras-tu, continueras-tu d'être homme de bien? (III, ix)

Such extravagance is all the more blatant because, in Dr. Peter France's phrase, "the gush is uncontrolled by the formal pattern of the alexandrine"[18]. Even in more restrained passages, where Diderot is no longer striving to reproduce a prose equivalent of Crébillon's frenzied manner, his soliloquies are still modelled on a literary, not a spoken, language:

> Ah, si je pouvais trouver en moi la force de sens et la supério-rité de lumières avec laquelle cette femme s'emparait de mon âme et la dominait, je verrais Rosalie, elle m'entendrait, et Clairville serait heureux... Mais pourquoi n'obtiendrais-je pas sur cette âme tendre et flexible le même ascendant que Constance a su prendre sur moi? Depuis quand la vertu a-t-elle perdu son empire?... Voyons-la, parlons-lui, et espérons tout de la vérité de son caractère et du sentiment qui m'anime. C'est moi qui ai égaré ses pas innocents; c'est moi qui l'ai plongée dans la douleur et dans l'abattement; c'est à moi de lui tendre la main, et à la ramener dans la voie du bonheur. (IV, vii)

These are the rhythms, the rhetorical devices, the sentimental emphasis of Rousseau's purple passages in texts like the *Rêveries* or the *Lettres à Malesherbes*:

> Ce sont là les jours qui ont fait le vrai bonheur de ma vie, bonheur sans amertume, sans ennuis, sans regrets, et auquel j'aurais borné volontiers tout celui de mon existence. Oui, Monsieur, que de pareils jours remplissent pour moi l'éternité,

je n'en demande point d'autres et n'imagine pas que je sois beaucoup moins heureux dans ces ravissantes contemplations que les intelligences célestes.[19]

It is a style from which Diderot's other writings are on the whole refreshingly free, and which he only seems to have felt compelled to adopt when writing for the theatre. Paradoxically, in the 'private theatre' of his philosophical dialogues he succeeds in capturing not only the fascination of a convincing intellectual discussion, but also the spontaneity of real speech. In *Le Fils naturel* and *Le Père de famille*, on the contrary, he shows himself to be a prisoner of the false rhetoric and the sentimental over-emphasis that affected most of the dramatists of his age. A page by Petit de Juleville hits the nail on the head (his examples are all taken from Act IV, scene iii of *Le Fils naturel*):

Un personnage de Diderot ne dit pas : Je suis sans amis. Il dit : « Abandonné presque en naissant entre le désert et la société, quand j'ouvris les yeux afin de reconnaître les liens qui pouvaient m'attacher aux hommes, à peine en trouvai-je des débris ». Il ne dit pas : J'ai songé à me marier. Il dit : « Je ne suis pas étranger à cette pente si générale et si douce qui entraîne les autres êtres et les porte à éterniser leur espèce ». Il ne dit point : L'homme aime naturellement les hommes. Il dit : « Une âme tendre n'envisage point le système général des êtres sensibles sans en désirer fortement le bonheur ».[20]

It is interesting in connection with Diderot's use of language in the theatre to examine his use of stage-directions. On the one hand we find a development of the tendency we have already noted in earlier plays towards the static pictorial tableau, which Diderot explicitly recommends in place of the contrived 'coup de théâtre'[21]; examples are the detailed domestic interior with which *Le Père de famille* opens, or the *larmoyant* tableau at the close of *Le Fils naturel*, in which the aged Lysimond embraces his two children and gives them his blessing. But elsewhere, stage-directions appear to be an acknowledgement of the inadequacy of the author's linguistic resources, as when he writes: "Il pousse l'accent inarticulé du désespoir", or: "Il se renverse dans un fauteuil. Il s'abîme dans la rêverie. Il jette ces mots par intervalles"—where it seems no longer to be physical gesture that is brought in to reinforce speech, but the reverse. A remarkable indication of Diderot's faith in gesture and 'la pantomime' is given in the passage in the *Entretiens* which contains the synopsis of an alternative, 'tragic' ending to *Le Fils naturel*:

> Cet acte s'ouvre par Dorval seul, qui se promène sur la scène, sans rien dire. On voit dans son vêtement, son geste, son silence, le projet de quitter la vie... Clairville n'en arrache que quelques monosyllabes. Le reste de l'action de Dorval est muette... Il se renverse quelquefois sur eux pour pleurer. Mais les larmes se refusent. Alors il se retire; il pousse des soupirs profonds; il fait quelques gestes lents et terribles; on voit sur ses lèvres des mouvements d'un ris passager, plus effrayants que ses soupirs et ses gestes.

And Diderot concludes: "Qu'on lui fasse dire quelques mots par intervalles, cela se peut; mais il ne faut pas oublier qu'il est rare que celui qui parle beaucoup se tue"[22].

If this seems to suggest the playwright in Diderot giving way to the choreographer, he was perceptive enough—and generous enough—to appreciate in the plays of other dramatists the effective writing of which he himself was incapable. It has been said that "*Le Philosophe sans le savoir* est le meilleur ouvrage de Sedaine, et Sedaine est le meilleur ouvrage de Diderot"[23]; and this is a relationship that both writers would surely have been glad to acknowledge. In a letter to Grimm, Diderot pays warm tribute to the naturalness of Sedaine's dialogue: "C'est le naturel sans aucun apprêt, c'est l'éloquence la plus vigoureuse sans l'ombre d'effort ni de rhétorique"[24]. Not that *Le Philosophe sans le savoir* completely eschews the devices—soliloquies, apostrophe, emotive phrasing—that we have seen are common to all these playwrights who aspire to produce a moral effect by sentimental means; but, being a true man of the theatre, Sedaine uses them sparingly. He writes with an altogether easier touch: even in moments of pathos he surprises us by using understatement rather than over-emphasis; and in any case, he does introduce scenes of genuine comic relief, with an appropriately lighter kind of dialogue. If Sedaine's plea against duelling is put across by an appeal to the audience's sensibility —we are made to feel not only indignation, but also distress, at the havoc that this barbarous custom can wreak with a happy family life—the other theme of the play, the attack on the 'préjugé nobiliaire', is presented by traditional comic means, and the snobbish aunt is a purely caricatural figure, straight out of Dancourt. Sedaine, therefore, is less fully representative of the trend of the times than for instance Mercier, whose *Déserteur*, called a 'drame', goes the full length of being a 'tragédie bourgeoise', and wrings all the effect it can from a situation of unrelieved pathos; or Beaumarchais, who genuinely believed— there seems to be no reason to doubt his word—that *Eugénie* and *Les Deux Amis* were far more worthwhile than his comedies, and that the first two Figaro plays were mere curtain-raisers for *La Mère coupable*: ". . . cet ouvrage terrible qui me consumait la poitrine"[25]. No doubt he thought that in this play he was obeying his precept: "la véritable éloquence est celle des situations, et le seul coloris qui soit permis est le langage vif, pressé, coupé, tumultueux et vrai des passions"[26]; but anyone who has read *La Mère coupable* knows how mediocre was the result.

Paradoxically it is in those works which made the largest claim of truth to nature that the harmful effect of *sensibilité* is the most acute, producing a new sort of 'style ampoulé' which is completely unnatural in its emphasis and extravagance. Yet Nodier reminds us, writing of this same style in Pixérécourt, that by the turn of the century this had become the pattern of popular speech: "On parlait faux, c'était le caractère distinctif de l'époque"[27]. He lays this at the door of the Revolutionary orators; yet their style is surely in its essentials very much the same as that which Diderot and others had introduced into the theatre: a sad case of life imitating art!

In tragedy proper, of course, there was no question of any concession being made to linguistic naturalism, and 'la hantise du sublime', in playwrights and public alike, preserved 'le style noble' virtually unchallenged throughout the century. It is true that La Motte, as early as 1729, had advocated the use of prose in tragedy; his arguments are those one would expect from a rationalist and a champion of the cause of the Moderns:

Les personnages tragiques doivent par la convenance de leur état parler avec plus de noblesse et d'élégance que les

comiques; mais ils n'en doivent pas parler moins naturellement; et leur dignité ne les rend pas poètes.

It is absurd to suggest, he says, that when an author has composed a tragedy one should say to him, in effect:

Réduisez toutes vos pensées sous une mesure uniforme.
Renfermez tous les membres de vos phrases en douze
syllabes, en leur ménageant encore un repos au milieu des
douze. Surtout quand vous aurez terminé une de ces mesures
par un mot d'une certaine désinence, terminez aussi la
suivante par une désinence pareille.[28]

These lines indicate clearly enough that La Motte considers the
writing of verse as a two-stage process: first the original act of
creative writing, then the secondary stage of 'translation' into an
artificial language, in order to achieve "le mérite accessoire de
la versification": indeed, the prose version of his *Œdipe* was
published, though never staged. What is perhaps even more
revealing is that Voltaire, when he comes to the defence of the
traditional use of verse against La Motte's attack, seems to
express an almost identical view of the poetic process. He takes
up La Motte's phrase: "un travail mécanique et méprisable",
but only appears to object to the second of these adjectives[29].
For him too the act of poetic creation is a mechanical process of
translation, to be justified by the notion of 'la difficulté vaincue'.
And in a very real sense, the language of verse tragedy was, if
not a foreign language, a different idiom from that in everyday
use: a second-hand language with inherited limitations on
vocabulary, with an accepted stock of clichés, standard pairs of
noun plus epithet, inherited rhymes; a language from which all
technical terms, and virtually all physical or material reference,
were banned; which took refuge from the concrete in the
abstract and the refined. "Des idées d'emprunt" was to be
Hugo's definition, "vêtues d'images de pacotille"[30].

Again, comparison with English drama is instructive. The
passage from the *Lettres philosophiques* is well known in which
Voltaire presents a translation of Hamlet's "To be or not to
be . . ." soliloquy into alexandrines consisting of colourless,
abstract clichés;[31] but there is a less familiar page, written
towards the end of his life, which perhaps offers an even clearer

indictment of the poverty of the poetic imagination in the eighteenth century. In it, Voltaire examines the exchange between Bernardo and Francisco at the beginning of the same play: "Have you had a quiet guard?"—"Not a mouse stirring", and compares it with the celebrated line from *Iphigénie* in which Racine also expresses the stillness of the night:

> Si vous me demandez pourquoi ce vers, « Mais tout dort, et l'armée, et les vents, et Neptune » est d'une beauté admirable, et pourquoi les vers suivants sont plus beaux encore, je vous dirai que c'est parce qu'ils expriment avec harmonie de grandes vérités, qui sont le fondement de la pièce. Je vous dirai qu'il n'y a ni harmonie ni vérité intéressante dans ce quolibet d'un soldat: « Je n'ai pas entendu une souris trotter ». Que ce soldat ait vu ou n'ait pas vu passer de souris, cet événement est très-inutile à la tragédie d'*Hamlet*; ce n'est qu'un discours de gilles, un proverbe bas qui ne peut faire aucun effet. Il y a toujours une raison pour laquelle toute beauté est beauté, et toute sottise est sottise. [32]

When he wrote this passage in the 1770s, Voltaire was perhaps already fighting something of a rearguard action with regard to the French attitude towards Shakespeare; but there is no doubt that as regards the writing of French verse drama, this concept of poetic diction prevailed throughout the century. That it was not incompatible with the achieving of real pathetic effect can be demonstrated in the cases of *Inès de Castro* or *Zaïre*—even of *Mélanide*. But where it inevitably had an inhibiting influence is in those fields in which Voltaire himself is usually credited with a certain importance as an innovator, namely in the adoption of mediaeval or modern historical subjects in tragedy, and in writing tragedies as vehicles for the philosophical ideas of the day.

To begin with, the accepted idiom imposed a considerable limitation on any possibility of conveying the sense of a particular period and local setting, with the result that Voltaire's Genghis-Khan, Mahomet, Orosmane and Alzire all speak the same language. This is of course a limitation of which *readers* of any historical play, lacking the resources of *mise en scène* and costume, must to some extent be conscious. On the other hand, even for a reader, the text of a play like *Lorenzaccio* or *Cyrano de*

Bergerac offers a great deal more help to the effort of the imagination; while without going beyond the Classical theatre, the examples of Roman plays such as *Horace* or *Cinna*, and of Biblical plays such as *Athalie*, show that a certain discreet use of local colour was possible even where the vocabulary concerned came within the accepted limits of 'le style noble'. But in the case of tragedies set in China, in Peru, in Palestine at the time of the Crusades, or at Mecca in the time of Mahomet, the public's knowledge of the background was not sufficient for such allusive reference to be meaningful, and anything more specific would have been unacceptable on grounds of *bienséance* or of linguistic harmony. In *Mahomet*, therefore, we have to be content with half-a-dozen proper names (*La Mecque* itself, *Médine*, *Arabie*, *Musulman*, *Alcoran*) and a handful of attempts at localization by reference to known facts about Mahomet or about his religion. Thus the prophet is referred to by an enemy as "de chameaux un grossier conducteur", and the Mohammedan practice of total abstinence is evoked in this laboured periphrasis:

J'ai banni loin de moi cette liqueur traîtresse,
Qui nourrit des humains la brutale mollesse. (II, iv)

For the rest, the local government of Mecca is called, by a conventional approximation, 'le Sénat', and Mahomet's military regime is referred to as 'l'aigle impérieux'. When he himself claims:

Je porte l'encensoir, et le sceptre, et les armes (*ibid.*)

this may be a very effective piece of writing, condensing as it does into one line, with three striking examples of metonymy, the notion that Mahomet combines the functions of high-priest, ruler and commander-in-chief; however, it will be obvious that each of these images has a generalizing, not a particularizing, force, which militates against the effect of local colour. And as for any attempt to come nearer home with their choice of subjects, if for example playwrights chose to write about modern warfare they were forced to refer to cannons and muskets in such terms as *bouches de feu*, *foudres mugissantes*, or *longs tubes d'airain*. As a result, the impact of 'historical' tragedy was bound to be

seriously diluted, even in plays like Voltaire's *Tancrède* or
De Belloy's *Le Siège de Calais*, whose authors claimed to be
pioneers in this field.

It has been suggested that in *Tancrède* "Voltaire . . . avait pris
grand soin que tout fût historiquement vrai, hors l'intrigue elle-
même"[33]; but in writing this play in 1760 in order to take
advantage of the removal of the spectators from the stage of the
Théâtre-Français in the previous year:

> ... C'est dans cet esprit, Madame, que je dessinai la faible
> esquisse que je soumets à vos lumières. Je la crayonnai dès que
> je sus que le théâtre de Paris était changé, et devenait un vrai
> spectacle[34]

—the playwright refrained (perhaps wisely) from even attempting to match the increased visual spectacle by the creation of
any specifically linguistic local colour. Apart from half-a-dozen
place-names, the setting remains completely vague, and the
atmosphere of *Tancrède* is no more 'mediaeval' than that of *Le
Cid*. If the dénouement of Voltaire's play does achieve a certain
poignant force, as Aménaïde curses the fatherland whose cruel
injustice has robbed her of her lover, this is because it sticks to
the rhetorical rhythms, and the cliché-like vocabulary, of the
past hundred years or more:

> Il meurt et vous pleurez...
> Vous, cruels; vous, tyrans, qui lui coûtez la vie!
> Que l'enfer engloutisse et vous et ma patrie!
> Et ce Sénat barbare, et ces horribles droits
> D'égorger l'innocence avec le fer des lois!
> Que ne puis-je expirer dans Syracuse en poudre,
> Sur vos corps tout sanglants écrasés par la foudre! (V, vi)[35]

One Frenchman of this period who recognized the inability
of traditional verse tragedy to take on the character of genuine
historical drama was Charles-Jean-François Hénault. His own
François II, a historical tragedy in prose, was no more than a
scholarly exercise (complete with marginal annotations indicating Hénault's sources in Mézerai, de Thou and other historians); but its Preface (1747) constitutes a landmark in the
appreciation of Shakespeare in France. Despite his passionate

interest in history, Hénault tells us, he had never been able to obtain from conventional historians a clear picture of the Wars of the Roses; but the reading of *Henry VI* had been a revelation to him:

> J'ai trouvé les faits à peu près à leurs dates; j'ai vu les princi-paux personnages de ce temps-là mis en action, ils ont joué devant moi; j'ai reconnu leurs mœurs, leurs intérêts, leurs passions qu'ils m'ont apprises eux-mêmes; et tout à coup oubliant que je lisais une tragédie, et Shakespeare lui-même aidant à mon erreur par l'extrême différence qu'il y a de sa pièce à une tragédie, je me suis cru avec un historien, et je me suis dit: Pourquoi notre histoire n'est-elle pas écrite ainsi?[36]

Later in the century, Sébastien Mercier was the first to com-bine a sense of history with effective dramatic writing in the new genre of historical drama in prose, and was further to exploit the subject of the French Wars of Religion, which, as Hénault had claimed, were just as fertile a source of material for the dramatist as England's Wars of the Roses. Although plays like *Jean Hennuyer, évêque de Lisieux* (1772) and *La Destruc-tion de la Ligue* (1782) remained, like *François II*, unstaged—for reasons of censorship in Mercier's case—they provide powerful support for their author's theoretical critique of the historical pretensions of contemporary tragedy. Mercier makes extensive use of reliable historical sources, but he was too much of a revolutionary for his interpretation of these sources to be im-partial; however, despite his anti-monarchical and anti-clerical bias, one can recognize in him, as in Hénault, a genuine appreciation of the distinguishing characteristic of Shake-speare's 'Histories': the historical event seen not as the pre-determined working-out of an individual's tragic fate, but the product of a complex relationship of cause and effect in par-ticular circumstances of time and place[37].

This is surely the crucial difference between tragedy and historical drama; and even without going outside tragedy itself, if this traditional genre was to achieve the 'historical' character with which Voltaire and others hoped to endow it, it must somehow develop the means of representing in a convincing manner the essential historical contingencies of time and place.

But such a development remained impossible without a real linguistic and stylistic revolution.

(iii) The 'philosophes' and the theatre

IF tragedies like *Mahomet, Tancrède* or *Le Siège de Calais* suffer such obvious limitations as regards their localization in time and place, it is also legitimate to wonder whether their philosophical message had the impact their authors hoped for, and which some later writers have been ready to allow.

While the remoteness of the tragic hero—both the historical or geographical 'éloignement' to which Racine refers in the Preface to *Bajazet*, and the elevation that Aristotelian theory requires of him—can be a powerful aid to the *tragic* effect of a play, it is by no means so with regard to its effect as propaganda. It is not for nothing that Mahomet's "Je veillerai sur vous comme sur l'univers" (II, iii) echoes Auguste's celebrated line from *Cinna*: such lines are proof of the heroic, the superhuman stature of these characters, which is a very necessary ingredient of the make-up of the tragic hero. But this same feature necessarily conflicts with what Fontaine calls "le caractère militant du théâtre, cette sorte de complicité de l'art dramatique et de la philosophie"[38]—unless, that is, we define 'la philosophie' in very vague and general terms. Mahomet, in fact, is in his way an impressive tragic figure, a sort of male version of Corneille's Cléopâtre, with touches of Crébillon's Atrée; we might say of him what Corneille says of Cléopâtre in *Rodogune*: "tous ses crimes sont accompagnés d'une grandeur d'âme qui a quelque chose de si haut, qu'en même temps qu'on déteste ses actions, on admire la source dont elles partent"[39]. But this is not the stuff of which *littérature engagée* is made: at best plays like this can only move us to righteous indignation; they cannot change men's minds, they can only confirm attitudes that the majority of the audience already subscribe to—at any rate in the form of general principles. Trahard says that in *Mahomet* "notre sensibilité n'est plus en jeu que sous la forme de l'indignation"[40]; but the converse is also true, that our indignation is aroused almost entirely by a sentimental appeal to generally held notions of right and wrong, not by a process of intellectual persuasion based on particular circumstances. Not only is Voltaire's plot totally lacking in historical basis, but the issue of

religious fanaticism is blurred by the introduction of incongruous elements of the same romanesque sort that we have
seen in Crébillon.

L'inceste était pour nous le prix du parricide

says one character to another at the climax of the play (IV, v);
it is very much the same mixture as before, and this melodramatic plot considerably dilutes even such force as this
distant and stylized treatment of the theme of 'le fanatisme'
might have had. Voltaire's prefatory letter to Frederick of
Prussia is infinitely more *engagé* than the play itself; and if
Mahomet did arouse any stir, this was surely because it was
adroitly surrounded by its author with the necessary provocative publicity. It is highly doubtful whether any of his 'philosophical' tragedies had a fraction of the effect on the minds of
his contemporaries that he was certainly able to achieve with
his pamphlets, his *contes* and his philosophical poems.[41]
Belief in the power of the theatre to change men's minds and
move their hearts was of course very central to the theory of
'drame bourgeois':

Le parterre de la comédie est le seul endroit où les larmes de
l'homme vertueux et du méchant soient confondues. Là, le
méchant s'irrite contre des injustices qu'il aurait commises;
compatit à des maux qu'il aurait occasionnés, et s'indigne
contre un homme de son propre caractère. Mais l'impression
est reçue; elle demeure en nous, malgré nous; et le méchant
sort de sa loge moins disposé à faire le mal, que s'il eût été
gourmandé par un orateur sévère et dur.[42]

But it would surely be optimistic to believe that any drama can
achieve the effect that Diderot writes of here; we react to a play
not as individuals, but as members of a 'public de théâtre'. The
gap may be considerable between the principles an audience
will support in public, and the behaviour of the members of that
audience in their private lives; and one does not have to be
excessively cynical in order to suspect that there was a good
deal of wishful thinking in the aspirations of Diderot and the
other *philosophe* dramatists. As Geoffroy pointed out, com-

menting on the vogue for serious comedy and 'drame' in the
1770s:

> Pour juger combien ces homélies sont infructueuses, il suffit
> de faire quelque attention au contraste frappant qui se trouve
> entre nos mœurs actuelles et le goût qui domine au théâtre.
> Jamais peut-être les hommes n'ont été aussi durs, aussi
> insensibles aux malheurs d'autrui; cependant le théâtre
> retentit sans cesse des noms d'humanité et de bienfaisance.[43]

How does Diderot hope to give the new 'genre sérieux' the
moral force he talks about? By a choice of plot and subject-
matter which allow for serious discussion:

> On discuterait au théâtre les points de moral les plus im-
> portants... Un poète agiterait la question du suicide, de
> l'honneur, du duel, de la fortune, des dignités et cent
> autres.[44]

In order to make such discussions less abstract and general in
their reference, and to give them more topicality and relevance
to the audience's own interests, playwrights must reject the
traditional preoccupation with 'caractères', and substitute for
this the study of 'conditions':

> C'est la condition, ses devoirs, ses avantages, ses embarras,
> qui doivent servir de base à l'ouvrage. Il me semble que cette
> source est plus féconde, plus étendue et plus utile que celle des
> caractères. Pour peu que le caractère fût chargé, un spec-
> tateur pouvait se dire à lui-même, ce n'est pas moi. Mais il ne
> peut se cacher que l'état qu'on joue devant lui ne soit le sien;
> il ne peut méconnaître ses devoirs. Il faut absolument qu'il
> s'applique ce qu'il entend.[45]

Thus, the new genre will present "l'homme de lettres, le
philosophe, le commerçant, le juge, l'avocat, le politique, le
citoyen, le magistrat, le financier, le grand seigneur, l'intendant"; and Diderot's list goes on to include, somewhat mis-
leadingly, "toutes les relations: le père de famille, l'époux, la
sœur, les frères". The most convincing examples of this new
development were to be produced by other dramatists: they are
to be found in Beaumarchais's *Les Deux Amis, ou le Négociant de*

Lyon, which portrays the 'conditions' of banker and business-man; in Mercier's *Le Déserteur* which, if its eloquent humani-tarian plea against militarism does depend rather too much on the detail of a highly-contrived plot, also presents an admirable study of the 'condition' of regular serving officer; and in Sedaine's *Le Philosophe sans le savoir*, which is built round a very successful embodiment of the 'condition' of *commerçant*. Diderot's own plays offer little support to his theory in this respect: the characters of *Le Fils naturel* and *Le Père de famille* are hardly any more closely related to a particular social context than those of La Chaussée's plays.

However, there is one respect in which Diderot does put his ideas into practice in *Le Fils naturel*: that is, in the use of the theatre to debate a serious issue. The ostensible theme of the play, to judge by its title—a Romantic *plaidoyer* for the rights of the illegitimate—is never developed at all, since Dorval is surrounded by characters completely devoid of any prejudice on this score; but Act IV scene iii, the philosophical kernel of the play, presents a sustained discussion between Constance and Dorval on another subject with strong pre-Romantic overtones: the individual's relationship to the society in which he lives. It is well known that Rousseau interpreted one line from this scene: "L'homme de bien est dans la société, et il n'y a que le méchant qui soit seul" as a disparaging reference to himself, and took such umbrage that this put an end to his cordial relations with Diderot; but it has recently been claimed that the whole of the scene was in fact directed against Rousseau, and is built on a fundamental conflict between the two men:

> To get the full impact of the situation, one has only to sub-stitute, in reading the scene in question, the name of Diderot for that of Constance, and the name of Rousseau for that of Dorval.[46]

Whether or not this argument holds good in detail, in a more general sense it does seem to be the case that Act IV scene iii can fairly be related, and was intended to be related by con-temporaries, to an important topical debate about the indivi-dual's duties towards society.

More than this: if Diderot had only had the courage of his

convictions, he could have made a most far-reaching dramaturgical innovation in this scene. In *The Quintessence of Ibsenism*,
Shaw writes of what he calls "the technical novelty in Ibsen's
plays":

> Formerly you had in what was called a well-made play an
> exposition in the first act, a situation in the second, an un-
> ravelling in the third. Now you have exposition, situation,
> and discussion; and discussion is the test of the playwright.[47]

Diderot is in fact on the threshold of such a breakthrough in
Le Fils naturel. Dorval embarks on his long discussion with
Constance, hating himself for having fallen in love with Rosalie,
the young fiancée of Clairville, his friend and benefactor, but
unable to bring himself to renounce her and persuade her to
return to her love for Clairville: by the end of the scene
Constance's precept and example have won him over from
Rousseauistic individualism to a sense of social responsibility
much more typical of Diderot's own form of *philosophie*, and he
is ready to pass the message on to Rosalie. The central scene of
Act V is devoted to this, and at the end of scene iii the dilemma
is resolved. Dorval and Rosalie have returned to the path of
reason, Clairville can now marry Rosalie, and Constance can
marry Dorval: a dénouement-by-discussion such as Shaw might
have approved of—when, to spoil it all, Rosalie's aged father
arrives from the West Indies and not only greets his daughter,
but also recognizes Dorval as his long-lost son. So Dorval and
Rosalie could not have married; their penchant satisfies, if only
in retrospect, the audience's salacious obsession with the incest-
motif; and for the Shavian dénouement-by-discussion is substituted the most hackneyed of dénouements by *deus ex machina*.

Writers of 'drame' as well as writers of tragedy remained
prisoners of the sentimental cliché with regard to motivation of
plot, just as much as they did in matters of linguistic expression.
In tragedy, there are almost no exceptions to this (though the
early *Alzire* among Voltaire's plays, and De Belloy's *Siège de
Calais*, seem to achieve a directness and a moral persuasiveness
seldom found elsewhere); while in 'drame bourgeois' Sedaine
was perhaps alone in freeing himself from the worst effects of the
sensibility of his age. The latter half of the eighteenth century

was not lacking in theoretical writings based on the premise that
the traditional forms were long outmoded; and in some cases—
Beaumarchais's 'Lettre sur le genre dramatique sérieux' (which
appeared in 1767, as the Preface to his *Eugénie*), or Mercier's
Du théâtre of 1773—one can even say that the limitations of neo-
classical tragedy are exposed with something of the vigour that
was to characterize the *Préface de Cromwell*. But the only playwright who triumphantly overcame these limitations in practice
was Beaumarchais, whose good sense fortunately sometimes
prevented him from taking his moralizing self too seriously. *Le
Mariage de Figaro* manages to combine a substantial *larmoyant*
element, a powerful feminist plea, and a keen attack on contemporary judicial, economic and administrative abuses; it
contains genuine appeal to sentiment alongside parody of the
sentimental tradition, and genuine moralizing alongside an
ironical critique of the moralizing attitude. Such eclecticism is
the mark of the man of genius; and with its remarkable variety
of tone and its dramaturgical originality, *Le Mariage* is not only
the one play which unquestionably redeems the mediocrity of
the eighteenth-century theatre, but is also more truly original
and forward-looking in its dramatic idiom than almost anything
the French theatre was to produce during the nineteenth
century.

Notes to Chapter One

1. Cf. H. C. Lancaster, *French Tragedy in the Time of Louis XV and
   Voltaire, 1715–1774*, Baltimore, 1950.
2. Cf. Lancaster, *op. cit.*; F. C. Green, *Minuet*, London, 1935.
3. Cf. Lancaster, *op. cit.*; Green, *op. cit.*; R. S. Ridgway, *La
   Propagande philosophique dans les tragédies de Voltaire* (Studies
   on Voltaire and the Eighteenth Century, XV), Geneva, 1961.
4. Cf. F. Gaiffe, *Le Drame en France au xviiie siècle*, Paris, 1910.
5. See R. Fargher, *Life and Letters in France: the Eighteenth Century*,
   London, 1970, pp. xiii–xx.
6. P. Trahard, *Les Maîtres de la sensibilité française au xviiie siècle*,
   Paris, 1931, I, pp. 14–15.
7. *Polyeucte*, l. 166.
8. G. Lanson, *Nivelle de La Chaussée et la comédie larmoyante*, Paris,
   1887, pp. 230–233.

9. *Op. cit.*, pp. 17ff.
10. *Ibid.*, p. 15.
11. On *Rhadamiste et Zénobie*, see M. Descotes, *Le Public de théâtre et son histoire*, Paris, 1964, ch. v.
12. *Œuvres*, Paris, 1754, V, p. 184.
13. *Notices sur les œuvres de théâtre*, ed. H. Lagrave (Studies on Voltaire and the Eighteenth Century, XLII), Geneva, 1966, p. 261.
14. Diderot, *Entretiens sur le Fils naturel*; in *Writings on the Theatre*, ed. F. C. Green, Cambridge, 1936, p. 51.
15. On *Mélanide*, see Descotes, *Le Public de théâtre . . .*, ch. vi; and the edition of the play by W. D. Howarth, Brighton, 1973.
16. *Mimesis: the Representation of Reality in Western Literature*, English translation, Princeton, 1953; see especially ch. xvi.
17. 'De la poésie dramatique'; *op. cit.*, p. 183.
18. In an unpublished paper, 'Diderot's Private Theatre'.
19. *Lettres à Malesherbes*, ed. G. Rudler, London, 1928, p. 45.
20. *Le Théâtre en France*, Paris, 1927, p. 319.
21. *Entretiens sur le Fils naturel*; *op. cit.*, p. 29.
22. *Ibid.*, pp. 81ff.
23. Petit de Juleville, *op. cit.*, p. 320.
24. Letter of 3.xii.1765.
25. 'Un Mot sur *La Mère coupable*' (1792).
26. *Essai sur le genre dramatique sérieux* (1767).
27. C. Nodier, Introduction to Pixérécourt, *Théâtre choisi*, Paris and Nancy, 1841–43, I, p. xi.
28. *Œuvres, ed. cit.*, V, p. 393; V, p. 409.
29. Preface to *Œdipe* (1729).
30. *Préface de Cromwell*, ed. M. Souriau, Paris, n.d., p. 275.
31. Letter 18.
32. *Lettre à l'Académie Française* (1776).
33. L. Breitholtz, *Le Théâtre historique en France jusqu'à la Révolution*, Uppsala, 1952, p. 184.
34. Dedicatory letter 'A Madame la Marquise de Pompadour' (1760).
35. It is noteworthy that at this emotional climax Voltaire almost completely abandons this play's one real stylistic innovation, the *vers croisés*—a medium of which he wrote in the 'Épître dédicatoire' that although it preserved "l'uniformité de la rime", nevertheless such verse "approche peut-être trop de la prose". Of the last thirty lines of the play, only four are *croisés*: the rest form couplets alternating in the normal way.
36. Quoted by Breitholtz, *op. cit.*, p. 136.

37. See W. D. Howarth, 'History in the Theatre: the French and English Traditions', *Trivium*, I, 1966, pp. 151–168.
38. L. Fontaine, *Le Théâtre et la philosophie au xviiie siècle*, Versailles, 1878, p. 13.
39. *Discours de l'utilité et des parties du poème dramatique* in *Trois Discours sur le poème dramatique*, ed. L. Forestier, Paris, 1963, p. 55.
40. *Op. cit.*, p. 256.
41. "Voltaire n'avait pas tort d'exprimer une philosophie sur la scène. Mais cette philosophie est aussi éloignée que possible de l'univers tragique qu'il voulait évoquer. Il y a là une contradiction fondamentale entre le génie de Voltaire et son moyen d'expression. Sa tentative de prolonger un genre qui ne pouvait survivre dans le climat intellectuel du siècle des lumières était condamnée inéluctablement à l'insuccès", Ridgway, *op. cit.*, pp. 239–240.
42. Diderot, *De la poésie dramatique*; *op. cit.*, p. 123.
43. *L'Année Littéraire*, 1778.
44. *De la poésie dramatique*; *op. cit.*, p. 124.
45. *Entretiens sur le Fils naturel*; *op. cit.*, p. 89.
46. Blandine McLaughlin, 'A New Look at Diderot's *Fils naturel*', *Diderot Studies*, X, 1968, p. 113.
47. London, 1913, p. 187.

2 Pre-Romanticism

(i) *The fortunes of the theatre during the Revolution*

AS the eighteenth century moves towards its close, the signposts pointing to the need for radical changes in the nature of French dramatic writing are even clearer. It now becomes necessary to look more closely at the material conditions prevailing in the theatre, for even in the Comédie-Française, where privilege, vested interests and the inertia of most of the *sociétaires* had maintained things virtually unaltered for a hundred years, change was suddenly accelerated[1].

The most significant event there in the years immediately preceding the Revolution was the début in 1787 of François-Joseph Talma, perhaps the greatest of all French actors. While still a relatively new member of the company Talma set himself, with the help of his friend the painter David, to study the costumes of the ancient world; and in 1789 he astonished his colleagues by rejecting the ostentatious silks and laces, wigs and gloves, of established theatrical tradition for the simple costume *à l'antique*, appropriate to the setting of the particular play being performed[2]. It was a long time before all his colleagues—particularly the actresses of the company—were converted to his way of thinking; but here was the first breach in a long-standing tradition which had always stood in the way of greater historical verisimilitude on the stage. More important, in the same year the young Talma became involved in a celebrated political controversy which split the Comédie-Française into two sharply opposed factions—the beginning of dissensions within this body which were to last throughout the Revolutionary period. Indeed, the company presented at this time a microcosm of society at large; and the conflict between reactionaries and radicals came to a head here almost independently of the explosive events of July 1789.

The occasion of this controversy was the production of Marie-Joseph Chénier's play *Charles IX, ou la Saint-Barthélemy*. We have seen that earlier plays on subjects taken from the Wars of Religion by Hénault and Mercier had remained unperformed: Chénier's play, based on the most provocative of all subjects from that troubled period, was accepted by the Comédie in 1788, but banned by the royal censor. After the events of July and August the authorities were unable to prevent its production: repeated demands from spectators in the theatre reinforced Chénier's own attempts to circumvent the hostility of the majority of the *comédiens*, and the play was finally performed in November 1789, after certain textual changes which reinforced references to the contemporary political climate. Public reaction was tumultuous—Danton is said to have observed that "si *Figaro* avait tué la noblesse, *Charles IX* tuerait la monarchie"[3] —but a highly successful run was interrupted after 33 performances when a deputation of bishops petitioned the King. Chénier had intended the role of the weak, decadent Charles for Saint-Fal, an established tragedian, but the latter refused a part so unrewarding in his eyes, opting for the safer Henri de Navarre. The part therefore came Talma's way, giving him his first opportunity to make his mark in a major role. His personal triumph, and the triumphant success of the play—a *succès de scandale*, hardly justified by the intrinsic qualities of Chénier's writing—merely served to intensify dissensions within the troupe[4].

In April 1790 Talma, as the most recently elected *sociétaire*, was entrusted with the *compliment d'ouverture* after the Easter recess. On this occasion the *compliment* was written by Chénier: although it could by no means be called subversive, it did contain indirect references to the banning of the play, and an assertion of the importance of the theatre as a reflection of public feeling in critical times; the effect of this alliance between Chénier and Talma, both men of radical sympathies, was to sharpen the opposition backstage between those who favoured the continuation of the social and political system as it was, and those who looked for change. In July matters came to a head, when a group of Provençal delegates to the States-General demanded a performance of *Charles IX* as part of the protracted celebrations of the first anniversary of the sacking of the Bastille. When a theatre full of excited spectators reiterated their demand, Naudet, one of the reactionary party among the *sociétaires*, was deputed to announce that it was impossible to perform the play because of the illness of two actors. Talma, however, followed Naudet on stage, and contradicted the official announcement—a step which led to a duel with Naudet, a performance of *Charles IX* in near-riot conditions the following evening, and Talma's expulsion from the company. Although this expulsion was rescinded in September, after repeated popular demonstrations had led to the intervention of Bailly, the mayor of Paris, the vindictiveness of his colleagues deprived Talma of any further major roles; and as soon as the Assemblée Nationale had passed its all-important decree of January 13th 1791, liberating the theatres in Paris from the monopolistic domination of the Comédie-Française (which gave it sole rights to the classical repertory), Talma and others—the 'rouges', or radicals, of the troupe—withdrew to form the nucleus of a new company at the Théâtre-Français de la rue de Richelieu (on the site of the present-day Comédie-Française)[5]. Healthy competition, the lack of which had inhibited experiment and reform throughout the century, was therefore created by a combination of political strife and enlightened legislation; but if this meant in theory that dramatists now had better chances of getting unorthodox new plays accepted, and that there was a much greater opportunity for producers and actors to rejuvenate the traditional manner of presenting the classical masterpieces, in practice one orthodoxy was soon replaced by another.

During the years 1791–92 the theatres of Paris continued to form a battleground for demonstrations of feeling between royalists and revolutionaries—for instance the *première* of Chénier's *Caïus Gracchus* at the Richelieu in February 1792, a phrase from which, "Des lois, et non du sang"[6], was to become a slogan for the moderates. For the 'rouges' such as Chénier and Talma were soon left far behind by the zeal of the extreme revolutionaries; and the establishment of the Republic in August 1792 meant that not only the conservative members of the Théâtre de la Nation (as the Comédie-Française itself was now called) but also those of the Théâtre de la République (the name adopted by the Richelieu theatre) had constantly to give renewed proof of their *civisme*. The classical repertory was thoroughly purged: not only were plays with an insufficiently democratic message banned, but in those that survived, titles like 'Seigneur', 'Monsieur' or 'Madame' had to be replaced by 'Citoyen' and 'Citoyenne', while for instance the closing line of *Tartuffe*, "Nous vivons sous un prince ennemi de la fraude", became:

Ces jours-là sont passés d'injustice et de fraude.

Dress and décor stressed patriotic motifs, however incongruously, while interludes and additions to the text introduced topical allusions[7]. As for new plays, the officially approved dramatic literature of this period, like the literature of more modern revolutions, was humourless, puritanical and heavily didactic; and the standard of this servile writing, as well as of production and acting, was dismally low. In August 1793 the Committee of Public Safety adopted a proposal that only 'patriotic' plays should henceforth be performed, and this remained in force until the end of the Terror.

At the République, Talma and others were already watched with suspicion as a result of an incident in October 1792, when Marat had denounced Talma's household as a "den of counter-revolutionaries". Nevertheless, by dint of prudence and the necessary professions of orthodoxy, the République stayed open. Not so the Théâtre de la Nation: as the repressive measures increased, after a campaign of persecution by Jacobin journalists, this theatre was closed in September 1792, and all the members of the company imprisoned. Saved by the fall of Robespierre, however, they were released soon after 9 Thermidor, and returned to the Comédie, which was reopened in August 1794[8].

In the years which followed, the position of the official theatres remained precarious, in the face of competition from a great variety of new establishments. Liberty flourished under the Convention, but the Directory reintroduced some of the repressive measures of the Jacobins, and the fortunes of Parisian theatres generally declined. Finally, after many vicissitudes, the survivors of the original Comédie-Française were reunited in May 1799 in the rue de Richelieu[9].

The Napoleonic régime paid considerable attention to the reorganization of the theatre, as of all other aspects of the intellectual and cultural life of the country; this culminated in a series of decrees (1806–7) which consolidated a state of affairs not unlike that of the *ancien régime*. No new theatres were to be established in Paris without a licence; all new plays were to be approved by a censor; there were to be three official companies: the Comédie (occupying what was now called the Théâtre de l'Empereur, with a subsidiary house, the Théâtre de l'Impératrice, newly built on the site of the Odéon), the Opéra, and the Opéra-comique—each with exclusive rights to its own traditional repertory; and all other theatres, designated as belonging to a 'secondary' category, were to be confined each to their own officially prescribed genre. Thus the Théâtre de la Porte-Saint-Martin, which was to play an important role in the history of Romantic drama, was to be "particularly committed to the genre called melodrama, to plays with great spectacle. As in all the secondary theatres, only scraps of song, to popular tunes, may be heard here." However, a further decree (July 1807) reduced the number of 'secondary' houses to four: the Gaîté and the Ambigu-Comique, devoted to melodrama, pantomime, *arlequinades* and farces; and the Variété and the Vaudeville, specializing in parodies, musical sketches, and short plays in the *grivois*, *poissard* or *villageois* genres[10]. Thus the old monopoly, which had favoured the Comédie-Française at the expense of its rivals, the Italians and the *théâtres de la foire*, all through the previous century, was now back in a new guise, and the theatre in Paris was once more submitted to rigid control:

So at last ended the capital's debilitating surplus of theatres by the restoration of the very checks and controls cast off so eagerly almost twenty years before. Out of the agonies of those twenty years emerged stronger and better organized national theatres, one significant new boulevard house, several new genres the importance of which was as yet little realized, and major innovations in acting, costume, and theatre architecture. Yet for all that, not a few Parisians felt that in the theatre a circle had come round, and if the famous sleeper Épiménide[11] were to awaken once again amid the theatre world of 1807, he might be forgiven for at first assuming that the *ancien régime* had come again.[12]

However, nothing could be quite the same again; and in the theatre as elsewhere the years of the Revolution had left their mark. Never again could five-act verse tragedy in its traditional form enjoy quite the same unrivalled prestige among connoisseurs as the apex of a hierarchy of genres, consecrated by the refinement of its subject-matter and the purity of its diction. If the works of the great classics, Corneille, Racine and Voltaire, did retain, or regain, a large part of their popularity, new works had to be more than mere imitations of these models if they were to impose themselves, and the most successful tragedies of the Revolutionary and post-Revolutionary periods were those which embodied an author's attempt to make the genre express topical ideas, and to bridge the gap between tragedy *à l'antique*, with its remote subject and stylized setting, and the events and issues of the day. Ideals of liberty, equality and fraternity; themes of patriotism and democracy; attacks on weak or tyrannical kings and their evil counsellors—these all became commonplaces in the tragedy of the Revolutionary years, while in the more domesticated genre of 'drame bourgeois' playwrights repeatedly denounced the iniquities of the priesthood, the evils of enforced celibacy, or the power and privilege of class, and upheld all the desirable civic virtues. And on both these genres, as on the ephemeral examples of more trivial forms of dramatic writing, 'la sensibilité révolutionnaire' left its peculiar stamp[13].

In its extreme form—the grim paradox, given such compelling imaginative treatment in Anatole France's *Les Dieux ont soif*, which enabled men who were themselves by no means lacking in sensibility to accept, and even to commit, the most inhuman atrocities in the name of 'humanity'—this is certainly to be seen at its clearest in the kind of ephemeral drama without any literary pretensions, which provided up-to-date comment on topical affairs. Thus, for instance, playwrights expressed at any rate the official, or public, mood of the times when they showed a parent welcoming the death of a young son in battle as proof of patriotic zeal, or when they glorified the actions of characters who informed on members of their own family, betraying them to the Revolutionary Tribunal, just as much as they did in paying tribute in dramatic form to humanitarian acts of charity[14]. But in a more general sense, all the dramatic literature of this period is marked by an intensification of the tendency, which had been apparent in most of the sentimental drama of the eighteenth century, towards the psychological simplification, and the crudity of characterization, which we associate with melodrama. Issues were reduced to elementary terms of right and wrong, and characters likewise became pasteboard embodiments of good and evil.

If the mood of the times was more favourable to melodrama than to genuine tragedy, it may also be true that the historical subject of Chénier's *Charles IX*, in spite of the author's opinion that it was "le sujet le plus tragique de l'histoire moderne"[15], was one in which it would have been difficult to avoid the black-and-white characterization proper to melodrama; and perhaps Chénier should be congratulated on having created, in between the criminal Catholics and the virtuous Protestants, the subtler portrayal of the weak and vacillating Charles. The play was preceded, in its published form, by a 'Discours préliminaire' in which Chénier showed himself to be inhibited by no sense of false modesty with regard to his standing as a writer of tragedy:

> J'ai du moins saisi la seule gloire à laquelle il m'était permis d'aspirer: celle d'ouvrir la route, et de composer le premier une tragédie vraiment nationale... On a écrit, dans ces derniers temps, quelques tragédies sur des sujets français; mais ces pièces sont une école de préjugés, de servitude et de mauvais style. Du Belloy (*sic*), calculateur d'effets de théâtre, a substitué aux grands intérêts publics des niaiseries chevaleresques, des rodomontades militaires; il a sacrifié sans cesse à la vanité de quelques maisons puissantes et à l'autorité arbitraire: il a donc fait des tragédies anti-nationales.[16]

What are the characteristics of 'la tragédie nationale' as Chénier interprets the term? First, it contains one structural innovation:

> J'ai banni de ma pièce ces confidents froids et parasites qui n'entrent jamais dans l'action et qui ne semblent admis sur la scène que pour écouter tout ce qu'on veut dire, et pour approuver tout ce qu'on veut faire. Les sept personnages les plus illustres de la France à la fin du seizième siècle servent à nouer et à dénouer mon intrigue importante.[17]

But this is the limit of his technical originality; and for all his political fervour, Chénier is no revolutionary in matters of style:

> Qu'on s'avise de faire des tragédies en prose; qu'on nous exhorte à laisser là Sophocle et Racine pour imiter les dégoûtantes absurdités du théâtre anglais et les niaiseries burlesques du théâtre allemand: ces sottises sans conséquence sont plus divertissantes que dangereuses; tout cela passe, et va bientôt du ridicule à l'oubli.[18]

In fact, the recipe remains virtually unchanged. When Henri de Navarre recounts his premonitory fears:

> Je goûte des plaisirs empoisonnés d'alarmes:
> Au milieu de ces jeux dont vous vantez les charmes,
> Dans l'épaisseur des nuits, au moment du repos,
> Dans le lit nuptial je me peins des complots;
> Le poison terminant les jours de votre frère,
> Et peut-être au tombeau précipitant ma mère;
> Des crimes, des malheurs, et les champs odieux
> Où Condé, ce grand homme, expira sous nos yeux;
> D'un carnage éternel nos régions fumantes,
> Et des princes lorrains les intrigues sanglantes...

the mere use of the proper terms *Condé* and *lorrains* is hardly enough to give the passage a genuinely specific or particularizing character: for the rest, these are the cliché-like hemistiches familiar to readers and spectators of French tragedy throughout the previous two hundred years. In fact, just as the tragic dramatists relied on a series of set pieces with which they filled in the framework of the play (*e.g.* this variant on the premonitory dream or nightmare, L'Hôpital's *récit* of the massacre itself (V, ii), or the closing speech in which the criminal king's remorse is expressed in the form of hallucinatory vision), so too for the more detailed fabric of their writing they often seem to have recourse to a stock of ready-made 'units'. This is not to deny the force of such writing; but it is a style whose impact depends to a considerable extent on the reader's recognition of literary reminiscences or echoes. Who could fail, for instance, to recognize the Racinian undertones of the following passage:

Cruels! à mes tourments soyez du moins unis.
C'est vous qui me coûtez des larmes éternelles.
Mes mains, vous le savez, n'étaient point criminelles;
Sans crainte et sans remords je contemplais les cieux;
Tout est changé pour moi: le jour m'est odieux.
Où fuir? où me cacher dans l'horreur des ténèbres?
O Nuit, couvre-moi bien de tes voiles funèbres! (V, iv)

Another of Chénier's successes in the early years of the
Revolution was *Jean Calas, ou l'École des juges* of 1791. Here,
perhaps even more than in *Charles IX*, was a subject ready-made
for sentimental emphasis and for black-and-white portrayal of
character. Although labelled a 'drame', the play is in verse; and
despite the novelty claimed by Chénier's patron Palissot in his
introductory letter ("avoir osé mettre en action, ce qui jusqu'
alors était sans exemple, un interrogatoire juridique, et en
avoir fait une des plus intéressantes scènes de la pièce")[19], the
structure is that of a regular tragedy: the action starts at the
moment of crisis, and unity of time is strictly observed. Portrayal
of grief is so conventional and stylized as to lose its direct impact;
and what strikes the reader most forcefully is the resemblance to
the rhetoric of Voltaire's philosophical poems. One can well
imagine the topicality of the anticlerical message, expressed
both in the satirical portrait of the priesthood:

Repoussez loin de vous ces prêtres sanguinaires,
Qui vous font désirer le trépas de vos frères,
Qui, d'orgueil enivrés, prêchent l'humilité,
Qui du sein des trésors prêchent la pauvreté,
Et qui, trompant toujours et dévastant la terre,
Servent le Dieu de paix en déclarant la guerre (I, iv)

and in the Voltairian evocation of a humanitarian ideal:

— Sans consumer ma vie au fond des sanctuaires,
Je tâche d'être humain: ce sont là mes prières.
— Vos vœux et votre encens sont les plus précieux:
Tout mortel bienfaisant est un prêtre des cieux.
Aimer le genre humain, secourir la misère,
C'est la religion; c'est la loi tout entière;

C'est le précepte saint que Dieu même a dicté:
Son culte véritable est dans l'humanité. (I, v)

But stirring as this appeal may have been, its nature is essentially non-dramatic[20]; and Chénier was not the dramatist to revolutionize neo-classical tragedy by matching novelty of form to originality of content.

In the case of Ducis, another friend and collaborator of Talma, potential originality of form and subject-matter was again accommodated to the ruling French taste. His adaptations of Shakespeare, for which he is generally remembered, were in any case made at second hand, for he knew no English, and worked from the bowdlerized 'translations' of La Place and Letourneur. The series, begun with *Hamlet* in 1769 and *Roméo et Juliette* in 1772, had continued with *Lear* in 1783 and *Macbeth* in 1784; Talma created the roles of John in *Jean sans Terre* (1791) and Othello in *Le Maure de Venise* (1792), but it was the production of a revised form of *Hamlet* in 1804 which provided him with one of the great successes of his career. Even in Ducis's version[21], despite the conventional nature of the alexandrines (here Cornelian, rather than Racinian, in inspiration):

Ah! je respire enfin, j'ai su dompter l'amour.
Je puis à ma fureur me livrer sans retour.
   (*en regardant l'urne:*)
Gage de mes serments, urne terrible et sainte,
Que j'invoque en pleurant, que j'embrasse avec crainte,
C'est à vous d'affermir mon bras prêt à frapper.
Barbare Claudius, ne crois pas m'échapper (V, iii)

the character of the "gloomy Dane" revealed literary qualities markedly different from those of the neo-classical tragedies based on Greek legend or Roman history. Ducis himself, indeed, spoke of combining in his *Hamlet* the inspiration of Shakespeare with that of Dante[22]; and, to take one example, the rendering of the "To be or not to be . . ." soliloquy, although less literal than Voltaire's[23], does manage to avoid his excess of rhetorical abstraction, and to achieve a more convincingly dramatic 'atmosphere':

Je ne sais que résoudre... immobile et troublé...
C'est rester trop longtemps de mon doute accablé;
C'est trop souffrir la vie et le poids qui me tue.
Hé! qu'offre donc la mort à mon âme abattue?
Un asile assuré, le plus doux des chemins
Qui conduit au repos les malheureux humains.
Mourons. Que craindre encor quand on a cessé d'être?
La mort... c'est le sommeil... c'est un réveil peut-être.
Peut-être... Ah! c'est ce mot qui glace épouvanté
L'homme au bord du cercueil par le doute arrêté.
Devant ce vaste abîme il se jette en arrière,
Ressaisit l'existence, et s'attache à la terre.
Dans nos troubles pressants qui peut nous avertir
Des secrets de ce monde où tout va s'engloutir?
Sans l'effroi qu'il inspire, et la terreur sacrée
Qui défend son passage et siège à son entrée,
Combien de malheureux iraient dans le tombeau
De leurs longues douleurs déposer le fardeau!
Ah! que ce port souvent est vu d'un œil d'envie
Par le faible agité sur les flots de la vie!
Mais il craint dans ses maux, au delà du trépas,
Des maux plus grands encore, et qu'il ne connaît pas.
Redoutable avenir, tu glaces mon courage!
Va, laisse à ma douleur achever son ouvrage... (IV, i)[24]

At all events, Talma seems to have had an intuitive understanding of the 'pre-Romantic' character of Shakespeare's heroes—the indecisive introspection of Hamlet, the daemonic passion of Othello—which went far beyond the timid compromises of Ducis's text. (He had of course a sound knowledge of Shakespeare in the original, dating from an early period of his life spent in England.) But this was to remain the only form in which Shakespeare was known to the playgoers of the Revolutionary generation; and if Ducis's alexandrines, and regular classical structure, gave little hint of the poetic genius, or the dramaturgical inventiveness, of the originals, nevertheless it is probably true to say that these 'Shakespearean' roles helped to develop in Talma that Romantic inspiration which his contemporaries remarked on in his playing of the classical repertory:

Cet artiste donne autant qu'il est possible à la tragédie française ce qu'à tort ou à raison les Allemands lui reprochent

de n'avoir pas, l'originalité et le naturel... Il y a dans sa
manière de déclamer Shakespeare et Racine artistement
combinés. Pourquoi les écrivains dramatiques n'essaieraient-
ils pas aussi de réunir dans leurs compositions ce que l'acteur
a su si bien amalgamer par son jeu?[25]

Apart from Chénier and Ducis, the tragic dramatist who
made the biggest mark during the post-Revolutionary era was
the precocious young Népomucène Lemercier, whose first
tragedy was accepted by the Comédie-Française when he was
only fifteen. Lemercier wrote a 'drame', *Lovelace* (based on
Richardson's novel) in 1792, and a satirical comedy, *Le
Tartuffe révolutionnaire*, in 1795; his biggest success, however,
was the *Agamemnon* of 1797, and there could be no better
illustration of the conservative taste of audiences at the
Comédie-Française throughout this period. For the play could
have been written at any time during the previous hundred
years: it adheres strictly to the unities; the killing of Agamemnon takes place off-stage; room is found for the conventional
set-pieces of recognition-scene and *récit*; and there are few
tragedies which better illustrate the 'second-hand' appeal of
imitative neo-classical tragedy through recognition of familiar
features. A cultured audience no doubt greatly appreciated
Lemercier's ingenious variations on the original legend, with
skilful *péripéties* which succeed in holding the spectator's
interest; but one is forced to assume that they also relished
the frequent textual reminiscences of Racine (the following
examples represent merely the more obvious echoes of lines
from *Phèdre*):

> Mais d'où vient sur ton front cette morne tristesse,
> Clytemnestre? pourquoi, dans de si doux moments,
> Ton trouble répond-il à mes embrassements? (II, vi)

> Sers notre amour, Égisthe, et non pas ma prudence (IV, i)

> Qui sait où la fureur aurait pu m'entraîner?
> Qui sait à quels remords j'allais me condamner? (V, iv)

This pastiche is carried to such lengths that even Vauthier,
Lemercier's biographer, in an otherwise fulsome commentary
on the play, is constrained to observe:

L'esprit y paraît plus que le cœur, et l'on y sent moins le poète que l'homme de talent qui se joue au milieu d'éléments divers et les assemble avec une rare expérience.[26]

This particular feature—the constant echoes from the repertory of previous generations of writers—is one we should not expect to find prominent in 'drame bourgeois', where spontaneous expression of feeling was not subject to the same limitations of vocabulary and versification. However, we must remember that the formal definition of this genre was still somewhat fluid, and as we have seen, some 'drames', like Chénier's *Calas*, were still being written in verse. One example of verse 'drame', held up by the censor since 1767 but now produced (in 1790) with considerable success, was Falbaire's *L'Honnête Criminel*, the dramatization of a *fait divers* in which a son had voluntarily taken the place of his father, a Protestant pastor condemned to the galleys for practising his religion. Here, the use of verse seems clearly to conflict with the author's attempt to be concrete and specific in his reference:

> Et toi, retourne sur ton bord.
> Tu ne peux aujourd'hui travailler sur le port.
> De la Marine ici j'attends deux Commissaires
> Qui viennent de Toulon visiter les Galères.
> André, sois à ton banc comme tous les forçats,
> Mais songe qu'avec eux je ne te confonds pas. (I, ii)

But in fact, Falbaire is less concerned with the naturalistic conviction of spontaneous dialogue than with the conventional 'sublime' of stylized attitudes. For this play illustrates the continuation into 'drame bourgeois' of the sentimental clichés of 'comédie larmoyante'; there is no nuance at all in the characterization: all the characters are moved by *bienfaisance* (André has taken his father's place in the galleys; Cécile shares her fortune with Amélie and d'Anplace, and is prepared to marry d'Olban because she is sorry for him; d'Olban generously gives up Cécile and hands her over to André; Lisimon comes in search of André to release him by taking his place . . .), and all are victims of a situation dependent on chance (apart from the original injustice of Lisimon's condemnation). In other words, this is the plot of a sentimental comedy, a completely inadequate vehicle for the humanitarian message it is meant to convey.

Another example of verse 'drame' was La Harpe's *Mélanie*, which had remained unperformed since 1770 because of its provocative theme (like the heroine of Diderot's *La Religieuse*, Mélanie is forced by her family to take religious vows). This was played at the Théâtre de la Nation in 1791 with Talma (who had played d'Anplace in *L'Honnête Criminel*) in the role of Monval, the young man who loves Mélanie, but fails to prevent her cruel father from carrying out his wish. We must assume that Mélanie's situation was not at all uncommon in pre-Revolutionary society; as the enlightened Curé says at the beginning of the play:

> Allons, je vais encor voir une infortunée
> Qu'un intérêt cruel au cloître a condamnée;
> Que l'on ensevelit au lieu de la doter;
> Qui pousse des soupirs que l'on craint d'écouter,
> Et donne, en détestant sa retraite profonde,
> Au Ciel des vœux forcés et des regrets au monde. (I, iii)

Indeed, for the first two acts the situation is highly credible, and the language not at all forced: the alexandrines are those of 'haute comédie', and although no doubt hemistiches are borrowed wholesale from earlier plays in this sort of writing as well as in tragedy, such echoes or reminiscences are not obtrusive, and the verse convention does not seriously impair the naturalism of the style. In Act III, however, the tone suddenly changes: Mélanie's brother (in whose interest the sacrifice of her future is being made) is killed in a duel, and meanwhile Mélanie herself has taken poison; at the same time, the style becomes that of high-flown tragedy:

> Levez-vous à ma voix, victimes malheureuses,
> Levez-vous, entendez mes plaintes douloureuses,
> Accablez avec moi l'oppresseur abhorré,
> Dont je n'ai pu fléchir le cœur dénaturé.
> Dieu! que le dernier cri de sa fille expirante
> Retentisse à jamais dans son âme tremblante!
> Et s'il t'ose implorer au jour de son trépas,
> Rejette sa prière et ne pardonne pas. (III, ix)

A moving drama, capable of expressing a humanitarian message with simple eloquence, turns into a sensational melodrama; and this play too fails because of the lack of *rapport* between theme and dramatic form.

One 'drame' in prose which fully typifies the tendencies of this period is Beaumarchais's *La Mère coupable*, produced at the new Théâtre du Marais in 1792. This third play in the Figaro trilogy has affinities as indicated by its full title, *L'Autre Tartuffe ou la Mère coupable*, with a crop of melodramatic versions of Molière's play which appeared in the closing decades of the century[27]. Like other dramatists, Beaumarchais saw the Tartuffe theme in terms of the social and political context of the Revolution, with false *civisme* on the hypocrite's part taking the place of *fausse dévotion*[28]; but his version derives from his private life as much as from public affairs of the moment, for his hypocrite, Bégearss, represents a personal enemy, the lawyer Bergasse. In his preface, the author draws attention to the play's originality: it consists, he says, of "une intrigue de comédie, fondue dans le pathétique d'un drame". Structurally, it is indeed something of a landmark: it is an early example of the formula of the 'well-made play' which Scribe was to develop, and which Sardou and other playwrights were to do to death[29]; but as regards conception of character and literary style, it is very much of its time. Bégearss, surely one of the blackest and most odious of all stage villains, is opposed by a Figaro who has become the ideal of the faithful retainer, motivated entirely by a highminded and selfless devotion to the interests of the Almaviva family. Here, Beaumarchais returns with a vengeance to the predilections which had marked his early career as a dramatist: there is no trace of the comic verve which distinguishes *Le Barbier de Séville* and *Le Mariage de Figaro*, and *La Mère coupable* is a final tribute to the eighteenth-century axiom that sensibility is a proof of virtue.

(ii) *Pixérécourt and 'le mélodrame'*

IF, as we have suggested, the established genres of tragedy and 'drame' were both characterized during the Revolutionary and post-Revolutionary periods by the development of certain tendencies towards melodrama, it is hardly surprising that 'le mélodrame' itself, as a separate, well-defined genre, should have come into being and flourished in this same period.

There has been some difference of opinion among the historians about the origins of 'mélodrame'. Geoffroy, for instance, writing as a contemporary, defined it as a debased form of eighteenth-century tragedy, "une sorte de tragédie à l'usage du peuple"; and saw Crébillon, Voltaire and Ducis as the forerunners of 'genuine' historical melodrama, which he distinguished from 'le drame bourgeois et populaire'[30]. For Gaiffe, however, 'mélodrame' was simply a product of the evolution of 'drame bourgeois' itself; and he details the various features which the two genres have in common: a taste for the exotic, a mixture of serious and comic scenes, rudimentary psychology—and above all "un style d'une solennelle platitude"[31]. However, the author of the most thoroughgoing treatment of this question, Pitou, while recognizing points of contact with both these genres, particularly the latter, insists on the importance of certain developments that had taken place with regard to more popular forms of dramatic entertainment in the decades preceding the Revolution. Whereas 'drame bourgeois' proper, as a genre with literary aspirations, was confined to the Comédie-Française and the Théâtre-Italien, there sprang up alongside it in the popular theatres (particularly at the Ambigu, opened in 1769) another new kind of entertainment known as 'la pantomime'. Beginning as a mimed performance—a mixture of comedy, fantasy and burlesque set to music—this rapidly developed in the direction of a rudimentary 'drame pathétique':

> Exaltation de la classe bourgeoise et paysanne, magnanimité mouillée de larmes, bras qui s'ouvrent et chaînes qui tombent, bénédictions et actions de grâces, voilà qui rappelle plutôt les drames et les opéras comiques sentimentaux que les Arlequinades et les féeries coutumières au Boulevard.[32]

From 1779 onwards, in spite of the restriction imposed on such popular establishments by the monopoly theatres, these 'pantomimes' became partly spoken; but throughout the 1780s exotic, historical or heroic subjects continued to predominate over domestic:

> Si brèves qu'elles soient, ces pièces échappées au contrôle des Comédiens français ne doivent pas être négligées: c'est par

leur intermédiaire que le Mélodrame apprendra peu à peu du Drame les fécondes ressources dramatiques de la sensiblerie.[33]

Finally, the 'décret de la liberté des théâtres' of 1791 helped this popular genre to become less of an ephemeral spectacle, and to acquire more solid literary connections; the year 1792 saw, for instance, as well as Loaisel de Tréogate's *Le Château du diable* (the first play of this nature to be fully 'dialogué'), Lamartelière's adaptation of Schiller's *Die Räuber*. The last decade of the century also produced an adaptation of Lewis's *Monk* (1797) and two versions of Anne Radcliffe's *Castle of Udolpho*, both in 1798 and one by Pixérécourt himself—a clear indication of the kind of blend of sentimentality and sensationalism that was to characterize all the work of "le Corneille du Boulevard".

Pitou's explanation, that 'mélodrame' was a development from 'la pantomime héroïque', modified by such influences as the gothic novel, is perhaps in its way as selective, and as doctrinaire, as those of Geoffroy and Des Granges or of Gaiffe and others. It seems that one should be prepared to recognize in the new genre the reflection of various tendencies in both serious and popular drama, and to agree with Marsan that in melodrama "s'achève l'évolution logique de tout le théâtre du XVIIIe siècle"[34]. We should also bear in mind a valuable comment made by Grimod de la Reynière, writing in 1797, on the evolution of the 'public de théâtre' towards the end of the century:

Il suffit d'assister à nos jeux scéniques pour être convaincu que jamais la classe des spectateurs ne fut plus inepte sous tous les rapports. Ces spectateurs, également étrangers aux connaissances préliminaires que le goût de la comédie nécessite et suppose, ignorent jusqu'aux premiers éléments de la grammaire et de la versification, ne savent point distinguer la prose des vers, le comique de la farce, l'enflure du sublime, le pathétique du larmoyant. La sublimité de Corneille les étourdit, ils bâillent aux vers de Racine, Molière n'est pour eux qu'un froid écrivain, la gaîté de Regnard les révolte, la raison de Destouches les ennuie, la naïveté de Dancourt les scandalise. Et c'est à de tels juges, bon Dieu, que sont confiées en France aujourd'hui les destinées de l'Art dramatique.[35]

If we can imagine the naive enthusiasm of this new class of spectator, uneducated and quite lacking in sophistication, it is perhaps no wonder that 'le mélodrame' should share so many obvious features with a popular art-form of the early years of our own century: the first silent films, addressed to an equally naive and unsophisticated audience[36].

In the thirty years or so during which Pixérécourt was the undisputed king of the Parisian theatre, he turned out over a hundred plays, the majority melodramas, almost all of them variations on the essential theme of 'l'innocence opprimée'. A brief analysis of the action of a handful of these will serve to illustrate the characteristic features of this genre (which was also, of course, represented by other equally prolific, if less well known, dramatists)[37].

We learn, in the artificial expository scenes at the beginning of *Cœlina, ou l'Enfant du mystère* (1800), that the heroine has two uncles: M. Dufour her guardian, whose son Stéphany she loves, and M. Truguelin, who wants to marry his own son to her for her money. Truguelin is expected at Dufour's house where, we also learn, a dumb beggar called Francisque has recently been given shelter. We are told how this unfortunate man had been found eight years earlier, the victim of a brutal attack, with his tongue cut out. He declines to reveal who his attackers were, but hints, in writing, that they are not unknown to Dufour. Truguelin arrives, and immediately recoils in horror at the sight of Francisque. Cœlina overhears Truguelin and his servant plotting to kill Francisque, and helps to save his life. Truguelin denounces Francisque as Cœlina's father, Cœlina herself as illegitimate and therefore not an heiress; whereupon Dufour turns them out of the house despite his son's pleas. Truguelin is recognized by a witness of the crime committed eight years earlier, and denounced to the police. He disguises himself as a peasant, and the last act is devoted to a chase in and out of a miller's cottage and up a waterfall:

> Truguelin fuit par le sentier qui borde le torrent et va traverser le pont du haut, quand un archer se présente le sabre élevé; Truguelin se jette sur lui, le désarme et le jette dans le torrent; alors il veut passer outre; mais plusieurs archers l'en empêchent, et il est forcé de redescendre précipitamment jusqu'auprès du moulin, où se livre un combat

1   The Théâtre-Français, early 19th century

2 Mérimée as Clara Gazul, by Delécluze

très-vif entre lui et les archers; il en renverse un et va échapper à l'autre, quand les paysans arrivent armés, se précipitent sur lui et se disposent à le frapper. (III, x).[38]

Francisque is proved to have been secretly married to Cœlina's mother: Dufour now accepts him just as impulsively as he had before rejected him: "Vous êtes un brave homme, et je vous rends mon estime"; and all ends happily.[39]

In *Le Pèlerin blanc, ou les Orphelins du hameau* (1801), we see the veneration in which the absent Count of Castelli is held by his tenants and villagers; his castle had burned down fourteen years earlier, leading to the death of his wife, the supposed death of his infant sons, and the Count's own disappearance. The sorrowing villagers presume that he is now dead; and we learn of the tyranny exercised by the present châtelaine, the Baronne (the Count's niece) and her evil *intendant* Roland. Two orphans arrive, and after being hospitably welcomed by the villagers, they are taken off to the castle by Roland. There, when evidence shows them to be the Count's missing sons, they are imprisoned on the Baronne's orders; while Roland administers (as he thinks) poison to the boys. However, he is foiled by a mysterious elderly retainer, who has recently entered the Baronne's service, and who manages to switch two bottles of wine at the crucial moment, so that it is Roland himself who drinks the poison. The boys escape, with the help of the old servant, and rejoin the friendly villagers; when Roland pursues them with armed guards, he is prevented from recapturing them by the intervention of a pilgrim dressed in white: he is none other than the Count, and it is he who has for the past month been disguised as a servant in his own castle, so as to collect evidence against his niece and Roland. The poison now takes its effect, and Roland dies, amid the rejoicing of the villagers.

Éliza, the heroine of *La Femme à deux maris* (1802), has for some time been happily married to Count Édouard, but we learn that she had earlier disobeyed her father to make a first marriage to a scoundrel, Isidore Fritz, who has since been in prison; she has married again on receiving documentary proof of his death. Her father is old and blind, and she has brought him as her *fermier* to the château, though he does not know her: he reveres her as a kind mistress, and her voice reminds him of the daughter he has still not forgiven. There is also a son by the first marriage, who lives with Éliza as her adopted son: she dare not reveal herself either to her father or to her son. The action opens with the arrival of Isidore Fritz, still alive and escaped from prison to claim the whole of his wife's property, which her second husband has settled on her; Éliza's father now recognizes her and curses her as a bigamist. The rest of the play is concerned with Fritz's arrest as a deserter from the army, Édouard's generous connivance in his escape, to save him from an ignominious death, and Fritz's determination to repay this by killing Édouard. Fritz's own accidental death frees Éliza, and her father pardons her now that she is free.

Valentine, ou le Séducteur (1821) shows certain modifications of the characteristic formula: the plot is much less sensational, characterization is more *nuancée*, and there is no happy ending[40]. The Count Édouard, inspired by his libertine friend Ernest, has seduced Valentine, the daughter of a blind old man, Albert; in order to overcome her virtue, he has had to arrange a mock marriage. The action begins on the following day. Valentine finds out that she has been deceived, and her father (whom she had disobeyed by listening to Édouard's advances, when he was disguised as a poor painter) now curses her. Édouard himself is full of remorse, and his wife, a gracious lady, befriends Valentine; but once she has made certain that her father will be well looked after, Valentine throws herself into a river.

In all four of these examples, it will be seen that a strong pathetic interest is aroused on behalf of persecuted virtue (represented by Cœlina and Francisque; the orphan children; Éliza; and Valentine) suffering at the hands of a villain or villains (Truguelin and his accomplice; the Baronne and Roland; Isidore Fritz; Édouard and Ernest). Sympathy for the heroine is reinforced by indignation at the injustice shown by those from whom she has a right to expect indulgence: Dufour, and the fathers of Éliza and Valentine, are all ready to deliver a paternal curse and to cast off their daughter (or adopted daughter) on the basis of a misconceived suspicion; while the prevalence of deaf-mutes and blind old men among the minor characters is also clearly intended to enhance the sentimental appeal of these plays.

Cœlina is much the most spectacular of the four plays analysed,

though the following stage-direction from the closing scene of
La Tête de mort (1827) is an even more extreme example of the
sensational effects Pixérécourt was capable of requiring of his
metteur-en-scène[41]. (This closing incident is quite independent of
any dramatic dénouement; in fact, Réginald, the villain of the
play, has just conveniently died of nothing more lethal than
remorse and shame! At this moment, "on entend le bruit du
Vésuve augmenter... Des foudres volcaniques sillonnent
l'atmosphère"...):

> Tous les personnages se tournent avec effroi vers la gauche
> et sont frappés de terreur; ils veulent fuir en poussant de
> grands cris; mais un torrent de lave se précipite des hauteurs
> à gauche dans les excavations du fond. Tout le monde recule
> à cette vue. Quand l'excavation est remplie, la lave déborde
> et s'avance dans la grande rue qu'elle inonde... Les soldats
> menacent les bandits, qui sont renversés et détruits par la
> lave. Le corps de Réginald en est couvert, et disparaît sous
> les scories brûlantes. Un torrent venant de la gauche traverse
> le théâtre dans sa largeur et va tomber à droite dans une
> cavité où s'étaient réfugiés quelques bandits. On entend leurs
> cris de détresse. Le théâtre est entièrement inondé par cette
> mer de bitume et de lave; une pluie de pierres embrasées
> et transparentes et de cendres rouges tombe de tous côtés...
> Tout concourt à former de cette effrayante convulsion de la
> nature un tableau horrible et tout à fait digne d'être comparé
> aux Enfers.[42]

Pixérécourt is said to have confessed: "J'écris pour ceux qui
ne savent pas lire"[43]; and if the visual appeal of his plays was
crude and unsophisticated, their style too was quite lacking
in subtlety. His text reads like a concentrated parody of
Crébillon, La Chaussée, Diderot and Mercier. *Sententiae* abound:
"L'homme vertueux punit, il n'assassine pas"; "Un père
offensé qui pardonne est la plus parfaite image de la divinité!";
and the whole tone of his dialogue is sententious and emphatic.
Characters address each other as "respectable vieillard", "vil
séducteur", "monstre inhumain", "noble épouse"; and at
moments of crisis they indulge in frenzied soliloquy:

> Ah! je suis trahie, déshonorée, perdue!... Victime des
> adroites séductions d'un imposteur, il ne me reste rien, plus

rien!... O mon père! la voilà donc accomplie votre terrible prédiction! la misère, la honte, l'opprobre, sont désormais l'unique partage de la malheureuse Valentine. (*Valentine*, II, xiii)

Motivation is of the most rudimentary, and the audience is not called on to show any measure of psychological penetration: asides to the *parterre* constantly reveal the villain's real thoughts, and *tableaux à la Diderot* play on the feelings of the simple-minded spectator, underlining a crudely moralistic message.

Of *Valentine*—which, as has been said, is less crude in its effects than most of Pixérécourt's plays—a contemporary wrote:

Cette pièce est presque une tragédie bourgeoise de la conception la plus hardie et de l'effet le plus vigoureux. Elle a produit sur les spectateurs une impression profonde.[44]

But if Édouard himself offers more psychological interest than usual, as a wrongdoer sincerely repentant, he can hardly be called an active character, and the plot of the play is the persecution of Valentine by Édouard's evil genius Ernest. As always, Good is opposed to Evil; and though for once the representative of Good is defeated, there is a saving morality not only in Édouard's remorse, but also in the punishment which we know to be in store for Ernest. It is this black-and-white attitude towards character and plot which above all distinguishes melodrama from tragedy. As Camus wrote in 'Sur l'avenir de la tragédie':

Les forces qui s'affrontent dans la tragédie sont également légitimes, également armées en raison. Dans le mélodrame ou le drame, au contraire, l'une seulement est légitime. Autrement dit, la tragédie est ambiguë, le drame simpliste. Dans la première, chaque force est en même temps bonne et mauvaise. Dans le second, l'une est le bien, l'autre le mal (et c'est pourquoi de nos jours le théâtre de propagande n'est rien d'autre que la résurrection du mélodrame). Antigone a raison, mais Créon n'a pas tort... La formule du mélodrame serait en somme: « Un seul est juste et justifiable » et la formule tragique par excellence: « Tous sont justifiables, personne n'est juste. »[45]

And this distinction of course applies just as much to genuine 'tragédie bourgeoise' as it does to any other form of tragedy. To take an example from English eighteenth-century drama: Lillo's *The Fatal Curiosity* (1736) presents the story, current in the folklore of many countries, to which Camus himself was to give rather more sophisticated form in *Le Malentendu,* and which he also related in *L'Étranger* as "un fait divers... qui avait dû se passer en Tchécoslovaquie":

> Un homme était parti d'un village tchèque pour faire fortune. Au bout de vingt-cinq ans, riche, il était revenu avec une femme et un enfant. Sa mère tenait un hôtel avec sa sœur dans son village natal. Pour les surprendre, il avait laissé sa femme et son enfant dans un autre établissement, était allé chez sa mère qui ne l'avait pas reconnu quand il était entré. Par plaisanterie, il avait eu l'idée de prendre une chambre. Il avait montré son argent. Dans la nuit, sa mère et sa sœur l'avaient assassiné à coups de marteau pour le voler et avaient jeté son corps dans la rivière. Le matin, la femme était venue, avait révélé sans le savoir l'identité du voyageur. La mère s'était pendue. La sœur s'était jetée dans un puits. J'ai dû lire cette histoire des milliers de fois. D'un côté, elle était invraisemblable. D'un autre, elle était naturelle. De toute façon, je trouvais que le voyageur l'avait un peu mérité et qu'il ne faut jamais jouer.[46]

Such a story, in the form given to it by Lillo (if not by Camus), obviously has much in common with Pixérécourt's plots: the same economy of means and crudity of effect. But at least we can see a real affinity, however primitive, with the basic relationship between character and fate which is the hallmark of all tragedy. Not only Lillo's murderers, but also the traveller-victim himself, are to blame; and the play communicates a powerful sense of a tragic force stronger than the characters themselves—whether one calls this Fate, as in Lillo's title, or whether one prefers, with Camus, to call it the Absurd. Melodrama offers nothing of the sort: Fate is replaced by trivial chance, and tragic catharsis by a tearful *pathétique*. For all its atrocities and its piled-up sensations, for all the violence of its language, the affinities of melodrama are not with genuine 'tragédie bourgeoise', but with 'comédie larmoyante' and the domestic drama of the eighteenth century.

What of the affinities between Pixérécourt's theatre and the Romantic drama of the 1830s? In this respect, Geoffroy's prophetic comment is well known but it is none the less valuable for that:

> Si on s'avise d'écrire le mélodrame en vers et en français, si on a l'audace de le jouer passablement, malheur à la tragédie!... Malheur au Théâtre-Français quand un homme de quelque talent s'avisera de faire des mélodrames![47]

This comment is full of irony, of course—and it is hardly complimentary to Pixérécourt; but it was no passing *boutade*. Geoffroy's rooted preference for regular tragedy is never in doubt, but he is enough of a pragmatist to make an accurate assessment of the taste of the contemporary public:

> Des gens qui payent ont droit d'exiger des amusements de leur goût, et s'embarrassent peu des règles de l'art: les lecteurs ne veulent point d'autres livres que des romans; les spectateurs ne demandent pas d'autres pièces que des drames, qui sont des romans en action. Ils ont tort, mais ils payent; et le théâtre doit entendre cette raison-là[48]

and to give credit to Pixérécourt for a highly successful attempt to cater for that taste:

> Le boulevard semble être aujourd'hui la grande sphère d'activité de notre poésie dramatique. Sur ce Parnasse nouveau, chaque mois voit éclore un chef-d'œuvre, tandis que nos plus nobles théâtres, frappés d'une stérilité honteuse, abusent du privilège de la noblesse, et vivent sur leur ancienne gloire. Il ne manque plus aux mélodrames, pour acquérir un titre vraiment littéraire, que la pompe de la représentation, l'éloquence et la dignité du style: du reste, on y trouve plus d'invention, quelquefois plus d'intérêt, souvent autant de régularité et de vraisemblance, que dans beaucoup de pièces soi-disant régulières.[49]

But it is the testimony of Charles Nodier, Pixérécourt's editor, which has the greatest value, since his Introduction to the four-volume *Théâtre choisi*, written in 1840, contains not prophecy, but critical appreciation based on an assessment of the contemporary theatrical scene. Nodier's views on the style of melodrama have already been quoted[50]; but even on this score, the comparison with Pixérécourt's successors is not entirely to the latter's advantage:

> Après tout, le style du mélodrame n'est pas aussi répréhensible que le prétendent aujourd'hui des gens qui n'ont jamais eu de style d'aucune espèce. Il a ses excuses, et peut-être ses avantages. Il enveloppe quelquefois la vérité d'ornements superflus, mais il ne la falsifie point; il la cèle à demi, mais il la contient; sa forme sentencieuse et quelque peu solennelle a quelque chose d'imposant qui lui donne un ascendant merveilleux sur l'esprit du vulgaire; ses tours ambitieux et mystiques semblent commander le respect; ses figures et ses images frappent l'imagination et se saisissent de la mémoire.

However, the main grounds on which Nodier defends Pixérécourt are the wholesomeness, and the effectiveness, of his moral teaching—and here he draws a very emphatic distinction between melodrama and the productions of 'la nouvelle école':

> Je lui sais moins de gré... de ces brillantes qualités dramatiques dont les distributeurs en titre de gloire littéraire auraient dû lui tenir compte avant moi, que du sentiment profond de bienséance et de moralité qui se manifeste dans toutes ses compositions. C'est que je les ai vues, dans l'absence du culte, suppléer aux instructions de la chaire muette, et porter, sous une forme attrayante qui ne manquait jamais son effet, des leçons graves et profitables dans l'âme des spectateurs; c'est que la représentation de ces œuvres vraiment *classiques*, dans l'acception élémentaire du mot, dans celle qui se rapporte aux influences morales de l'art, n'inspirait que des idées de justice et d'humanité, ne faisait naître que des émulations vertueuses, n'éveillait que de tendres et généreuses sympathies, et qu'on en sortait rarement sans se trouver meilleur; c'est qu'à cette époque difficile, où le peuple ne pouvait recommencer son éducation religieuse et sociale qu'au Théâtre, il y avait dans cette application du mélodrame au développement des principes fondamentaux de toute espèce de civilisation, une vue providentielle.

Some of Nodier's comments show the same naive optimism in the power of the theatre as we have already commented on in the case of Diderot:

> Les méchants n'auraient osé se présenter dans un lieu de divertissement où tout les entretenait de remords déchirants et de châtiments inévitables. Un trouble invincible les aurait trahis... Il n'est personne qui n'ait pu lire dans son journal ce mot profond d'un témoin en matière criminelle qui racontait qu'on lui avait proposé un crime, et qu'il s'était écrié pour toute réponse: « Malheureux, tu n'es donc jamais allé à la Gaîté! tu n'as donc jamais vu représenter une pièce de Pixérécourt! » Je dis qu'un Théâtre pareil est sublime.

Yet it would be wrong to doubt the sincerity of his conviction that the moral standards of society had declined sharply since the restoration of the Monarchy, and that this decline was mirrored in the dramatic literature of the 1830s:

> Le Théâtre est devenu l'école de toutes les passions mauvaises que son institution le destinait à corriger. Envoyez au Théâtre qu'on nous a fait, un homme qui n'a point de principes... il aiguisera le soir un poignard pour se donner un air dramatique, et vous le verrez dans un mois sur le chemin du bagne, se draper fièrement des haillons de Robert-Macaire.

Nor should we be misled by the reference to Robert Macaire: it was not Pixérécourt's successors on the 'Boulevard du Crime' who were the principal target of Nodier's attack, and the following passage makes it quite clear that he had in mind plays with more ambitious literary aspirations:

> La tragédie et le drame de la nouvelle école ne sont guère autre chose que des mélodrames relevés de la pompe artificielle du lyrisme; heureux les auteurs de ces productions d'ailleurs fort remarquables, s'ils avaient été aussi fidèles au but primitif du mélodrame qu'à sa forme![51]

At a distance of a century and a half, the reader might be forgiven for thinking that such a *rapprochement* with Hugo and his contemporaries does too much honour to Pixérécourt and the genre he created. But this was not Nodier's view, it would

seem; and it was emphatically not the view of Pixérécourt himself, who insisted on concluding the final volume of his *Théâtre
choisi* with this energetic disclaimer:

> Jadis on choisissait seulement ce qui était bon; mais dans les
> drames modernes, on ne trouve que des crimes monstrueux
> qui révoltent la morale et la pudeur. Toujours et partout
> l'adultère, le viol, l'inceste, le parricide, la prostitution, les
> vices les plus éhontés, plus sales, plus dégoûtants l'un que
> l'autre... J'ai vu, pendant plus de trente ans, toute la
> France accourir aux représentations multipliées de mes
> ouvrages. Hommes, femmes, enfants, riches et pauvres, tous
> venaient rire et pleurer aux mélodrames bien faits. Hélas! ce
> temps est passé. Le théâtre est abandonné pour toujours...
> Depuis dix ans, on a donc produit un très-grand nombre
> de pièces romantiques, c'est-à-dire, mauvaises, dangereuses,
> immorales, dépourvues d'intérêt et de vérité. Hé bien! au
> plus fort de ce mauvais genre, j'ai composé *Latude* avec le
> même goût, les mêmes idées et les mêmes principes qui m'ont
> dirigé pendant plus de trente ans. Cette pièce a obtenu le
> même succès que les anciennes... Pourquoi donc les auteurs
> d'aujourd'hui ne font-ils pas comme moi? Pourquoi leurs
> pièces ne ressemblent-elles pas aux miennes? C'est qu'ils
> n'ont rien de semblable à moi, ni les idées, ni le dialogue, ni
> la manière de faire un plan; c'est qu'ils n'ont ni mon cœur,
> ni ma sensibilité, ni ma conscience. Ce n'est donc pas moi qui
> ai établi le genre romantique. Je le demande maintenant avec
> assurance, ce que l'on a fait depuis et même avant 1830, est-il
> semblable à ce que j'ai produit pendant les trente années
> précédentes? Il est très-pénible pour moi, malade et presque
> aveugle, de m'être trouvé dans la nécessité de toucher cette
> corde brûlante. Mais on m'y a forcé. La question est là. Les
> faits sont là. Je laisse au public impartial le soin de me
> juger.[52]

We can only admire the earnestness with which the playwright
expresses his convictions, and the sincerity of his belief in the
moral utility of the theatre. But Gide's dictum that "c'est avec
les beaux sentiments qu'on fait de la mauvaise littérature"
applies to dramatic writing just as much as to any other kind;
and there could be no better example than Pixérécourt and his
melodrama.

(*iii*) *Shakespeare and Schiller*

"PENDANT une vingtaine d'années, le mélodrame sera tout
notre théâtre; par lui, lentement, se préparera la Révolution de
1827." Marsan's assertion[53] is hardly an exaggeration: the
period 1800–25, during which Pixérécourt flourished, were lean
years indeed for French drama with more serious literary pretensions[54]. It was not only dramatists who were scarce, of
course: French literary and cultural life as a whole were very
slow to recover from the ravages of the Revolution and the
Napoleonic Wars. To quote Alexandre Dumas:

> Pendant dix-neuf ans le canon ennemi passa dans la généra-
> tion des hommes de quinze à trente-six ans. Il en résulta que
> lorsque les poètes de la fin du dix-huitième siècle et ceux du
> commencement du dix-neuvième furent en face les uns des
> autres, ils se trouvaient de chaque côté d'un ravin immense
> creusé par la mitraille de cinq coalitions; au fond de ce ravin
> était couché un million d'hommes, et parmi ce million
> d'hommes violemment arrachés à la génération, se trouvaient
> ces douze poètes que Napoléon avait toujours demandé
> vainement à M. de Fontanes.[55]

Everywhere, however, the feeling was growing among
Frenchmen of taste and discernment that the traditional form
of regular classical tragedy was played out, and that new
energy and inspiration needed to be injected into it; and the
quarter of a century which was to elapse before "la Révolution
de 1827" produced a number of important contributions from
writers, not themselves practising dramatists but conscious of
such a need, capable of analysing it effectively, and willing to
suggest to their readers where sources of new inspiration might
be found. None of these texts had anything like the impact that
the *Préface de Cromwell* was to have, and none possesses the
historical importance of Hugo's challenging manifesto; but
they each reflect the impatience felt by a writer of broad cosmopolitan culture with the limitations of a narrowly insular art-
form, and together they helped to condition the public to accept
the coming 'revolution'.

Madame de Staël's *De la littérature* (1800) is no doubt more
significant as a landmark in the general history of literary

criticism—as the definitive embodiment of that relativism in literary matters towards which progressive thinkers had been groping throughout the eighteenth century—than for any specific promotion of the greater understanding of Shakespeare in France; though P. Van Tieghem has called her chapter 'Des tragédies de Shakespeare' "certainement la contribution la plus ample et la plus substantielle que la critique française eût apportée jusque-là à la découverte de Shakespeare"[56]. Madame de Staël applies to the field of literary creation the same approach that Montesquieu had adopted in *De l'esprit des lois*: just as national characteristics, produced by differences of 'climate', determine the nature of those social and political institutions which vary from one country to another, so these institutions will themselves in turn, together with the more fundamental differences of national temperament which they reflect, impose differences of aesthetic taste. A.-M. Rousseau reminds us that Voltaire himself had early been attracted by this 'relativist' approach:

> Sa meilleure expression est *l'Essay upon epick poetry* de 1727[57] (la version française de 1733 amorce déjà un recul). A chaque peuple ou climat (à chaque culture, nation ou tradition littéraire, dirions-nous aujourd'hui, sans modifier vraiment l'idée) correspond une forme d'art qui lui est propre, entité relativement absolue, pour ainsi dire, qu'il nous faut simplement comprendre, non juger, encore moins tronquer.[58]

But Voltaire's attitude had soon hardened into the aesthetic absolutism which is characteristic of his later years, when references to Shakespeare are marked by real animosity:

> Ce qu'il y a d'affreux, c'est que le monstre a un parti en France; et pour comble de calamité et d'horreur, c'est moi qui autrefois parlai le premier de ce Shakespeare; c'est moi qui le premier montrai aux Français quelques perles que j'avais trouvées dans son énorme fumier. Je ne m'attendais pas que je servirais un jour à fouler aux pieds les couronnes de Racine et de Corneille pour en orner le front d'un histrion barbare.[59]

Voltaire is alluding here to the prospectus issued in 1776 for Letourneur's translation; but it could hardly be said that

Shakespeare had yet done much damage to the reputation of
his French rivals, and references to the English playwright still
tend to be equivocal. Mercier, for instance, although he was
capable of expressing extravagant praise[60], makes only a couple
of passing mentions of Shakespeare in *Du théâtre*; and Jaucourt,
the author of the article 'Stratford' in the *Encyclopédie*, while
claiming that "il s'agit du premier auteur dramatique d'entre
les modernes", follows this with the sort of qualification which
might have come from Voltaire:

> En admirant Shakespeare, nous ne devons pas fermer les
> yeux sur ses défauts; s'il étonne par la beauté de son génie, il
> révolte quelquefois par son comique trivial, ses pointes et ses
> mauvaises plaisanteries... Il écrivit d'abord pour le peuple
> sans secours, sans avis, et sans aucune vue de réputation; mais
> après que ses ouvrages eurent mérité les applaudissements de
> la cour et de la ville, il perfectionna ses productions, et
> respecta davantage son auditoire.

Madame de Staël's criticism, therefore, based on a genuine
effort at historical understanding, really does break new
ground, though it must be said that her attempt to relate
Shakespeare to his historical and social background is hardly a
convincing one. For instance, when she writes:

> Une nation devenue libre, dont les passions ont été fortement
> agitées par les horreurs des guerres civiles, est beaucoup plus
> susceptible de l'émotion excitée par Shakespeare, que de
> celle causée par Racine[61]

she obviously overlooks the fact that the gap separating Racine
from the French Wars of Religion was less than that which
separated Shakespeare from the Wars of the Roses[62]; and, more
generally, the background to which Shakespeare is related
remains vague and conventional:

> Les peuples du nord ont existé, pendant plusieurs siècles, dans
> un état tout à la fois social et barbare, qui a dû longtemps
> laisser parmi les hommes beaucoup de souvenirs grossiers et
> féroces. Shakespeare conserve encore des traces de ces
> souvenirs. Plusieurs de ses caractères sont peints avec les seuls

traits admirés dans ces siècles où l'on ne vivait que pour les combats, la force physique et le courage militaire.[63]

It is also true that for all her understanding of "les littératures du nord", Madame de Staël cannot disguise her preference for the more polished and more regular works of French literature; witness the title of one of her chapters: 'Pourquoi la nation française était-elle la nation de l'Europe qui avait le plus de grâce, de goût et de gaîté?' Nevertheless, in 1800, any attempt to interpret a foreign playwright sympathetically in terms of a historical relationship with the culture which produced him and the audience for which he wrote, was a great step forward. The next step may also be said to have been taken by Madame de Staël in her *De l'Allemagne* (1813), which consolidated the ideas of the earlier work in the celebrated opposition between the 'classical' *littérature du midi* and the 'romantic' *littérature du nord*, each with its own historical justification:

> Je n'examinerai point ici lequel de ces deux genres de poésie mérite la préférence: il suffit de montrer que la diversité des goûts, à cet égard, dérive non seulement de causes accidentelles, mais aussi des sources primitives de l'imagination et de la pensée.[64]

Madame de Staël emphatically rejects the chauvinistic suggestion of French critics that the Germanic literatures are still "dans l'enfance de l'art"; as for the authors of these countries:

> leur caractère, leurs habitudes et leurs raisonnements les ont conduits à préférer la littérature fondée sur les souvenirs de la chevalerie, sur le merveilleux du moyen âge, à celle dont la mythologie des Grecs est la base.

Moreover—and here we can almost recognize the tone, as well as a central theme, of the *Préface de Cromwell*—'classical' culture, however splendid its achievements, is really a foreign importation, which has remained alien to the French people:

> La littérature romantique est la seule qui soit susceptible encore d'être perfectionnée, parce qu'ayant ses racines dans notre propre sol, elle est la seule qui puisse croître et se

vivifier de nouveau: elle exprime notre religion; elle rappelle
notre histoire; son origine est ancienne, mais non antique.[65]

Benjamin Constant, adapting Schiller's *Wallenstein* trilogy in
his own tragedy *Wallstein* (1809), made his intentions quite
clear: "(emprunter) de la scène allemande un de ses ouvrages
les plus célèbres, pour l'adapter aux formes reçues dans notre
littérature"[66]. He was no iconoclast, but prided himself on the
eclecticism of his taste:

> La tragédie française est, selon moi, plus parfaite que celle
> des autres peuples; mais il y a toujours quelque chose d'étroit
> dans l'obstination qui se refuse à comprendre l'esprit des
> nations étrangères. Sentir les beautés partout où elles se
> trouvent, n'est pas une délicatesse de moins, mais une faculté
> de plus.[67]

Schiller's material ("a dramatic prelude and two massive
plays")[68] is not only compressed into the five-act form of a
single play, but also translated into the style and idiom of
Voltairian tragedy: "aux lecteurs de Racine, et surtout de
Voltaire, les tirades de Constant offrent comme un air de
famille. *Wallstein* a été écrit par un homme dont les vers
classiques obsédaient les oreilles et la mémoire"[69]. In spite of
Madame de Staël's eulogy: "Aucune tragédie, depuis la mort
de Voltaire, n'a réuni autant de beautés de divers genres que le
Wallstein français"[70]—the play had been written when its author
and she were living together, so that perhaps she had a vested
interest in its excellence—Constant's tragedy was never performed, and it was only the accompanying treatise *Quelques
Réflexions sur la tragédie de Wallstein et sur le théâtre allemand* which
attracted more than a passing interest. In this brief text, which
was to have considerably more influence than its modest twenty
pages might suggest, Constant offers a perceptive analysis of
the essential character of German historical tragedy, of which
Wallenstein is the masterpiece; and shows himself a generous
admirer of Schiller, in spite of the timidity of his own adaptation
(his appreciation of *Wallenstein* is, for instance, a good deal more
sympathetic than Madame de Staël's in *De l'Allemagne*).
Constant recognizes the sterility of French tragic diction, compared with the resources of the German poets:

Les auteurs allemands peuvent employer, pour le développement des caractères, une quantité de circonstances accessoires qu'il serait impossible de mettre sur notre théâtre sans déroger à la dignité requise: et cependant ces petites circonstances répandent dans le tableau présenté de la sorte beaucoup de vie et de vérité. Dans le *Goetz de Berlichingen* de Goethe, ce guerrier, assiégé dans son château par une armée impériale, donne à ces soldats un dernier repas pour les encourager. Vers la fin de ce repas, il demande du vin à sa femme, qui suivant les usages de ce temps, est à la fois la dame et la ménagère du château. Elle lui répond à demi-voix qu'il n'en reste plus qu'une seule cruche qu'elle a réservée pour lui. Aucune tournure poétique ne permettrait de transporter ce détail sur notre théâtre: l'emphase des paroles ne ferait que gâter le naturel de la situation, et ce qui est touchant en allemand, ne serait en français que ridicule.[71]

He compares Schiller's use of 'personnages subalternes' with the effects Greek dramatists gained from a chorus:

Il y a, sur un second plan, une seconde espèce d'acteurs, spectateurs eux-mêmes, en quelque sorte, de l'action principale, qui n'exerce sur eux qu'une influence très-indirecte. L'impression que produit, sur cette classe de personnages, la situation des personnages principaux, m'a paru souvent ajouter à celle qu'en reçoivent les spectateurs proprement dits. Leur opinion est, pour ainsi dire, devancée et dirigée par un public intermédiaire, plus voisin de ce qui se passe, et non moins impartial qu'eux.[72]

And by the same token, the more comprehensive approach to the portrayal of principal characters, on the part of Schiller and Shakespeare, is contrasted favourably with the selective concentration by French dramatists on a single passion: such concentration may produce "des effets plus constamment tragiques", but the characters resulting from it are conventional stereotypes:

Il y a bien peu de différence entre les caractères d'Aménaïde et d'Alzire. Celui de Polyphonte convient à presque tous les tyrans mis sur notre théâtre, tandis que celui de Richard III, dans Shakespeare, ne convient qu'à Richard III.[73]

Although Constant claims to have preserved this breadth of approach in his *Wallstein*, in other respects he adopts a somewhat defeatist attitude, and it looks as though when it came to the point he lacked the courage of his more radical convictions. For instance, he says that the imagination of German playwrights is always restrained by a "conscience littéraire" and a "sensibilité naturelle" which he fears are lacking in France; so that there would be too many dangers in the imitation of foreign models:

> Il serait à craindre, si ces ressources étaient admises, que nous ne vissions bientôt plus sur notre théâtre que des échafauds, des combats, des fêtes, des spectres et des changements de décoration.[74]

Likewise, though he catalogues the defects produced by observance of the Unities, he has preferred to write his own *Wallstein* as a regular tragedy, and recommends the same course to others: "malgré les gênes qu'elles imposent et les fautes qu'elles peuvent occasionner, les unités me semblent une loi sage"[75]. It was hardly to Constant, therefore, that contemporaries could look for the breakthrough that many were beginning to think was long overdue. However appreciative he might be of the greater 'truth to nature' to be found in Schiller than in Voltaire and other French imitators of Racine, he too, when forced to choose, came down on the side of "la dignité de la tragédie"[76].

Guizot's *Shakespeare et son temps* (1821), the most academic in tone of these precursors of the *Préface de Cromwell*, was written as the introduction to a new translation of Shakespeare based on that of Letourneur, published in 1776–83. A historian with a particular interest in Tudor and Stuart England, Guizot brought his specialist knowledge to bear on the background to Shakespeare's theatre; and altogether, this was the fullest, most scholarly and most sympathetic introduction to Shakespeare yet to appear in France. It also takes us furthest along the road leading to the *Préface de Cromwell*, for instance when Guizot's analysis of Shakespeare's comic genius, compared with that of Aristophanes and Molière, closely anticipates Hugo's theory of the 'grotesque'; for him as for Hugo, 'le mélange des genres' is a natural characteristic of modern art:

Les représentations religieuses, origine du théâtre européen, n'avaient pas échappé à ce mélange. Le christianisme est une religion populaire; c'est dans l'abîme des misères terrestres que son divin fondateur est venu chercher les hommes pour les attirer à lui... Les premiers mystères amenèrent en même temps sur la scène les émotions de la terreur et de la tendresse religieuses et les bouffonneries d'un comique vulgaire; et ainsi, dans le berceau même de la poésie drama-tique, la tragédie et la comédie contractèrent l'alliance que devait leur imposer l'état général des peuples et des esprits.[77]

Unlike Constant, Guizot comes out clearly in opposition to the Unities: the one unity which matters, he argues, is "l'unité d'impression":

L'unité d'impression, ce premier secret de l'art dramatique, a été l'âme des grandes conceptions de Shakespeare et l'objet instinctif de son travail assidu, comme elle est le but de toutes les règles inventées par tous les systèmes. Les partisans exclusifs du système classique ont cru qu'on ne pouvait arriver à l'unité d'impression qu'à la faveur de ce qu'on appelle les trois unités. Shakespeare y est parvenu par d'autres moyens.[78]

The essential criterion in his view is that the focus of interest and the focal point of the action must be identical; in this respect he claims that *Richard III*, where such is the case, com-pares favourably with *Andromaque*, where he finds that although Andromaque is the centre of interest, the action of the play is centred on Hermione.

But however favourable to Shakespeare such comparisons may be, Guizot's remains a detached and objective survey—and it is all the more valuable for that: compare the early attacks on classical tragedy made by such writers as Beaumarchais or Mercier, whose bias was so pronounced that their theoretical treatises became partisan pamphlets in favour of 'le genre sérieux'. Shakespeare, for Guizot (as for Hugo in the *Préface*), was to be an example to playwrights of the sort of way in which they might liberate themselves from a crippling tradition, not a model to be followed uncritically:

Le système classique est né de la vie de son temps; ce temps est passé: son image subsiste brillante dans ses œuvres, mais ne peut plus se reproduire. Près des monuments des siècles écoulés, commencent maintenant à s'élever les monuments d'un autre âge. Quelle en sera la forme? Je l'ignore; mais le terrain où peuvent s'asseoir leurs fondements se laisse déjà découvrir. Ce terrain n'est pas celui de Corneille et de Racine; ce n'est pas celui de Shakespeare; c'est le nôtre; mais le système de Shakespeare peut fournir, ce me semble, les plans d'après lesquels le génie doit maintenant travailler.[79]

It was of course this very point to which Stendhal was to give such challenging expression in his famous formula:

Le *romanticisme* est l'art de présenter aux peuples les œuvres littéraires qui, dans l'état actuel de leurs habitudes et de leurs croyances, sont susceptibles de leur donner le plus de plaisir possible. Le *classicisme*, au contraire, leur présente la littérature qui donnait le plus grand plaisir possible à leurs arrière-grands-pères.[80]

Relativism of time rather than of place forms the basis of Stendhal's argument in *Racine et Shakespeare* (1823). The aspiring playwright must remain independent not only of his French classical predecessors, but also of "le galimatias allemand, que beaucoup de gens appellent romantique aujourd'hui"[81]; and if "la nouvelle tragédie française" were to happen to resemble Shakespearean drama, "ce serait uniquement parce que nos circonstances sont les mêmes que celles de l'Angleterre en 1590"[82].

However, when it comes to the deficiencies of the traditional forms of tragedy, Stendhal is more outspoken than any of these other writers. If we still derive pleasure from works written in this idiom, he says, it is "un plaisir épique, et non plus dramatique"[83]:

Le public va chercher au théâtre français actuel une suite d'odes bien pompeuses, et d'ailleurs exprimant avec force des sentiments généreux.[84]

Such tragedies can appeal only to spectators with a nostalgia for the past:

Je prétends qu'il faut désormais faire des tragédies pour nous, jeunes gens raisonneurs, sérieux et un peu envieux, de l'an de grâce 1823. Ces tragédies-là doivent être en prose. De nos jours, le vers alexandrin n'est le plus souvent qu'un cache-sottise.[85]

The word *pistolet* for instance, says Stendhal, "ne peut absolument pas entrer dans un vers tragique"; and he cites as a most effective example of the 'anti-Romantic' in contemporary drama the dilemma of the poet Legouvé, unable to render Henri IV's famous saying: "Je voudrais que le plus pauvre paysan de mon royaume pût du moins avoir la poule au pot le dimanche" otherwise than by this laboured periphrasis:

Je veux enfin qu'au jour marqué pour le repos
L'hôte laborieux des modestes hameaux
Sur sa table moins humble ait, par ma bienfaisance,
Quelques-uns de ces mets réservés à l'aisance.[86]

Finally, in the second version of *Racine et Shakespeare* (1825), he formulates this challenging definition:

Le Romantisme appliqué au genre tragique, c'est une tragédie en prose qui dure plusieurs mois et se passe en divers lieux.[87]

A good deal of this second version is devoted to a satirical attack on the Academy, a repository of conservatism, says Stendhal, worthy of those original members whose petty criticism of *Le Cid* had made them ridiculous in the eyes of posterity. He quotes from a hostile manifesto by Auger, one of the *quarante*, these words of warning:

Un nouveau schisme se manifeste aujourd'hui. Beaucoup d'hommes élevés dans un respect religieux pour d'antiques doctrines s'effrayent des progrès de la secte naissante, et semblent demander qu'on les rassure... Le danger n'est pas grand encore, et l'on pourrait craindre de l'augmenter en y attachant trop d'importance... Mais faut-il donc attendre que la secte entraînée elle-même au delà du but où elle tend, en vienne jusque-là qu'elle pervertisse par d'illégitimes

succès cette masse flottante d'opinions dont toujours la
fortune dispose?[88]

Already in 1822 the *Annales de la Littérature et des Arts* had shown
how firm a hold the subversive opinions of the progressives had
gained:

> Demandez quel est le poète qui règne sur notre Parnasse par
> la force de son mâle génie. On vous répondra: c'est Byron. —
> Quel est le romancier dont les productions touchantes savent
> intéresser, instruire et émouvoir? — C'est Walter Scott. —
> Enfin quelles sont les tragédies nouvelles qui occupent l'atten-
> tion et divisent les suffrages du monde littéraire? — C'est le
> théâtre de Schiller et celui de Shakespeare.[89]

But Lamartine was there to challenge the supremacy of Byron,
and the Romantic novel had already been launched by Nodier's
Jean Sbogar (1818) and Hugo's *Han d'Islande* (1823); only in
drama were no French names forthcoming. In one very effective
page of his attack on the Academy, Stendhal lists sixteen
nonentities from among its forty members, and invites his
readers to compare these "sous le rapport de l'esprit et du
talent" with his own list of sixteen "sectaires"[90]. Stendhal's
choice is a tribute to his critical acumen and perspicacity: in the
light of subsequent reputation, his nominee wins handsomely
nearly every time; and alongside such relatively safe academic
names as Daunou, Guizot or Fauriel, and writers with a reputation already established like Constant or Lamartine, it is
interesting to see that his list of 'moderns' includes much more
controversial figures such as Béranger, Courier and Lamennais.
But the most striking feature is the dearth of playwrights: the
only dramatist Stendhal can find to include in his right-hand
column is Scribe: Scribe, of whom he was to write a few pages
further on:

> Le genre dramatique, celui de tous qui a le plus illustré la
> France, est stérile depuis bien des années; l'on ne traduit à
> Londres et à Naples que les charmantes pièces de M. Scribe
> ou les mélodrames. Que faut-il faire?[91]

It needed no great foresight in 1825 to recognize that the theatre
was to be the vital battleground. Indeed, the rebel troops were

already gathering: but where was the general who was to lead them into action?

Notes to Chapter Two

1. See A. Pougin, *La Comédie-Française et la Révolution*, Paris, 1902; M. Carlson, *The Theatre of the French Revolution*, Ithaca, N.Y., 1966.
2. See H. F. Collins, *Talma: A Biography of an Actor*, London, 1964, pp. 43ff.
3. Quoted by A. Lieby, *Étude sur le théâtre de M.-J. Chénier*, Paris, 1901, p. 62.
4. Collins, *op. cit.*, pp. 48–50.
5. *Ibid.*, pp. 51–65; Carlson, *op. cit.*, pp. 7–79.
6. Des lois, et non du sang; ne souillez point vos mains.
   Romains, vous oseriez égorger des Romains!
   Ah! du Sénat plutôt périssons les victimes;
   Gardons l'humanité, laissons-lui tous les crimes. (II, iii)
7. Even the dénouement of Voltaire's *Mort de César* was changed in 1792; the sight of the dead Caesar's body was deemed insufficiently stirring, and instead, a curtain was drawn aside revealing "la statue de la Liberté entourée d'un cercle de peuple", while Cassius declaimed:

   Républicains, voilà votre divinité;
   C'est le dieu de Brutus, le mien, la Liberté.

   Cf. Ridgway, *op. cit.*, p. 89.
8. Carlson, *op. cit.*, pp. 155–161.
9. See Carlson, *op. cit.*; Pougin, *op. cit.*; J. Hérissay, *Le Monde des théâtres pendant la Révolution, 1789–1800*, Paris, 1922; E. Lunel, *Le Théâtre et la Révolution*, Paris, 1910.
10. See *Carlson, op. cit.*, pp. 285–287.
11. This character had appeared in *Le Réveil d'Épiménide* and in *L'Épiménide français*, both of 1790.
12. Carlson, *op. cit.*, p. 287.
13. See P. Trahard, *La Sensibilité révolutionnaire (1789–94)*, Paris, 1936.
14. Cf. Carlson, *op. cit.*, p. 217; pp. 194, 196–197; p. 210.
15. *Œuvres*, Paris, 1826, I, p. 173.
16. *Ibid.*, I, pp. 162–163.
17. *Ibid.*, I, p. 173.

18. *Ibid.*, I, pp. 176–177.
19. *Ibid.*, II, pp. 78–79.
20. In this respect it resembles one of the most successful tragedies of the period immediately preceding the Revolution, Lemierre's *La Veuve du Malabar, ou l'Empire des coutumes* (1770). In this tragedy, dealing with the overthrowing of the religious ritual by which a widow was required to sacrifice herself on her husband's funeral pyre, an absurdly romanesque plot leads to a highly contrived happy ending. The melodramatic polarization of characters, the conventional stylization of the language, prevent any emotional involvement with the protagonists; what does perhaps come across effectively is the humanitarian ideal, expressed in Voltairian tones, as something quite divorced from the dramatic context:

> Ce n'est point seulement par la haine et le crime
> Que la cruauté règne, et proscrit le bonheur;
> C'est sous les noms sacrés de justice, d'honneur,
> De piété, de loi; la coutume bizarre
> A su légitimer l'excès le plus barbare;
> Et par un pacte affreux, le préjugé hautain
> A soumis l'être faible au mortel inhumain. (I, iii)

21. The unities are strictly adhered to, and in order to observe the *bienséances*, Claudius and Gertrude are not yet married; Ophélie is the daughter of Claudius, not Polonius (so that Hamlet is faced with a 'Cornelian' conflict between love and duty). There are no gravediggers; the Ghost is retained, but appears only to Hamlet's mind's eye: it is not visible to the audience; and the player-scene is replaced by a *récit* of the murder of a king of England in circumstances similar to that of Hamlet's father. Hamlet renounces his love for Ophélie, and having confronted his mother in the 'closet scene' with an urn containing his father's ashes, kills Claudius, with the help of Norceste (Horatio). Gertrude takes her own life, and Hamlet is proclaimed king. For a more detailed analysis of Ducis's *Hamlet*, see H. P. Bailey, *Hamlet in France*, Geneva, 1964, pp. 14ff., 25ff.; and J. D. Golder, '*Hamlet* in France 200 years ago' in *Shakespeare Survey*, XXIV, 1971, pp. 79–86.
22. See Collins, *op. cit.*, p. 157.
23. *Lettres philosophiques*, no. 18.
24. Ducis's version of this soliloquy was added in 1804; it is missing in the 1769 text.

25. Mme de Staël, *De l'Allemagne* (1810), ch. xxvii.

26. G. Vauthier, *Essai sur la vie et les œuvres de N. Lemercier*, Toulouse, 1886, p. 70.

27. See W. D. Howarth, 'The Theme of *Tartuffe* in Eighteenth-century Comedy', *French Studies*, IV, 1950, pp. 113–127.

28. For an interesting analysis of *La Mère coupable*, see Péguy, *Œuvres en prose, 1909–1914*, Paris, 1961, pp. 157–179.

29. See A. R. Pugh, 'Beaumarchais, the *drame bourgeois* and the *pièce bien faite*', *Modern Language Review*, LXI, 1966, pp. 416–421.

30. This view is endorsed by the author of a thesis on Geoffroy, C.-M. Des Granges (*Geoffroy et la critique dramatique*, Paris, 1897, pp. 404ff.).

31. F. Gaiffe, *op. cit.*, p. 550.

32. A. Pitou, 'Les Origines du mélodrame français à la fin du XVIIIe siècle', *Revue d'Histoire Littéraire de la France*, XVIII, 1911, p. 260.

33. *Ibid.*, p. 266.

34. J. Marsan, 'Le Mélodrame et Guilbert de Pixérécourt', *Revue d'Histoire Littéraire de la France*, VII, 1900, p. 196.

35. Quoted by W. G. Hartog, *Guilbert de Pixérécourt, sa vie, son mélodrame, sa technique et son influence*, Paris, 1913, p. 71.

36. M. Descotes, *op. cit.*, ch. vii ('*Cœlina, ou l'Enfant du mystère* de Pixérécourt: Le Public renouvelé') makes an extended comparison, on a rather different basis, between melodrama and 'le western cinématographique' (pp. 225–226).

37. For a brief comment on the melodramas of Ducange, for instance, see J. Guex, *Le Théâtre et la société française de 1815 à 1848*, Vevey, 1900, pp. 19–24.

38. F. Rahill, *The World of Melodrama*, University Park, Pa., 1967, p. 38, refers to this scene as "one of the most important in the whole range of the modern theatre. With *Cœlina*, action—action integrated with an elaborate, built set—came on the French stage from the pantomime to galvanize a spoken play. Realistic settings and properties had been used before this at the Boulevard theatres, and romantic effects in scenic investiture and machines were developed to a high degree of perfection in the court pageants and opera of the Baroque era in Italy, France and England. What *Cœlina* did was recapitulate this progress in a theatrical piece which combined the everyday and the romantic."

39. See *Cœlina, ou l'Enfant du mystère*, édition critique par Norma Perry, Exeter, 1972.

40. It was also less popular: in the Foreword to Vol. I of his *Théâtre*

choisi (Nancy, 1841–43), Pixérécourt claims a total of 1,533 attested performances for *Le Pèlerin blanc*, 1,476 for *Cœlina*, and 1,346 for *La Femme à deux maris* (these were the three most popular plays, judged by this criterion)—but only 131 for *Valentine*.

41. "Il faut que l'auteur dramatique sache mettre lui-même sa pièce en scène... J'ai été redevable de la moitié de mes succès au soin minutieux et sévère avec lequel j'ai constamment présidé aux répétitions" (*Théâtre choisi, ed. cit.*, IV, pp. 495–496).

42. *Ibid.*, IV, pp. 358–359. It should be remembered that this taste for lavish spectacle in the popular boulevard theatres had been to some extent anticipated by the Théâtre-Français itself, once the stage had been freed of its spectators in 1759. Voltaire's *Olimpie* (1764) ends with the heroine throwing herself into a "bûcher enflammé", while in Act V of the unstaged *Lois de Minos* "On voit le temple en feu, et une partie qui tombe dans le fond du théâtre".

43. Hartog, *op. cit.*, p. 191.

44. Quoted in *Théâtre choisi, ed. cit.*, IV, p. 113. The same point is made by F. Rahill, who writes of *Valentine* as "the finest thing Pixérécourt ever did, the only one of his plays which rises above the limitations of the genre in which he worked . . . The play is actually not a melodrama at all; its affinities are all with the earlier *drame* or the later plays of Dumas *fils*" (*op. cit.*, pp. 64–65).

45. *Théâtre, récits, nouvelles*, Paris, 1962, p. 1703.

46. *Ibid.*, p. 1180. On the theme of *The Fatal Curiosity*, see M. Frauenrath, *Le Fils assassiné*, Munich, 1974.

47. Quoted by Marsan, *art. cit.*, p. 216.

48. 'Notice sur *La Rose blanche et la rose rouge*' in Pixérécourt, *Théâtre choisi, ed. cit.*, II, p. 507.

49. 'Notice sur *La Femme à deux maris*', *ibid.*, I, p. 243.

50. See p. 33.

51. *Théâtre choisi, ed. cit.*, I, pp. xiii, ii, iii–vi, vi–vii, vii.

52. *Ibid.*, IV, pp. 497–499.

53. *Art. cit.*, p. 201.

54. Pixérécourt himself was extremely modest in this respect: not only did he resist pressure from friends to stand for election to the Academy, but having once offered one of his plays to the Théâtre-Français and had it accepted, he withdrew it before it was staged.

55. Quoted in Guex, *op. cit.*, p. 25.

56. P. Van Tieghem, *Le Préromantisme*, Vol. III: *La Découverte de Shakespeare sur le Continent*, Paris, 1947, p. 333.

57. "There are not more Revolutions in governments than in arts. They are shifting, and gliding away from our pursuit, when we endeavour to fix them by our rules and definitions", quoted by T. Besterman, *Voltaire on Shakespeare* (Studies on Voltaire and the Eighteenth Century, LIV), Geneva, 1967, p. 41.

58. Introduction to Voltaire, *La Mort de César*, Paris, 1964, pp. 15–16.

59. Besterman, *op. cit.*, p. 175.

60. For instance, he calls the scene between Brutus and Cassius (*Julius Caesar*, IV, iii) "la scène la plus sublime qui ait jamais été tracée sur aucun théâtre; n'eût-il fait que cette scène, il serait immortel" (quoted by P. Van Tieghem, *op. cit.*, III, p. 325).

61. *De la littérature, considérée dans ses rapports avec les institutions sociales*, ed. P. Van Tieghem, Paris, 1959, I, p. 194.

62. See Van Tieghem, *Le Préromantisme*, III, p. 332.

63. *De la littérature, ed. cit.*, I, p. 202.

64. *De l'Allemagne*, ed. H. W. Eve, Oxford, 1906, p. 33.

65. *Ibid.*, p. 35.

66. *Wallstein, tragédie en cinq actes et en vers, précédée de quelques réflexions sur le théâtre allemand*, ed. J.-R. Derré, Paris, 1965, p. 67.

67. *Ibid.*

68. G. Steiner, *The Death of Tragedy*, London, 1963, p. 158.

69. Derré, Introduction to *Wallstein, ed. cit.*, p. 10.

70. Quoted in Derré, *op. cit.*, p. 41.

71. *Op. cit.*, pp. 52–53.

72. *Ibid.*, p. 54.

73. *Ibid.*, p. 62.

74. *Ibid.*, p. 57.

75. *Ibid.*, p. 60.

76. *Ibid.*

77. *Shakespeare et son temps*, ed. Paris, 1852, pp. 80–81.

78. *Ibid.*, pp. 152–153.

79. *Ibid.*, pp. 177–178.

80. *Racine et Shakespeare*, ed. H. Martineau, Paris, 1928, p. 43.

81. *Ibid.*, p. 52.

82. *Ibid.*, p. 51.

83. *Ibid.*, p. 8.

84. *Ibid.*, p. 9.

85. *Ibid.*, p. 3.

86. *Ibid.*, p. 47.

87. *Ibid.*, p. 113.

88. *Ibid.*, pp. 146–147.

89. Quoted by R. Bray, *Chronologie du romantisme, 1804–1830*, Paris, 1932, p. 67.
90. *Op. cit.*, p. 148.
91. *Op. cit.*, p. 155.

3 Preparations for Battle: The 1820s

(i) The battleground: theatres and audiences

WE have seen that the Napoleonic decrees had left the organization of the theatres much as it had been before the Revolution:
the official theatres retained their strict monopoly, and the
Gymnase, Ambigu-Comique and similar houses where Pixérécourt and the other authors of melodrama achieved their
popular successes remained worlds apart from the Théâtre-
Français and the Odéon. Not only the repertory, but also the
composition of the audience, was different[1]; yet the greater
vigour and inventiveness of the boulevard theatres was reflected,
year after year, in declining numbers at the Théâtre-Français,
and if a popular dramatist like Pixérécourt may often seem over-
ready to accept an established and unchanging order of things,
this was perhaps not entirely due to lack of ambition:

> *Benserade, ou Madame de la Vallière*, comédie en un acte et en
> vers, reçue au Théâtre-Français le 28 août 1818. Quoique la
> réception eût été unanime et très flatteuse pour l'auteur, il n'a
> jamais voulu faire jouer cette pièce de peur que la représenta-
> tion n'obtînt pas à son gré un succès pareil à ceux qu'il avait
> coutume d'obtenir depuis vingt ans.[2]

Just as much as conservative taste on the part of the 'connoisseurs' in the audience, it was the traditionalism and vested
interests among the actors which, as they had done before the
Revolution, stood in the way of change. The rigid hierarchy of
the organization, whereby effective power was preserved in the
hands of a committee of senior *sociétaires*; the strict demarcation
of the kind of parts each actor was entitled to play; even the
system of 'association', which discouraged lavishness of décor
and costumes, in the interests of a higher 'share' for each

sociétaire—witness this complaint on the occasion of a spectacular
production in 1828:

> Les immenses frais d'études, de costumes, de décors, de mise
> en scène ont eu pour résultat de rabaisser à 9 600 francs la
> part entière d'un comédien[3]

and, finally, a genuine reluctance to compete with the boulevard
actors on their own ground:

> Nous savons bien qu'en énergie âpre et sauvage, notre
> camarade Frédérick Lemaître l'emportera sur nous, qu'en
> larmes amères, qu'en accents de l'âme, Mme Allan-Dorval
> luttera avec avantage contre Mlle Mars[4]

—all these factors helped to preserve the Théâtre-Français as
the last retreat of the classical tradition, the symbol of the *ancien
régime* in the arts. The grievances of the *modernes* are summed up
in this *cri de cœur* of Émile Deschamps, defining his ideal theatre
as everything that the Théâtre-Français was not:

> la direction d'un entrepreneur intelligent, sans comité de
> lecture ni d'administration, sans cet encombrement d'ou-
> vrages reçus depuis trente ans et vieillis avant de naître, avec
> des acteurs jeunes, disposés à jouer tous les rôles, en étudiant
> la pantomime expressive et la déclamation naturelle des
> grands acteurs anglais... avec la ferme volonté de ne
> représenter, en fait de pièces nouvelles, que des pièces
> vraiment neuves, et d'un caractère homogène.[5]

Far from being content with easier victories in less tradi-
tionalist surroundings, the partisans of the new drama were
agreed that nothing would be achieved until this Bastille of the
arts had fallen; and it is no coincidence that the 'bataille
d'*Hernani*', by far the most significant single event in the establishing of Romantic drama in the Parisian theatre, was to take
place in the Théâtre-Français: although other Romantic plays
of the stature of *Hernani* were put on elsewhere, this was the
conquest that counted.

In retrospect, however, signs of the coming changes can be
discerned even here; and of the three principal factors which

historians generally recognize as having accelerated the acceptance of Romantic drama in 1830, two concern the Théâtre-Français very directly. The first of these was the appointment in 1825 of a new Commissaire Royal, Baron Taylor, to fill the post which had been set up (with the title of Commissaire Impérial) by the Napoleonic reforms of 1812, to ensure effective governmental control of the theatre. Taylor was still a young man, in his middle thirties; and in addition to having had three years' experience as administrator of the Panorama Dramatique, he was also an author (in collaboration with Nodier) of a melodrama based on a gothic novel by Maturin, and had studied painting and practised as a *décorateur*. Moreover, he admired Shakespeare, and was already on friendly terms with Hugo and Vigny. The formal powers of the Commissaire Royal had always been fairly limited: he handled the budget, dealt with matters of 'external relations', and acted as arbitrator in the not infrequent cases of dispute between members. Policy as regards choice and production of plays remained in the hands of the Committee, but the extent to which this could be influenced by the Commissaire depended very much on the latter's individual personality. What influence Taylor was able to assert was bound to be a liberalizing one, and the significance of this was soon recognized both within the Théâtre-Français, where he antagonized the more reactionary *comédiens*, of whom one Pierre-Victor made himself the spokesman:

> Vous qui, depuis six ans, avez tout mis en œuvre pour perdre [les tragédies classiques]; vous qui les laissez représenter de manière à les rendre méconnaissables; vous qui les faites journellement décrier par les feuilles romantiques de votre coterie, et qui les avez sacrifiées aux pièces les plus indignes de la Scène Française[6]

—and outside, where Émile Deschamps, for instance, hailed him as the white hope of the Romantics:

> Il faut espérer que la Comédie-Française ouvrira enfin les yeux. Avec les chefs-d'œuvre de son magnifique répertoire, secourus des chefs-d'œuvre de Shakespeare, avec l'ensemble satisfaisant qu'elle peut encore donner à ses représentations,

avec la sollicitude éclairée de M. Taylor (si elle sait y reconnaître sa providence), la Comédie-Française reprendrait bientôt cet éclat et cette popularité qui s'effacent et se perdent de jour en jour dans les pâleurs de l'imitation et dans les déviations de la routine.[7]

It would be wrong, however, to suggest that this was simply a case of Taylor championing the Romantics, opposed by the conservatism of his colleagues. Several of the *sociétaires* defended him against Pierre-Victor's attacks, and perhaps what Taylor's appointment in 1825 did do was to precipitate the divisions and dissensions within the Théâtre-Français which, as M. Descotes has so convincingly shown, were to make the establishing of Romantic drama such a delicate enterprise.

One senior *sociétaire* who did welcome Taylor's appointment was Talma:

Nous avons en ce moment un jeune homme à notre tête, comme commissaire royal, le baron Taylor, amoureux du théâtre, artiste, dessinateur, plein de zèle, de talents, auteur lui-même d'un grand voyage pittoresque en France; s'il ne parvient pas à relever le théâtre, il faudra y renoncer.[8]

But any possibility of a fruitful collaboration between the new Commissaire and the *doyen* of the company soon disappeared, for little more than a year elapsed before Talma's death (October 1826). The precise effect of this, the second significant event of the middle 1820s, on the relations between the Romantic dramatists and the Théâtre-Français has been much debated. On the one hand, Talma possessed a 'Romantic' sensibility[9], admired Kemble and other English actors, and had a feeling for Shakespeare which went far beyond Ducis's adaptations. "A combination of Racine and Shakespeare" had been Madame de Staël's description of his acting; and she had looked forward to the day when French dramatists should "réunir dans leurs compositions ce que l'acteur a su si bien amalgamer par son jeu"[10]; as if to confirm her prophecy, Talma is said to have given an enthusiastic reception, shortly before his death, to a reading of the first Act of Hugo's *Cromwell*. On the other hand, it was to Talma above all that playwrights and actors had looked to bolster up the shaky fortunes of the

Théâtre-Français in the early 1820s; and such tragedies as did succeed—Jouy's *Sylla* (1821), for instance, in which Talma modelled his portrayal of the hero on the physical appearance and manner of Napoleon—did so as vehicles for his personal triumph. Delécluze, the painter with Romantic sympathies, wrote this comment on Talma's death:

> Il est vrai de dire que la tragédie n'était tolérée en France qu'à cause de lui. Il est curieux de savoir ce qu'il en adviendra après sa mort. [11]

and the extraordinary petition which a group of playwrights addressed to the King in 1829, asking him to intervene in order to prevent the Théâtre-Français from being handed over to Romantic innovators, explicitly adduces Talma's death as a primary cause of the failure of tragedy to hold its own:

> La mort de l'acteur qui rivalisait de talent avec les acteurs les plus parfaits de quelque époque que ce soit, a porté plus d'un dommage au noble genre dont il était le soutien. Soit par dépravation de goût, soit par conscience de leur impuissance à le remplacer, quelques sociétaires du Théâtre-Français prétendant que le genre où Talma excellait ne pouvait plus être utilement exploité, se sont efforcés d'exclure la tragédie de la scène, et de lui substituer des drames. [12]

It seems on balance that Descotes is probably justified in concluding that "par sa mort, frappant de paralysie le genre traditionnel, Talma ouvrait au drame les portes du Théâtre-Français beaucoup plus sûrement que s'il avait vécu jusqu'en 1830" [13].

The third event took place outside the Théâtre-Français, though under the auspices of the 'Commission des Théâtres royaux': this was the visit of a company of English actors, headed by Kemble, Kean, Macready and Miss Smithson, in September 1827. An earlier visit in 1822 had met with a predominantly hostile reception, usually ascribed to the fact that political relations between the two countries had still not recovered from the aftermath of 1815: prevented from completing even a single performance at the Théâtre de la Porte-Saint-Martin, the English troupe had on that occasion been forced to withdraw to a private theatre and play to a small public of connoisseurs. In 1827, however, an improvement in the political situation, the outstanding talent and reputation of the performers, and no doubt a desire on the part of a wider public to experience at first hand this Shakespeare about whom so much was now being written, combined to make the visit as much a success as the previous one had been a failure. Performances were shared between the Odéon, the Salle Favart, and the Théâtre-Italien; and although it had originally been arranged for four months, the season was extended to nearly a year.

Since the censorship laws in Charles X's reign prohibited all reference to kings and queens in too disparaging a light, and were indeed very sensitive on the subject of any allusions to politics or religion, it was still not possible to show Shakespeare complete and unabridged; thus in *Hamlet*, Claudius and Gertrude became duke and duchess, and all reference to the Church's attitude to suicide and similar delicate topics had to be omitted[14]. But if not complete and uncensored, this was at least authentic Shakespeare[15], and the public was able for the first time to see what lay behind the conventional alexandrines of Ducis. Reaction was naturally mixed. The diehards, represented by the *Journal des Débats*, the *Courrier Français*, the *Mercure de France* and the *Réunion*, reiterated the standard reactions of their predecessors: occasional 'beautés' were contrasted with prevailing horrors, monstrosities, and flagrant breaches of good taste[16]. Not only the grave-diggers' scene in Hamlet, but also the hero's behaviour during the players' scene, were found offensive: "Rien sur notre scène ne paraîtrait moins tragique qu'un héros se roulant par terre comme le fait Hamlet"[17]. Clearly, for such spectators nothing had changed in the century which had elapsed since Voltaire's *Lettres philosophiques*: the mixture of comic and tragic scenes was still "une monstruosité qui ne peut convenir aux nations civilisées"; and *Hamlet*, although a "grande création", was, taken as a whole, an "amalgame indigeste de beautés inimitables et de trivialités choquantes"[18].

On the other hand, there is abundant testimony to the effect of these performances of Shakespeare and other dramatists in the English players' repertory on those who were willing to be

3   Costume for *Amy Robsart,* by Delacroix

4 'La Bataille d'*Hernani*', by Granville

impressed. The most striking evidence is this passage from
Dumas's 'Comment je devins auteur dramatique':

> Vers ce temps, les acteurs anglais arrivèrent à Paris. Je
> n'avais jamais lu une seule pièce du théâtre étranger. Ils
> annoncèrent *Hamlet*. Je ne connaissais que celui de Ducis.
> J'allai voir celui de Shakespeare.[19]
>
> Supposez un aveugle-né auquel on rend la vue, qui
> découvre un monde tout entier dont il n'avait aucune idée;
> supposez Adam s'éveillant après sa création, et trouvant sous
> ses pieds la terre émaillée, sur sa tête le ciel flamboyant, au-
> tour de lui des arbres à fruits d'or, dans le lointain un fleuve,
> un beau et large fleuve d'argent, à ses côtés la femme jeune,
> chaste et nue, et vous aurez une idée de l'Éden enchanté dont
> cette représentation m'ouvrit la porte.
>
> Oh! c'était donc cela que je cherchais, qui me manquait,
> que me devait venir; c'était ces hommes de théâtre, oubliant
> qu'ils sont sur un théâtre; c'était cette vie factice, rentrant
> dans la vie positive à force d'art; c'était cette réalité de la
> parole et des gestes qui faisaient, des acteurs, des créatures de
> Dieu, avec leurs vertus, leurs passions, leurs faiblesses, et non
> pas des héros guindés, impassibles, déclamateurs et senten-
> cieux. O Shakespeare, merci! O Kemble et Smithson,
> merci! Merci à mon Dieu! merci à mes anges de poésie!
>
> Je vis ainsi *Roméo*, *Virginius*, *Shylock*, *Guillaume Tell*, *Othello*;
> je vis Macready, Kean, Young. Je lus, je dévorai le répertoire
> étranger, et je reconnus que, dans le monde théâtral, tout
> émanait de Shakespeare, comme, dans le monde réel, tout
> émane du soleil; que nul ne pouvait lui être comparé, car il
> était aussi dramatique que Corneille, aussi comique que
> Molière, aussi original que Calderon, aussi penseur que
> Goethe, aussi passionné que Schiller. Je reconnus que ses
> ouvrages, à lui seul, renfermaient autant de types que les
> ouvrages de tous les autres réunis. Je reconnus enfin que
> c'était l'homme qui avait le plus créé après Dieu.
>
> Dès lors ma vocation fut décidée...[20]

The literal-minded reader may well object that Dumas's vocation must surely have been at least adumbrated by this time,
since he had already had two one-act vaudevilles produced (*La
Chasse et l'amour* at the Ambigu-Comique in September 1825,
and *La Noce et l'enterrement* at the Porte-Saint-Martin in November 1826); but there is no reason to doubt the sincerity of this

eloquent tribute to the powerful effect that the revelation of Shakespeare at first hand was capable of producing on the imagination of a young creative writer.

Berlioz was another young Romantic who recorded a lyrical account of his enthusiasm for Shakespeare—an enthusiasm no doubt particularly tinged in his case (at least in retrospect) with a personal admiration for the Ophelia of Miss Smithson, whom he was to marry in 1833:

> Shakespeare, en tombant ainsi sur moi à l'improviste, me foudroya. Son éclair, en m'ouvrant le ciel de l'art avec un fracas sublime, m'illumina les plus lointaines profondeurs. Je reconnus la vraie grandeur, la vraie beauté, la vérité drama-tique. Je mesurai en même temps l'immense ridicule des idées répandues en France sur Shakespeare par Voltaire... et la pitoyable mesquinerie de notre vieille poétique de pédagogues et de frères ignorantins. Je vis... je compris... je sentis... que j'étais vivant et qu'il fallait me lever et marcher.[21]

But it was not only this impact of Shakespeare on impressionable young men of letters, or even on the cultured public at large, which had such a powerful effect. There was also the revelation of a new style of acting; and numerous are the tributes paid by delighted spectators to the 'naturalness' of this English style, and the realism with which the English actors expressed emotion. This time, the *Courrier Français* echoed the favourable opinion:

> Il faut absolument que nos acteurs, et c'est déjà l'avis de Mlle Mars, empruntent aux acteurs anglais l'usage commode et raisonnable de se tenir sur la scène comme on se tient dans un salon. Chez nous, quand cinq ou six personnages se trouvent à la fois sur le théâtre, ces personnages forment un demi-cercle devant la rampe, et trop souvent celui qui ne parle pas, regarde dans les loges, ce qui détruit toute espèce d'illusion. En Angleterre, les acteurs vont et viennent sur la scène. Quand ils ne doivent pas prendre part à la conversation, ils se retirent au fond du théâtre, ils font enfin ce qu'on fait dans les salons de Paris et de Londres.[22]

Some discerning playgoers, it is true, did protest at the excessive use of *pantomime*, which reminded them of the style of

melodrama, and at the excessive realism—or at any rate conviction—with which death-agonies and other extremes of
suffering were conveyed; and critics were not slow to ridicule
the imitation of such mannerisms, which became fashionable
even at the Théâtre-Français:

> Comme les extrêmes se touchent, on s'aperçoit depuis
> quelques mois d'une certaine velléité qu'aurait ce premier
> théâtre de marcher sur les brisées du Cirque-Olympique et
> de produire de l'effet à sa manière, car le comité n'exclut pas
> tout à fait la tragédie, mais il la voudrait comme il l'entend,
> c'est-à-dire avec marches, changements à vue, coups de
> sabres, assaut, enfin avec tout l'attirail dramatique; c'est
> ainsi que l'ont décidé les membres les plus influents de la
> Comédie, qui depuis quelque temps ne jurent que par
> Shakespeare, et, tout ébahis de la pantomime des acteurs
> anglais à Paris, veulent une agonie de cinq bonnes minutes
> après un coup de poignard et des haut-le-cœur après un
> empoisonnement. Déjà une de ses principales actrices, devant
> singer la folie, a reçu l'ordre d'aller dans une maison de santé
> prendre sur le fait les grimaces et les aberrations de gestes et
> d'idées les plus en usage dans les cas d'aliénation mentale;
> déjà, dit-on, un acteur qui doit avaler une coupe de ciguë
> dans un drame reçu par acclamation, s'exerce depuis un mois
> sur son tapis à faire des sauts de carpe devant sa psyché et à
> se débattre avec son traversin.[23]

However, there is no doubt that the technique of the English
visitors was much admired—and imitated—by the French
actors themselves; and more important from the point of view
of the form that Romantic drama was to take than any attempt
on the part of the established tragedians of the rue de Richelieu
to modify their style in an effort to give new life to a dying
genre, was the fact that the young actors of the next *promotion*—
Bocage, Lemaître, Marie Dorval—who were to give flesh and
blood to Romantic drama outside the Théâtre-Français, were
all much influenced by Kean and Kemble, Smithson and
Macready.

Comparison with the early days of the Italian actors in France
is surely instructive. Playing before audiences whose language
they could speak only imperfectly, the Italians had been forced

to perfect an art of pantomime and significant gesture. Now, the English company of 1827–28 were acting in a language only imperfectly understood by their audiences; and if Dr. Baldick's estimate of the extent of this understanding is correct:

> Ignoring the beauty of the verse, which they could not appreciate, and fastening instead on the more sensational pieces of stage business, such as Miss Smithson's grimaces, Kean's convulsions and Kemble's sardonic laughter, they saw little more in Shakespeare than a combination of picturesque costumes, crude contrasts and violent action[24]

—it is perhaps hardly surprising that one important influence of their visit, paradoxical though this may seem, should have been to turn the long-awaited Romantic drama in the direction of melodrama and spectacle.

(ii) *The classical camp: reactionaries and progressives*

BY 1825, as can be seen from *Racine et Shakespeare*, the idea of the coming 'bataille romantique' was very much in the air. Indeed, with the advantage of hindsight, it is not difficult to recognize that the issue throughout the 1820s was not whether a Romantic version of historical drama would sooner or later supplant traditional tragedy on the French stage, but what form the new kind of drama would take: whether it would be an imaginative, poetic form in which the pull towards drama would be stronger than that towards history, or a sober, documentary genre inspired by fidelity towards historical fact. The two attitudes towards history may be roughly attributed, respectively, to the rival 'Romanticisms' of the middle 1820s: on the one hand, the royalist Catholics grouped round Nodier and Hugo, poets and imaginative writers, and on the other the liberals who gravitated round Stendhal.

It was in 1824 that Charles Nodier became librarian at the Arsenal, and began to hold regular Sunday gatherings at his home. We have seen that by the early 1840s, disillusioned with the achievements of Romanticism in the theatre, Nodier was prepared to adopt a very critical attitude towards his former associates[25]; but the Cénacle at the Arsenal was of the greatest importance in these formative years, and the personal relation-

ship between Nodier and Hugo has been hailed as a major
influence in shaping the ideas which the latter was to express in
the *Préface de Cromwell*[26]. In the early 1820s, however, the leading members of this group do not seem to have displayed any
very direct interest in historical drama: the outlet which their
imaginative approach to history found lay rather in the direction of prose fiction: cf. Nodier's *Jean Sbogar* (1818), and Hugo's
Bug-Jargal (written in 1818 and published in 1826) and *Han
d'Islande* (1823). However, champions of the poetic, imaginative
treatment of history in the theatre were to be found in Lebrun,
whose very successful adaptation of Schiller's *Maria Stuart*
(1820) even Stendhal was prepared to call "à demi romantique";
and in Manzoni, whose *Conte di Carmagnola* and *Adelchi* were
published in 1823 in Fauriel's translation, accompanied by
Manzoni's own 'Lettre à M. Chauvet sur l'unité de temps et de
lieu dans la tragédie'. In this treatise, the Italian playwright
defends his own dramatic formula, a blend of responsible
historical reconstruction with more imaginative poetic interpretation; and demonstrates, by a detailed analysis of Shakespeare's *Richard II*, that serious historical drama, dealing
responsibly with the relationship between cause and effect, must
be free of the limitations imposed by the unities of time and
place[27].

This current was fed by Scott's novels, and it fused with the
more imaginative influence of the Byron of *Manfred*; Shakespeare was beginning to be better known among a circle of
literary *cognoscenti*, and here were all the forces capable of
combining to produce the formula for that kind of Romantic
drama of which *Hernani* was to be the supreme example. But the
headway made by this movement in the theatre, to begin with,
was slow indeed. A translation of Byron's *Marino Faliero* was just
as much a failure at the Théâtre-Français in 1821 as the original
had been in London; and as for the dramatic productions with
which the members of Nodier's group tried to revitalize the
theatre, these were a long way from suggesting the sort of
inspiration which was to produce *Hernani*. The melodramatic
'tragedy' which Nodier himself composed (in collaboration
with Taylor, the future administrator of the Théâtre-Français)
—*Bertram, ou le Château de Saint-Aldobrand, tragédie en cinq actes
traduite librement de l'anglais du Révérend C.-R. Maturin* (1821)—

was, as he admitted in the Preface, "comme les rêveries déli-
rantes des fiévreux", and only to be considered as the "distraction innocente d'une étude plus sérieuse". But what of Alexandre
Soumet, whose name must occupy a prominent position in any
list of the 'Romantiques' of 1820–25?

Soumet provides perhaps the clearest example of the dilemma
faced by this group of monarchist Romantics. Prominent as one
of their leaders from the early 1820s, and one of the founder-
members of *La Muse Française* which represented in 1823–24 the
principal target of their opponents, he was in fact much more
ready to compromise with his literary leanings than with his
political beliefs: the real enemy for him was not classicism, but
liberalism. As regards the theatre, he now appears distinctly
conservative; his career as a dramatist is an excellent illustration
of the efforts of those 'reformers', or conciliators, whose aim was
to modify classical tragedy rather than to overthrow it. His
Clytemnestre, played at the Théâtre-Français in 1822 with Talma
as Oreste, is outstanding among the latter-day tragedies on
traditional subjects both structurally (there is some particularly
effective use of dramatic irony) and as regards the quality of the
writing. The verse is forceful and fluent—witness the opening
speech by Électre:

> Soleil qui reparaît sans ramener Oreste,
> J'ouvre en pleurant mes yeux à la clarté céleste,
> Et la nuit à son tour, témoin de mes douleurs,
> Près de ce monument retrouve Électre en pleurs,
> Avec des traits meurtris, et des chants lamentables,
> Visitant, évoquant des mânes redoutables;
> Sans cortège de deuil, sans pompe, sans flambeau,
> Prêtresse dévouée au culte d'un tombeau,
> Je viens, faible et mourante, à son auguste cendre,
> Demander le vengeur que m'a promis Cassandre

—but it contains virtually no concessions, either in vocabulary
or in versification, to the ideas of the new school. By any
standards, this is a distinguished example of neo-classical
tragedy on one of the greatest of all tragic themes; but if it
manages to transcend the derivative and mechanical quality of
so much eighteenth-century verse, it does this by capturing the

harmonies of André Chénier or Lamartine, not by anticipating the iconoclastic effects of Hugo.

Saül, performed in the same year at the Odéon, has more to offer in the way of innovation, or at least has a more recognizably Romantic flavour, even if this largely means the importation of certain features reminiscent of melodrama. The chief of these are the appearance among the *dramatis personae* of Achimelech, "vieillard aveugle âgé de 90 ans, gardien du temple de Nobé", and the large role given to the 'Pythonisse', the Witch of Endor; while the character of Saül himself shares something of the daemonic quality of the Byronic hero.

His reputation established by these two successes, Soumet was all the more careful to avoid giving offence, for his sights were now fixed on election to the Academy; and when a vacancy occurred in 1824 he not only forsook the *Muse Française* (his defection, with that of Deschamps, was the principal cause of the demise of that journal) but went over almost completely to the literary 'establishment'. However, he did write one more play which is of interest in the context of the Classical/Romantic controversy of the 'twenties. This is *Élisabeth de France*, performed at the Théâtre-Français in 1828: a historical tragedy with features recalling both the spectacular setting of melodrama (in Act I "le théâtre représente une vue de l'ermitage d'Alvarès, placé sur des rochers élevés. Un torrent descend de ces rochers") and also its 'style haletant'. The characterization, too, is melodramatic, in the opposition between the princess Élisabeth and her lover Carlos on the one hand, innocent victims of a 'raison d'état', and Carlos's tyrannical father Philip II of Spain and a sinister Chef du Tribunal (another "vieillard aveugle, âgé de 90 ans") on the other. All depends on the contrived working-out of situation: there is no dramatic development of character; and while this play does succeed in modifying the classical formula in certain superficial respects, it falls far short, not only of the aims, but also of the best achievements, of the Romantic dramatists who were to follow.

Two other dramatists of the 1820s occupy a somewhat similar position to that of Soumet: that is, without challenging the supremacy of neo-classical tragedy, they made a conscious effort to renovate and revitalize it. The first of these is Népomucène Lemercier, whose débuts during the Revolutionary era

we have already noted. His *Agamemnon* was followed by a group
of tragedies on subjects taken from early French history:
Charlemagne (1803, but not produced until 1816), *Clovis* (1820)
and *Frédégonde et Brunéhaut* (1821); and his attempt to renew
classical tragedy hardly goes beyond his choice of subject-
matter: "l'image des discordes de la France encore informe et
partagée entre les princes mérovingiens". He will be happy, he
says, "si la couleur et le dessin des tableaux que j'ai composés
sur *le grand gothique* les placent en digne parallèle à côté des
imitations du *beau antique*"[28]. As regards the dramaturgical
formula of traditional tragedy, he is adamant:

> Me ferait-on un autre tort de ne vouloir jamais dégrader par
> des inventions romanesques des tragédies tout historiques et
> d'avoir manifesté de nouveau, en observant le respect des
> trois unités grecques et latines, que les écarts et l'indépen-
> dance du genre nommé romantique ne produisent point
> d'émotions plus profondes et plus vives que n'en fournit la
> seule application exacte de nos classiques règles dans les
> mouvements passionnés artistement circonscrits en de sages
> limites? Quand je m'en écartai, ce ne fut spécialement que
> dans le drame, et non dans la tragédie ni dans la haute
> comédie qui les commandent, et que toute licence fait
> déchoir de leur rang ou dénature.[29]

Frédégonde et Brunéhaut is no more, therefore, than a revamped
version of *Rodogune*, with a heroine who is both thoroughly evil
and strong enough to impose her will on others. All these
characters are artificial, personifying not so much an idea as a
single dramatic motive; and the play is little more than a melodrama ("la moralité de l'action", writes Lemercier, "résulte . . .
de la seule horreur qu'inspire la victoire des méchants, et de
l'intérêt qui s'attache à l'infortune des bons") with certain
literary pretensions. The horror which he hopes to evoke with
this "modern equivalent of the Atreides theme" is largely
described, not enacted:

> Je ne vois que poignards, que breuvages perfides;
> Mon sommeil inquiet ne rêve qu'homicides...
> Des astres inconnus roulent au Ciel leurs flammes;
> La terre tremble, s'ouvre, et de plaintives âmes

Laissent en s'échappant les sépulcres déserts;
Des traits contagieux empoisonnent les airs (II, v)

—and described, moreover, in the hackneyed language of the
previous century. Even in his *Richard III et Jeanne Shore, drame
historique imité de Shakespeare et de Rowe* (1825) Lemercier retains
the derivative jargon of verse tragedy:

> D'un opprimé devenez le sauveur.
> Sur mes propres dangers ma triste indifférence
> N'eût point sitôt osé chercher votre présence;
> Mais d'un mortel bien cher à mon cœur gémissant
> M'amène devant vous le malheur plus pressant.
> De l'époux honoré par mon deuil funéraire
> L'horreur d'une prison enlève encor le père! (III, iv)

—and virtually the only liberty he permits himself in departing
from "le genre supérieur de la tragédie" is to change the scene
between the acts!

Casimir Delavigne, the other leading playwright of this
decade who retained the classical formula, appears to be at once
nearer to the views of the Romantics, and more capable of
writing genuine tragedy, than Lemercier. The position he takes
up in his 'Discours de réception' shows an eclecticism which, if
it looks timid when compared with the utterances of the
declared Romantics, is nevertheless very adventurous by the
side of Lemercier's uncompromising conservatism:

> Admirateurs ardents de Sophocle, sachons donc admirer
> Shakespeare et Goethe, moins pour les reproduire en nous,
> que pour apprendre en eux à rester ce que la nature nous a
> faits. Quel que soit le parti littéraire qui nous adopte ou nous
> rejette, cherchons le vrai en évitant la barbarie; sans con-
> fondre la liberté avec la licence, obéissons aux besoins d'un
> sujet dont le développement nous emporte; mais ne nous
> attachons pas au char d'un écrivain fameux, pour nous faire
> traîner à la réputation sous sa livrée. Ce qui est vrai en lui est
> faux en nous; ce qui le jette hors des rangs nous confond avec
> la foule. Soyons nous-mêmes; nos idées et nos sentiments
> sauront se revêtir, en naissant, de couleurs inusitées, et voilà
> l'originalité véritable.[30]

Les Vêpres siciliennes (1819), the play with which Delavigne made
his reputation, could be said to be a tragedy in the Cornelian
manner, in the sense that it presents a conflict between love and
duty against a background of heroism and patriotism. Delavigne
retains the strict observance of the unities, the roles of confidants,
the austere verse-form and the sparse vocabulary of traditional
tragedy; what gives this play a more Romantic character than
those of Lemercier or Soumet is the original twist given to the
Cornelian theme. For this is a sort of 'Horace à rebours':
Lorédan, the hero, dies a tragic victim of those heroic attitudes
which are traditionally glorified in tragedy, and *Les Vêpres
siciliennes* thus becomes an effective expression of anti-militaristic
idealism, a plea to set the brotherhood of man above the narrow
call of nationalism. Whatever response it evoked, this was
surely a theme of considerable topicality in these immediately
post-Napoleonic years.

Delavigne's language is simpler and more forceful than
Lemercier's; and while it cannot be said to be particularly
forward-looking, it is dramatically effective; it suggests the
vigorous manner of Corneille, rather than the derivative jargon
of so many of his successors:

> Arrêtez, ma victoire est un assassinat:
> Je vois avec horreur vos maximes d'État.
> Croyez-vous m'abuser? Couverts de noms sublimes,
> Ces crimes consacrés en sont-ils moins des crimes?
> Mon pays, dites-vous, me défend de pleurer;
> Eh! m'a-t-il défendu de me déshonorer?...
> Vous m'avez entraîné dans ce complot funeste;
> J'ai tout perdu pour vous, le remords seul me reste.
> Farouche liberté, que me demandes-tu?
> Laisse-moi mes remords, ou rends-moi ma vertu. (V, v)

At the end of his 'Discours de réception', Delavigne turns to
the question of language:

> La langue française, si rigoureuse dans ses aversions, ennemie
> impitoyable de toute obscurité, est la plus universelle et la
> plus calomniée; elle n'admet, il faut l'avouer, que les
> hardiesses qui se cachent; elle n'accepte que les dons qu'on
> lui déguise: mais Corneille et Racine ont prouvé qu'au

théâtre il n'est point de hauteurs inaccessibles pour elle,
point d'humbles familiarités où elle ne puisse descendre, et la
plus singulière des innovations, la création de toutes la plus
sublime et la plus inattendue serait encore d'écrire comme
eux.[31]

If *Les Vêpres siciliennes*, judged by this criterion, deserves to rank
as an original creation, the same cannot be said of *Le Paria*
(1821). Whilst the theme of this play may possess a superficial
novelty—Idamore, the hero, is the pariah of the title, the
unclean outcast who is put to death at the instigation of the
fanatical Brahmin high-priest, although he has saved the people
by his military exploits—the treatment is thoroughly conventional. Conventional, that is, both as regards plot—almost
inevitably, the humanitarian theme is marred by a sentimental
complication, in which Idamore loves the daughter of the high-
priest Akébar—and as regards language; for here we are
reminded at every turn of the cliché-ridden idiom of the
previous century. If Delavigne does on occasion achieve a
strikingly elegiac tone:

> Mais c'en est fait, Alvar, non, je ne dois plus voir
> Les étendards flottants dans les airs se mouvoir;
> Non, je n'entendrai plus le signal des batailles;
> Je ne dois plus rentrer vainqueur dans ces murailles,
> Et, déposant mon glaive à l'ombre des drapeaux,
> Goûter près d'une épouse un glorieux repos!...   (V, ii)

—he is here, like André Chénier in his *Iambes*, merely making
effective use of the poetic resources of the *ancien régime*: this is
very different from Hugo's manner, with its technical virtuosity
and lyrical freshness.

Marino Faliero, performed at the Porte-Saint-Martin in May
1829, not only takes us to the eve of the 'bataille d'*Hernani*', but
also goes a long way towards bridging the gap which separates
classical tragedy from 'drame romantique'. Indeed, on the basis
of this play, it would be necessary to treat Casimir Delavigne as
one of the first successful contributors to the new genre itself,
were it not for his explicit disclaimer, which repeats the position
he had taken up in his 'Discours de réception':

Deux systèmes partagent la littérature. Dans lequel des deux
cet ouvrage a-t-il été composé? C'est ce que je ne déciderai
pas, et ce qui d'ailleurs me paraît être de peu d'importance.
La raison la plus vulgaire veut aujourd'hui de la tolérance
en tout: pourquoi nos plaisirs seraient-ils seuls exclus de
cette loi commune?[32]

Marino Faliero, then, is no 'œuvre de combat'; but seen as the
attempt by an intelligent and skilful dramatist to carry modification of the existing system as far as was possible without dis-
rupting that system, it occupies an important place, from the
historical point of view, in the drama of the period. Nor are its
intrinsic merits entirely to be disregarded; for this is no uneasy
compromise, but a convincing attempt to exploit a new style
within the classical formula. The subject-matter, for instance,
breaks completely with the traditions of neo-classical tragedy;
the plot, as George Steiner remarks of Byron's play on the same
subject, "turns upon private affront and public conspiracy"[33]:
it is, therefore, the sort of plot which in the seventeenth century
would have been considered proper to tragicomedy, not
tragedy. The real subject-matter, in fact, is not the personal
dilemma of a single tragic hero, but the portrayal of the life of
fourteenth-century Venice, with its corruption and intrigues.
Delavigne captures something of the atmosphere which
characterizes *Lorenzaccio*: the spectator's sympathetic interest
and involvement is spread over several characters, and the
impact is that of 'drame' rather than of tragedy.

   Characterization, too, is refreshingly unconventional. Unlike
Lemercier's attempts to rejuvenate well-tried characters and
situations by transferring them from the house of Atreus to the
Merovingian dynasty—and unlike his own practice in *Le Paria*
—Delavigne has here created a group of characters who are not
predictable stereotypes: whose motivation is complex, or at
least ambiguous. Marino Faliero himself, the elderly doge who
embarks on a conspiracy against the Council of Ten in order to
avenge a personal insult to his wife's honour, but who also has
the interests of the common people at heart; Éléna, his wife,
and Fernando, his adopted son, whose love for each other has
made them guilty towards him, but who remain loyally devoted
to him in spite of their fault; Bertram, the traitor who betrays

the conspirators not out of self-seeking, but to repay the generosity of Lioni, one of the Ten: these are not the black-and-white clichés familiar to spectators of melodrama and of contemporary tragedy alike, but represent a genuine attempt to express the complexity of motivation that we encounter in life itself.

As for the language, this perhaps reveals the biggest break with past tradition: it is as if Delavigne modelled himself on the freer vocabulary and the more flexible rhythms of 'haute comédie', rather than on the much more restricted, if more 'elevated', alexandrine of tragedy. As a result, for every case of awkward, stilted versification along traditional lines:

> Eh quoi! vous êtes seul? Venez: de cette fête
> Si le vain bruit vous pèse à le fuir je suis prête (II, x)

> A ce sublime aveu qui pouvait s'élever
> De cette trahison ne fut jamais capable (IV, iv)

one can cite examples of a much bolder and more inventive handling of the alexandrine:

> — Vous abusez de tout.
>
>   — Il le faut à notre âge:
> Le seul abus d'un bien en fait aimer l'usage.
> Quoi de plus ennuyeux que vos plaisirs sensés?
> Ils rappellent aux cœurs, trop doucement bercés
> Par un retour prévu d'émotions communes,
> Ce fade mouvement qu'on sent sur les lagunes.
> En ôtez-vous l'excès, le plaisir perd son goût.
> Mais l'excès nous réveille, il donne un charme à tout.
> Un amour vous suffit; moi, le mien se promène
> D'un esclave de Smyrne à la noble Romaine,
> Et de la courtisane il remonte aux beautés
> Que votre bal promet à mes yeux enchantés.
> Le jeu du casino me pique et m'intéresse;
> Mais j'y prodigue l'or, ou j'y meurs de tristesse.
> Si la liqueur de Chypre est un heureux poison,
> C'est alors qu'affranchi d'un reste de raison,
> Mon esprit pétillant, qui fermente comme elle,
> Des éclairs qu'il lui doit dans l'ivresse étincelle.

Mes jours, je les dépense au hasard, sans compter.
Qu'en faire? on en a tant! Peut-on les regretter?
Pour les renouveler, cette vie où je puise
Est un trésor sans fond qui jamais ne s'épuise;
Ils passent pour renaître, et mon plus cher désir
Serait d'en dire autant de l'or et du plaisir.
Je parle en philosophe.

                      — Et je réponds en sage.
Vous ne pouvez rester. (II, iv)

Act II scene v shows a skilful use of the alexandrine to represent
the general conversation of a number of characters at a ball;
and similarly there is effective handling of 'broken' sticho-
mythia in II, xiii, where a quarrel leads to a challenge to a duel.
Here at last is a style of dramatic writing which looks forward
to Hugo rather than backward to Crébillon or Voltaire.[34]

    (*iii*) *Romantic skirmishers: Mérimée and the 'scène historique'*
AS we have seen, the young Romantics with royalist leanings
grouped round Nodier had to begin with either displayed little
active interest in the theatre, or else, like Soumet, been far too
conservative to make any substantial changes to the traditional
formula of classical tragedy. It was a different matter, however,
with Stendhal and his fellow-liberals. If one landmark of 1824
was the formation of the 'Cénacle' round Nodier at the Arsenal,
another was the founding of the liberal review *Le Globe*. An
early contribution by Vitet announced the programme of the
new journal:

Notre ordre social et nos mœurs ont été rajeunis, l'industrie
et la pensée affranchies, le gouvernement mitigé; en un mot
les Philosophes ont gagné leur procès: mais la cause qu'ils
avaient oublié d'instruire est encore en suspens, les parties
sont encore en présence, et le jugement se fait attendre... le
goût en France attend son 14 juillet. Pour préparer cette
nouvelle révolution, de nouveaux encyclopédistes se sont
élevés: on les appelle *romantiques*. Héritiers non des doctrines,
mais du rôle de leurs devanciers, ils plaident pour cette
indépendance trop longtemps négligée, et qui pourtant est le
complément nécessaire de la liberté individuelle, l'indépendance en matière de goût... Tel est le romantisme pour ceux

qui le comprennent dans son acception la plus large et la plus générale, ou, pour mieux dire, d'une manière philosophique. C'est, en deux mots, le protestantisme dans les lettres et les arts.[35]

Le Globe took a special interest in the coming revolution in the theatre: "La tragédie historique et libre", proclaimed an early issue, "n'est pas à coup sûr le romantisme tout entier, mais elle en est l'une des branches les plus importantes, celle peut-être vers laquelle la direction actuelle des esprits nous pousse irrésistiblement, celle qui nous permet les jouissances les plus vives"[36]. But historical *tragedy* was only one of the possible ways of treating historical subjects in the theatre; in the opinion of some, the ideas of 'history' and of 'tragedy' were conflicting, if not incompatible, ideas, and what was needed was an altogether freer form of dramatic composition, capable of allowing full scope to the arbitrary and unpredictable pattern of historical events, without seeking to compress these into the significant mould of tragedy. Népomucène Lemercier, writing his *Pinto, ou la Journée d'une conspiration, comédie historique*, in 1799, had shown himself aware of this problem:

> Mon but en composant cette comédie a été de dépouiller une grande action de tout ornement poétique qui la déguise, de présenter des personnages parlant, agissant comme on le fait dans la vie, et de rejeter le prestige, quelquefois infidèle, de la tragédie et des vers.[37]

As Scribe was later to do in historical comedies like *Le Verre d'eau*, Lemercier set out to show the way in which great events can depend on very trivial causes: here, the revolution of 1640 which drove the Spaniards from Portugal is at least partly caused by the Admiral's infatuation for the Duchesse de Bragance, which plays into the conspirators' hands; an early editor comments that "le sujet et le but de ce drame d'un genre tout nouveau appartiennent à la tragédie, les détails et les moyens à la comédie"[38]. But in a way, this was merely substituting one 'pattern' for another: history ran just as much risk of being falsified in a 'comédie historique' as in tragedy. What was wanted was a more documentary portrayal of an episode from history, aiming at realism and local colour, and emphasizing the interaction of characters in a given situation rather than highlighting the dilemma of a hero or central character.

It was perhaps inevitable that such an approach should chiefly commend itself to literary circles outside the theatre; and it was in fact a young friend of Stendhal's, and a contributor to *Le Globe*, who produced the first important essay in this genre. Mérimée's *Théâtre de Clara Gazul* was published in 1825,[39] with no intention for the time being of actual performance in the theatre; it was a collection of six plays—two 'comédies en trois journées', the rest one-acters[40]—attributed to an imaginary Spanish actress with literary pretensions. The interest of these plays—apart from the anecdotal interest which always attaches to a successful literary hoax, and the light they throw on the young Mérimée's knowledge of Spain and Spanish literature[41] —is that they embody the theories current in Stendhal's circle. Mérimée had read them all before publication[42] in the salon of the painter Delécluze, who was to execute the 'portrait' of Doña Clara for the first edition (in fact, a portrait of Mérimée himself wearing a mantilla), and they can be seen as the vindication of the theory of the 'scène historique', on which this group of young Romantics pinned their hopes for a new kind of theatre:

> Ce nouveau « genre » — car on crut bien pendant quelques années que c'en était un — naissait du grand succès du roman historique et du goût récent pour la lecture des *Mémoires* historiques, contemporains ou anciens; il suffisait, pour y réussir, de découper dans les plus vivants de ces mémoires les scènes les plus pittoresques, de les dialoguer, d'entasser les propos qui pouvaient donner l'impression de la couleur locale; on écrivait en bonne prose, on brouillait les genres, on mélangeait les tons... Pour satisfaire la passion politique on n'avait qu'à chercher la matière dans l'histoire des diverses révolutions médiévales ou modernes, portugaise, française ou anglaise, dans l'histoire de l'Inquisition. Tout un théâtre nouveau pouvait sortir de là.[43]

At first sight, *Les Espagnols en Danemarck* may not strike the modern reader as very different in tone from Pixérécourt; much of the dialogue has the same melodramatic emphasis. Mérimée's characters, however, are more ambivalent than Pixérécourt's, and the play certainly does not point any simplistic moral.

Indeed, the story (an incident from the Napoleonic Wars) is handled with a certain ironical detachment, and prompts the reader to reflect, like *Pinto* or *Le Verre d'eau*, on the role of chance in determining the outcome of historical events.

Les Espagnols is neither comedy nor tragedy, but belongs to the intermediate category of historical 'drame'. None of the other five playlets in this collection is related in the same way to a specific historical event, and if they can be called 'scènes historiques' it is because they all portray certain aspects of Spanish *mœurs* in a given historical period. The picture which emerges is colourful and violent: the clash of human passion with Christian asceticism (*Une Femme est un diable*), the interplay of passion and jealousy with the religious fanaticism of the Inquisition (*Le Ciel et l'Enfer*), and the triumph of primitive feelings of honour and vengeance over love and friendship (*L'Amour africain*) are all presented in brief sketches with a simple dramatic structure and a violent ending; while as regards the two pieces bearing the title *Inès Mendo*, the first, *Le Préjugé vaincu*, portraying the triumph of love over class prejudice and of humanitarian feeling over tradition, serves as a prologue to the second, in which the more primitive instincts of passion, ambition and revenge reassert themselves. In a foreword to *Inès Mendo*, Mérimée writes:

> L'auteur, qui s'est étudié à imiter les anciens comiques espagnols, n'a nullement cherché à éviter leurs défauts ordinaires, tels que le trop de rapidité dans l'action, le manque de développements, etc.[44]

and there is certainly a lack of subtlety, both in the revelation of character and in the producing of dramatic effect, which is reminiscent of the Spanish *comedia*, or of pre-classical French drama. Indeed, it is often concluded from this that the playwright must have been indulging in parody; to quote a recent study:

> Si l'action est violente à souhait et ressortit au mélodrame, la forme en est parfois discrètement parodique. Le moyen, par exemple, de prendre tout à fait au sérieux Antonio, qui, dans *Une Femme est un diable*, hurle à son rival, un moine, comme il

se doit: « Marie-moi ou je te tue! » Car le libéralisme anti-
clérical de Mérimée se donne ici joyeusement carrière et
s'acharne à plaisir sur des gens d'église, passionnés et libertins,
dont la galanterie paillarde trouve son correctif dans l'ou-
trance caricaturale.[45]

While there can be no doubt of Mérimée's anticlericalism, it is
not nearly so certain what degree of literary parody is meant to
underlie these portraits; and despite the element of *mystification*
which accompanied the publication of the *Théâtre de Clara
Gazul*, it seems quite likely that the pastiche of primitive
dramatic forms, as well as the vivid portrayal of Spanish *mœurs*,
was meant to be taken seriously.

M. Baschet seems to be equally indulgent towards these short
pieces when he writes:

L'on est ravi de constater que ces pièces du *Théâtre de Clara
Gazul*, tout de même que les pièces de Musset, qui, elles non
plus, n'ont pas été écrites pour la scène, se trouvent être, de
toute la production théâtrale des romantiques, le plus naturellement dramatiques.[46]

Certainly, the two plays of this collection still capable of arousing some interest today are those written with more obvious
irony and detachment: *Les Espagnols en Danemarck*, and especially one of the two plays added in the 1829 edition, *Le Carrosse
du Saint-Sacrement*, in which the portrait of Spanish (in this
case Spanish-American) *mœurs* takes the form of highly amusing
social satire, as the actress La Périchole twists her lover the
Viceroy round her little finger and scores off the hypocritical
churchmen and the jealous prudes[47].

For the greater part of his career as a writer, Mérimée chose
to embody the most intense and vivid of his imaginative creations not in dramatic form, but in that of the short story—
though the innate dramatic power of a 'nouvelle' like *Carmen*
comes out very strongly in the libretto which Meilhac and
Halévy were to write for Bizet's opera. However, he did write
two further works in dramatic form during these years which
saw the birth of Romanticism in the theatre: *La Jaquerie,
scènes féodales* and *La Famille de Carvajal, drame*, which were
published together in 1828[48]. The latter shows the same in-

spiration as the shorter Clara Gazul pieces: a mixture of honour and cruelty, passion and horror; it is like a gothic novel transported to a sixteenth-century Spanish-American setting. What distinguishes this play, however, is the more sustained attention given to characterization: whereas *Une Femme est un diable*, or even *Inès Mendo*, present no more than a dramatized situation, with little attempt to develop character, both the character of Don José de Carvajal, whose incestuous passion leads him to crown a life of crime by killing his wife and attempting to ravish his daughter, and especially that of Catalina herself, are something more than the conventional melodramatic stereotypes. The latter, far from being a passive victim *à la Pixérécourt*, is given a strength and independence of mind which enable her to stand up to her father, and (when she has killed him in order to preserve her honour) to face abandonment by Don Alonso, her lover. The closing lines, when Catalina is left alone with the Indians who have arrived with Alonso too late to prevent the catastrophe:

LE CACIQUE: Femme, où faut-il te conduire?

CATALINA: Menez-moi dans la forêt.

LE CACIQUE: Mais... tu y seras bientôt dévorée par les tigres.

CATALINA: Plutôt des tigres que des hommes! Partons!

do perhaps suggest a Romantic pose; and here again, editors and commentators have concluded that Mérimée must have had his tongue in his cheek: "une parodie de certain théâtre romantique"[49], "mélodrame à la Pixérécourt, parodie sans pitié, charge exemplaire du drame romantique"[50]. However tempting it may be to attribute to these early essays the astringent irony of Mérimée's later writing, it would surely be pertinent to ask what this 'drame romantique' was, which Mérimée was already so obviously parodying in 1828? The case does not appear to be proved; and *La Famille de Carvajal* seems to be a particularly good illustration of the difficulty that exists with so much Romantic writing in distinguishing between tongue-in-cheek pastiche and enthusiasm for the real thing[51]. It might be prudent, therefore, to keep an open mind about

Mérimée's intentions in writing the Clara Gazul plays and *La
Famille de Carvajal*; but there can be no doubt that *La Jaquerie*
was meant seriously as a contribution to the genre of the 'scène
historique'. Of all these 'dramatic' writings of Mérimée's, this
is by far the most interesting and original, in the context of the
current search for new forms. It represents a much more determined attempt at the sort of historical drama for which
eighteenth-century writers like Hénault had felt the need; and
although it is very much of its time in drawing on the kind of
mediaeval material for which Scott's novels had created such
a vogue, it does make very definite borrowings from the
technique of the Shakespearean historical play. The effect
produced by a rapid succession of short scenes, for instance, is
thoroughly Shakespearean, as is the way in which Mérimée
handles the battle-scenes (scenes xix–xxii); the following stage-
directions might easily come from any of the 'Histories': "Une
petite colline près du champ de bataille. On entend dans le
lointain le bruit du combat... Une autre partie du champ de
bataille... Bivouac des insurgés sur le champ de bataille"[52].

But in fact Mérimée goes further than Shakespeare: not only
does he set out to convey the impression of history as the
product of a complex process of cause and effect—of deliberately
planned policies upset by personal relationships, self-interest
and pure chance—but he does this without Shakespeare's concentration on a central figure or figures. Whereas the character
of Richard II or Henry V, for instance, provides the unity of the
play, here the only unity is that provided by the historical event
itself: if we choose to assign to Frère Jean the role of central
character, this is because he is the leader of the rebels, not
because the dramatist makes him stand out from other characters by any distinctive treatment[53]. By the same token, the
construction of the play anticipates the naturalists' 'tranche de
vie': there is a minimum of preparation or arrangement of
events, and Mérimée clearly wanted to produce the impression
of an unselective chronicle. The result, not surprisingly, is that
lack of artistic focus from which any 'slice of life' must inevitably
suffer: however interesting it is as an experiment, *La Jaquerie*
remains dramatized history, it does not succeed as historical
drama.

Other exponents of the 'scène historique', as Marsan shows in

an important study of this topic[54], were even more remote than
Mérimée from the active professional theatre. Thus Roederer, a
frustrated politician, devoted the years of his retirement to
cultivating the amateur theatre, producing Carmontelle's
'proverbes' and his own 'scènes historiques' (published in 1827,
these included *Le Marguillier de Saint-Eustache*, written some years
earlier). Far from supporting the aspirations of the Romantics,
Roederer thought that historical drama should repudiate any
connection with "la comédie romantique, genre bâtard et
ignoble"[55]; but although the Preface to *Le Marguillier* accumulates references to documentary sources (and acknowledges the
influence of Hénault), the manner of Scribe's 'comédies historiques' is not wholly absent from the play itself. There were
those, however, who moved in the same circle as Stendhal and
other contributors to *Le Globe*: for instance Gain-Montaignac,
the Preface to whose *Théâtre*, published in 1820, had anticipated
some of the ideas expressed in *Racine et Shakespeare*:

Que peuvent maintenant nous apprendre des poèmes écrits
dans un langage conventionnel, nous offrant des personnages
qui portent plus souvent un masque habilement colorié
qu'une figure vivante? Vieillis par une longue et dure
expérience, il nous est devenu impossible d'être intéressés par
des ouvrages qui ne reposeraient que sur un idéal convenu; et
le langage magnifiquement vague de la tragédie en vers, sa
froide pompe et ses narrations épiques ont usé en France tout
leur effet. Nous avons besoin désormais d'un art plus simple,
plus près de la nature et de la vérité.[56]

Another was Rémusat, author of two lost plays, *La Féodalité* and
L'Insurrection de Saint-Domingue, and of a *Saint-Barthélemy* which
belongs to the same period (1824–28), but was published only
half a century later: a play whose fifty-odd named characters
and close on 400 pages of octavo text put it in the same class as
Hugo's *Cromwell*; while a pair of collaborators, Dittmer and
Cavé, publishing their 'tableaux dramatiques' under the title
of *Soirées de Neuilly* and under the pseudonym of M. de Fongeray
(1827–28), achieved in one of these, *La Conspiration de Malet*, a
dramatized version of a historical *fait divers* which was frequently
to be hailed as a model of its kind. Finally, Vitet, whom we have
already met as a journalist associated with *Le Globe*, published

three volumes of dramatized episodes from the Wars of Religion: *Les Barricades, scènes historiques* (1826), *Les États de Blois* (1827) and *La Mort de Henri III* (1829). Here is an author who explicitly acknowledges the limitations that we have referred to in connection with *La Jaquerie*:

> Ce n'est point une pièce de théâtre que l'on va lire, ce sont des faits historiques présentés sous la forme dramatique, mais sans la prétention d'en composer un drame... Si j'eusse voulu faire un drame, au contraire, il eût fallu songer avant tout à la marche de l'action; sacrifier, pour la rendre plus vive, une foule de détails et d'accessoires; piquer la curiosité par des réticences; mettre en relief, aux dépens de la vérité, quelques personnages et quelques événements principaux et ne faire voir les choses qu'en perspective: j'ai préféré laisser les choses telles que je les trouvais.[57]

Interesting as these experiments are, they lie in the final analysis outside the main lines of development of genuine historical drama, and they are of limited importance in view of the form which Romantic dramatists were to choose in the 1830s (though it is perhaps worth observing that these 'scènes historiques' of the 1820s have a good deal more in common with some of the experimental dramatizations of historical events that we have seen in both the French and the British theatres in the 1960s and 1970s). It is true that *Lorenzaccio*, the masterpiece of Romantic historical drama, was to be based on a 'scène historique', George Sand's *Une Conspiration en 1537*—but it is also true that it needed the creative talent of a Musset to convert this dramatized chronicle into a dramatic masterpiece.

Notes to Chapter Three

1. Some indication of the difference in composition of the audiences may be seen in the fact that in 1827 the prices of seats at the Théâtre-Français ran from 1 fr. 80 to 6 frs 60, while at the Ambigu-Comique they ranged from 0 fr. 60 to 3 frs 60 (quoted by Descotes, *Le Drame romantique et ses grands créateurs*, Paris, P.U.F., n.d., p. 9).
2. Pixérécourt, *Théâtre choisi, ed. cit.*, I, p. lxxii.

3. *Nouvelle Année Littéraire*, 15.iii.1828 (quoted by Descotes, *Le Drame . . .*, p. 55).

4. *Journal des Comédiens*, 17.v.1829 (Descotes, *ibid.*).

5. Preface to *Études françaises et étrangères*, Paris, 1828, p. 35 (Descotes, p. 54).

6. Pierre-Victor, *Documents pour servir à l'histoire du Théâtre-Français sous la Restauration*, Paris, 1834, p. 102 (Descotes, p. 89).

7. *Op. cit.*, p. 52 (Descotes, p. 86).

8. *Correspondance avec Madame de Staël*, ed. G. de la Batut, Paris, 1928, p. 160.

9. In *Quelques Réflexions sur Lekain et sur l'art théâtral* (1826) he set out to demolish the notion, subscribed to by Diderot in his *Paradoxe sur le comédien*, that sensibility in an actor is a mark of mediocrity.

10. *De l'Allemagne, ed. cit.*, pp. 240–241.

11. *Journal* for 21.x.1826 (quoted by Descotes, *Le Drame . . .*, p. 34).

12. *Au Roi* (January 1829), quoted by Descotes, p. 35.

13. *Op. cit.*, p. 35.

14. See H. P. Bailey, *op. cit.*, pp. 36ff., 68ff.; J. L. Borgerhoff, *Le Théâtre anglais à Paris sous la Restauration*, Paris, 1912, pp. 56ff.

15. Or at any rate, authentic Shakespeare as currently presented to the playgoing public in London: for instance, *Romeo and Juliet* included Garrick's adaptation of the dénouement, with Juliet regaining consciousness before Romeo's death.

16. See Borgerhoff, *op. cit.*, p. 76.

17. *Courrier Français*, 13.ix.1827 (quoted by Borgerhoff, *op. cit.*, p. 78).

18. *Réunion*, 13.ix.1827 (Borgerhoff, p. 79).

19. In a later text, Dumas claimed that he knew *Hamlet* almost by heart in Letourneur's version, and was able to follow the English "translating Hamlet's words as Kemble spoke them" (*Mémoires*, Paris, 1868–83, IV, p. 280, quoted by Bailey, *op. cit.*, p. 69).

20. *Théâtre complet*, Paris, 1863–65, I, pp. 14–15.

21. Quoted by Borgerhoff, *op. cit.*, p. 188.

22. 13.ix.1827 (Borgerhoff, pp. 169–170).

23. *Le Corsaire*, 23.i.1828 (Borgerhoff, pp. 172–173).

24. R. A. E. Baldick, *The Life and Times of Frédérick Lemaître*, London, 1959, p. 50.

25. See pp. 71–72.

26. See E. M. Schenck, *La Part de Charles Nodier dans la formation des idées romantiques de V. Hugo jusqu'à la Préface de Cromwell*, Paris, 1914.

27. *Tutte le opere*, a cura di G. Lesca, Florence, 1923, pp. 239–279.

28. Preface to *Frédégonde et Brunéhaut*.
29. *Ibid*.
30. *Œuvres complètes*, Brussels, 1832, III, pp. 172–173.
31. *Ibid*., p. 174.
32. *Ibid*., I, p. 205.
33. *Op. cit*., p. 204.
34. P. J. Yarrow ('Three Plays of 1829, or Doubts about 1830', *Symposium*, XXIII, 1969, pp. 373–383) ascribes a good deal more importance to Romantic features of *Marino Faliero*, though his analysis perhaps tends to overlook the more conservative elements in the play.
35. Quoted by R. Bray, *op. cit*., p. 129.
36. Quoted by P. Martino, Introduction to Mérimée, *Théâtre de Clara Gazul*, Paris, 1929, p. x.
37. Quoted in *Chefs-d'œuvre des auteurs comiques*, Paris, Firmin-Didot, n.d., VIII, p. 3.
38. *Ibid*.
39. "It is the first published attempt in French to create plays which would exemplify the new aesthetic, antedating Hugo's *Cromwell* by two years, Dumas's *Henri III et sa cour* by four years, and Hugo's *Hernani* by five years. In retrospect it appears—as it did at the time to a small but influential body of literary opinion —as a date in the history of the French theatre", A. W. Raitt, *Prosper Mérimée*, London, 1970, pp. 46–47.
40. Two more plays, *L'Occasion* and *Le Carrosse du Saint-Sacrement*, were added in the 1830 edition.
41. The Spanish theatre was beginning to benefit, alongside the English and the German theatres, from the enthusiasm for foreign drama. In 1821 the publisher Ladvocat inaugurated the publication of his *Chefs-d'œuvre des théâtres étrangers* with an issue devoted to Lope de Vega and Spanish drama; and in 1824 Mérimée himself published four articles in *Le Globe* on the Spanish theatre. It was also, of course, a subject of which Hugo was to display first-hand knowledge in the *Préface de Cromwell*.
42. As he had also read, at about the same time, a *Cromwell* that has not survived. The form of this work—a 'play within a play', performed as a puppet-show—suggests affinities with Corneille's *Illusion comique* rather than with Shakespearean historical drama. See Bray, *op. cit*., pp. 124–125.
43. Martino, *op. cit*., p. xii.
44. *Théâtre de Clara Gazul, ed. cit*., p. 177.
45. R. Baschet, *Du Romantisme au Second Empire: Mérimée (1803–70)*, Paris, 1958, p. 31.

46. *Ibid.*
47. *Le Carrosse du Saint-Sacrement* was staged at the Comédie-Française in 1850; given six performances, it had a very hostile reception. However, it was produced with great success by Copeau at the Vieux-Colombier in 1920 and subsequently at the Comédie-Française in 1946. *Les Espagnols en Danemarck* was first produced at the Comédie-Française in 1948 (see Baschet, *op. cit.*, pp. 33, 159).
48. As well as a *comédie de mœurs* with a satirical flavour, *Les Mécontents*, published in the *Revue de Paris* in 1830.
49. P. Jourda, 'Avant-propos' to *La Jaquerie, suivie de la Famille de Carvajal*, Paris, 1931, p. xxxi. For a full statement of the case that Mérimée was writing in a spirit of parody, see pp. xxiv-xxx.
50. Baschet, *op. cit.*, p. 41.
51. Marsan's judgement seems more dependable, and to take more account of contemporary comment: "Libre, capricieux, pittoresque, impatient de toute contrainte, dépouillé de tendresse, indifférent, et d'autant plus émouvant, le *Théâtre de Clara Gazul* est la première œuvre de ce théâtre réaliste que réclame, sous le nom de romantisme, le cénacle stendhalien", 'Le Théâtre historique et le romantisme', *Revue d'Histoire Littéraire de la France*, XVII, 1910, p. 18.
52. *La Jaquerie*, ed. cit., pp. 204, 206, 212.
53. "If any one of these characters were visibly to become the hero, we should see these scenes as a play, whereas they are meant as an imaginative re-creation of history", Raitt, *op. cit.*, p. 85.
54. *Art. cit.*, pp. 1-33. See also M. Trotain, *Les Scènes historiques: étude du théâtre livresque à la veille du drame romantique*, Paris, 1923.
55. Quoted by Marsan, *art. cit.*, p. 12.
56. *Ibid.*, p. 13.
57. *Ibid.*, p. 23.

4 Hostilities Begin

(i) *Hugo and 'Amy Robsart'*

— Seigneur, abandonnez une telle entreprise.
En attaquant Actor, vous attaquez Cambyse.
Il est beau, je le sais, de périr pour son roi:
Mais avez-vous songé (j'en frissonne d'effroi)
Aux dangers où ce zèle expose votre vie!
Que deviendrait, hélas! la triste Phalérie
Si...

— Madame, cessez de craindre pour mes jours,
Cessez de m'offenser par de pareils discours;
Quoi! baissant sous le joug une tête soumise,
J'irais ramper aux pieds d'un soldat de Cambyse,
Et, trahissant l'espoir d'un héros que je sers,
Je baiserais la main qui nous donne des fers![1]

THIS exchange, which—*mutatis mutandis*—might have come from any of the hundreds of derivative neo-classical tragedies of the previous 150 years, in fact constitutes the opening lines of Victor Hugo's earliest play. For when, by publishing the *Préface de Cromwell* in 1827, Hugo staked his claim to the vacant position of leader of the Romantic poets in their challenge to the classical tradition, this was far from being his first venture into dramatic writing. His precocious talent—if not his genius—had found expression here, as it had in other literary genres, and the three texts surviving from his schoolboy years explore, as it were, the range of existing dramatic forms[2]. *Irtamène, tragédie* (written in 1816, when Hugo was only fourteen), presents conventional characters in a conventionally imprecise setting: despotic usurper, magnanimous hero placed in a vaguely 'Cornelian' dilemma, and so on. The young Hugo's alexandrine is a mechanical copy of the formula established by his predecessors, and in the brief extract quoted above we can recognize such familiar features as the tyranny of the caesura; unimaginative rhyming (particularly the reliance on the proper name at the rhyming position); sententious abstraction; and a pervading impression of *déjà vu* produced by some of the cliché-like hemistiches. *A quelque chose hasard est bon* (1817) is a simple *vaudeville*, not very ambitious in its aims; it accumulates so many coincidences and clichés of plot that it almost parodies the genre, but it does demonstrate a certain modernity of style by distinct reminders of the manner of Beaumarchais's Figaro:

> C'est pourtant la pure réalité: né par hasard je ne sais où, confié par hasard à un notaire, condamné par hasard (il est vrai que celui-là a été bien conduit) à payer je ne sais quelle dette, duelliste par hasard, amoureux par hasard, tu conviendras que je ne puis être de l'avis de ceux qui prétendent que le hasard n'est rien.[3]

The third example of Hugo's juvenilia, *Inez de Castro* (1818) presents the material of La Motte's tragedy of 1723, but in the manner of Pixérécourt. That is to say, it retains the black-and-white characterization of Inez and Don Pèdre, persecuted by the evil Queen (who is abetted in this version by an equally evil Alcade d'Alpunar), but the poetry and the pathos of La Motte's play have disappeared, and in their place we have a prosaic, if more eventful and more spectacular, example of the 'mélodrame historique'.

None of these plays indicates any particular aptitude for the dramatic medium, and there is certainly no suggestion here of those structural and stylistic innovations which were to characterize the plays of Hugo's maturity. But these were no more than adolescent literary exercises, deliberate pastiches of the existing genres, composed without a thought of possible stage performance. The first play to make its mark, however ephemerally, on the Parisian stage was *Amy Robsart*, performed at the Odéon in February 1828. Though this places it after the publication of the *Préface de Cromwell*, nevertheless the date of its composition, six years earlier, makes it appropriate to deal with *Amy Robsart* as Hugo's first notable contribution to the new form of drama.

The play had originally been planned as a joint undertaking by Hugo and Soumet, but the latter disapproved of his collaborator's tendency towards a 'Shakespearean' mixture of comic and tragic:

> M. Victor Hugo avait fait sa part; mais lorsqu'il avait lu ses trois actes, M. Soumet n'en avait été content qu'à moitié; il n'admettait pas le mélange du tragique et du comique, et il voulait effacer tout ce qui n'était pas grave et sérieux. M. Victor Hugo avait objecté l'exemple de Shakespeare; mais alors les acteurs anglais ne l'avaient pas encore fait applaudir à Paris, et M. Soumet avait répondu que Shakespeare, bon à lire, ne supporterait pas la représentation.[4]

Each author had therefore gone on to complete his own version separately: Soumet's *Émilia* had been performed at the Théâtre-Français in 1827[5], but Hugo's play had remained unpublished and unacted until his brother-in-law, Paul Foucher, persuaded him to allow it to be offered to the Odéon under his (Foucher's) name. The disguise was transparent, for it was generally known in literary and theatrical circles that this was Hugo's own 'ballon d'essai'.

Amy Robsart is another example of 'mélodrame historique' according to Pixérécourt's formula; but the fact that its source was Scott's novel (rather than a regular tragedy, as in the case of *Inez de Castro*) gives it a much greater degree of complication. Indeed, Hugo's version of *Kenilworth* not only condenses, but in places elaborates on Scott, and produces an action-packed melodrama very much in the gothic idiom, with secret doors, poisonings, and a spectacular dénouement in which the castle keep is consumed by fire. One can only assume that the failure of the play—there was no second performance, and Hugo wrote to the press acknowledging full responsibility for the passages which had been particularly objected to—was due to the Paris playgoer's 'hierarchical' attitude to dramatic genres: whereas the 'mélodrames' of Pixérécourt and others were still pleasing other audiences, the 'second Théâtre-Français' was expected to aim higher than this. But *Amy Robsart* retains a certain interest, if only from a historical point of view. It had marked, as early as 1822, the parting of the ways between Hugo and Soumet, the timid reformer[6]; and in 1828 it provided the occasion for the first collaboration between Hugo and Delacroix, who designed the costumes for the production at the Odéon. If in theme and style it conforms to the formula of Pixérécourt's *Valentine*—Amy, like Valentine herself, represents innocence persecuted, while Leicester, like Édouard, is weak rather than wicked, and is led on by the unscrupulous Varney—the attempt at an authentic historical background brings it a good deal nearer to what is usually meant by 'Romantic drama' than any of the plays we have so far considered. The relationship between history and 'historical drama' is one we shall have to return to in later chapters; here, let it suffice to suggest that whatever alterations of the facts concerning the historical Leicester's first marriage with Amy Robsart have been introduced by Scott and other imaginative writers, the sources used by Hugo retain enough of what he himself was later to call "la couleur des temps" for his play to carry conviction as the treatment of a genuine episode from history. Leicester, Varney and Elizabeth, in other words, are not merely characters from a melodrama *à la Pixérécourt*, but plausible embodiments (however crude) of the types of statesman, courtier and ruler produced by the particular historical circumstances of the Tudor period in England. It would no doubt have been a better play if there had been more responsible and detailed use of local colour, with less of the trappings of the gothic novel, and fewer gratuitous intrusions of the kind of grotesque element represented by the improbable Flibbertigibbet; in some of his later plays Hugo was certainly able to achieve a better *dosage* of these ingredients, but *Amy Robsart* at any rate suggests the possibility of a viable dramatic alternative to the over-academic 'scène historique'.

(ii) The 'Préface de Cromwell'

"LA *Préface de Cromwell* n'est pas la préface de *Cromwell*": this is no mere superficial *boutade*, for more than almost any of the major treatises which have been published as prefaces to creative works of imagination, Hugo's *Préface* demands to be considered on its own as a self-contained piece of writing, independent of the play to which it is attached. And there is no doubt about it: this is one of the major theoretical writings of the century, one of the outstanding manifestos of an age which set great store by literary manifestos. Like that other Romantic preface which completely overshadows the work to which it is nominally an introduction, Gautier's *Préface de Mademoiselle de Maupin*, it condenses controversial views which were in the air at the time into provocative formulae for the purposes of polemic; and it makes brilliant use of journalistic techniques in order to create something of much more than ephemeral, journalistic importance. "Œuvre polémique, certes, mais avant tout œuvre d'art": this comment of a modern editor of Gautier's *Préface*[7] would apply with equal force to Hugo's. It is a masterpiece of theoretical writing, which not only provided the young Romantics with the rallying-point they were looking for but, in addition, going beyond the context of the contemporary polemic in the theatre expressed something fundamental to the Romantic aesthetic in a challenging and permanently memorable way.

The play *Cromwell* was finished towards the end of September 1827; the Preface was written during October, and read before a gathering of enthusiastic friends at Nodier's apartment at the Arsenal; and play and Preface were published together in December.

Brunetière's epigram: "Ce qu'il y a de propre à Hugo dans cette célèbre *Préface* est faux; et ce qu'elle contient de vérité, tout le monde l'avait dit avant lui"[8] merely formulates more neatly a criticism expressed by countless other commentators, and it has become a commonplace to denigrate both the originality and the validity of Hugo's ideas. However, the question of Hugo's indebtedness to earlier writers was thoroughly investigated by Maurice Souriau in his scholarly introduction to the *Préface*, first published in 1897[9]; and while Souriau certainly indicates substantial borrowings from, or affinities with, other thinkers such as Madame de Staël, Manzoni or Schlegel with regard to most of the important ideas of the *Préface*, he also pays sincere tribute to the range of Hugo's own erudition, as well as to that genuine kind of originality which consisted in giving forceful expression to ideas currently 'in the air'[10]. Souriau also points to the remarkable maturity and authority shown by Hugo's earlier theoretical and critical writings on aesthetic matters, in such periodicals as the *Conservateur Littéraire* and the *Muse Française*, and in writings like *Le*

Journal d'un jeune Jacobite de 1819: Hugo was only 25 when he wrote the *Préface de Cromwell*, but his apprenticeship as a literary and dramatic critic and theorist, from his teens onwards, had been more assiduously, and fruitfully, pursued than his formation as a practising dramatist. It is perhaps not inappropriate to see him emerging from this period of apprenticeship in 1827, and offering the *Préface de Cromwell*, quite literally, as his masterpiece.

The *Préface* opens with a conventional apology for what is to follow: "Le drame qu'on va lire n'a rien qui le recommande à l'attention ou à la bienveillance du public"[11]; Hugo's real standpoint, however, is expressed in the proud declaration of independence which follows, standing out by its brevity from the longer paragraphs which surround it, and much more typical of his colourful, challenging style:

Il s'offre donc aux regards, seul, pauvre et nu, comme l'infirme de l'Évangile, *solus, pauper, nudus.*[12]

The opening paragraphs make clear the tendentious nature of what is to come, though (with another conventional disclaimer) he insists that the Preface is not written in a spirit of hostility:

Voici sa fronde et sa pierre; mais d'autres les jetteront à la tête des Goliaths *classiques.*[13]

With these preambles out of the way, Hugo begins by harking back to the 'Querelle des Anciens et des Modernes', with a restatement of one of the favourite analogies of the modernists. The history of human society, he says, is like the life-story of an individual:

Le genre humain dans son ensemble a grandi, s'est développé, a mûri comme un de nous. Il a été enfant, il a été homme: nous assistons maintenant à son imposante vieillesse.[14]

And the rhetorician's favourite ternary phrasing is matched by the systematic thinker's tripartite division of the history of civilization: there have been three great ages in the evolution of mankind, Hugo claims—"les temps primitifs, les temps antiques, les temps modernes"[15]—each with its characteristic form of literature. His imaginative development of this theme (which certainly owes something to the *Génie du christianisme*) is the product of a poet's vision rather than of a historian's regard for factual truth. Hugo's first age is that of the waking human consciousness, surrounded by the marvels of creation; it is the world of Genesis, and its characteristic literature is the ode:

> Voilà le premier homme, voilà le premier poète. Il est jeune, il est lyrique. La prière est toute sa religion, l'ode est toute sa poésie.[16]

The second age is no longer 'patriarchal', but 'theocratic': the idyllic pastoral life has given way to wars and the clash of empires. The epic is now the characteristic form, Homer the poet *par excellence* of this age; for even in ancient tragedy, "ses personnages sont encore des héros, des demi-dieux, des dieux; ses ressorts, des songes, des oracles, des fatalités..."[17]. The scale, the ritual character, the subject-matter of Greek tragedy all illustrate this affinity with the epic:

> Mêmes fables, mêmes catastrophes, mêmes héros. Tous puisent au fleuve homérique. C'est toujours l'*Iliade* et l'*Odyssée*. Comme Achille traînant Hector, la tragédie grecque tourne autour de Troie.[18]

Roman civilization, which saw the decline of this second age, was the birthplace of the third; and Hugo's stirring delineation of the character of the literature of the Christian era forms the climax of this first section of the *Préface*:

> Cette religion est complète, parce qu'elle est vraie; entre son dogme et son culte, elle scelle profondément la morale. Et d'abord, pour premières vérités, elle enseigne à l'homme qu'il a deux vies à vivre, l'une passagère, l'autre immortelle; l'une de la terre, l'autre du ciel. Elle lui montre qu'il est double comme sa destinée, qu'il y a en lui un animal et une intelligence, une âme et un corps; en un mot, qu'il est le point d'intersection, l'anneau commun des deux chaînes d'êtres qui embrassent la création, de la série des êtres matériels et de la

série des êtres incorporels, la première partant de la pierre pour arriver à l'homme, la seconde partant de l'homme pour arriver à Dieu.[19]

Here, too, Chateaubriand is an important source; for instance, "un sentiment nouveau, inconnu chez les anciens et singulièrement développé chez les modernes, un sentiment qui est plus que la gravité et moins que la tristesse, la mélancolie"[20] corresponds quite closely to the notion of "le vague des passions" in the *Génie*[21]—although the purpose of Hugo's survey is not moral, as with Chateaubriand, but aesthetic. For Hugo, the moral and spiritual essence of Christianity provides the basis of a new aesthetic doctrine:

La muse purement épique des anciens n'avait étudié la nature que sous une seule face, rejetant sans pitié de l'art presque tout ce qui, dans le monde soumis à son imitation, ne se rapportait pas à un certain type du beau. Type d'abord magnifique, mais, comme il arrive toujours de ce qui est systématique, devenu dans les derniers temps faux, mesquin et conventionnel. Le christianisme amène la poésie à la vérité. Comme lui, la muse moderne verra les choses d'un coup d'œil plus haut et plus large. Elle sentira que tout dans la création n'est pas humainement *beau*, que le laid y existe à côté du beau, le difforme près du gracieux, le grotesque au revers du sublime, le mal avec le bien, l'ombre avec la lumière.[22]

This is the core of the message of the *Préface de Cromwell*: a profoundly original message—however shaky its historical foundations—which takes us to the very heart of Hugo's aesthetic. Under the impulse of Christianity, says Hugo, "la poésie fera un grand pas, un pas décisif, un pas qui, pareil à la secousse d'un tremblement de terre, changera toute la face du monde intellectuel":

Elle se mettra à faire comme la nature, à mêler dans ses créations, sans pourtant les confondre, l'ombre à la lumière, le grotesque au sublime, en d'autres termes, le corps à l'âme, la bête à l'esprit; car le point de départ de la religion est toujours le point de départ de la poésie.[23]

Between the recognition of this new aesthetic and the refusal to recognize it lies the watershed between 'classical' and 'Romantic': between archaic tragedy, wedded to an obsolete view of the world, and 'le drame' which alone can represent the complexity of life as seen through Christian eyes. For it is 'le drame' which is the characteristic literary form of the modern age:

> Du jour où le christianisme a dit à l'homme: Tu es double, tu es composé de deux êtres, l'un périssable, l'autre immortel, l'un charnel, l'autre éthéré, l'un enchaîné par les appétits, les besoins et les passions, l'autre emporté sur les ailes de l'enthousiasme et de la rêverie, celui-ci enfin toujours courbé vers la terre, sa mère, celui-là sans cesse élancé vers le ciel, sa patrie; de ce jour le drame a été créé. Est-ce autre chose en effet que ce contraste de tous les jours, que cette lutte de tous les instants entre deux principes opposés qui sont toujours en présence dans la vie, et qui se disputent l'homme depuis le berceau jusqu'à la tombe?
>
> La poésie née du christianisme, la poésie de notre temps est donc le drame; le caractère du drame est donc le réel; le réel résulte de la combinaison toute naturelle de deux types, le sublime et le grotesque, qui se croisent dans le drame, comme ils se croisent dans la vie et dans la création. Car la poésie vraie, la poésie complète, est dans l'harmonie des contraires. Puis, il est temps de le dire hautement, et c'est ici surtout que les exceptions confirmeraient la règle, tout ce qui est dans la nature est dans l'art.[24]

It is not, therefore, the moral aspect of Christian dualism—the challenge to man to subordinate his physical, earthy nature to his finer spiritual self—which appeals to Hugo, but the aesthetic possibilities offered by the dramatic contrast between these two sides of our make-up. Not that this new aesthetic is peculiar to Hugo: though he was to exploit the possibilities of the contrast between 'sublime' and 'grotesque' much more systematically than any of his contemporaries[25], the same insight surely underlies, for instance, the following passage from Musset's *On ne badine pas avec l'amour*:

> Tous les hommes sont menteurs, inconstants, faux, bavards, hypocrites, orgueilleux et lâches, méprisables et sensuels;

toutes les femmes sont perfides, artificieuses, vaniteuses,
curieuses et dépravées; le monde n'est qu'un égout sans fond
où les phoques les plus informes rampent et se tordent sur des
montagnes de fange; mais il y a au monde une chose sainte et
sublime, c'est l'union de deux de ces êtres si imparfaits et si
affreux.[26]

Likewise, Hugo's feeling for dramatic contrast is reflected—
more subtly, and with genuine spiritual anguish, yet nevertheless
in unmistakably similar terms—in Baudelaire's fundamental
antithesis between 'Spleen' and 'Idéal':

Dans tout homme, à toute heure, il y a deux postulations
simultanées, l'une vers Dieu, l'autre vers Satan. L'invocation
à Dieu, ou spiritualité, est un désir de monter en grade; celle
de Satan, ou animalité, est une joie de descendre.[27]

The whole of the 'Études philosophiques' section of Balzac's
Comédie humaine is based on a highly personal adaptation of the
fundamental Romantic dichotomy between the spiritual
aspirations of man and his physical limitations; while the same
theme was expressed most memorably, perhaps, in Romantic
versions of the Faust legend, which was so important to Nerval,
Berlioz and Gounod as well as to Goethe.

When Hugo writes, therefore, that "tout ce qui est dans la
nature est dans l'art", he does not mean that art must be the
servile copy of nature. Far from it: he insists on the "limite
infranchissable" which separates the two[28]; and, in a paragraph
devoted to the notion of realism in the theatre, he takes issue
(though he does not name him) with Diderot:

D'autres, ce nous semble, l'ont déjà dit, le drame est un
miroir où se réfléchit la nature. Mais si ce miroir est un
miroir ordinaire, une surface plane et unie, il ne renverra des
objets qu'une image terne et sans relief, fidèle, mais dé-
colorée; on sait ce que la couleur et la lumière perdent à la
réflexion simple. Il faut donc que le drame soit un miroir de
concentration qui, loin de les affaiblir, ramasse et condense
les rayons colorants, qui fasse d'une lueur une lumière, d'une
lumière une flamme. Alors seulement le drame est avoué de
l'art.[29]

The 'reality' of the 'drame', then, as envisaged by Hugo, could not be more different from that of 'drame bourgeois'; and the one playwright he points to as a precursor is Shakespeare:

> L'ode vit de l'idéal, l'épopée du grandiose, le drame du réel. Enfin, cette triple poésie découle de trois grandes sources, la Bible, Homère, Shakespeare[30]

—Shakespeare, as he writes in another passage, "ce dieu du théâtre, en qui semblent réunis, comme dans une trinité, les trois grands génies caractéristiques de notre scène, Corneille, Molière, Beaumarchais"[31]. For it is in Shakespeare that Hugo finds the richest store of examples of the *grotesque* contrasted with the *sublime*:

> Il s'infiltre partout, car de même que les plus vulgaires ont maintes fois leurs accès de sublime, les plus élevés paient fréquemment tribut au trivial et au ridicule. Aussi, souvent insaisissable, souvent imperceptible, est-il toujours présent sur la scène, même quand il se tait, même quand il se cache. Grâce à lui, point d'impressions monotones. Tantôt il jette du rire, tantôt de l'horreur dans la tragédie. Il fera rencontrer l'apothicaire à Roméo, les trois sorcières à Macbeth, les fossoyeurs à Hamlet. Parfois enfin il peut sans discordance, comme dans la scène du roi Lear et de son fou, mêler sa voix criarde aux plus sublimes, aux plus lugubres, aux plus rêveuses musiques de l'âme.[32]

The new 'drame', like that of Shakespeare, will seek to re-create reality by an artistic synthesis, not by attempting a slavish copy. And Hugo is very scornful of those products of classical 'reason' which attempt to minimize the distance between reality and illusion, "l'arbitraire distinction des genres" and "la prétendue règle des deux unités":

> Nous disons deux et non *trois* unités, l'unité d'action ou d'ensemble, la seule vraie et fondée, étant depuis longtemps hors de cause.[33]

In a passage which illustrates the attractive variety of his style, he subjects the classical conventions to the test of common sense:

Quoi de plus invraisemblable et de plus absurde en effet que
ce vestibule, ce péristyle, cette antichambre, lieu banal où nos
tragédies ont la complaisance de venir se dérouler, où
arrivent, on ne sait comment, les conspirateurs pour déclamer
contre le tyran, le tyran pour déclamer contre les conspirateurs, chacun à leur tour... Il résulte de là que tout ce qui
est trop caractéristique, trop intime, trop local, pour se passer
dans l'antichambre ou dans le carrefour, c'est-à-dire tout le
drame, se passe dans la coulisse. Nous ne voyons en quelque
sorte sur le théâtre que les coudes de l'action; ses mains sont
ailleurs. Au lieu de scènes, nous avons des récits; au lieu de
tableaux, des descriptions. De graves personnages placés,
comme le chœur antique, entre le drame et nous, viennent
nous raconter ce qui se fait dans le temple, dans le palais,
dans la place publique, de façon que souventes fois nous
sommes tentés de leur crier: — Vraiment! mais conduisez-
nous donc là-bas! On s'y doit bien amuser, cela doit être beau
à voir![34]

Finally, having defined the genre, and sketched the form, of
the new drama, Hugo turns his attention to the language in
which it is written. Unlike Stendhal, and in keeping with his
own views on the relationship between art and nature, he
insists on the retention of verse:

Nous n'hésitons pas à considérer le vers comme un des
moyens les plus propres à préserver le drame du fléau que
nous venons de signaler, comme une des digues les plus
puissantes contre l'irruption du commun, qui, ainsi que la
démocratie, coule toujours à pleins bords dans les esprits.[35]

And it is on the subject of verse that he gives his most detailed
prescription to the aspiring playwright:

Que si nous avions le droit de dire quel pourrait être, à notre
gré, le style du drame, nous voudrions un vers libre, franc,
loyal, osant tout dire sans pruderie, tout exprimer sans
recherche; passant d'une naturelle allure de la comédie à la
tragédie, du sublime au grotesque; tour à tour positif et
poétique, tout ensemble artiste et inspiré, profond et soudain,
large et vrai; sachant briser à propos et déplacer la césure
pour déguiser sa monotonie d'alexandrin; plus ami de

l'enjambement qui l'allonge que de l'inversion qui l'embrouille; fidèle à la rime, cette esclave reine, cette suprême grâce de notre poésie, ce générateur de notre mètre; inépuisable dans ses secrets d'élégance et de facture; prenant, comme Protée, mille formes sans changer de type et de caractère; fuyant la *tirade*; se jouant dans le dialogue; se cachant toujours derrière le personnage; s'occupant avant tout d'être à sa place, et lorsqu'il lui adviendrait d'être *beau*, n'étant beau en quelque sorte que par hasard, malgré lui et sans le savoir; lyrique, épique, dramatique selon le besoin; pouvant parcourir toute la gamme poétique, aller de haut en bas, des idées les plus élevées aux plus vulgaires, des plus bouffonnes aux plus graves, des plus extérieures aux plus abstraites, sans jamais sortir des limites d'une scène parlée; en un mot, tel que le ferait l'homme qu'une fée aurait doué de l'âme de Corneille et de la tête de Molière. Il nous semble que ce vers-là serait bien *aussi beau que de la prose.*[36]

This capital text, with its forceful style and its positive message, does more for French verse than has been achieved by a century or more of timid and ineffectual protests. Hugo not only preserves the alexandrine, but strengthens it immeasurably by freeing it from the tyranny of 'le style noble'; and this paragraph should be read in conjunction with his poem 'Réponse à un acte d'accusation' (1834) in which he prides himself on his achievement in more picturesque terms:

Je fis souffler un vent révolutionnaire.
Je mis un bonnet rouge au vieux dictionnaire.
Plus de mot sénateur! plus de mot roturier!
Je fis une tempête au fond de l'encrier,
Et je mêlai, parmi les ombres débordées,
Au peuple noir des mots l'essaim blanc des idées...
Je massacrai l'albâtre, et la neige, et l'ivoire;
Je retirai le jais de la prunelle noire,
Et j'osai dire au bras: Sois blanc, tout simplement.
Je violai du vers le cadavre fumant;
J'y fis entrer le chiffre; ô terreur! Mithridate
Du siège de Cyzique eût pu citer la date...
J'ai dit aux mots: Soyez république! soyez
La fourmilière immense, et travaillez! croyez,
Aimez, vivez! — J'ai mis tout en branle, et, morose,
J'ai jeté le vers noble aux chiens noirs de la prose.[37]

This is Hugo's real triumph. In the theatre as elsewhere, the linguistic breakthrough was the one aspect of the Romantic 'revolution' which really mattered; and before the *Orientales* and the *Feuilles d'automne*, before the plays which were to put the new verse-form to the test in the theatre—in other words, with only the *Odes et ballades* behind him—*Cromwell* and its Preface provided Hugo with the opportunity to experiment with the reinvigorated alexandrine and to proclaim it confidently as the vehicle for the new verse drama.

The last section of the *Préface*, in which Hugo turns to analysis and justification of the play itself, contains an interesting commentary on the character of Cromwell seen as an example of the *grotesque/sublime* antithesis. From the mass of seventeenth-century pamphlets and memoirs that he read, says Hugo, there emerged "un Cromwell tout nouveau":

> Ce n'était plus seulement le Cromwell militaire, le Cromwell politique de Bossuet; c'était un être complexe, hétérogène, multiple, composé de tous les contraires, mêlé de beaucoup de mal et de beaucoup de bien, plein de génie et de petitesse; une sorte de Tibère-Dandin, tyran de l'Europe et jouet de sa famille...

A long antithetical portrait follows, and Hugo concludes:

> Celui qui écrit ceci, en présence de ce rare et frappant ensemble, sentit que la silhouette passionnée de Bossuet ne lui suffisait plus. Il se mit à tourner autour de cette haute figure, et il fut pris alors d'une ardente tentation de peindre le géant sous toutes ses faces, sous tous ses aspects. La matière était riche. A côté de l'homme de guerre et de l'homme d'État, il restait à crayonner le théologien, le pédant, le mauvais poète, le visionnaire, le bouffon, le père, le mari, l'homme-Protée, en un mot le Cromwell double, *homo et vir*.[38]

The *Préface* closes with a plea for a change in the attitudes of French playgoers and critics. If his play were ever modified for stage production, Hugo says, "une pièce extraite de *Cromwell* n'occuperait toujours pas moins de la durée d'une représentation. Il est difficile qu'un théâtre *romantique* s'établisse autrement"[39]. In place of a two-hour tragedy, in which "un ou deux personnages, types abstraits d'une idée purement métaphysique, se promènent solennellement sur un fond sans profondeur, à peine occupé par quelques têtes de confidents, pâles contre-calques des héros, chargés de remplir les vides d'une action simple, uniforme et monocorde"[40], followed by an even shorter *opéra-comique* or farce to fill out the bill, why not copy the English and German theatres, where a whole evening is devoted to a single play—and let that play combine the essence of the two genres so artificially separated:

> [Le drame romantique] broierait et mêlerait artistement ensemble ces deux espèces de plaisir. Il ferait passer à chaque instant l'auditoire du sérieux au rire, des excitations bouffonnes aux émotions déchirantes, *du grave au doux, du plaisant au sévère...* La scène romantique ferait un mets piquant, varié, savoureux, de ce qui sur le théâtre classique est une médecine divisée en deux pilules.[41]

And finally, Hugo appeals for a new generation of critics: not like the academic critics of the eighteenth century, forever on the look-out for departures from a narrow doctrinal orthodoxy, but prepared to interpret new works in a spirit of generous understanding:

> On quittera, et c'est M. de Chateaubriand qui parle ici, *la critique mesquine des défauts pour la grande et féconde critique des beautés.*[42]

A brief analysis cannot do full justice either to the range of ideas covered by Hugo (and the variety of the texts adduced in support of his argument) or to the astonishing virtuosity of his style. To appreciate the impact of this style, one need only compare the *Préface de Cromwell* with those earlier treatises by Guizot, Constant and Stendhal, and see how the conventional abstract rhetoric of serious French prose is here enriched by a poet's imagination. The rhetorical devices are there—we note above all that predilection for forceful antithesis which was to characterize Hugo's poetic manner throughout his career—but they are transformed by bold, provocative imagery into something vital and dynamic: a style which persuades by a powerful appeal to the imagination as much as by a formal, logical appeal to the reason.

Some of Hugo's historical assumptions can no doubt be shown to be inaccurate—the role of the chorus in Greek tragedy, for instance, or the notion of Corneille's genius unwillingly confined in the straitjacket of the unities—and as Souriau shows, he can sometimes be caught out in the practice of manipulating the evidence to suit his argument. But in the broad sweep of his historical survey, in the confidence of his critical judgements, and in his intuition of concepts so central to the Romantic revolution in literature, the *Préface* is a remarkable *tour de force*. For Hugo's young contemporaries, it was no doubt welcomed chiefly as a critical weapon, expressing with devastating effect their common anti-classical sentiments. But for readers 150 years on, its topical and polemical character is less important. For us, Hugo's intuitive perception, and challenging formulation, of the contrast between the sublime and the grotesque as the essential characteristic of the literature of the modern era gives the *Préface de Cromwell* a much wider significance. However fallible as a generalization in the larger historical context to which Hugo assigns it, this concept could not be more pertinent, or more meaningful, as a key to the working of the Romantic imagination in broad terms, and more particularly to the creative principle underlying the drama of Hugo and his contemporaries.

(iii) 'Cromwell': the play

TALMA, meeting Hugo in 1827 when he was working on *Cromwell*, had urged the young poet to complete his play, in the hope that it would provide him with the sort of role for which he had always vainly hoped: "un personnage qui eût la variété et le mouvement de la vie, qui ne fût pas tout d'une pièce, qui fût tragique et familier, un roi qui fût un homme"[43]. But the actor had died shortly after their meeting; and there may be some truth in Madame Hugo's suggestion that this radically affected the character of the play, since it need no longer be written with stage performance in mind: "M. Victor Hugo . . . put donner à son drame des développements que n'aurait pas comportés la représentation"[44]. It is interesting to speculate on the possible fortunes of a *Cromwell* produced by the collaboration of Hugo and Talma, and scaled down to the requirements of performance at the Théâtre-Français; as published, however, *Cromwell* could not hope to be more than an academic illustration of the ideas of the *Préface*, and it was the latter which was recognized, by friend and foe alike, as the really vital challenge to the established order of things.

How well does *Cromwell* the play represent the ideas put forward in its Preface? In particular, how successfully does the central character embody the formula based on the antithesis of sublime and grotesque, and how does Hugo's verse measure up to the requirements of the Romantic alexandrine as defined in the *Préface*? In both respects, the answer must be that Hugo's achievement in practice still fell at this stage some way behind the originality of his theoretical programme. For all that he writes about "l'homme-Protée, en un mot le Cromwell double, *homo et vir*", his hero is little more than a novel variant of the hero of classical tragedy, faced with a stereotyped dilemma; and his verse-form, too, falls short of the flexibility and variety of his mature alexandrine.

What the play does offer is an immensely rich kaleidoscope of "la couleur des temps": a motley parade of eccentrics in the guise of Royalist conspirators, Puritan fanatics, Court jesters, Roundheads, Cavaliers—over seventy speaking parts, and a veritable army of supernumeraries—in colourful settings designed to illustrate the constant contrast between serious issues of state and absurd, or trivial, personal preoccupations. It may well be that this gives a convincing—if at times over-erudite— picture of the ambience of Cromwell's court; but it is in this picture of an environment, rather than in the portrayal of Cromwell himself, that Hugo's penchant for antithesis finds expression. It is clear, of course, that these external trappings— including the caricatural portraits of his supporters, rivals, and enemies, his co-religionaries and his hangers-on—are intended to symbolize aspects of Cromwell's own character. But they remain an *external* representation, more easily appreciated by the reader than by the hypothetical spectator; and in strictly dramatic terms, the portrayal of the man himself could hardly be simpler. As Hugo says in the Preface, the unities of time and place are observed with almost classical rigour—"[Mon] drame ne sort pas de Londres, il commence le 25 juin 1657 à trois heures du matin et finit le 26 à midi"[45]—and in keeping with this, the plot presents an action taken at crisis-point. Will Cromwell yield to the temptation to declare himself King, thereby inviting almost certain death at the conspirators' hands? The problem is posed at the conspirators' rendezvous in Act I, and Cromwell himself faces up to his dilemma in Act II. Acts III and IV give him the chance to turn the tables on the conspirators, but it is the victory over himself which matters, and this is resolved, in true classical manner, in Act V. The rest is window-dressing: the essential plot is as classical, both in its conception and in its handling, as that of *Cinna*. True to the recommendations of the Preface, Hugo has dispensed with the colourless confidant; but he makes conventional use of soliloquy to explore his hero's dilemma[46], and what we do learn about Cromwell we learn in this way, rather than through the relationships with his family, courtiers, jesters and the rest. In short, the notion of Cromwell as an "homme-Protée" may reflect Hugo's reaction to the historical figure; but disappointingly little of this has passed into the play.

When we come to examine the language of *Cromwell*, it is necessary to distinguish between Hugo's on the whole quite conventional handling of the alexandrine from the metrical point of view, and his complete rejection of convention with regard to vocabulary. He makes sparing use of *enjambement*; and there are few genuine ternary lines without a median caesura, on the pattern:

Malheur à vous! Malheur à moi! Malheur à tous! (V, vi)

J'ai faim; j'ai soif; l'été, j'ai chaud; j'ai froid, l'hiver. (V, xiv)

It is true that, compared with almost any dramatist of the previous 150 years, he achieves far greater flexibility within the 'classical' alexandrine by exploiting the variability of the subsidiary *coupes*, and by frequently making these more prominent than the caesura itself:

Mon père... Mais d'où vient ce trouble inattendu?
Quel est sur votre front ce nuage épandu,
Mylord? où doit tomber la foudre qu'il recèle
Et dont l'éclair sinistre en vos yeux étincelle?

Qu'avez-vous? Qu'a-t-on fait? Parlez: que craignez-vous?
Qui peut vous attrister dans le bonheur de tous?
Demain, des anciens rois rejoignant les fantômes,
La république meurt, vous léguant trois royaumes;
Demain votre grandeur sur le trône s'accroît;
Demain, dans Westminster proclamant votre droit,
Jetant à vos rivaux son gant héréditaire,
Le champion armé de la vieille Angleterre,
Aux salves des canons, au branle du beffroi,
Doit défier le monde au nom d'Olivier roi.
Qui vous manque? l'Europe, et l'Angleterre, et Londre,
Votre famille, tout semble à vos vœux répondre.
Si j'osais me nommer, mon père et mon seigneur,
Je n'ai, moi, de souci que pour votre bonheur,
Vos jours, votre santé... (II, xix)

—but then these were precisely the means by which Racine had overcome the limitations of the seventeenth-century line and made it such a supple and harmonious verse-form.

Not that 'harmony' was Hugo's object here, at least in any conventional sense. Flexibility and variety certainly were his aims, however; and the most striking thing about the style of *Cromwell* is the range and scope of the vocabulary. The barriers between 'style noble' and 'style bas', between 'poetic' and 'prosaic', have been overthrown, and from the celebrated first line:

Demain, vingt-cinq juin mil six cent cinquante-sept[47]

onwards, Hugo seems to be trying to rise to a challenge, attempting the *tour de force* of accommodating the alexandrine to the most outlandish vocabulary possible. The use of proper names—particularly Biblical names in the mouths of the Puritans—foreshadows his practice in the *Légende des siècles*, much later; it is most successful when combined with his characteristic virtuosity with regard to rhymes:

Oui, messieurs, sa fortune aveugle ce Cromwell,
Qui semble un Attila fait par Machiavel (V, iv)

Huzza, grand juge Hale! — Huzza, sergent Wallop!
— Voici des colonels qui passent au galop (V, xi)

> Ah! comment nomme-t-on
> L'orateur? — C'est, je crois, sir Thomas Widdrington. (*ibid.*)

For, as these examples show, there is a world of difference
between the banal stereotypes of the *Oreste/funeste* variety and the
amusing, suggestive or provocative effects achieved by Hugo's
inventive rhyming. But the erudition and the economical
allusiveness of Hugo's style frequently make him difficult to
follow; and it is clear that in the theatre such a text would have
run into serious difficulties—that certain passages would not
easily have been able to 'passer la rampe'. Take, for instance,
the following:

> Souviens-toi d'Isboseth. Ce roi vain et peu sage
> Fit ranger le premier le peuple à son passage;
> Il mit sur des chevaux cent guerriers d'Issachar
> Qui sans cesse couraient en avant de son char.
> Mais Dieu fait toujours naître, et c'est l'effroi de l'âme,
> Le malheur du bonheur, la cendre de la flamme.
> Or Isboseth tomba, tel qu'un fruit avorté,
> Tel qu'un bruit sans écho par le vent emporté.
> Songe à Salmanasar. Sur ses coursiers rapides,
> Ce roi, qu'environnaient les grands argyraspides,
> Passa, comme l'été, sous la nue enchaîné,
> Passe un éclair du soir — sans même avoir tonné. (V, xiv)

The modern reader finds the condensed imagery and the jarring
rhythms of a passage such as this disconcerting enough; and it
is not difficult to imagine what would have been the effect, on
a generation of playgoers whose ears were still attuned to the
familiar abstractions and the well-worn clichés hallowed by a
century's use, of a vigorous, colourful vocabulary and a new
kind of dramatic rhetoric. For the rhythm is no longer that of
the classical dramatist, for whom the syntactical unit of the
sentence had normally corresponded to the single line, the
couplet, or the four-line 'stanza', but rather the shapeless
sentence of irregular length, accumulating phrases and clauses
quite haphazardly. This can be seen most clearly, perhaps, in
the long harangue of Cromwell to the Parliament (V, xii) or
Carr's vituperative tirade (V, xiv)—but the same irregular and
unpredictable rhythms characterize all the longer speeches

throughout the play (and the same is true of the later plays, too, written for stage performance). At the other extreme is the equally disconcerting effect produced by the attempt to reproduce rapid, broken dialogue, seen at its most striking in the 'Voix dans la foule' passages of Act V, scenes xi and xii:

> Quoi! c'est la Protectrice! Elle a l'air bien épais.
> — La fille d'un certain Bourchier.   — C'est un beau rêve
> Qu'elle fait là.   — Monsieur, quelle est cette jeune Ève
> A sa droite?   — Ici?   — Non; là.   — C'est lady Francis.
> — Sa fille?   — Oui.   — Le vieux Noll en a donc cinq ou
> six?
> — Non, quatre. Vous voyez.   — La plus jeune est charmante.
> — Qu'il fait chaud!   — Qu'on est mal!   — La foule encore augmente.
> — On est pressé ici comme ces fils d'enfer
> Dont le nombre égalait le sable de la mer.
> — Les oiseaux sont heureux avec leur paire d'ailes.
> — On m'écrase! (V, xi)

The virtuosity here is more apparent than real, however: while such writing may convey a vivid effect on the printed page, it must be evident that it would be impossible to achieve the same effect in the theatre without completely sacrificing any sense of the alexandrine line.

If it does not completely vindicate the dramatic and linguistic programme of the *Préface*, at least the text of *Cromwell* illustrates it in a challenging way. Over-ambitious it certainly is: far exceeding the resources of any theatre management, and anticipating the techniques of the cinema with such things as the contrasting of groups of actors, or some of the crowd-effects. But it is also over-academic; for an essentially simple dramatic theme is overlaid with detail which, far from helping to delineate character, merely provides an erudite commentary on Cromwell's times. This is a fault which can possibly be excused in a historical novel—though it is obtrusive enough in *Notre-Dame de Paris*; in a historical drama, however, there is no room for superfluous erudition, and Hugo's lack of selection and control in handling detail makes *Cromwell* in its bizarre way yet another 'scène historique'.

(iv) Vigny and 'Le More de Venise'

DESPITE the very real impact of its Preface, *Cromwell* must have been for Hugo's contemporaries, as it has remained from a historical point of view, a literary experiment rather than a valid contribution to the life of the theatre. Nor was Hugo himself destined to be the first Romantic dramatist to gain acceptance at the Théâtre-Français. This honour fell, strictly speaking, to Vigny, whose *Roméo et Juliette*, prepared in collaboration with Émile Deschamps, was accepted by the *comité de lecture* in April 1828. However, Vigny was to lose no time in experiencing at first hand the difficulties awaiting any playwright working with the Théâtre-Français; for although the *comédiens* had been willing enough to accept *Roméo et Juliette*, the play was never performed. According to Vigny himself, this was because Mlle Mars was afraid of appearing ridiculous in a part as young as that of Juliet[48]; though a subsidiary factor was no doubt the actors' unwillingness to compete with a rival *Roméo* by Soulié, which was produced at the Odéon shortly after the acceptance of Vigny's and Deschamps's version at the Théâtre-Français.

Besides Vigny, another aspiring dramatist with Romantic leanings also found the Théâtre-Français well-disposed towards the new drama in this same year, 1828. If we are to believe Alexandre Dumas's own account, his *Christine* was accepted enthusiastically by Baron Taylor, and with unanimous acclaim by the *comité de lecture*; though M. Descotes suggests that the facts were perhaps not so outstandingly favourable to the young playwright[49]. At all events, *Christine* was accepted—but only to undergo in its turn a fate very similar to that of *Roméo et Juliette*. It is likely that in this instance there were some misgivings on the part of influential *sociétaires* about certain features of Dumas's play; but once more, rivalries and jealousies held up the casting of the play, until competition with a rival *Christine* (a play by one Brault, also accepted at the Salle Richelieu) was alleged as a pretext for deferring production. However, at this point Dumas, with the support of Taylor, had a second play, his *Henri III et sa cour*, accepted; and as a *quid pro quo* for the shelving of *Christine*, *Henri III* was given preferential treatment and produced ahead of Brault's *Christine*.

Henri III et sa cour thus became the first play by an author whom history regards as one of the major Romantic dramatists to be produced at the Théâtre-Français. Put on in February 1829, it ran for 38 performances, and was withdrawn only because Mlle Mars insisted on her right to her annual leave[50]. It was an undoubted success, in other words—and a much more spontaneous success than that of *Hernani* a year later. For Dumas had no need to pack the theatre with his friends in order to win the day—if only, perhaps, because his play did not arouse the intense opposition aroused by *Hernani*[51]. Neither the Romantic faction nor their opponents, in fact, regarded *Henri III* as a vital challenge to the classical orthodoxy: although it was a notable achievement for Dumas to get his play performed at the Théâtre-Français, the very fact that it was in prose meant that comparisons were made with Pixérécourt's melodramas rather than with traditional verse tragedy. Critics may have complained of the debasing of the first theatre of France, of a deplorable pandering to popular taste[52]—but such were the more obvious literary and dramatic affiliations of *Henri III* that neither its friends nor its enemies saw it as a serious threat to the classical tradition[53].

It was hard on the heels of the success of *Henri III* that Hugo finished *Marion de Lorme*: his first play, apart from the youthful *Amy Robsart*, designed for stage performance. A semi-public reading of the play took place in July 1829 "devant une réunion nombreuse", Mme Hugo tells us, "dans laquelle on remarquait MM de Balzac, Eugène Delacroix, Alfred de Musset, Alexandre Dumas, Alfred de Vigny, Sainte-Beuve, Villemain, Mérimée, Armand et Édouard Bertin, Louis Boulanger, Frédéric Soulié, Taylor, Soumet, Émile et Antony Deschamps, les Dévéria, Charles Magnin, Mme Tastu, etc."[54]—an evocative roll-call of all the most illustrious names among the young Romantics. The enthusiasm of Hugo's audience was tinged with relief:

> Un des étonnements de l'auditoire fut que M. Victor Hugo eût fait un drame jouable: le développement excessif de *Cromwell* avait fait craindre qu'il ne sût pas plier sa pensée aux exigences de la représentation; *Marion de Lorme* démentait cette peur et faisait décidément de lui un auteur dramatique.[55]

Confirmation followed swiftly: in the space of two days, Taylor demanded a reading before the *comité de lecture* at the Théâtre-Français, Jouslin de la Salle wrote requesting the play for the Porte-Saint-Martin, and Harel of the Odéon offered to put it on unconditionally, without a reading. Taylor, and the prestige of the Théâtre-Français, carried the day: Hugo promptly read his play, and *Marion de Lorme* triumphed again; in Taylor's memorable words, as reported by Mme Hugo: "Il est inutile d'aller aux voix: M. Hugo ne présente pas sa pièce, c'est nous qui la lui demandons"[56].

All was set for a successful opening in November, but like Vigny and Dumas before him, Hugo saw his first hopes frustrated. This time it was the censor who banned the play, citing the disparaging portrait of Louis XIII in Act IV as an indirect attack on Charles I. First Taylor, then Hugo himself, obtained audiences with the King: but his ministers were adamant, and the ban was confirmed. This was followed, shortly afterwards, by the offer of a new royal pension for the poet—an offer which Hugo refused, much to the gratification of the opposition press. Hugo's own reaction to this setback was to write *Hernani*—in three weeks, according to Mme Hugo. But in the meantime, the Théâtre-Français had filled an awkward gap by putting on, with the minimum of delay (in October 1829), *Le More de Venise*, Vigny's adaptation of *Othello*, which they had accepted in July.

If Dumas brought to the *métier* of dramatist the natural gifts of a man of the theatre, and Hugo those of a poet, Vigny's endowments were rather those of a scholar. Assuming that his first acquaintance with Shakespeare dates from the period when, as a young officer, he had tried his hand at an *Antoine et Cléopâtre*[57], this interest was greatly consolidated during the early 1820s by his friendly relations with a distant cousin by marriage, Bruguière de Sorsum, who was then at work on a translation of six of Shakespeare's plays. Bruguière died in 1823, but a collection of his works which appeared in 1826, edited by Chênedollé, included the four translations he had completed: those of *The Tempest*, *A Midsummer Night's Dream*, *Macbeth* and *Coriolanus*. This publication had been heralded in 1824 by an article written by Vigny for the *Muse Française*: 'Œuvres posthumes de M. le baron de Sorsum'—and the contents of this

article, together with the fact that the two plays whose translation remained unfinished on the latter's death (*Romeo and Juliet*
and *Othello*) were two of the three translated by Vigny himself,
are sufficient indication of the important role played by
Bruguière de Sorsum, not only in giving Vigny an active
interest in Shakespeare, but in determining the scholarly nature
of that interest.

For Bruguière's translation differed completely from Letourneur's, and from Guizot's revision of Letourneur's, in that it
attempted faithfully to reproduce the formal variety to be
found in the original: for the first time, Shakespeare's prose was
translated into French prose, his blank verse into non-rhyming
alexandrines, and his rhyming verse into alexandrine couplets.
The result was not an unqualified success, and Vigny ascribed
this to the unsatisfactory impression produced by the 'blank'
alexandrine: the variable stresses of the English blank-verse line
do of course convey a richness and variety to Shakespeare's
verse-rhythms which the alexandrine, with its much less flexible
tonic accent, cannot possess, but for which the pattern of the
rhyme-scheme in the alexandrine provides some compensation.
However, Vigny had a high regard for the scholarly aims of
Bruguière's translations, and there is little doubt that when he
came in his turn to translate Shakespeare, he set himself to
uphold the same standard of fidelity to the original, in versions
intended for stage performance[58].

If further stimulus was needed to turn Vigny from lyric poet
into dramatist, this was provided by the visit of the English
actors in 1827–28. Vigny inevitably shared in the general
enthusiasm[59], and immediately set himself, with Deschamps, to
translate *Romeo and Juliet*. As has been seen, this version was
accepted, but not produced; nor has it ever been published,
except piecemeal by modern scholars[60]. *Shylock*, completed in
1828, was published in 1839, but without having been performed; so that *Le More de Venise* was the only one of Vigny's
versions of a Shakespeare play to be produced at this period[61].

However scholarly a translator might be by temperament,
and however high his regard for the peculiar genius of Shakespeare, it would have been impossible to translate him with a
view to performance at the Théâtre-Français in 1829 without
making certain concessions to the taste of the audience. It is true

that *Othello* offered the advantage of being the play nearest in spirit to the French ideal of tragedy: it fails, of course, to conform to the unities of time and place, but it comes nearer to satisfying the unity of action than any other of Shakespeare's major tragedies—one has only to think of the relative diffuseness of *Hamlet* or *Lear*, or of the shift of tragic focus in *Julius Caesar*, to say nothing of the jarring variations of tone in *Coriolanus* or *Macbeth*. Shakespeare's *Othello* already largely satisfied the classical requirement of a single passion, taken at its crisis; but the *Othello* played by Macready and his colleagues during their Paris visit had embodied certain traditional modifications: in particular, the role of Bianca had been cut out. Vigny goes further, suppressing all mention of Bianca (the result being that Othello's jealousy lacks even the semblance of proof provided by the opening scenes of Act IV of Shakespeare's play), and making the dénouement crisper and less long-drawn-out[62]. But these and other omissions apart, the translation is as faithful as the rhythms of the alexandrine and the conventions of the 'style noble' would permit. Vigny did show the courage of his convictions, and kept the controversial 'handkerchief' (just as he persists in having Desdemona smothered by a pillow, unlike Letourneur, whose Othello had used a sword)—but the "salt and sorry rheum" of Shakespeare's Act III scene iv has gone, in favour of the relatively inoffensive:

Je souffre. Prêtez-moi, mon amie, un mouchoir.

The "Anthropophagi, and men whose heads / Do grow beneath their shoulders" have also disappeared; and throughout, the colour and imagery of the original have given way to the abstractions and the rhetoric typical of eighteenth-century tragedy. Indeed, the reader of Othello's final speech:

> Écrivez tout au Doge,
> Ou partez pour Venise et, s'il vous interroge,
> Dites: « C'est par honneur qu'il lui perça le sein ».
> Nommez-moi hardiment honorable assassin!
> On lira dans ma vie un crime, et non des vices.
> J'ai peut-être à l'État rendu d'heureux services,

> N'en parlons plus jamais: racontez seulement
> Que je n'aimai que trop cette femme, et comment,
> Dans un piège infernal lentement enlacée,
> Jusqu'à l'assassinat mon âme fut poussée.
> Racontez qu'un soldat qui ne pleura jamais
> Vous a montré des yeux vaincus et, désormais,
> Versant des larmes, plus que les palmiers d'Asie
> De leurs flancs parfumés ne versent d'ambroisie.
> Parlez ainsi de moi; puis racontez encor
> Que dans Alep un jour, dérobant un trésor,
> Un Turc au turban vert profanait une église,
> Insultait un chrétien; le More de Venise
> L'arrêta; vainement il demanda merci,
> Il le prit à la gorge en le frappant ainsi

—might be forgiven for wondering if this shows very much advance on Voltaire's translation of the soliloquy from *Hamlet*[63]. Vigny was no doubt right to choose the traditional alexandrine couplet rather than Bruguière's attempt at 'blank verse'; but having chosen the traditional metre, he was no more able to escape from its conventions than was any other poet before Hugo.

(v) The 'bataille d'Hernani'

VIGNY'S play achieved a modest success, with sixteen performances to its credit. The production had its share of difficulties and frustrations, some of them inherent in any dealings with a company structured on such rigidly hierarchical lines, some due to the poet's own susceptibilities and to his very demanding view of the relationship between a playwright and the actors interpreting his text. Certain sections of the press, as expected, showed their hostility; and Vigny had no option but to recruit teams of "conjurés", as he called them, to defeat the organized opposition within the theatre:

> Je pense que le serpent écrasé sifflera encore demain. Venez mettre aussi le pied sur lui. Que vos amis, cher Victor, viennent à quatre heures et demie, je les ferai entrer avant le public. Après cinq heures, je ne le pourrai plus.[64]

However, the result justified the effort; he was very ably served by Mlle Mars as Desdemona, by Joanny as Othello, and by

Périer as Iago; and the success of *Le More de Venise*, following
that of *Henri III*, was clear enough proof that the actors of the
Comédie-Française were no longer deliberately hostile to
'drames romantiques'[65]. On the other hand, *Henri III* had been
a 'mélodrame' in all but name; *Le More de Venise*, however
provocative the name of Shakespeare, was not an original work;
and there is little doubt that if only the banned *Marion de
Lorme* could have been put on when it was accepted, Hugo's
play would have received a much stormier reception at the
hands of critics and cabal. Hugo was the number one target for
which the enemy were reserving their fire. Already, before the
première of Vigny's play, Hugo's next offering had been
accepted by the *comédiens*. By the end of the year rehearsals were
under way; and the 'bataille d'*Hernani*' was being prepared on
both sides, amidst an unprecedented publicity campaign.

The launching of *Hernani*, and the battle to get it accepted by
the public of the Théâtre-Français, is one of the best-known
episodes of French literary history. It is richly documented in
the accounts given by Hugo's own partisans (Mme Adèle Hugo,
Gautier, Dumas), by more or less neutral observers such as the
actor Samson, and by those who were not particularly well-
disposed (*e.g.* Alexandre Duval)—as well as in the press of the
period and the correspondence of the principal protagonists[66].
This time, there was certainly reluctance, if not downright
hostility, on the part of some of the actors to be overcome.
Although *Hernani* had been "reçu par acclamations", and the
actors had no right to require textual changes that had not been
stipulated as a condition of acceptance, there were many
passages which they feared—and as events were to show, their
fears were not without justification—would provoke laughter
and ribald comment from spectators unused to bold imagery
and determined to scoff. Michelot, playing Don Carlos, and
Mlle Mars, playing the seventeen-year-old Doña Sol at the age
of 52, were the most critical. Michelot found the long session in
the cupboard in Act I an affront to his dignity, and the length of
the Act IV monologue, as well as some of its more outlandish
conceits, a source of likely trouble; while Mlle Mars kept up a
long feud with the author, vainly trying to force him to re-write
such lines as "Vous êtes mon lion superbe et généreux!" After
putting up with weeks of provocation and obstructive behaviour

from his leading lady, the young author was finally moved to threaten to have her replaced; this unprecedented threat did put a stop to the disruptive tactics, but even then (according to Dumas's account, repeated by Mme Hugo), the situation remained little better:

> Elle ne fut plus impertinente, en effet, mais elle fut muette. Elle protesta par une attitude glaciale. Son exemple refroidit les autres. A part M. Joanny, qui resta sympathique au moins en apparence, l'auteur se vit de jour en jour plus isolé.[67]

M. Descotes is of the opinion, setting Dumas's vivid but obviously 'embroidered' account against those of Samson and others, that the opposition of the troupe was a good deal less pronounced than this tradition would have it. In any case, it requires very little imagination to conceive the unpleasantness of the situation, from the point of view of the *comédiens*. When we read Gautier's delightfully nostalgic evocation, in his *Histoire du romantisme*, of what for a nineteen-year-old art-student must have been a glorious adventure, mixing with the already great and helping to create theatrical history:

> Cette soirée devait être, selon nous et avec raison, le plus grand événement du siècle, puisque c'était l'inauguration de la libre, jeune et nouvelle Pensée sur les débris des vieilles routines, et nous désirions la solenniser par quelque toilette d'apparat, quelque costume bizarre et splendide faisant honneur au maître, à l'école et à la pièce... Nous voulions la vie, la lumière, le mouvement, l'audace de pensée et d'exécution, le retour aux belles époques de la Renaissance et à la vraie antiquité, et nous rejetions le coloris effacé, le dessin maigre et sec... que l'Empire avait légués à la Restauration[68]

we tend to be so carried away by his enthusiasm and idealism that it is easy to forget those actors and actresses who had to struggle loyally with Hugo's text night after night against a noisy hubbub of jeering, cat-calls, insults, threats and open fighting—a situation in which the supporters of the play were almost as much concerned to make their voices heard as their opponents. One might well think, indeed, that the most difficult thing to hear must have been the text of the play itself—a text which in any case was often prudently adapted to circumstances, as actors modified or deleted passages which had been shown to cause trouble at previous performances. Thus Firmin, for instance, who played Hernani, had evolved his own tactics for avoiding the all-too-predictable uproar provoked by the line: "Oui, de ta suite, ô roi! de ta suite! J'en suis":

> Il prononce *de ta suite*, puis il trépigne, il se démène, il court sur le théâtre, à droite, à gauche, revient, et saisit dans tout cela un moment pour prononcer clandestinement le *j'en suis*.[69]

For the first three performances—the story is familiar enough, from the accounts of Gautier and others—Hugo had dispensed with the services of the professional *claque*, counting instead on the support of his friends and young supporters: the painters, sculptors, poets and musicians enrolled by such lieutenants as Gérard de Nerval, Pétrus Borel or Gautier. This hand-picked audience entered thoroughly into the spirit of the thing; and as long as the author could command enough free seats the issue was not in doubt. But it was after these initial exchanges—the legendary 'bataille d'*Hernani*'—were over that the real battle started. And this was much more like a war of attrition, evening after evening, with the *comédiens*, whether they liked it or not, in the front line, until the opposition were wearied and the flamboyant eccentricities of the new drama were finally allowed to pass unchallenged. Apart from a break imposed by the illness of Joanny (Hugo's warmest supporter among the leading actors, who played Don Ruy Gomez), the play ran from 25 February to 22 June, 1830: a total of 39 performances. It broke all records for box-office takings[70]—but if this was evidence of a well-sustained, hard-fought campaign, it was hardly proof of real, durable success.

When *Hernani* finally came off, Hugo and his friends had gained the symbolic victory that they had set so much store by: the Théâtre-Français had been taken by storm and conquered. But it was something of an empty victory; neither the press nor the public of the Français had been won over, and as for the actors themselves, their relations with Hugo (and with Vigny over *Le More de Venise*) left them with as little desire to repeat the experience in a hurry, as the Romantic poets themselves felt to renew contact with such a hierarchical and tradition-ridden body. From this point onwards, with the exception of a few further isolated attempts to conquer the Théâtre-Français (*Le Roi s'amuse*, *Chatterton*, *Angelo*, *Caligula* and *Les Burgraves*), the history of Romantic drama was to be made elsewhere.

Notes to Chapter Four

1. V. Hugo, *Théâtre complet*, ed. J. J. Thierry and J. Mélèze, Paris, 1963, I, p. 7.

2. I am deliberately excluding *Le Château du diable*, an early melodrama which has also survived, and whose text was first published by J. Montargis in the *Nouvelle Revue Française* in 1939. While *Le Château du diable* is a remarkable example of precocious talent (in dedicating the MS to Juliette Drouet in 1834, Hugo stated that he had written it in 1812, *i.e.* at the age of ten), it can hardly be counted as an original composition. Dr. R. Fargher has shown quite conclusively ('Victor Hugo's first melodrama', *Balzac and the Nineteenth Century, Studies . . . presented to Herbert J. Hunt*, ed. D. G. Charlton and others, Leicester, 1972, pp. 297–310) that it was a re-writing, in three-act form, of the four-act melodrama of the same name by Loaisel de Tréogate, performed in 1792 and published in 1793. I am grateful to Dr. Fargher for allowing me to see the typescript of the above article before publication.

3. *Théâtre complet, ed. cit.*, I, pp. 87–88.

4. Mme Adèle Hugo, *Victor Hugo raconté par un témoin de sa vie* in *Œuvres complètes de Victor Hugo*, Paris, Hetzel, n.d., II, p. 234.

5. Scott's *Kenilworth* had also provided the source for a *Leicester* at the Opéra-Comique and a *Château de Kenilworth* at the Porte-Saint-Martin.

6. Mme Adèle Hugo tells this anecdote of Soumet's relations with Hugo in 1822: "M. Soumet confia un jour à Victor la perplexité où il était. Il avait fait ce vers dans sa *Clytemnestre*: «Quelle hospitalité funeste je te rends». — Eh bien? demande Victor. — J'hésite à laisser dire ce vers à la représentation. — Pourquoi? — N'êtes-vous pas effrayé de cette épithète qui enjambe l'hémistiche? — Ah bien! dit Victor, je leur ferai faire d'autres enjambées!" But such was Soumet's timidity that he replaced the offending line with "Quelle hospitalité, Pylade, je te rends" (*Op. cit.*, I, pp. 137–138).

7. Ed. G. Matoré, Paris, 1946, p. lxxiii.
8. *L'Évolution des genres*, Paris, 1910, p. 191.
9. *La Préface de Cromwell: Introduction, texte et notes*, Paris, 1897. Page references to the *Préface* are to this edition.
10. Among other discussions of the question of Hugo's sources for the ideas expressed in the *Préface de Cromwell*, cf. *Poetic Genesis: Sébastien Mercier into Victor Hugo* by H. Temple Patterson (Studies on Voltaire and the Eighteenth Century, XI), Geneva, 1960.
11. p. 169.
12. p. 170.
13. p. 175.
14. pp. 175–176.
15. p. 176.
16. p. 177.
17. pp. 180–181.
18. p. 183.
19. pp. 183–184.
20. p. 187.
21. Part II, Book iii, ch. ix.
22. pp. 190–191.
23. p. 191.
24. pp. 222–223.
25. And not only in his dramas: Quasimodo in *Notre-Dame de Paris* (1831) and Gwynplaine in *L'Homme qui rit* (1869) are further examples of characters constructed on the basis of this kind of antithesis.
26. Act II, scene v.
27. *Juvenilia, œuvres posthumes, reliquae*, ed. J. Crépet, Paris, 1952, II, p. 93.
28. p. 260.
29. pp. 262–263.
30. p. 215.
31. p. 231.
32. pp. 230–231.
33. p. 231.
34. pp. 232–233.
35. p. 267. There is an interesting comparison to be made here with Gide's *Évolution du théâtre* (1911), which contains a warning in similar terms against what Gide calls "l'épisodisme", or triviality in art.
36. pp. 279–282.
37. *Contemplations*, 'Autrefois', I, vii.

38. pp. 294–298.
39. pp. 308–309.
40. p. 309.
41. pp. 312–313. Hugo's italics indicate a quotation from Boileau (*Art poétique*, I, 76).
42. p. 319. For the Chateaubriand quotation, cf. *Œuvres complètes*, Paris, 1843, V, p. 471.
43. *Victor Hugo raconté . . .*, ed. cit., II, p. 222.
44. *Ibid.*, p. 224. For a sceptical reaction to the tradition that *Cromwell* was originally conceived with performance by Talma in mind, see E. Biré, *Victor Hugo avant 1830*, Paris, 1902, pp. 422–423.
45. p. 304.
46. Cromwell has soliloquies in III, xiii; III, xvii; IV, ii and IV, v.
47. This line is doubly provocative: the unpoetic content is matched by a metrical 'barbarism', in that the caesura falls in a totally unacceptable place, between *mil* and the remainder of the numeral.
48. See Descotes, *Le Drame . . .*, pp. 93–94. In 1828, Mlle Mars was aged 49: for a résumé of her career and personality, see Descotes, pp. 72–75.
49. As well as the account in 'Comment je devins auteur dramatique' (*Théâtre*, I, 1–34), there are two other accounts of his early career by Dumas himself (*Souvenirs dramatiques*, I and *Mémoires*, première série, XI). Descotes compares these with the account of the negotiations over *Christine* given by the actor Samson (*Mémoires*, Paris, 1882, pp. 255ff.).
50. Hoping, apparently, that the administration of the theatre would bargain with her, and offer her monetary compensation instead of the holiday she was entitled to. This did not happen, and no other actress could replace her, as she had a monopoly of the *premiers rôles*. There were five further performances later in the year, on Mlle Mars's return.
51. "Presque inconnu la veille, et n'ayant pas de passé qui suscitât de haines, il avait surpris le parti classique qui, non préparé, n'avait pu se défendre... Ç'avait été un triomphe sans lutte..." (*Victor Hugo raconté . . .*, II, p. 267).
52. Cf. Descotes, *Le Drame . . .*, p. 105.
53. For a detailed appreciation of *Henri III*, see Chapter VI.
54. *Victor Hugo raconté . . .*, II, pp. 258–259.
55. *Ibid.*, p. 259.
56. *Ibid.*, p. 261.
57. Vigny had written two tragedies, *Julien l'Apostat* and *Roland*, at

the age of nineteen; and *Antoine et Cléopâtre* dates from approximately the same period. All three of these MSS were destroyed by Vigny himself in 1832.

58. See A. Sessely, *L'Influence de Shakespeare sur Alfred de Vigny*, Paris, 1928, ch. ii: 'Bruguière de Sorsum et l'article de la *Muse Française*'.

59. *Ibid.*, ch. iii: 'Le Théâtre anglais à Paris'.

60. For details see Sessely, *op. cit.*, p. 56.

61. *Shylock* was in fact produced at the Comédie-Française in 1905.

62. "J'ai recomposé et resserré ce dénouement tout entier depuis la scène iii; il m'a fallu rassembler des traits épars, en ajouter quelques-uns et retrancher de trop lentes explications, parce que c'est aujourd'hui, pour la France surtout, une nécessité que la dernière émotion soit la plus vive et la plus profonde. J'ai tâché seulement de ne perdre aucun des grands traits de Shakespeare", *Œuvres complètes*, édition définitive, Paris (Delagrave), n.d., Théâtre, II, p. 276.

63. Indeed, the closing couplets of *Zaïre*, which Voltaire based on this final speech by Othello (and which represent one of the closest imitations of Shakespeare to be found in his whole theatre):

> Porte aux tiens ce poignard, que mon bras égaré
> A plongé dans un sein qui dut m'être sacré;
> Dis-leur que j'ai donné la mort la plus affreuse
> A la plus digne femme, à la plus vertueuse
> Dont le ciel ait formé les innocents appas:
> Dis-leur qu'à ses genoux j'avais mis mes états;
> Dis-leur que dans mon sang cette main s'est plongée;
> Dis que je l'adorais, et que je l'ai vengée. (*Il se tue*)

succeed by dint of their rhetorical rhythms, and in spite of the wholly 'classical' flavour of their vocabulary, in creating a pathetic effect which seems quite lacking in Vigny's translation.

64. Letter to Victor Hugo, 27.x.1829.

65. On the relations between Vigny and his actors, see Descotes, *Le Drame . . .*, pp. 109–118.

66. For an objective account by a modern historian, see Descotes, *ibid.*, pp. 119–135.

67. *Victor Hugo raconté . . .*, II, p. 272.

68. *Histoire du romantisme*, Paris (Librairie des Bibliophiles), n.d., pp. 79–80.

69. J. Olivier, *Paris en 1830, journal*, quoted by Descotes, *Le Drame . . .*, p. 122.

70. See Descotes, *Le Drame . . .*, pp. 131–135; *Hernani*, ed. H. F.

Collins, London, 1968, p. xlv. As regards the number of performances, Hugo himself gives a figure of 53 (Preface to *Le Roi s'amuse*), while other authorities give 45 (Biré, *op. cit.*, p. 507; G. Lote, *En préface à Hernani*, Paris, 1930, p. 69; A. Sleumer, *Die Dramen Victor Hugos*, Berlin, 1901, p. 89). The correct figure of 39 is given by Descotes (*Le Drame . . .*, p. 135) as well as by A. Joannidès (*La Comédie-Française de 1680 à 1900*, Paris, 1921), who remains the most reliable source for information of this sort. I am grateful to Mme Sylvie Chevalley for her kind assistance in checking these and other figures in the *Registre* of the Comédie-Française.

Hugo and the Romantic Drama in Verse

(i) 'Hernani'

IN view of the prominence we have given to the novelty of Hugo's dramatic formula as defined in the *Préface de Cromwell*, perhaps the most important critical question to consider with regard to *Hernani* is the success with which that formula is embodied in the play. As far as structure and dramatic craftsmanship are concerned, the new play certainly marks a significant advance on *Cromwell*: how well does it illustrate the theory of the *Préface*?

To begin with, unlike *Cromwell*, *Hernani* is irregular in structure: that is, it infringes the unities both of time and place. Hugo here claims considerable freedom, and the scene ranges from Saragossa and the mountains of Aragon to Aix-la-Chapelle; while the time-span must be at least sufficient to allow for journeys from Spain to Aix and back (according to history, the death of Maximilian, reported in Act I, and the election of Charles V (Act IV) were separated by five months). Hugo had referred in the *Préface* to the unity of action as "la seule vraie et fondée"; and although commentators may debate whether the sub-plot in *Hernani* does, or does not, technically conform to the notion of a 'unified' action, the play possesses a tight, coherent structure. There is a close interlinking of plot (the love of three men for Doña Sol) and sub-plot (Carlos's ambitions for the Empire), while the sub-title (*L'Honneur castillan*) may be seen as indicating the source of the various *péripéties*, the relations between the three men being determined by the interplay of their love and honour, as follows:

Act I is almost entirely expository. We learn that Doña Sol is loved by three men, each of whom has something in his favour: Don Carlos, royal power; Don Ruy Gomez, the fact that she is due to marry him; Hernani, the fact that she returns his love. There is little development, though Hernani's desire for vengeance on the King is revealed, as is Carlos's ambition to be elected to the Empire. A rendezvous is arranged between the lovers for the following evening, and at the end of the Act Carlos saves Hernani from detection by Ruy Gomez.

In *Act II* Carlos impersonates Hernani at the rendezvous, and tries to abduct Doña Sol. Hernani spares Carlos's life.

Act III. Hernani offends against the code of honour by making love to Doña Sol after accepting Ruy Gomez's hospitality; but Ruy Gomez saves his life by refusing to hand him over to the King. Carlos abducts Doña Sol instead. Hernani accepts that his life is forfeit to Ruy Gomez, but demands a chance to avenge himself on Carlos; he offers to lay down his life when Ruy Gomez claims it.

In *Act IV* Hernani refuses Ruy Gomez's offer of his life in exchange for the right to kill Carlos. But Carlos's election as Emperor is announced, whereupon he pardons the conspirators (including Ruy Gomez and Hernani), reinstates Hernani in his rank and titles, and bestows Doña Sol on him. Hernani accepts, abandoning his desire for vengeance.

Act V opens with the marriage celebrations. But Ruy Gomez arrives, reminding Hernani of his promise, and claiming his life. The lovers die together; Ruy Gomez kills himself.

The interplay of these two forces leads to the crisis (IV, iii), which is resolved by an apparently happy ending with the removal of the material obstacle to the marriage. The hidden obstacle remains, however, and Ruy Gomez's implacable jealousy brings about not only the deaths of the two lovers, but also his own.

But structural cohesion, while it may make for dramatic effectiveness, is no guarantee of other, more valuable qualities: the fortunes of the term 'well-made play' show clearly enough that dramaturgical competence on its own cannot redeem mediocrity of content. It has often been said of *Hernani* that it is like Pixérécourt's plays: well constructed, 'good theatre', but vitiated by absurd or arbitrary *données* of characterization or plot. Certainly many contemporaries thought so, and this view is popular among modern commentators[1].

At first sight, *Cromwell* certainly appears the more serious of the two plays, the more ambitious. It is easier to recognize in the dramatic treatment of a major historical subject like that of *Cromwell* that moral purpose which Hugo was later to insist on as an essential feature of 'drame'[2]: despite some of the bizarre elements—the Puritans, the clowns—surrounding Cromwell himself, the portrait of the Protector remains a responsible and a recognizable one. That of Don Carlos, by comparison, is much more difficult to accept. The gratuitousness of the first scene spent in a cupboard, and the striking contrast between the King of Acts I–III and the same man as Emperor in Acts IV and V, appear to do violence to all credibility; and although Hugo prepared the ground before the first performance with the following text:

Il est peut-être à propos de mettre sous les yeux du public ce que dit la chronique espagnole de Alaya... touchant la jeunesse de Charles-Quint, lequel figure comme on sait dans *Hernani*: « Don Carlos, tant qu'il ne fut qu'archiduc d'Autriche et roi d'Espagne, fut un jeune prince amoureux de son plaisir, grand coureur d'aventures, sérénades et estocades, sous les balcons de Saragosse, ravissant volontiers les belles aux galants et les femmes aux maris, voluptueux et cruel au besoin. Mais, du jour où il fut empereur, une révolution se fit en lui (*se hizo una revolucion en el*), et le débauché Don Carlos devint ce monarque habile, sage, clément, hautain, glorieux, hardi avec prudence, que l'Europe a admiré sous le nom de Charles-Quint » (*Grandezas de España*, descanso 24)[3]

no trace has ever been discovered of the authority here referred to, and one can only conclude that this was an example of deliberate *mystification*[4]. Whatever Hugo may claim about the serious historical foundations of the play:

Par le sens historique,... *Ruy Blas* se rattache à *Hernani*. Le grand fait de la noblesse se montre, dans *Hernani* comme dans *Ruy Blas*, à côté du grand fait de la royauté. Seulement, dans *Hernani*, comme la royauté absolue n'est pas faite, la noblesse lutte encore contre le roi, ici avec l'orgueil, là avec l'épée; à demi féodale, à demi rebelle. En 1519, le seigneur vit loin de la cour, dans la montagne, en bandit comme Hernani, ou en patriarche comme Ruy Gomez. Deux cents ans plus tard, la question est retournée. Les vassaux sont devenus des courti-sans[5]

these are really of the vaguest. The 'sens historique', like the Spanish local colour, which, according to *Victor Hugo raconté par un témoin de sa vie*, derived from the poet's childhood memories[6], is either very approximative, or else reflects second-hand *idées reçues* about Spain and the Spanish.

If the moral earnestness which Hugo claims hardly seems to be justified by an examination of the historical sources, is it possible instead to see in *Hernani* a more topical message, addressed to his politically-minded contemporaries? The Preface to the play contains this stirring call:

> Le romantisme... n'est... que le *libéralisme* en littérature... La liberté dans l'art, la liberté dans la société, voilà le double but auquel doivent tendre d'un même pas tous les esprits conséquents et logiques; voilà la double bannière qui rallie... toute la jeunesse si patiente et si forte d'aujourd'hui... Les *Ultras* de tout genre, classiques ou monarchiques, auront beau se prêter secours pour refaire l'ancien régime de toutes pièces, société et littérature; chaque progrès du pays, chaque développement des intelligences, chaque pas de la liberté fera crouler tout ce qu'ils auront échafaudé

—and it was hardly a coincidence that less than three months after publication of this text (dated 9th March 1830), the July Revolution had taken place and Charles X been forced to abdicate[7]. At first sight, one might be tempted to compare *Hernani* with Schiller's *Die Räuber*, as expressing the political idealism which animated many of the 'Jeunes-France', as of the 'Stürmer-und-Dränger'. But Hernani is no Karl Moor: although like Schiller's hero he is a 'noble bandit', his quarrel is with his King, Don Carlos, not with society. He is motivated by a personal vendetta, and once Carlos has decided to mark his election to the Empire by a signal act of clemency, the bandit-chief is ready enough to renounce his way of life, accept the Order of the Golden Fleece, and settle down to married bliss as a 'grand d'Espagne'[8]. It would be difficult not to conclude that the literary affinities with Corneille's *Cinna* are stronger than any ideological link with Schiller's Karl Moor.

5　*Antony:* the final curtain, by A. Johannot

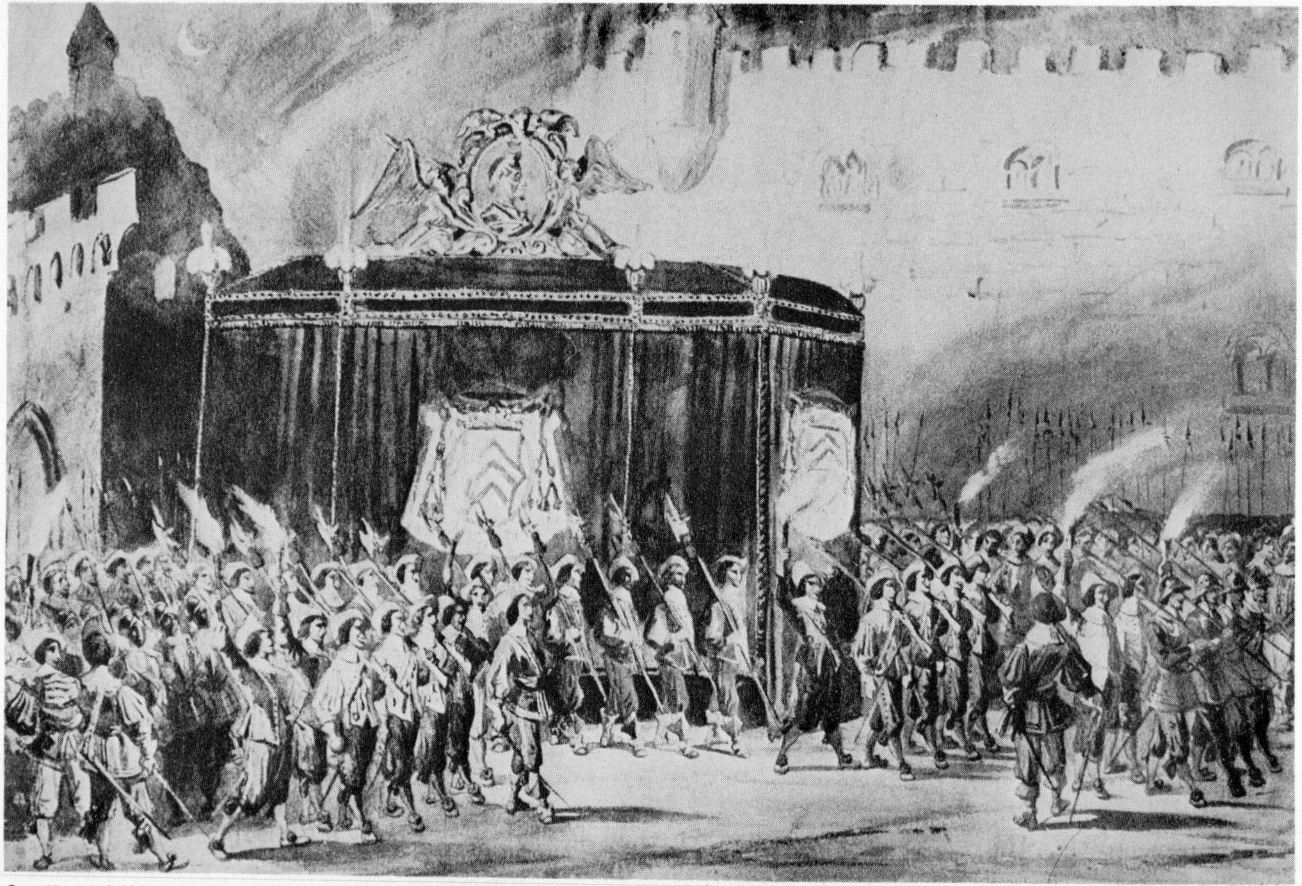

6 'La Litière de Richelieu' (*Marion de Lorme,* Act V) by Boulanger

Indeed, if we are looking for reflections of topical ideas in *Hernani*, the most obvious example is provided, not by Hernani himself as a representative of the ideology of the 1830 Revolution, but by Charles V, saluting Charlemagne as an embodiment of the Napoleonic legend:

> Quoi donc! avoir été prince, empereur et roi!
> Avoir été l'épée, avoir été la loi!
> Géant, pour piédestal avoir eu l'Allemagne!
> Quoi! pour titre césar et pour nom Charlemagne!
> Avoir été plus grand qu'Annibal, qu'Attila,
> Aussi grand que le monde... (ll. 1495–1500)[9]

But both topical allusion and historical reference are of subsidiary importance: it is above all contemporary literary influences that the play reflects. The central theme, 'l'honneur castillan', had come into fashion with the recent revival of Spanish themes and motifs[10]: Mérimée's Clara Gazul plays had been one notable example of this, while Hugo himself says in the Preface to *Hernani* that "le *Romancero general* est la véritable clef [de ce drame]". G. Lote declares confidently: "En dehors du *Romancero*, presque toute la documentation historique d'*Hernani* sort des pièces du théâtre espagnol et du livre de Sismondi: *De la littérature du Midi de l'Europe*"[11]; and if the source of one important scene (III, vi, the 'scène des portraits') has been shown to be a contemporary English tragedy set in Italy[12], the twist given to the original by Hugo in order to accommodate it to the currently fashionable 'honour theme' seems just as significant as the English borrowing itself.

Into this Spanish framework, of highly conventional character, has been placed a hero who is the very embodiment of that Romantic fatalism which is often ascribed to Byron's influence (but which had already been seen in such heroes as Chateaubriand's René or Nodier's Jean Sbogar—to say nothing of eighteenth-century precursors such as Crébillon's Rhadamiste or Prévost's Des Grieux); and those young Romantics among Hugo's supporters who identified themselves with Hernani seem less likely to have done so because he represented a political or social ideal, than because they saw in him a fellow-sufferer from *le mal du siècle*.

If we analyse Hernani's particular form of *mal du siècle*, we can easily see that he expresses no coherent philosophy: neither nihilistic resignation, nor committed anti-social individualism. Although, as we have noted, he has not irrevocably turned his back on society, he feels himself to be an outcast, "[Un] malheureux que tout abandonne et repousse" (l. 48). He neither finds consolation in religious faith nor feels the anguish of rejection by God: his despair is quite without metaphysical overtones, and it is 'le ciel'—nature—not 'le Ciel' which provides the bare necessities of the life of hardship to which he is reduced:

> Je n'ai reçu du ciel jaloux
> Que l'air, le jour et l'eau, la dot qu'il donne à tous.
> (ll. 121–22)

Though the challenge from the King rouses him at the end of Act I to a positive expression of the one dynamic passion—the desire for vengeance—by which he is animated, elsewhere, even in his relationship with Doña Sol, his despair makes of him a predominantly passive character. He may attribute to himself daemonic qualities:

> Je suis une force qui va!
> Agent aveugle et sourd de mystères funèbres!
> Une âme de malheur faite avec des ténèbres!
> Où vais-je? je ne sais. Mais je me sens poussé
> D'un souffle impétueux, d'un destin insensé.
> Je descends, je descends, et jamais ne m'arrête (ll. 992–97)

—but what he actually displays is more like a brooding melancholy. In his extreme absorption in his own sufferings, now he insults Doña Sol, doubting her constancy, now he indulges in an orgy of masochistic self-abasement:

> Tu vis et je suis mort. Je ne vois pas pourquoi
> Tu te ferais murer dans ma tombe avec moi. (ll. 971–72)[13]

The change in his fortunes at the end of Act IV leaves Hernani—almost literally—speechless; then for a brief spell, in V, iii, he enjoys the opposite extreme of exalted euphoria, before the appearance of the masked Ruy Gomez plunges him into the depths of fatalistic despair.

What we have here, therefore, is not so much the coherent expression of an attitude to life, as an impressionistic succession of moods. Hugo's conception of character is poetic, not rationalistic: he shows a poet's intuitive grasp of essential human feelings, and expresses these, like Shakespeare in his soliloquies, in a manner which transcends the particular and the contingent, to achieve an appeal that is truly universal. Those critics who fault Hugo on the minutiae of character-portrayal, taking as their criterion the rationalistic concept of realism, fail to understand the true nature of his poetic drama. George Steiner has expressed very clearly the position of the Romantic poet in this respect:

> Until the advent of rational empiricism the controlling habits of the Western mind were symbolic and allegoric. Available evidence regarding the natural world, the course of history, and the variety of human action was translated into imaginative designs or mythologies . . . After Shakespeare the master spirits of western consciousness are no longer the blind seers, the poets, or Orpheus performing his art in the face of hell. They are Descartes, Newton, and Voltaire. And their chroniclers are not the dramatic poets but the prose novelists.
>
> The Romantics were the inheritors of this tremendous change. They were not yet prepared to accept it as irremediable. Rousseau's primitivism, the anti-Newtonian mythology of Blake, Coleridge's organic metaphysics, Victor Hugo's image of the poets as the Magi, and Shelley's "unacknowledged legislators" are related elements in the rearguard action fought by the Romantics against the new scientific rationalism.[14]

Even the tragedy of Corneille had abandoned the poetic, the suggestive: its appeal had been to the spectator's reason, not to his imagination. The rhetoric and the dialectic of eighteenth-century tragedy, while not excluding, as we have seen, a strong appeal to the sensibility of the spectator, made few demands on his imagination: their domain was the prosaic domain of the rationalist, not that of the poet. It may well be true that in his

conception of character Hugo shares something of the primi-
tivism of Pixérécourt and other popular dramatists: his
characters, like theirs, remain relatively unsophisticated. But
whereas in prose melodrama the banality of the language, or the
turgid sentimental clichés, add nothing to these elementary
données, in Hugo at his best the simplicity of this basic concept of
character is embroidered with the rich texture of his imagery,
so that—the comparison with Shakespeare is not entirely out
of place—generalizations about love, death, old age or honour
become, not banal commonplaces, but moving, evocative or
exciting poetic utterances.

In any case, Hugo's characterization, however systematic,
does not reproduce the naive black-and-white confrontations of
a Pixérécourt. True to the spirit of the *Préface de Cromwell*, he
seeks the dramatic opposition between contrary elements not in
pairs of contrasting characters, but within the same character;
thus, each of the three male protagonists exhibits some conflict
between the instinct of love and the principle of honour. In
Carlos, the debauched monarch gives way to the magnanimous
Emperor; Ruy Gomez's proud refusal to betray Hernani
contrasts with the vengeance dictated by his jealousy; and
Hernani's noble bearing is compromised by the deceit that he
practises in Act III. But such contrasts are less crudely systematic than in some of the later plays; and while the same antithetical principle of the contrast between sublime and grotesque
does clearly underlie Hugo's conception of his characters
(bandit and outlaw / 'grand d'Espagne'; king hiding in
cupboard / emperor at vigil in Charlemagne's tomb), it is not
applied in *Hernani* in such a doctrinaire fashion.

With Hugo, rationalistic concepts of plausibility of characterization are not really appropriate. In this play perhaps more
than anywhere else in Hugo's theatre, characters are above all
vehicles for poetic developments of a lyrical, elegiac, or satirical
nature. It is impossible not to be struck, from this, the first of
Hugo's major plays, onwards, by the distinctly *operatic* character
of Hugo's dramatic writing. For the playwright has rejected the
linear plot-development of the traditional serious drama of the
rationalist neo-classical era, in which even soliloquies normally
fulfilled a dialectical function; in place of this, we have a
structure in which 'plot' is a framework for a series of solos and

duets, arias and recitatives, of a very much more static nature. Static, because—unlike the case of the classical soliloquy, which although it may slow down the action in a physical sense, does advance the psychological action[15]—here the dramatic context is often only a pretext. Instead of being intensely inward-looking like the classical hero, bounded by the confines of his particular predicament, Hugo's characters, like Shakespeare's, look outward from the particular to the universal[16]; their imaginative flights transcend the limitations of context, and it is the function of the imagery, like that of the music in opera, to give memorable, striking form to these passages, which are poetic rather than strictly speaking dramatic, at any rate in the conventional sense of the word.

The lyrical quality of Hugo's writing in *Hernani* has often been appreciated—but usually as if it were a question of isolated passages which constitute a superficial adornment and help to redeem the triviality, or absurdity, of the rest of the play. On the contrary, the kind of imaginative writing exemplified by such varied passages as Hernani's lyrical description of the bandit's life (ll. 125–46), his invective against Carlos (ll. 381–414), Ruy Gomez's elegy on old age (III, i), Carlos's Act IV monologue, or the marvellous love-duet of the last Act, is no superficial decoration; it permeates the whole of Hugo's drama. As in Romantic opera, these virtuoso passages—together with the flow and sparkle of imaginative writing, in lower key, throughout the play—are what really counts. Hugo offers us, not the logical conviction of a chain of events leading up to an intellectually satisfying catastrophe, but the intuitive recognition of the poetic power of universal tragic themes. The irrational Romantic death-wish, the poignant self-knowledge of old age, young love doomed to early death: these may be clichés, and there is no doubt something arbitrary in the way Hugo presents them to us; but it is by his 'operatic' treatment of these perennial themes, which denotes a concept of drama totally different from the worn-out neo-classical formula, that Hugo the tragic poet has succeeded in creating a new 'sublime':

Quand passe un jeune pâtre — oui, c'en est là! — souvent,
Tandis que nous allons, lui chantant, moi rêvant,
Lui dans son pré vert, moi dans mes noires allées,

Souvent je dis tout bas: — O mes tours crénelées,
Mon vieux donjon ducal, que je vous donnerais,
Oh! que je donnerais mes blés et mes forêts,
Et les vastes troupeaux qui tondent mes collines,
Mon vieux nom, mon vieux titre, et toutes mes ruines,
Et tous mes vieux aïeux qui bientôt m'attendront,
Pour sa chaumière neuve et pour son jeune front!
Car ses cheveux sont noirs, car son œil reluit comme
Le tien, tu peux le voir, et dire: Ce jeune homme!
Et puis, penser à moi qui suis vieux. Je le sais!
Pourtant j'ai nom Silva, mais ce n'est plus assez!
Oui, je me dis cela. Vois à quel point je t'aime!
Le tout, pour être jeune et beau, comme toi-même!
Mais à quoi vais-je ici rêver? Moi, jeune et beau!
Qui te dois de si loin devancer au tombeau! (ll. 735–52)

The effects are simple, as befits all true lyric verse, based on the
requirements of oral delivery. But it is these simple devices—the
repetitions (*que je vous donnerais, Oh! que je donnerais; Mon vieux
nom, mon vieux titre; et toutes mes ruines, Et tous mes vieux aïeux;
jeune et beau... Moi, jeune et beau!*), the alliterations (*Mon vieux
donjon ducal, que je vous donnerais; Et les vastes troupeaux qui tondent
mes collines*), the insistent play on the antithesis *jeune/vieux*—
which impart a genuinely musical character to Ruy Gomez's
reflections on old age and death. Such a passage is far from
being a *hors-d'œuvre*; it expresses the very essence of the character's situation throughout the play. It does this, however, not by
means of the inward-looking dialectic of 'Cartesian' drama, but
in the expansive, outward-looking manner of Shakespeare.
These are not gratuitous 'lyrical' embellishments, in other
words, on the surface of a conventionally 'dramatic' plot: the
two elements are integrated into a new concept of 'lyrical
drama', and the term fits Hugo's tragedies just as well as the
opera to which it is more often applied. George Steiner's comment on the "natural relationship" between Romantic drama
and opera:

In the French Romantic theatre, the core of drama is buried
beneath the mechanics of passionate presentation. The basic
quality of the work suffers no violence through the addition
of music. On the contrary, music rationalizes and completes

the elements of pure gesture and fantasy inherent in the
material. Melodic lines can safely carry a great burden of
absurdity. Thus it is in the operas of Donizetti, Meyerbeer
and Verdi that Victor Hugo's conception of dramatic form
was most fully realized[17]

surely fails to do justice to the lyrical, or imaginative, quality of
Hugo's plays, and takes no account of the way in which 'melodic
lines' have already been provided by the poet himself, fulfilling
very much the function that is here attributed to music.[18]

Thus, the sustained duet of Act V, scene iii lifts the emotional
tone of the finale on to a level that would be unattainable in the
medium of prose: for a brief moment, the hero's obsessive
death-wish seems to have been exorcized, and he gives himself
up to the lyrical celebration of his joy, with the image of
physical homecoming symbolizing a kind of spiritual rebirth:

> Que m'importe
> Les haillons qu'en entrant j'ai laissés à la porte!
> Voici que je reviens à mon palais en deuil.
> Un ange du Seigneur m'attendait sur le seuil.
> J'entre, et remets debout les colonnes brisées,
> Je rallume le feu, je rouvre les croisées,
> Je fais arracher l'herbe au pavé de la cour,
> Je ne suis plus que joie, enchantement, amour. (ll. 1927–34)

But we are not allowed to forget for long that this is only an
interlude, and it is Doña Sol who gives unwitting expression to
the theme of the death-wish; first in a figure of speech, charged
with unconscious irony, at the climax of her own lyrical
response:

> Mon duc, rien qu'un moment!
> Le temps de respirer et de voir seulement.
> Tout s'est éteint, flambeaux et musique de fête.
> Rien que la nuit et nous. Félicité parfaite!
> Dis, ne le crois-tu pas? sur nous, tout en dormant,
> La nature à demi veille amoureusement.
> Pas un nuage au ciel. Tout, comme nous, repose.
> Viens, respire avec moi l'air embaumé de rose!
> Regarde. Plus de feux, plus de bruit. Tout se tait.
> La lune tout à l'heure à l'horizon montait;

Tandis que tu parlais, sa lumière qui tremble
Et ta voix, toutes deux m'allaient au cœur ensemble,
Je me sentais joyeuse et calme, ô mon amant,
Et j'aurais bien voulu mourir en ce moment! (ll. 1949–62)

—and then in the flight of fancy which ironically heralds Ruy
Gomez's summons on the horn:

— Ce silence est trop noir, ce calme est trop profond.
Dis, ne voudrais-tu pas voir une étoile au fond?
Ou qu'une voix des nuits, tendre et délicieuse,
S'élevant tout à coup, chantât?

                             — Capricieuse!
Tout à l'heure on fuyait la lumière et les chants!

— Le bal! Mais un oiseau qui chanterait aux champs!
Un rossignol perdu dans l'ombre et dans la mousse,
Ou quelque flûte au loin!... Car la musique est douce,
Fait l'âme harmonieuse, et, comme un divin chœur,
Éveille mille voix qui chantent dans le cœur!
Ah! ce serait charmant!
        (*On entend le bruit lointain d'un cor dans l'ombre.*)
                   Dieu! je suis exaucée!
                        (ll. 1969–79)

Judged by purely rational analysis, this moment of tragic irony
may seem no more than a highly contrived example of Steiner's
"absurdity"; but Hugo's poetry makes it so appropriate to its
context, as the climactic point of a lyrical drama in which the
themes of love, honour and death are inseparably interrelated,
that his technique cannot be faulted.

Not all the writing is of this quality, of course; nor is it
intended that the same lyrical appeal should be expressed by
every scene. Ruy Gomez's entry abruptly changes the tone: he
is not meant to compete with the lovers for our sympathy at this
point, and it is hard not to see him now, in melodramatic terms,
as the *traître*, or villain of the piece. But once the necessary
dramatic exchanges have taken place and the lovers have shared
the phial of poison, their final duet at once resumes the same
fluent musicality. The lyrical exaltation of the preceding
passages is now muted into the elegiac, as the imagery, pro-

claiming the identification of the lovers' "nuit de noces" with
their death-bed, nevertheless attenuates the harshness of death
by welcoming it as sleep:

Oh! béni soit le ciel qui m'a fait une vie
D'abîmes entourée et de spectres suivie,
Mais qui permet que, las d'un si rude chemin,
Je puisse m'endormir ma bouche sur ta main. (ll. 2155-58)

The supreme Romantic myth of twin souls finding perfect
communion in a shared, unblemished love perhaps necessarily
carries with it, in its most sublime manifestations, an unconscious death-wish: there must be no harsh awakening to the
realities of life to follow the ideal happiness of the wedding-
night. If this is so, the last twenty lines of *Hernani*, seen as an
expression of Romantic idealism, have an aesthetic rightness
that makes them as moving and as satisfying as those other
magnificent embodiments of this myth, the closing pages of
Keller's *Romeo und Julia auf dem Dorfe* or the finale of Verdi's
Aïda.[19]

(ii) 'Marion de Lorme'

Marion de Lorme, shelved by order of the censor in 1829, was
performed in August 1831. Hugo had declined an offer to
produce the play at the Théâtre-Français in 1830; he now took
the step of withdrawing his manuscript because of the threatened reintroduction of censorship at the national theatres,
and decided to offer it to the Théâtre de la Porte-Saint-Martin
on hearing that two other plays had been completed on the
same subject.[20] Reception of the new play was much less
turbulent than had been the case with *Hernani*. Although the
press was predominantly hostile, audiences at the Porte-Saint-
Martin showed less prejudice against the new kind of drama
than those of the Théâtre-Français, and the play was an
honourable, though not a spectacular, success. It ran for 68
performances, despite temporary interruptions of its run due to
the indisposition of Bocage (who played Didier) and to the
threat of riots in the quarter in which the theatre was situated.[21]

The title had been changed from the original *Un Duel sous
Richelieu* on the instances of Marie Dorval, who was to follow

up her success in Dumas's *Antony* three months earlier by playing
Hugo's heroine, and wanted due prominence to be given to her
role[22]; and the text of the play, too, had undergone some significant changes. In particular, the dénouement was changed so
as to allow Marion to be pardoned by her lover: in the 1829
text Didier had gone to his death without expressing the love
and the forgiveness which provide such a touching finale in the
definitive version. All accounts agree that Mme Dorval was the
ideal Romantic heroine; and whereas Mlle Mars, as we have
seen, had reacted unfavourably to what she had considered to
be lapses from the style appropriate to tragedy, the nature of
Marie Dorval's previous experience made her much more
adaptable. She had been a member of the Porte-Saint-Martin
company since 1818, and by 1829 was "une des reines du
boulevard"[23]. She excelled in the delivery of simple, prosaic
'mots nature', and had a well-developed taste for mime and
significant gesture—in short, precisely those attributes by which
Harriet Smithson had impressed her French admirers in 1827.
The role of Adèle in *Antony* had been well within her range: how
well equipped was she to play Marion?

She had in fact come to verse drama for the first time in 1829,
in Delavigne's *Marino Faliero*, when she had found the traditional alexandrine somewhat uncongenial. M. Descotes,
examining various changes introduced in the MS text of *Marion
de Lorme* in the course of rehearsals, comments:

> Il faut admettre, en étudiant le manuscrit, que certaines
> scènes furent remaniées pour permettre à Dorval de tirer
> meilleur parti de sa voix, de son style. Elle amenait ainsi
> Hugo à rendre son vers plus coupé, plus heurté, plus pro-
> saïque. Les interprètes du Théâtre-Français n'étaient plus là
> pour l'empêcher de multiplier les « Oh! dis... », les « Sais-
> tu ? », les « N'est-ce pas ? » qui, directement venus du langage
> parlé, faisaient partie du « ton Dorval ».

Analysing in particular Marion's long speech in Act IV, scene
vii (which originally consisted of only four and a half lines):

> Ah! sire! à notre deuil que le roi compatisse.
> Savez-vous ce que c'est? Deux jeunes insensés,
> Par un duel jusqu'au fond de l'abîme poussés!

Mourir, grand Dieu! mourir sur un gibet infâme!
Vous aurez pitié d'eux! — Je ne sais pas, moi femme,
Comment on parle aux rois. Pleurer peut-être est mal;
Mais c'est un monstre enfin que votre cardinal!
Pourquoi leur en veut-il? Qu'ont-ils fait? Il n'a même
Jamais vu mon Didier. — Hélas! qui l'a vu, l'aime.
— A leur âge, tous deux! les tuer, pour un duel!
Leurs mères! songez donc! — Ah! c'est horrible! — O ciel!
Vous ne le voudrez pas!... — Ah! femmes que nous sommes,
Nous ne savons pas bien parler comme les hommes,
Nous n'avons que des pleurs, des cris, et des genoux
Que le regard d'un roi ploie et brise sous nous!
Ils ont eu tort, c'est vrai! Si leur faute vous blesse,
Tenez, pardonnez-leur. Vous savez? la jeunesse!
Mon Dieu! les jeunes gens savent-ils ce qu'ils font?
Pour un geste, un coup d'œil, un mot — souvent au fond
Ce n'est rien, — on se blesse, on s'irrite, on s'emporte.
Les choses tous les jours se passent de la sorte;
Chacun de ces messieurs le sait. Demandez-leur,
Sire. — Est-ce pas, messieurs? — Ah! Dieu! l'affreux
    malheur!
Dire que vous pouvez d'un mot sauver deux têtes!
Oh! je vous aimerai, sire, si vous le faites!
Grâce! grâce! — Oh! mon Dieu! si je savais parler,
Vous verriez, vous diriez: Il faut la consoler,
C'est une pauvre enfant, son Didier, c'est son âme...
J'étouffe. Ayez pitié!

Descotes concludes:

> Le prosaïsme sentimental et pathétique éclate dans ces
> phrases courtes, ces formules banales, ces constructions très
> lâches, ces exclamations. Et le texte permet les jeux de scène
> les plus *anglais*: supplications à genoux, mains qui se tordent,
> voix qui s'étrangle. Dorval devait remporter dans cette scène
> faite pour elle tout le succès qu'elle pouvait espérer.[24]

It is a fact that the style of *Marion de Lorme* is less obviously
poetic than that of *Hernani*, and the reason indicated by M.
Descotes is clearly in part responsible. This is not the whole of
the story, however; and one of the first things that strikes the
reader of *Marion de Lorme* is a strong resemblance to *Cromwell*.
Not only do both plays contain a much more thoroughgoing

and conscientious evocation of a historical setting than *Hernani* can offer, but the tone of the dialogue throughout much of *Marion de Lorme*—and not only in passages involving the heroine herself—is closer to the lively colloquialism, and the inventive virtuosity, of *Cromwell* than to the imaginative lyricism of *Hernani*.

There is in fact a greater variety of tone and style than in either of the earlier verse plays. At one extreme we have, for instance, the inventive word-play of the dialogue in Act II, in which the fashionable conversation of Court and capital is brilliantly rendered, with enough caricatural exaggeration for comic effect, but without destroying the credibility of these volatile, hot-blooded young aristocrats:

> — Moi je te dis que non!
>
> > — Moi je te dis que si!
>
> — Le Corneille est mauvais!
>
> > > — Traiter Corneille ainsi!
> Corneille enfin, l'auteur du *Cid* et de *Mélite*!
>
> — *Mélite*, soit! j'en dois avouer le mérite;
> Mais Corneille n'a fait que descendre depuis,
> Comme ils font tous! Pour toi je fais ce que je puis.
> Parle-moi de *Mélite* et de *La Galerie*
> *Du Palais*! Mais *Le Cid*, qu'est cela, je te prie?
>
> — Monsieur est modéré.
>
> > > — *Le Cid* est bon!
>
> > > > — Méchant!
> Ton *Cid*, mais Scudéry l'écrase en le touchant!
> Quel style! ce ne sont que choses singulières,
> Que façons de parler basses et familières.
> Il nomme à tout propos les choses par leurs noms.
> Puis *Le Cid* est obscène et blesse les canons.
> Le Cid n'a pas le droit d'épouser son amante.
> Tiens, mon cher, as-tu lu *Pyrame* et *Bradamante*?
> Quand Corneille en fera de pareils, donne m'en.
>
> — Lisez aussi *Le Grand et Dernier Soliman*
> De monsieur Mairet. C'est la grande tragédie.
> Mais *Le Cid*! (II, i)

At the other extreme comes the brooding introspection of Didier, like Hernani another sufferer from *le mal du siècle* with a marked death-wish:

> La mort a mille aspects. Le gibet en est un.
> Sans doute ce doit être un moment importun
> Quand ce nœud vous éteint comme on souffle une flamme,
> Et vous serre la gorge, et vous fait jaillir l'âme!
> Mais après tout, qu'importe! et, si tout est bien noir,
> Pourvu que sur la terre on ne puisse rien voir, —
> Qu'on soit sous un tombeau qui vous pèse et vous loue,
> Ou que le vent des nuits vous tourmente, et se joue
> A rouler des débris de vous, que les corbeaux
> Ont du gibet de pierre arrachés par lambeaux, —
> Qu'est-ce que cela fait? (V, iii)

In Act V, scenes iii–v, where the tension mounts towards the pathetic climax, these two contrasting styles are brought together, and there is a very effective counterpoint between Didier's sombre soliloquies and the inconsequential, lighthearted *panache* of Saverny, who has just quixotically sacrificed his life to die alongside him—an attitude which we readily accept, not so much because Saverny is a rounded character who has already been fully portrayed, as because he is a representative of his class, whose ethos has been so effectively characterized, by means of dialogue, from the beginning of the play.

Didier is, of course, something of a Romantic stereotype: the foundling, marked by the fatal sign that sets him apart from the rest of humanity. Though he lacks Hernani's lyrical expansiveness, the latter's "Fuis ma contagion" is echoed in Didier's words to Saverny:

> Vous viviez heureux, il m'a suffi
> De toucher votre vie, hélas! pour la corrompre.
> Votre sort sous le mien a ployé jusqu'à rompre. (V, v)

So long as we are not troubled by the anachronism the character is a convincing representative of a common Romantic type. He is far from being over-idealized: indeed, there is something objectionably self-righteous in his spurning of the repentant Marion right up to the last minute, and this certainly adds a realistic nuance to his character.

For her part, Marion is much the most successful of the
characters created by Hugo according to the antithetical
formula of the *Préface de Cromwell*. The fallen woman regenerated
by a pure, self-sacrificing love was to become another Romantic
stereotype[25]; but the contrast between the *grotesque*, or moral
ugliness, of Marion's past life and the *sublime*, or ideal purity,
of her present love for Didier is a good deal less contrived than
some of the syntheses of black and white that we shall meet in
later plays. Here, the basic *données* of the character do not strain
our credulity unduly, and the dramatic character built on these
données is a compellingly plausible one. It is true that we actually
see in action only one side of the 'double' Marion; though her
past life is adequately evoked by means of the ribald remarks of
Saverny and others, sceptical of her 'conversion', and in the
very effective scene at the climax of Act I where, just as Marion
is moving haltingly towards a confession of her true identity,
Didier catches sight of the volume left behind by Saverny, *La
Guirlande d'amour, à Marion de Lorme*, and vehemently denounces
the infamous courtesan[26]:

> Ah vile créature, impure entre les femmes!
> ... Que faites-vous de ces livres infâmes?
> Comment sont-ils ici? ...Savez-vous,
> Vous dont l'œil est si pur, dont le front est si doux,
> Savez-vous ce que c'est que Marion de Lorme?
> Une femme, de corps belle, et de cœur difforme,
> Une Phryné qui vend à tout homme, en tout lieu,
> Son amour qui fait honte et fait horreur! (I, ii)

Altogether, the structure of the play is impressive. Plot
matters in *Marion de Lorme* much more than in *Hernani*, and one
might perhaps be the more inclined to invoke the pejorative
designation of 'well-made play'. But there is much more here
than the skilful mechanics of plot-construction: the stages by
which the plot is advanced—the finding of the copy of *La
Guirlande d'amour*; Saverny's careless gossiping about Marion,
which not only alerts Laffemas, but reveals Marion's true
identity to Didier; Marion being forced to give herself to the
evil Laffemas in an attempt to save her love; Didier's obstinate
rejection of the chance to escape—none of these are fortuitous
elements, manipulated by the dramatist. They can all be

accepted as inescapable consequences of Marion's past. Thus, from the beginning of the play, the lovers' precarious happiness is threatened not only by Didier's arbitrary, subjective premonition of doom:

Mais je dois t'avertir, oui, mon astre est mauvais.
J'ignore d'où je viens et j'ignore où je vais.
Mon ciel est noir. Marie, écoute une prière.
Il en est temps encor, toi, retourne en arrière.
Laisse-moi suivre seul ma sombre route; hélas!
Après ce dur voyage, et quand je serai las,
La couche qui m'attend, froide d'un froid de glace,
Est étroite, et pour deux n'a pas assez de place (III, vi)

—but also by the inexorable logic of cause and effect. We are conscious from the first scene onwards that Marion is staking everything on the dream of an ideal happiness that can never be realized. The *locus classicus* for the tragic defeat of the Romantic ideal by the sober facts of life is no doubt, for most readers or playgoers, represented by *La Dame aux camélias* (or *La Traviata*); but *Marion de Lorme*, twenty years earlier, not only provides Dumas *fils* with his principal literary source, but constitutes in its own right a powerful and moving treatment of the same theme.

Though less obvious, those affinities with opera that have been discussed with regard to *Hernani* can still be seen in *Marion de Lorme*. Here, it is less a question of the overall structure of the play—as we have seen, this is more traditionally 'linear', and makes more of an appeal to the intellectual faculties of reader or spectator[27]—than of 'operatic' set-pieces which, though less numerous and perhaps less striking, do show the same inspiration as corresponding passages of *Hernani*.

Examples of this illustrate the wider range of Hugo's style in this play. The following speech by an episodic minor character, Gassé, for instance, may be compared to the comic 'patter-songs' of opera (and anticipates the style used to such brilliant effect by Rostand in *Cyrano de Bergerac*):

Monsieur vient de Paris?

              — Dit-on quelques nouvelles?

— Point. — Corneille toujours met en l'air les cervelles.
Guiche à l'ordre. Ast est duc. Puis des riens à foison.
De trente huguenots on a fait pendaison.
Toujours nombre de duels. Le trois, c'était d'Angennes
Contre Arquien pour avoir porté du point de Gênes;
Lavardin avec Pons s'est rencontré le dix
Pour avoir pris à Pons la femme de Sourdis;
Sourdis avec d'Ailly pour une du théâtre
De Mondori. Le neuf, Nogent avec Lachâtre
Pour avoir mal écrit trois vers de Colletet;
Gorde avec Margaillan, pour l'heure qu'il était;
D'Humière avec Gondi, pour le pas à l'église;
Et puis tous les Brissac avec tous les Soubise
A propos du pari d'un cheval contre un chien.
Enfin, Caussade avec Latournelle, pour rien;
Pour le plaisir. Caussade a tué Latournelle. (II, i)

Act IV is the most episodic in construction of the five. It contains two outstanding virtuoso 'arias': the plea by the elderly
Marquis de Nangis for clemency towards Saverny, his nephew,
beginning:

Je dis qu'il est bien temps que vous y songiez, sire;
Que le cardinal-duc a de sombres projets,
Et qu'il boit le meilleur du sang de vos sujets... (IV, vii)

—and, following closely on this, Marion's plea on behalf of
Didier (quoted above); in addition to these two speeches, there
is also much in the portrayal of the weak Louis XIII in this Act
that is static and dramatically *hors-d'œuvre*. But it is the final
duet in Act V, expressing mutual forgiveness and reconciliation,
which has the most obvious affinities with opera, and which
challenges a comparison with the lyrical finale of *Hernani*. In
this long development, too extensive to quote (V, vii), Marion's
humiliation and self-sacrifice are at last vindicated, if not by
Didier's release, at least by the brief ecstatic reunion of the two
lovers before he is led away to the scaffold. The scene will not,
of course, stand up to logical analysis: that the action should be
held up at the moment of crisis for a protracted display of
Romantic passion calls for a suspension of disbelief every bit as
willing as that required by the lusty death-bed arias of grand

opera. Nor is there any logical reason why we should accept without intellectual protest the waste of two young lives; but we are so carried away by the lyrical *élan* of the scene that we not only acquiesce in Didier's death as inevitable, but accept it, in the context, as desirable:

> Non, laisse-moi mourir. Cela vaut mieux, vois-tu?
> Ma blessure est profonde, amie! Elle aurait eu
> Trop de peine à guérir. Il vaut mieux que je meure!
> Seulement si jamais — vois-tu comme je pleure! —
> Un autre vient vers toi, plus heureux ou plus beau,
> Songe à ton pauvre ami couché dans le tombeau!

After the lyrical duet comes the grim economy of the closing lines. Richelieu makes his single brief appearance, refusing Marion's plea for a reprieve; and apart from the last two couplets spoken by Marion in a state of incoherent grief, the message of the finale is conveyed by visual spectacle, with the crowd flocking back on stage after the execution, while the blood-red palanquin of the sinister Cardinal crosses slowly again upstage. There is the same sort of aesthetic rightness about this ending to *Marion de Lorme* that we feel at the end of *Aïda*, *Tosca*, or *La Traviata*. It is a product not of logical persuasion or intellectual conviction, but of emotional exaltation: a combination of the imaginative appeal of the lovers' situation —mutual forgiveness and idealized love in the face of imminent death—and the simple directness of the writing:

> Écoutez tous: A l'heure où je suis, cette terre
> S'efface comme une ombre, et la bouche est sincère!
> Eh bien, en ce moment, du haut de l'échafaud —
> Quand l'innocent y meurt, il n'est rien de plus haut —
> Marie, ange du ciel que la terre a flétrie,
> Mon amour, mon épouse — écoute-moi, Marie —
> Au nom du Dieu vers qui la mort va m'entraînant,
> Je te pardonne!
>
>   — O ciel!
>
>   — A ton tour maintenant,
> Pardonne-moi!
>   — Didier!

> — Pardonne-moi, te dis-je!
> C'est moi qui fus méchant. Dieu te frappe et t'afflige
> Par moi. Tu daigneras encor pleurer ma mort.
> Avoir fait ton malheur, va, c'est un grand remords.
> Ne me laisse pas, pardonne-moi, Marie!
>
> — Ah!...
>
> —Dis un mot, tes mains sur mon front, je t'en prie.
> Fais-moi signe... Je meurs, il faut me consoler!
> (*Marion lui impose les mains sur le front. Il se relève et l'embrasse
> étroitement, avec un sourire de joie céleste.*)
> Adieu! Marchons, messieurs! (V, vii)

It is difficult to agree with the opinion expressed by Nebout in
his otherwise admirable appreciation of the play, that Hugo's
original dénouement would have been preferable:

> D'une manière et de l'autre le poète pardonne et aussi le
> spectateur; Marion est lavée parce qu'elle a souffert; mais le
> premier dénouement, Didier inflexible, est plus grand, plus
> antique, car il y a dans ce drame quelque chose de la fatalité
> impitoyable des anciens![28]

For this is not simply the tragedy of Marion herself, but of the
couple Marion/Didier. The earlier ending, with Didier, for
whom Marion's ultimate sacrifice has been made, acting to the
end as her inflexible judge, would have left a distinctly repug-
nant impression. As it is, though the 'antique' theme of retribution is still central to the play, the final emphasis is on the
Romantic theme of the incompatibility of ideal love with the
real world; and for this it is necessary that the two lovers—even
if they are not to die together, like Pyramus and Thisbe, Romeo
and Juliet, or Hernani and Doña Sol—should be reconciled
before Didier goes to his death.[29]

(iii) 'Le Roi s'amuse'

HUGO'S next play, *Le Roi s'amuse*, was produced at the
Théâtre-Français in November 1832: in spite of his uneasy
relations with the company over *Hernani*, he was determined to
aim higher than the Porte-Saint-Martin. This time, he had to
contend both with the opposition of those who disapproved on

aesthetic grounds[30] and with arbitrary political censorship. The play was given a disastrous reception on the first night, and the following morning Hugo was informed that the management of the theatre had been instructed to suspend further performances—a suspension which was soon turned into a definitive ban[31]. According to Mme Hugo, the political ban was not unconnected with professional jealousies:

> Le prétexte de la suspension était l'immoralité; la vérité était qu'un certain nombre d'auteurs classiques, dont plusieurs étaient députés, étaient allés trouver M. d'Argout et lui avaient dit qu'on ne pouvait tolérer une pièce dont le sujet était l'assassinat d'un roi, le lendemain du jour où le roi avait failli être assassiné; que *Le Roi s'amuse* était l'apologie du régicide.[32]

As for the author himself, although he was at pains, in the Preface he wrote for the publication of *Le Roi s'amuse* later in the same year, to thank his literary opponents for the loyalty they had shown on this occasion:

> Le pouvoir s'est trompé. Son acte brutal a révolté les hommes honnêtes dans tous les camps. L'auteur a vu se rallier à lui, pour faire face à l'arbitraire et à l'injustice, ceux-là mêmes qui l'attaquaient le plus violemment la veille. Si par hasard quelques haines invétérées ont persisté, elles regrettent maintenant le secours momentané qu'elles ont apporté au pouvoir. Tout ce qu'il y a d'honorable et de loyal parmi les ennemis de l'auteur est venu lui tendre la main, quitte à recommencer le combat littéraire aussitôt que le combat politique sera fini

—he made it quite clear elsewhere that he saw the ban on *Le Roi s'amuse* as being "une persécution littéraire cachée sous une tracasserie politique":[33]

> Le gouvernement prêtant main-forte à l'Académie en 1832! Aristote redevenu loi de l'État! une imperceptible contre-révolution littéraire manœuvrant à fleur d'eau au milieu de nos grandes révolutions politiques! des députés qui ont déposé Charles X travaillant dans un petit coin à restaurer Boileau! quelle pauvreté![34]

It seems likely that the persecution Hugo complains of here was
not purely imaginary, and that in attempting to impose his new
kind of drama on the public of the Théâtre-Français, he had to
face determined opposition on doctrinaire grounds that had
little to do with the intrinsic merits of his plays. At all events,
whether the censor's ban on this occasion was imposed for
genuinely political reasons, or whether the machinery of
government was being used to promote the ends of literary
rivalry and cultural prejudice, both the preface to the play and
the speech Hugo made before the Tribunal de Commerce in his
unsuccessful appeal against the ban, are a clear and courageous
statement of the case against censorship. The former in particular contains some excellent early examples—all the more
effective because dignified and restrained—of the satirical
invective that he was to use so devastatingly in *Les Châtiments*.

Even in 1832 there were those who suggested that the ban
was maladroit from the government's own point of view, and
that it would have been better to trust to the judgement of the
public and wait for the play to fail. By general agreement, *Le
Roi s'amuse* is inferior to both *Hernani* and *Marion de Lorme*, an
obvious example of creation according to an *a priori* formula.
Ligier (who was cast as Triboulet) found the play extremely
moving when it was read to the *comédiens*, especially the fifth
Act—but he also testified to the exceptional difficulty of this
same Act from the point of view of the actor playing the central
role[35]. It must indeed be a very demanding part, both in its
unusual length and in the emotional intensity called for: from
the end of Act II onwards, when Triboulet discovers the
abduction of his daughter, there is a sustained intensity of
feeling, with only a brief respite in Act IV. The whole of the
last Act is a series of impassioned, or frenzied, soliloquies, with
a minimum of contribution from other characters; and
although here the writing attains genuine imaginative power—
for instance where Triboulet's exultation over the prospective
murder of the King turns into *folie de grandeur*:

> Quel temps! nuit de mystère!
> Une tempête au ciel! un meurtre sur la terre!
> Que je suis grand ici! ma colère de feu
> Va de pair cette nuit avec celle de Dieu.

Quel roi je tue! — Un roi dont vingt autres dépendent,
Des mains de qui la paix ou la guerre s'épandent!
Il porte maintenant le poids du monde entier.
Quand il n'y sera plus, comme tout va plier!
Quand j'aurai retiré ce pivot, la secousse
Sera forte et terrible, et ma main qui la pousse
Ébranlera longtemps toute l'Europe en pleurs,
Contrainte de chercher son équilibre ailleurs!
Songer que si demain Dieu disait à la terre:
— O terre, quel volcan vient d'ouvrir son cratère?
Qui donc émeut ainsi le chrétien, l'ottoman,
Clément-Sept, Doria, Charles-Quint, Soliman?
Quel César, quel Jésus, quel guerrier, quel apôtre,
Jette les nations ainsi l'une sur l'autre?
Quel bras te fait trembler, terre, comme il lui plaît?
La terre avec terreur répondrait: Triboulet! —
Oh! jouis, vil bouffon, dans ta fierté profonde.
La vengeance d'un fou fait osciller le monde! (V, i)

—the character never really recovers from the lack of cohesion
of the first two Acts. For here we can see an example of characterization by the synthesis not only of antithetical, but even of
apparently quite incompatible elements. As we see him in Act I,
Triboulet is the epitome of physical and moral deformity, his
misanthropy and cruelty symbolized by his hunched back as he
gloats over the misfortunes of the noblemen whose wives and
daughters have been seduced by the King. This Act closes with
Saint-Vallier's curse on him; and the rest of the plot concerns
the working-out of the curse, the retribution which awaits
Triboulet. In the Preface, Hugo refers to the ancient concept of
Fatality underlying *Notre-Dame de Paris*:

Au fond de l'un des autres ouvrages de l'auteur, il y a de la
fatalité. Au fond de celui-ci il y a la providence.

—but another phrase from the Preface provides an unconscious
clue to the reason why this does not really work in *Le Roi
s'amuse*:

Cette malédiction, sur qui est-elle tombée? Sur Triboulet fou
du roi? Non. Sur Triboulet qui est homme, qui est père, qui
a un cœur, qui a une fille.

The dualism on which Triboulet's character is based is no longer discreet, as with Marion de Lorme, but a glaring juxtaposition of opposites. The devoted father of Blanche whom we see in Act II is just as idealized as the perverted pander of Act I is a caricature: both *sublime* and *grotesque* are too extreme, and since we scarcely see more than a flicker of the Triboulet of Act I through the remainder of the play, we can hardly accept this as a viable synthesis. It really is almost as if retribution were falling on an innocent person—as if the sins of the court jester were being visited on a complete stranger in Blanche's father.

The historical aspect of the subject-matter is treated in a thoroughly cavalier fashion, and the effect is totally different from that produced by *Marion de Lorme*. The King is something of a travesty of the real François I, and local colour amounts to little more than the dropping of a few proper names; while for the character lent to Triboulet (who was a historical person), there is of course no justification at all. In addition, the *mise en scène* is that of melodrama. The setting of *Cromwell* and of *Marion de Lorme* had both been perfectly straightforward (a single, simple set for each Act), and even that of *Hernani* had called for nothing more complicated than a conventional place of concealment (the cupboard in Act I, the hiding-place behind the portrait in Act III, Charlemagne's tomb in Act IV)[36]; but *Le Roi s'amuse* calls for a complex set, such as had been developed in the popular boulevard theatres for Pixérécourt and other authors of melodrama. At one point in Act II, the action is carried on simultaneously by groups of characters both inside the garden of Triboulet's house and in the street outside; while in Act IV, the set needs to show simultaneous action not only both inside and outside Saltabadil's hovel, but upstairs as well as downstairs indoors[37].

Altogether, it is easy to see that even without the censor's ban, *Le Roi s'amuse* could hardly have hoped for an easy passage at the Théâtre-Français; and it is somewhat ironical that of the three plays produced so far, the one which would almost certainly have given least offence to the purists at the Salle Richelieu was the one which had been staged elsewhere. For whereas *Hernani* and *Le Roi s'amuse* were both calculated to shock, by their stage effects as well as by their style, *Marion de Lorme* was much more sober in inspiration; as a version of a historical subject it was a great deal more responsible; and it is likely, moreover, that it would have been given a more accomplished production at the Théâtre-Français than it received at the Porte-Saint-Martin[38]. A performance of *Marion de Lorme* at the Théâtre-Français in 1831 would probably have given Hugo the best possible chance of imposing himself on the audience that he made repeated, but unsuccessful, attempts to conquer; and this might well have made a significant difference to the future history of Romanticism in the theatre.

More than any other of Hugo's verse plays, *Le Roi s'amuse* justifies the description, often applied indiscriminately to them all, of 'versified melodrama'. Yet the epithet here is by no means lightly to be disregarded: the fact that Hugo chose the medium of verse is all-important[39]. Once again, as with *Hernani*, the most impressive passages are set-pieces whose effect depends only to a limited extent on context. Indeed, here it is perhaps not merely, as with *Hernani*, a question of independence of dramatic context: the *morceaux de bravoure* which go some way towards redeeming *Le Roi s'amuse* also stand independent of consistent, or even convincing, characterization. Quoting from Triboulet's tirade in Act III, and from the final soliloquy over his daughter's body, Berret comments:

Sans doute ces sentiments perdent-ils à être exprimés contre toute vérité historique, ou quelquefois même contre toute vraisemblance psychologique: qu'importe, ils nous émeuvent, hors du personnage. Je ne crois pas qu'ils gagnent quelque chose à être sentis et exprimés par un monstre difforme et par ailleurs de cœur méchant, mais je ne sais pas non plus s'ils seraient plus émouvants dits par un personnage dont toute l'âme serait en harmonie avec eux. Ils portent en eux-mêmes, et grâce au miracle de l'expression, leur vertu émotive.[40]

One could hardly ask for a more telling characterization of the 'operatic' quality of Hugo's writing. And it is perhaps no coincidence that out of this play was to be produced the most successful of all the operas based on any of Hugo's plays: the brightest future of *Le Roi s'amuse*, in fact, lay ahead of it as *Rigoletto*.

(iv) 'Ruy Blas'

IF the characterization of Triboulet constitutes a major obstacle to the spectator's, or reader's, ready acceptance of *Le Roi s'amuse*, at first sight the role of the central character of *Ruy Blas* presents a similar difficulty. Morally, and in dramatic terms, the character of Ruy Blas is plausible and consistent: the internal psychological aspect of the *grotesque/sublime* antithesis has been handled here with a good deal more discretion than in the case of Triboulet. But socially and historically, the character seems thoroughly absurd, and we find it difficult to take seriously, particularly in a seventeenth-century Spanish setting, the notion of a lackey who becomes prime minister and who loves, and is loved by, a queen. In other words, within the dramatic context established by the playwright, Ruy Blas is plausible enough, but the acceptance of that particular contextual framework requires a considerable suspension of disbelief.

More attention has been given to the sources of *Ruy Blas* than is the case with any other of Hugo's plays. For the theme of revenge by means of a valet disguised as a nobleman in love, Molière's *Précieuses ridicules*, Edward Bulwer Lytton's romantic comedy *The Lady of Lyons* (1838), and L. de Wailly's novel *Angelica Kaufmann* (1838) have been cited; for the Spanish background and intrigues at the court of Charles II, the anecdotal memoirs of Mme d'Aulnoy, *Mémoires de la cour d'Espagne* (1690) and *Voyage d'Espagne* (1692), and the play *La Reine d'Espagne* by Hippolyte de Latouche (1831); Lemercier's *Pinto* (1800) for the characters of Don Salluste and Don César, as well as, for the latter, Maurin de Pompigny's comedy *Le Ramoneur-Prince* (1784); and for the rise of a man of humble birth to a position of supreme political power (coupled with the favours of a queen) Gaillardet's play *Struensée* (1833)[41]. The hunt for sources *qua* sources has very little to do with appreciation of the intrinsic qualities of Hugo's play; what the more interesting of these comparisons do show, however (leaving aside such fortuitous coincidence of plot as that with *Les Précieuses ridicules*), is that the twin themes of *Ruy Blas* were justified not only by analogues within the romanesque literature of the period, but also by historically authenticated parallels.

The marriage of Angelica Kaufmann, the Swiss painter, to a valet posing as a Swedish nobleman—possibly engineered by a disappointed lover—had actually taken place in 1767; and as for examples of a sudden rise from obscurity to a position of political power, in the second of Mme d'Aulnoy's volumes Hugo could have found an account of the career of Fernando de Valenzuela (1630–92), the son of an impoverished nobleman, who began life as a humble page in a duke's household, and not only rapidly rose to be prime minister, but was made a grandee of Spain and generally supposed to be the lover of the Queen Regent, while the meteoric career of Johann Struensee (1731–72) followed a similar pattern: a German physician who knew no Danish, he nevertheless became prime minister and dictator of Denmark, and lover of Queen Carolina Matilda.

It is evident, then, that Hugo could have defended himself against charges of improbability by invoking the sort of argument used by Corneille, for whom the 'possible improbable' was always preferable to the Aristotelian 'probable', and who declared that "le sujet d'une belle tragédie doit n'être pas vraisemblable"[42]. Like Corneille in *Héraclius* or *Pertharite*, he chose a subject which, however unlikely, could be justified by an appeal to analogous cases from real life. But of course it is not only the choice of general theme in *Ruy Blas* which makes it difficult to take the play seriously; it is also the trivialization of a 'serious' subject by an excessive reliance on material accessories[43], and the fact that the final catastrophe depends less on character or on tragic fate than on chance (the roles of Don César, Don Guritan). It is not even as if Hugo set out deliberately, like Scribe in *Le Verre d'eau*, to illustrate the role of chance in determining the course of history; there seems little doubt that he intended *Ruy Blas* to be every bit as serious a contribution to historical drama as *Marion de Lorme*, for instance, had been: we have only to look at the passage in the Preface where he refers to:

l'impression particulière que pourrait laisser ce drame, s'il valait la peine d'être étudié, à l'esprit grave et consciencieux qui l'examinerait, par exemple, du point de vue de la philosophie de l'histoire.

Although Hugo went out of his way to claim fidelity to historical details[44], the only kind of historical truth the play possesses is that broad epic conception of "la couleur des temps", that intuitive grasp of the moral character of an age, that was later to be so characteristic of the *Légende des siècles*. From a strictly dramatic point of view, in terms of character and plot, *Ruy Blas* is the least 'historical' of Hugo's plays so far[45].

In fact it is another case, like *Hernani*, of the historical setting being chosen after the event[46], in order to provide a framework for an abstract, *a priori* theme, which constitutes the *raison d'être* of the play. This is the attitude to history of Corneille or of Voltaire—very different from the method of the authors of the 'scènes historiques', which Hugo himself had approached much more closely in *Cromwell* and *Marion de Lorme*.

The plot of *Ruy Blas*—more obviously melodramatic than that of *Hernani* or *Le Roi s'amuse*—serves as a vehicle, once more, for a highly operatic treatment of the principal theme—the incompatibility of an ideal love with the demands of the real world—together with the subsidiary themes of political ambition, honour and revenge. Again, the lyrical quality of its 'arias' and 'duets' is the play's most attractive feature, and it is this which has led many commentators to prefer *Ruy Blas* to all the rest of Hugo's theatre[47]. But alongside its Romantic *pathétique* and its lyrical *élan*, this play possesses a much stronger comic element than any of the other plays since *Cromwell*; and the role of Don César de Bazan probably represents Hugo's masterpiece as a creator of comedy. This is no dramatic *hors-d'œuvre*[48], for Hugo is quite right in claiming that *Ruy Blas* exemplifies more fully than preceding plays the conception of 'le drame romantique' as a synthesis of the recognized dramatic genres:

> Les trois formes souveraines de l'art pourraient y paraître personnifiées et résumées. Don Salluste serait le drame, don César la comédie, Ruy Blas la tragédie. Le drame noue l'action, la comédie l'embrouille, la tragédie la tranche.[49]

Nor, despite César's celebrated entry via the chimney, is his role merely to be regarded as a concession to the popular taste for farce; and Sarcey has left a very shrewd analysis of the nature of the comedy created by this character:

C'est que, dans ce quatrième acte, le comique n'est ni dans la situation, ni même dans l'esprit du dialogue. C'est un comique tout particulier qui résulte tout entier de la sonorité de l'alexandrin et du contraste de cette sonorité avec l'idée exprimée par le vers ou les mots employés par lui. Il y a là, comme dans tout contraste, une source de comique qui n'est à l'usage que des excellents ouvriers en vers, et Victor Hugo est le premier de tous. Gautier s'en est servi également dans le *Tricorne enchanté*, et Banville en a repris la tradition dans ses *Odes funambulesques*. Ce dernier a fait en ce genre des chefs-d'œuvre d'excellente bouffonnerie. Aucun n'approche du quatrième acte de Victor Hugo.[50]

Sarcey's paragraph was written before Rostand's *Cyrano de Bergerac*, which perhaps illustrates an even more striking development of this particular manner; but César is a very worthy predecessor of Cyrano, and none, apart from Hugo's conservative contemporaries, have doubted the contribution this character makes to the overall success of *Ruy Blas*.

For the staging of *Ruy Blas* in 1838—it followed the series of three plays in prose which will be discussed in Chapter 7—Hugo chose neither the Théâtre-Français nor the Odéon, but the Théâtre de la Renaissance. The former Salle Ventadour had recently been acquired by the manager Anténor Joly, and was refitted and decorated for its opening in November 1838 with Hugo's play. For Ruy Blas, Hugo and Joly chose Frédérick Lemaître, whose reputation had been made on the 'boulevard du crime', but who had already by this time acted with success in Hugo's *Lucrèce Borgia* and in Dumas's *Kean*. The role of the Queen had been written with Hugo's mistress Juliette Drouet in mind (as will be seen, she had already played a small part in *Lucrèce Borgia* (1833), and had failed completely in the role of Jane in *Marie Tudor* in the same year). But Mme Hugo took advantage of a short absence on her husband's part to write to Joly expressing her doubts about Juliette's talent; the letter had the desired effect, and the part was given to Atala Beauchêne, Frédérick's own current mistress[51]. Despite the by now familiar opposition of the critics, the reception given to the play was very favourable; it ran for 50 performances before being taken off to please Villeneuve, Joly's business associate in the Renaissance, who was a partisan of musical comedy and had had a clause inserted in their agreement providing for equally favourable treatment of this genre. Once again, therefore, a play by Hugo was denied the complete success it might have had, through factors which had nothing to do with its intrinsic merits.

Frédérick toured the provinces with *Ruy Blas* in 1839, and when the play was revived at the Porte-Saint-Martin in 1841 he again played the lead; he regarded it as one of his finest parts, and the impression he made on audiences as Ruy Blas was sensational[52]. In terms of its impact on the contemporary public, this must count as the greatest success in the history of Romantic drama; moreover, *Ruy Blas* is of all the works of the Romantic dramatists the one which really proved an unqualified success when taken into the repertory of the national theatres. This happened in very favourable circumstances, for both at the Odéon in 1872 and at the Théâtre-Français in 1879 the part of the Queen was played by Sarah Bernhardt[53]. On the latter occasion, with Mounet-Sully as Ruy Blas and Coquelin as César, the play obtained from Sarcey the sort of enthusiastic review which consecrated it as a classic of the French theatre, and compensated in large measure for the scorn, or animosity, of the critics of Hugo's own generation[54]:

> Il a suffi d'un demi-siècle pour balayer toute cette poussière de critiques, et *Ruy Blas* est entré glorieusement dans cette région sereine où planent les véritables chefs-d'œuvre. Personne ne s'inquiète plus de marquer les invraisemblances ni les absurdités de ce conte de fées étrange sur lequel Victor Hugo s'est plu à jeter la pourpre de sa poésie. ...On a passé condamnation sur tout cela; on n'y fait plus attention. On prend même en pitié les retardataires qui s'amusent à ces objections inutiles. On est tout entier et sans partage aux beautés qui ont fait, avec l'aide du temps, de l'œuvre du poète un éternel chef-d'œuvre.[55]

Whatever the significance of such a passage may be from a historical point of view, and despite the perception shown in Sarcey's analysis of Hugo's poetic style, it is important to remember that this critic's standpoint was in its way as biased as that of Gustave Planche or any other anti-Romantic of the 1830s. Sarcey's criterion was above all theatrical effectiveness;

he prized the neat, logical construction of the best examples of Romantic drama, but was much less concerned with the subtler aesthetic of Romantic tragedy.

For in two plays at least, Hugo had brought 'le drame romantique' to a higher and more ambitious artistic level, where it could challenge the greatest classical tragedies on their own ground of a pure, refined *sublime*. If *Hernani* and *Marion de Lorme* had not quite succeeded in achieving this, they had been magnificent failures: plays in which, as in Shakespeare, the grotesque element serves merely to enhance the sublime, and in which any subsidiary, discordant reactions on the audience's part are subsumed in an overall response that can be compared without any doubt to the response we make to genuine tragedy. *Ruy Blas* is perhaps the best of the plays in which the dramatist —consciously or unconsciously—aimed less high: the plays in which the mixture of sublime and grotesque is more blatant[56], the juxtaposition of comic and serious elements more obtrusive. Dr. Ubersfeld, in her 'Notes pour une étude littéraire', examines Hugo's notion of an "esthétique de la totalité", adumbrated in the Preface to *Ruy Blas*, and suggests that the effect of diffuseness or dispersion we experience here is one we normally associate with non-dramatic fiction: "l'esthétique de *Ruy Blas* se rapproche de l'esthétique du roman"[57]. There are, indeed, first-class scenes of suspense, or of pathos; there are magnificent virtuoso passages such as Ruy Blas's hundred-line tirade of Act III:

> Bon appétit, messieurs! O ministres intègres!
> Conseillers vertueux! voilà votre façon
> De servir, serviteurs qui pillez la maison!
> Donc vous n'avez pas honte et vous choisissez l'heure,
> L'heure sombre où l'Espagne agonisante pleure!... (ll. 1058ff.)

The whole, in fact, may be superb theatrical entertainment; but in the final analysis, *Ruy Blas* is completely lacking in the cathartic power of real tragedy. We have no difficulty in identifying ourselves with Hernani and Doña Sol, with Marion de Lorme and Didier—but such an identification, so essential to the tragic process, is as impossible with Ruy Blas and his Queen as it is with Triboulet. In the latter case I have suggested that it is the internal cohesion of the character that is at fault, but with the central characters of *Ruy Blas* the fault seems rather to be that the dramatic framework which surrounds them fails to carry conviction. It is interesting to see that both Sarcey and Dr. Ubersfeld use the same term to describe the 'unreality' of *Ruy Blas*, the latter echoing Sarcey when she talks of "un canevas de conte de fée". There is indeed something "onirique", as she says, in this fable in which "le héros délivre la reine prisonnière du méchant enchanteur, extermine les forces du mal et meurt"[58]. The robust nature of Hugo's creative imagination did not, of course, allow him to leave his characters in the diaphanous dream-world of a Novalis or a Maeterlinck, where a myth of such universal appeal might have been able to achieve a very different sort of tragic effect, no less genuine; but the transposition to the real world has been only imperfectly realized, so that instead of being moved by a poetically valid re-creation of the world of reality, we must resign ourselves to being intrigued by the gratuitous extravagance of a dreamer's fancy.

(v) Summary

THIS is a suitable point at which to attempt to assess Hugo's achievement in verse drama. *Ruy Blas* had been in many ways the most successful of his plays, while the only remaining play to be staged, *Les Burgraves*, was such a failure that 1843 is usually taken as representing the end of Romantic drama.

Hugo's contemporaries stood too close to him for an objective critical reaction to be possible. Are we now able to do justice to the merits, as well as to the faults, of his plays? P.-A. Touchard, writing in 1967, is of the opinion that "il est difficile de se montrer juste devant le théâtre de Hugo". He blames this on Hugo's lack of 'sincerity'—not in the sense of the conviction with which he held his beliefs, for Touchard distinguishes *sincérité* from *croyances*—but in that, as a man of the theatre, Hugo "utilise... ces commodes conventions théâtrales dont il a lui-même dénoncé les grossièretés", and therefore offends our sense of artistic integrity[59]. This may be so; but such an assessment surely represents a one-sided view of the dramatist. To prefer *Ruy Blas* to the rest of Hugo's theatre because it best exemplifies "un théâtre engagé"[60] and prefigures *Torquemada*, to which Touchard devotes some highly appreciative lines: this is to sacrifice Hugo the poet to Hugo the thinker, and the early verse plays are surely above all the work of the poet. Hugo's major achievement in these plays is unquestionably the liberation of the alexandrine and the emancipation of poetic vocabulary, and it is this part of the programme of the *Préface de Cromwell* that has been the most successfully realized.

The range of Hugo's vocabulary in these plays, like the variety of his poetic effects, is immense. A passage like the following, taken at random from *Hernani* (Act IV, scene iii, where the conspirators are about to draw lots), combines the precise realism of the *mot propre* with a verse-form whose rhythms express the speaker's fanatical exaltation more economically than any prose could do:

> Que l'élu croie en Dieu,
> Frappe comme un romain, meure comme un hébreu!
> Il faut qu'il brave roue et tenailles mordantes,
> Qu'il chante aux chevalets, rie aux lampes ardentes,
> Enfin que pour tuer et mourir, résigné,
> Il fasse tout! (ll. 1623–28)

Elsewhere (*Ruy Blas*, IV, ii), in a passage consisting of nothing but the most ordinary and pedestrian of words, the ingenious rhymes and bizarre conjunctions of images operate on a level of comic fantasy to create an idiosyncratic style which is poles apart from the prosaic:

> C'est égal, me voilà revenu. Tout va bien.
> Ah! mon très cher cousin, vous voulez que j'émigre
> Dans cette Afrique où l'homme est la souris du tigre!
> Mais je vais me venger de vous, cousin damné,
> Épouvantablement, quand j'aurai déjeuné.
> J'irai, sous mon vrai nom, chez vous, traînant ma queue
> D'affreux vauriens sentant le gibet d'une lieue,
> Et je vous livrerai vivant aux appétits
> De tous mes créanciers — suivis de leurs petits. (ll. 1506–14)

Even technical terms are accommodated to the alexandrine with masterly ease to produce a richly comic effect, as in Saverny's imaginative description of his own presumed death for Laffemas's benefit:

— Bien mort!...
D'une botte poussée en tierce, qui d'abord
A rompu le pourpoint, puis s'est fait une voie
Entre les côtes, par le poumon, jusqu'au foie,
Qui fait le sang, ainsi que vous devez savoir,
Si bien que la blessure était horrible à voir!

— Est-il mort sur le coup?

— A peu près. Son martyre
A peu duré. J'ai vu succéder au délire
Le spasme, puis au spasme un affreux tétanos,
Et l'emprostothonos à l'opistothonos.

— Diable!

— D'après cela, voyez-vous, je calcule
Qu'il est faux que le sang passe par la jugule...
                        (*Marion de Lorme*, III, i)

As in his most characteristic lyric verse, or his epic poems,
here too the Word is endowed by Hugo with an autonomous
life of its own; and it is the creative use he makes of the dynamic
image which really sets the seal of his inimitable manner on the
language of the verse plays. A passage like the following, for
instance (which concludes Ruy Blas's tirade beginning "Bon
appétit, messieurs!") achieves its effect by a striking juxtaposition of what in a lesser poet would no doubt be called mixed
metaphors:

Il nous faut ton bras! au secours, Charles-Quint!
Car l'Espagne se meurt, car l'Espagne s'éteint!
Ton globe, qui brillait dans ta droite profonde,
Soleil éblouissant qui faisait croire au monde
Que le jour désormais se levait à Madrid,
Maintenant, astre mort, dans l'ombre s'amoindrit,
Lune aux trois quarts rongée et qui décroît encore,
Et que d'un autre peuple effacera l'aurore!
Hélas! ton héritage est en proie aux vendeurs.
Tes rayons, ils en font des piastres! Tes splendeurs,
On les souille! — O géant! se peut-il que tu dormes?
On vend ton sceptre au poids! un tas de nains difformes
Se taillent des pourpoints dans ton manteau de roi;
Et l'aigle impérial, qui, jadis, sous ta loi,

7   Sketch for décor of *Le Roi s'amuse,* Act II, by Victor Hugo

8 (a) Frédérick Lemaître as Robert Macaire

(b) 'Louis-Philippe en Robert Macaire', by Daumier

Couvrait le monde entier de tonnerre et de flamme,
Cuit, pauvre oiseau plumé, dans leur marmite infâme.

(ll. 1143–58)

In the following lines, on the other hand, the power of a
grotesque imagination is conveyed by the sustained development of a single image:

O mon Dieu! voilà donc les choses qui se font!
Bâtir une machine effroyable dans l'ombre,
L'armer hideusement de rouages sans nombre,
Puis, sous la meule, afin de voir comment elle est,
Jeter une livrée, une chose, un valet,
Puis la faire mouvoir, et soudain sous la roue
Voir sortir des lambeaux teints de sang et de boue,
Une tête brisée, un cœur tiède et fumant,
Et ne pas frissonner alors qu'en ce moment
On reconnaît, malgré le mot dont on le nomme,
Que ce laquais était l'enveloppe d'un homme.

(*Ruy Blas*, ll. 1448–58)

The hierarchical attitude to the vocabulary of poetry has
gone for ever: the distinction between 'noble' and 'bas' has
quite simply been abolished. As we have seen, Hugo boasted
elsewhere of the lengths to which his revolution had gone:

Je violai du vers le cadavre fumant;
J'y fis entrer le chiffre; O terreur! Mithridate
Du siège de Cyzique eût pu citer la date...

But of course, things are not quite as simple as that, and the
emancipation of poetic diction was achieved only at a certain
cost. The opening line of Hugo's first verse play:

Demain, vingt-cinq juin mil six cent cinquante-sept

symbolizes, in its challenge to the accepted conventions, the
whole linguistic revolution that was to come. George Steiner
comments on this line:

It drew tragic verse down to the gross world of clocks and
calendars. Like wealth, in the poetics of Henry James and

Proust, verse relieves the personages of tragic drama from the complication of material and physical need . . . In a very real sense, the tragic hero lets the servants live for him. It is they who assume the corrupting burdens of hunger, sleep, and ailment. This is one of the decisive differences between the world of the novel, which is that of prose, and the world of the tragic theatre, which is that of verse. In prose fiction, as D. H. Lawrence remarked, "you know there is a water-closet on the premises". We are not called upon to envisage such facilities at Mycenae and Elsinore. If there are bathrooms in the houses of tragedy, they are for Agamemnon to be murdered in.[61]

The entry of the contingent and the circumstantial into poetic drama inevitably meant the forfeiting of that aesthetic purity which we associate with the best classical tragedy. In *Phèdre*, for instance, the coherence of the imagery, economical and concentrated on a few salient themes or leitmotifs, makes a powerful contribution to the tragic effect; there are no discordant or distracting images, and there is no evoking of material reality for its own sake. In Hugo, on the other hand, everything—the looser, more episodic structure, the passages deliberately aiming at a comic effect, the concrete, pictorial nature of much of the imagery, and the crude vigour of some of the linguistic devices—leads to a fragmentation, a dislocation of the aesthetic experience. Not that the appeal to a purer, more refined *sublime* is non-existent: the impression that the genuinely lyrical passages make by their simpler vocabulary and less extravagant imagery is perhaps even enhanced by the contrast with other more violent or colourful passages. In the 'mixed' aesthetic of Romantic drama—as in nineteenth-century Romantic opera—the unified, concentrated impact of *Œdipus* or of *Phèdre* is lacking. But let us not forget that two centuries earlier a similar mixed aesthetic had not only given rise to the tragedies of Théophile, Rotrou and other French dramatists whom we label 'baroque', but had also produced *King Lear*.

Notes to Chapter Five

1. E.g. *Hernani*, ed. Collins, p. xv; Biré, *op. cit.*, pp. 498ff.

2. "Le poète aussi a charge d'âmes. Il ne faut pas que la multitude sorte du théâtre sans emporter avec elle quelque moralité austère et profonde. Aussi espère-t-il bien, Dieu aidant, ne développer jamais sur la scène... que des choses pleines de leçons et de conseils" (Préface to *Lucrèce Borgia*, dated Feb. 1833).

3. This text was published in *Le Constitutionnel*, 25.ii.1830, and also distributed in the theatre.

4. G. Lote, *op. cit.*, p. 109, asserts that the traits of the dissolute Don Carlos belonged in reality to a later Don Carlos (grandson of Charles V, and hero of plays by Schiller and others), who also had a tutor called Ruy Gomez de Silva.

5. Preface to *Ruy Blas*, dated November 1838.

6. See e.g. I, pp. 111–112, 125, 139.

7. Cf. Sainte-Beuve's comment: "La carrière poétique de Victor Hugo a été toute une révolution... *Hernani*, ça a été pour moi la fin de l'Assemblée Législative" (quoted by Sleumer, *op. cit.*, p. 88).

8. Cf. Sleumer's comment: "Es scheint, als ob Hernani in der Nähe der Geliebten Klugheit, Männlichkeit, Scharfblick und Thatkraft, kurz alle Eigenschaften, die einem Räuberanführer vonnöten sind, verliere", *op. cit.*, p. 95.

9. Cf. Lote, *op. cit.*, pp. 183ff. See also M. Descotes, 'L'Obsession de Napoléon dans le *Cromwell* de Victor Hugo', *Archives des lettres modernes*, no. 78, Paris, 1967.

10. M. A. Williams, 'A Precursor of Hernani', *French Studies*, XIII, 1959, pp. 18–27, suggests that the war years had had a "darkening effect" on the conventional portrait of the Spaniard, "obliterating most traces of the gaiety Beaumarchais depicts and emphasizing the more sombre tones of jealousy and revengefulness".

11. *Op. cit.*, p. 116.

12. The play is R. L. Shiel's *Evadne, or the Statue* (1819). Cf. G. Rudler, 'La Source de la scène des portraits dans *Hernani*', *Modern Language Review*, XIII, 1918, pp. 329–332.

13. "Il a l'âme malade à force de désespérer du bonheur, et presque sans le vouloir, malgré lui, il trouve comme une âpre volupté à souffrir, sans se laisser arrêter par la crainte de faire souffrir", P. Nebout, *Le Drame romantique*, Paris, 1895, p. 254.

14. *Op. cit.*, pp. 196–198.

15. Even the so-called 'lyrical' *stances* of *Le Cid* (I, vi), which may seem to represent a static elegiac development in a manner very like Hugo's, are a device to enable Rodrigue to analyse his motives and strengthen his resolve.

16. Cf. F. C. Green, *Minuet*, ch. ii: 'The Philosopher and the Dramatist'.

17. *Op. cit.*, pp. 165–166.

18. From this point of view, Sarcey's appreciation shows a shrewder critical insight: "Tout l'art de Victor Hugo consiste à mettre violemment ses personnages dans une position où il puisse aisément, lui poète, s'épancher en odes, en élégies, en imprécations, et, d'un seul mot, en pièces de vers. Il se prépare, comme un habile librettiste à un compositeur, des airs de bravoure, des duos, des trios, des finales. Plusieurs de ses drames sont devenus des opéras; c'est qu'ils avaient été coupés pour être des opéras, où le vers tiendrait lieu de la musique. Y a-t-il rien de plus étrange que le quatrième acte d'*Hernani*, si l'on y cherche une œuvre sérieuse de théâtre? C'est une suite de scènes insensées, qui tombent les unes par-dessus les autres, sans lien, comme sans raison. Mais n'y voyez, pour un instant, qu'un livret d'opéra: comme cela est fait!", *Quarante Ans de théâtre*, Paris, 1901, IV, p. 2. See also the curious essay by P. and V. Glachant, 'Notes sur Victor Hugo et la musique' in *Le Théâtre de Victor Hugo: Les drames en vers*, Paris, 1902, pp. 377–401; and A. R. Oliver, 'Romanticism and Opera', *Symposium*, XXIII, 1969, pp. 325–332. For a detailed comparison between Hugo's *Hernani* and the libretto written by Piave for Verdi's *Ernani*, see C. Osborne, *The Complete Operas of Verdi*, London, 1973, pp. 82–91.

19. For a most perceptive treatment of the function of Hugo's poetry in *Hernani*, see C. Affron, *A Stage for Poets: Studies in the Theatre of Hugo and Musset*, Princeton, 1971, ch. ii: 'The Time of the Lyric'.

20. Letter to Mlle Mars, quoted in *Théâtre complet, ed. cit.*, I, p. 1757.

21. For details of this and other productions of *Marion de Lorme*, see Descotes, *Le Drame . . .*, pp. 215–223, and Sleumer, *op. cit.*, pp. 6off. Hugo himself (Preface to *Le Roi s'amuse*) gives the figure of 61 for the number of performances during the first run; while G. Lote unaccountably writes that "*Marion de Lorme . . .* n'a eu que quatre représentations, au milieu d'un effroyable vacarme", *op. cit.*, p. 70.

22. *Victor Hugo raconté . . .*, II, pp. 317–318.

23. Descotes, *Le Drame* . . ., p. 188.

24. *Ibid.*, pp. 217–218.

25. "La grande ambition des poètes romantiques, c'est d'agrandir, de purifier l'amour, c'est de transformer une passion qui était une source de faiblesse en un sentiment vertueux qui ramène l'homme à Dieu, à la conscience de son immortalité", Nebout, *op. cit.*, p. 182.

26. Needless to say, there is little in common between Hugo's idealized portrait of his heroine and the historical Marion de Lorme. Cf. Tallemant des Réaux, *Historiettes*, ed. A. Adam, Paris, 1961, pp. 30, 34–36, etc.

27. Though the plot must have been sufficiently promising from the operatic point of view for it to give rise to three adaptations (Bottesini, 1862; Pedrotti, 1865; Ponchielli, 1885)—as many as any other of Hugo's plays with the exception of *Ruy Blas*. Cf. Glachant, *op. cit.*, p. 399.

28. *Op. cit.*, p. 186.

29. See the very sympathetic commentary on *Marion de Lorme* by P. Berret, *Victor Hugo*, Paris (Garnier), n.d., pp. 291–301.

30. Incompetence on the part of some actors appears to have been a contributory factor: "M. Samson (Clément Marot) omit ces deux vers:

> Vous pouvez crier haut et marcher d'un pas lourd;
> Le bandeau que voilà le rend aveugle et sourd

— de sorte qu'on ne s'expliqua pas comment Triboulet ne voyait pas que l'échelle était à son mur et n'entendait pas les cris de sa fille. En outre, l'enlèvement de Blanche se fit maladroitement: Mme Anaïs fut emportée tête en bas et jambes en l'air, et cette gaucherie d'un figurant parut un tel défaut de la pièce que le deuxième acte finit sous une grêle de sifflets", *Victor Hugo raconté* . . ., II, pp. 331–332.

31. The second performance of *Le Roi s'amuse* was in fact given on 22 November 1882, fifty years to the day after the opening night.

32. *Victor Hugo raconté*..., II, p. 334. News of the attempted assassination had in fact been received as the first performance was about to begin.

33. *Théâtre complet*, I, p. 1689.

34. 'Discours prononcé par M. Victor Hugo devant le Tribunal de Commerce . . .', *ibid.*, p. 1668.

35. Descotes, *Le Drame* . . ., p. 242.

36. These are all examples of what M. Jacques Scherer terms "le

troisième lieu" (*La Dramaturgie de Beaumarchais*, Paris, 1954, pp. 172ff.).

37. On the subject of the spectacular appeal of Hugo's plays, it is worth remarking that the author himself took a first-hand interest in the design of sets and costumes. This participation was particularly important in the case of *Le Roi s'amuse* and *Ruy Blas*: see Plates 7 and 12, and cf. Marie-Antoinette Allevy, *La Mise en scène en France dans la première moitié du dix-neuvième siècle*, Paris, 1938, pp. 121–126.

38. M. Descotes comments as follows on the production at the Porte-Saint-Martin: "Les leçons que Hugo pouvait tirer de ce premier contact avec la Porte-Saint-Martin se dégagent aisément. D'une part, il éprouvait une sorte de déception: il n'avait pas encore trouvé le théâtre idéal. D'autre part, il gardait le souvenir très vivant de Mme Dorval dont les conseils et l'interprétation avaient grandement servi la pièce. Il n'est pas étonnant que Hugo se soit repris à regarder du côté de la rue Richelieu: ce serait, un an plus tard, l'expérience du *Roi s'amuse*. Mais le Théâtre-Français ne lui paraîtrait vraiment sûr que lorsque Dorval y aurait trouvé sa place: en 1835, pour *Angelo*, cette condition serait remplie", *Le Drame . . .*, pp. 222–223.

39. Cf. Sainte-Beuve's comment on hearing an early reading of the play: "J'ai bien quelques petites opinions personnelles sur ce genre de drame et sur son degré de vérité humaine, mais je n'ai aucun doute sur l'impression qui sera produite, et sur l'immense talent déployé dans cette œuvre radieuse de beaux vers" (letter to Pavie, quoted by Berret, *op. cit.*, p. 305).

40. *Op. cit.*, pp. 306–307.

41. See in particular E. Biré, *Victor Hugo après 1830*, Paris, 1891, I, pp. 236–251; E. Rigal, 'La Genèse d'un drame romantique: *Ruy Blas*', *Revue d'Histoire Littéraire de la France*, XX, 1913, pp. 753–788; G. Lanson, 'Victor Hugo et Angélica Kauffmann', *ibid.*, XXII, 1915, pp. 392–401; H. C. Lancaster, 'The Genesis of *Ruy Blas*', *Modern Philology*, XIV, 1917, pp. 129–134; H. de Latouche, *La Reine d'Espagne*, ed. F. Ségu, Paris, 1928, pp. lvii–lxvi; *Ruy Blas*, ed. H. F. Collins, London, 1966, pp. xxiv–xxvii; ed. A. Ubersfeld, Vol. I, Besançon and Paris, 1971, pp. 11–55.

42. 'Au lecteur' to *Héraclius*.

43. The letter written by Ruy Blas at Salluste's dictation; the key; the money; Don César's cloak, etc. See *Ruy Blas*, ed. Ubersfeld, pp. 69–70, 'Une Dramaturgie de l'objet'.

44. In the 'Note' attached to the first edition of the play (1838).
45. "*Ruy Blas*, pas plus qu'*Hernani* qui lui ressemble tant, n'est un drame véritablement historique" (*Ruy Blas*, ed. Ubersfeld, I, p. 78). And cf. the remarks of a contemporary reviewer: "M. Hugo se contente d'emprunter le nom de ses principaux personnages et ne consulte en les dessinant que sa fantaisie. M. Hugo ignore, oublie, ou méprise l'histoire... il est évident que l'histoire ne joue aucun rôle dans les drames de M. Hugo" (quoted by D. O. Evans, *Le Drame moderne à l'époque romantique*, Paris, 1923, p. 17).
46. Lancaster (*art. cit.*) quotes a remark of Hugo's made much later, in Guernsey, as evidence that the idea of the sudden rise of "a minister invested with absolute power", and his equally sudden fall at the bidding of an unknown man who commands him as his master, preceded the selection of the historical setting that was to serve as a framework.
47. See e.g. Berret, *op. cit.*, p. 316; Bellessort, *op. cit.*, pp. 61ff.; P. A. Touchard, 'Le Dramatique', in *Victor Hugo*, by J. de Lacretelle and others, Paris, 1967, pp. 87ff.
48. *Pace* M. Descotes, who refers to Act IV as "cet intermède gratuit et provocant", *Le Drame . . .*, p. 323.
49. Preface to *Ruy Blas*.
50. *Op. cit.*, IV, p. 53.
51. See R. A. E. Baldick, *The Life and Times of Frédérick Lemaître*, London, 1959, pp. 161–173.
52. See Baldick, *ibid.* Hugo himself published a generous appreciation of Frédérick's performance as Ruy Blas (as well as of that of other actors): "Dans *Ruy Blas*, M. Frédérick réalise pour nous l'idéal du grand acteur... Pour M. Frédérick, la soirée du 8 novembre 1838 n'a pas été une représentation, mais une transfiguration".
53. "Hugo ne devait trouver sa véritable interprète que beaucoup plus tard, avec Sarah Bernhardt qui sut mettre en valeur toute la poésie du personnage; lors de la reprise, Hugo devait déclarer que c'était la première fois que le rôle était joué", Descotes, *Le Drame . . .*, p. 324.
54. Cf. *Ruy Blas*, ed. Ubersfeld, I, pp. 107–118.
55. *Op. cit.*, pp. 49–50.
56. "Le fait le plus saillant peut-être de la dramaturgie de Hugo dans *Ruy Blas* est le retour offensif du grotesque", *Ruy Blas*, ed. Ubersfeld, p. 70.
57. *Ibid.*, p. 60. Dr. Ubersfeld quotes (p. 59) Hugo's article on Scott in the *Muse Française* of 1823: "Supposons un roman...

qui... soit un long drame... où les personnages pourraient se peindre par eux-mêmes et représenter par leurs chocs divers et multipliés toutes les formes de l'idée unique de l'ouvrage"; and it is interesting to compare Stendhal's comment on Scott in the same year: "de la tragédie romantique, entremêlée de longues descriptions" (*Racine et Shakespeare, ed. cit.*, p. 8).

58. *Ibid.*, p. 80.
59. *Op. cit.*, pp. 76–79.
60. *Ibid.*, p. 93.
61. *Op. cit.*, p. 243.

6 Dumas, Vigny and the Historical Drama

(i) 'Christine' and Dumas's verse drama

> L'école romantique, il est vrai, opposait les deux termes de *drame* et de *tragédie*; mais, à son insu, c'est de la tragédie qu'elle faisait.[1]

IF Nebout is right, and the kind of Romantic drama considered in the last chapter should more properly be called Romantic *tragedy*, there existed alongside it another type, of a much more prosaic nature, whose origins in the melodrama of the early years of the century it is not difficult to detect. While the former is associated almost exclusively with the name of Victor Hugo, the name we think of most readily in connection with the latter is that of Alexandre Dumas. Among Dumas's prodigious output, his plays alone number over ninety; of these, a large proportion were historical dramas; and of the latter, all but a handful were written in prose. Many, it is true, were in fact written—as were most of his lighter productions in the popular genre of *vaudeville* —in collaboration with others: this is particularly the case with those historical dramas, mostly dramatized versions of his successful novels, that he produced with Auguste Maquet from the middle 1840s onwards. For alone of the three major Romantic dramatists active in the early 1830s, Dumas was still writing for the theatre twenty years later—writing, even, at an increased rate of production[2]—according to the formula for historical melodrama that he had inherited from Pixérécourt and adapted to the requirements of the theatregoing public of the reign of Louis-Philippe. It would be unfair to be too patronizing about Dumas's commercialism: his formula did of course pay more regard to popular taste than to more genuinely literary qualities, but several of these plays were put on at the Théâtre-Français, and in any case the literary aspirations of

other practising dramatists were hardly more conspicuous in
the 1840s. Apart from the splendid failure of *Les Burgraves* in
1843, the revival of more traditional forms with Ponsard and
Augier, and the staging of some of Musset's comedies in the
latter years of this decade, the 'literary' theatre was by now in
retreat. Louis-Philippe's reign saw a considerable growth of
the theatre as popular entertainment—witness not only the
increase in the number of theatres in Paris[3], but also the considerable narrowing of the gap between the typical productions
of the 'boulevard' theatres and many of the new works produced
at the Théâtre-Français itself.

But Dumas—whose opportunism finally had the effect of
putting him on much the same level as Scribe as a popular
entertainer—had of course started out with quite other ambitions. We have already quoted his moving account of the
impression made by the revelation of Shakespeare on a young
idealist; and we have also seen that his first full-length play had
been written in verse. *Christine*, accepted by the Théâtre-
Français in 1828, had not been performed on that occasion; but
a revised version, offered to the Odéon, was performed there in
March 1830. The Odéon also staged *Charles VII chez ses grands
vassaux* in October 1831; while *Caligula* was performed at the
Théâtre-Français in December 1837, and *L'Alchimiste* (in which
Dumas enjoyed the collaboration of Gérard de Nerval) at the
Renaissance in April 1839[4].

Though these verse plays may not represent a very significant
proportion of Dumas's total output as a dramatist, the fact that
he adopted this medium for two of his earliest 'drames' indicates that he, too, set out with more exalted literary aims than
that of mere commercial success; and that he should later return
to the alexandrine, even if only occasionally, suggests that these
ambitions had not been entirely abandoned.

Christine, the first of these plays, ran for 50 performances in
1830; to begin with there was some turbulence, but this never
reached the proportions of the 'bataille d'*Hernani*': the audience
at the Odéon was different from that at the Théâtre-Français,
and Dumas was not Hugo. Nor was *Christine* a very distinguished
play, compared with Dumas's best work for the theatre. If we
attempt to 'place' this example of verse drama by reference to
Hugo's romantic tragedy on the one hand, and Dumas's own

'drame historique' on the other, we must conclude that it had a much greater affinity with the latter, and that the verse is mere external ornament, which fails to give the play any truly poetic quality. Certain passages, it is true, may appear at first sight to reproduce something of the lyricism of *Hernani*:

O Christine! pourquoi me faire cette injure?
Moi, t'aimer pour ton rang? Oh! non, je te le jure,
Que, quel que fût le rang que le ciel t'eût donné,
J'aurais aimé ton front même découronné,
Partout... Oui, si j'avais vu dans l'Andalousie
Tes yeux noirs à travers la verte jalousie,
J'aurais aimé tes yeux! Le théorbe à la main,
Assise au fût brisé d'un vieux tombeau romain,
Chantant un chant d'amour, si je t'avais trouvée,
J'aurais aimé ton chant, car je t'avais rêvée!
Je croyais te connaître avant que de te voir.
Oh! oui, j'avais osé, dans mes songes de l'âme,
Créer un ange à moi sous des formes de femme;
Il avait ce regard et ce sourire-là,
Et, lorsque je te vis, je me dis: « Le voilà! » (II, iv)

and there are others which really do anticipate the verbal dexterity Hugo was to show in *Marion de Lorme*:

— Les comédiens du roi donnaient, le mois dernier,
Un drame de Corneille — ou, je crois, de Garnier;
Non, c'était de Corneille.
     — Et son titre est...?
          — *Horace.*

— Qu'en dit-on?
      — Que l'auteur n'a pas suivi la trace
Des grands maîtres; qu'il est et trivial et bas;
Que ce n'est point ainsi que parlent Dubartas,
Desmarets, Saint-Sorlin, Bois-Robert et Jodelle,
Qui du suprême goût ont offert le modèle.

— Et qui donc dit cela?
        — L'Académie.
           — Encor!

— Oui, Votre Majesté; ses membres sont d'accord
Que c'est un novateur dont le culte idolâtre
Sacrifie à Baal et perd le beau théâtre;
Qu'eux seuls sont du bon goût arbitres signalés,
Et que *Cid*, et qu'*Horace* à bon droit sont sifflés. (I, i)

But far too often the verse is awkward, mechanical, or just
uninspired and prosaic. Harel, the director of the Odéon, had
from the beginning criticized Dumas's use of verse, and had
made strenuous efforts to get the play re-written in prose: he
may well not have been so very wide of the mark.

It is not only the language that is artificial and awkward in
Christine. As elsewhere in Dumas's historical plays, local colour
is often applied very crudely, by stilted conversation containing
forced allusions; and the minor characters Descartes, Corneille
and La Calprenède exist merely to fulfil a similar purpose.
Structurally, the play is extremely episodic, the alternative title
Stockholm, Fontainebleau et Rome indicating clearly enough the
three stages in the career of Queen Christina of Sweden that the
playwright chose to dramatize; though in fact, its essential plot
—the unmasking of the unscrupulous ambition of Monaldeschi,
Christine's Italian favourite, leading up to his assassination on
her orders—would probably have gained from being treated in
a more concentrated dramatic manner. Characterization is
weak, for 'character' amounts to little more than a series of
related actions, without sufficient consistent motivation. None
of the principal characters carries conviction, and *Christine*
perhaps illustrates the opposite tendency from the one we have
observed in some of Hugo's plays. Whereas a character like
Triboulet, though very much larger than life, is given a real
consistency in dramatic terms by the *a priori* idea which animates
him, Dumas's characters in this play are featureless marionettes
responding to the demands of the plot.

Dumas's second verse play illustrates the remarkable
eclecticism of this prolific dramatist (the eighteen months
between *Christine* and *Charles VII* had seen the appearance of
both *Napoléon Bonaparte* and *Antony*, while two months later he
was to produce *Richard Darlington*, and *Térésa* in February 1832
was to bring the total to six full-length plays produced in less
than two years). In subject-matter and setting, *Charles VII chez*

ses grands vassaux illustrates the vogue for the French Middle Ages, stimulated by Scott's novels and Hugo's *Notre-Dame de Paris*. In a Preface, Dumas indicates, in fact, that his source was a passage from Alain Chartier's *Chronique du roi Charles VII*; but he goes on to claim that the structure of the play is deliberately 'classique'—the unities of both time and place are observed—and admits that he has borrowed from Racine the dénouement of *Andromaque* (Bérengère, wife of Comte Charles Robert de Savoisy, repudiated by her husband because their marriage is barren, has him killed by the Saracen captive Yaqoub, then takes her own life). Dramatically, this concentration is effective, and *Charles VII* makes much better theatre than *Christine*[5]. But the characterization, though more distinctive, is hardly less arbitrary: in particular, the change in Bérengère from meek and submissive loving wife to frenzied murderess is unprepared and completely unconvincing, and Yaqoub fails to become a credible embodiment of the fatalistic Romantic hero. As for Dumas's handling of the alexandrine, this is so mechanical and undistinguished that the play might as well have been written in prose. Although it was certainly successful in the theatre, therefore, *Charles VII* cannot be said to depart in any essential way from the formula which characterizes historical melodrama[6].

With *Caligula*, Dumas set his sights much higher, aiming at 'la tragédie à l'antique'. His Preface speaks, in a style remarkably like that of Hugo's Prefaces, of the preparatory study he had undertaken before writing the play; and it must be admitted that the evocation of the atmosphere of ancient Rome is to say the least more convincing than that of modern periods, such as the Middle Ages or the Renaissance, in most of Dumas's other historical plays. He has chosen here to present "cette lutte du paganisme mourant et de la foi naissante"; and both the corruption, debauch and tyrannical cruelty embodied in Caligula and Messalina, and on the other hand the simple eager faith of the new convert Stella, are treated in such a way as to be historically and dramatically credible. Moreover—possibly due to collaboration with Gérard de Nerval[7]—there are passages in which verse seems to be used more effectively: Stella's exposition to her mother of her new faith, based on the Gospel narrative of the raising of Lazarus (I, ii), for instance, or her prayer for protection against Caligula's lust:

Seigneur miséricordieux,
Seigneur, ferez-vous moins que n'ont fait de faux dieux?
Quand, fuyant d'Apollon la poursuite profane,
Daphné tomba mourante en invoquant Diane,
Diane l'entendit, et d'un laurier soudain
L'écorce, chaste armure, enveloppa son sein;
De même, lorsque Pan d'une course hardie
Allait joindre Syrinx, la nymphe d'Arcadie,
Syrinx, pour échapper aux désirs ravisseurs,
A son aide appela les naïades ses sœurs;
Et l'on dit qu'aussitôt la nymphe fugitive
Sentit ses pieds lassés s'attacher à la rive,
Et, selon son désir, transformée en roseaux,
Mêla son dernier souffle au murmure des eaux.
En vous donc, Dieu puissant, je me fie et j'espère,
Car les faibles en vous trouvent un second père... (IV, i)

But Dumas's formula has not changed: this is not tragedy, but historical drama. Indeed, the fact that the treatment of the ancient world in this play is more responsible merely makes *Caligula* a better example of that genre: Dumas does succeed in persuading us, however fleetingly, that these events could only have been brought about by a unique combination of circumstances of time and place. In other words, our response to the play depends on the portrayal of the complex contingencies of a given historical moment, rather than on the personal fortunes of a tragic protagonist.

And the play is still thoroughly Romantic in its inspiration, for all its deliberate setting in the ancient world. Beneath the historical externals, however plausible, the black-and-white characterization of melodrama is clear enough: virtuous innocence in Stella is persecuted by unrelieved villainy in Caligula and his henchmen[8]. And as regards the stage effects, the comic naivety of such devices as the sign 'Bibulus tonsor' outside the barber's shop in the Prologue, combined with the lavish spectacle aimed at in stage-directions such as this:

Le cortège commence à défiler. Les Soldats, portant les trophées, entrent les premiers; puis Incitatus, le cheval de guerre de César, conduit par deux Sénateurs; puis des Enfants couronnés de roses, qui jettent des fleurs; puis enfin

César, sur un char d'ivoire et d'or, attelé de quatre chevaux blancs conduits par les Heures du jour et de la nuit. Derrière le char, les Prisonniers vaincus; derrière les Prisonniers, les Soldats[9]

—suggests nothing so much as one of Hollywood's historical or biblical 'epics'. In fact, it seems that the lavish staging of *Caligula* (which cost 40,000 francs, compared with 10,000 for *Marion de Lorme*) did a disservice not only to Dumas himself, but also to the fortunes of Romantic drama at the Théâtre-Français, to judge by the comment of Philoclès Régnier, who was acting Director of the theatre at the time:

Par suite de tous ces chefs-d'œuvre, nous faisons fort peu d'argent... Nos auteurs nous abandonnent; l'invasion de Hugo et de Dumas les fait reculer, et ces deux messieurs nous demandent le double de ce qu'on donnait aux autres, et ne nous font pas faire la moitié des recettes que nous donnaient C. Delavigne et Scribe.[10]

Ligier earned praise from reviewers for his performance as Caligula, but the interpretation of the female roles was almost universally criticized: both that of Mlle Noblet as Messaline, and that of Ida Ferrier as Stella[11]. The play ran for twenty performances.

When we turn to *L'Alchimiste*, it is a case of passing from a genuine historical drama, with convincing characters and a real sense of period, to a preposterous melodrama with cardboard characters, full of the worst clichés of the genre. The scene is set in sixteenth-century Florence, but the local colour is reduced to a handful of superficial references; and in fact, this background is less important for its own sake than as an appropriate setting for a version of the Faust legend. Fasio the alchemist is the Faust-figure, Francesca is his Gretchen, and the courtesan Maddalena his Helen, whom he hopes to procure with the treasures provided by the Mephisophelian Lelio. But the play never achieves the extra dimension of the myth: the suggestive poetic quality is lacking, and instead we have the most prosaic banality. Indeed, the best that can be said of the verse is that it is unobtrusive: one might have expected collaboration with

Nerval to give the play a certain lightness of touch and a genuine poetic flavour, but *L'Alchimiste* was on the contrary the least ambitious of Dumas's verse plays, the one in which he seems to have been most content to accept the conventional stereotypes of the melodramatic formula; and even the fact that Frédérick Lemaître played the central role did not enable it to run for more than seventeen performances[12].

To conclude, therefore, Dumas's ventures into verse drama produced one very mediocre melodrama, two moderately successful examples of the genre of 'mélodrame historique', and one play, *Caligula*, which though unsuccessful at the time and generally dismissed by subsequent commentators[13], seems to offer the most interest to the modern reader not only on account of its more sensitive and perceptive treatment of a historical period, but also because it comes nearest to justifying the use of verse.

(ii) 'Henri III et sa cour' and the historical melodrama

THE normal medium for the historical melodrama, with Dumas as with his predecessors, was prose; and from *Henri III et sa cour* through to the end of his life, the historical drama in prose constitutes the most substantial part of Dumas's output. Though the respective proportions of 'history' and melodrama may vary from play to play, the basic formula remains the same: unsubtle black-and-white characterization, a strong visual appeal achieved through both settings and spectacular *coups de théâtre*, and an abuse of emphatic diction.

In all these respects, *Henri III* continues an existing tradition, and altogether it marks much less of a new departure than a play like *Hernani*. If *Henri III* is to be considered a 'Romantic' play, therefore, this is largely due to such external factors as Dumas's declared support for the aspirations of Hugo and his friends in the field of drama, and to the iconoclastic challenge constituted by the production of a historical melodrama at the Théâtre-Français: the affinities of the play are nearly all with Pixérécourt and Ducange, rather than with the *Préface de Cromwell*. Whereas a coherent aesthetic underlies all Hugo's dramas—the prose plays as well as those written in verse— Dumas on the other hand was bound by no *a priori* convictions, and was free to adopt Hugo's manner when it suited the tactical requirements of the moment, or reject it in favour of a less ambitious formula. Thus *Henri III et sa cour* shows no more awareness than had *Christine* of the Romantic theories of characterization formulated in the *Préface*: in place of Hugo's antithesis between conflicting elements within the single personality, the principal protagonists are simple characters, ranged without any ambiguity on one side or the other of a dividing-line separating good and evil—or at any rate, sympathetic and unsympathetic. Essentially, this is a conjugal drama, with the Duchesse de Guise and her lover Saint-Mégrin faced by the powerful, brutal Duc de Guise; the fact that the 'guilty' partners are the sympathetic characters does perhaps suggest the moral atmosphere of Romantic literature rather than that of Pixérécourt's melodramas, although compared with what was to come later, *Henri III* is only a timid step in the direction of immoral licence: the adulterous love remains unconsummated, and the sympathy we feel for the lovers is largely a negative one, the strong positive reaction being one of revulsion from the Duke. Saint-Mégrin, in fact, is little more than a functional hero, responding to the dictates of plot rather than to any distinctive psychological motivation; it is difficult not to feel that Dumas neglected an obvious opportunity in failing to develop the romantic potential of his ill-starred hero, and in not making Saint-Mégrin into something more like an Hernani or a Didier.

But Dumas was no more sensitive to Romantic 'mood' than he was concerned with the finer points of the representation of history. The historical plot—the domination of the weak Henri III by his mother, and the assumption of power by the Ligue—remains subsidiary to the main conjugal drama, but the two are linked in that Guise is the head of the *ligueurs*, while Saint-Mégrin is a devoted supporter of the King. But there is no attempt to offer any interpretation of sixteenth-century events, whether in the manner of a historian, as in the 'scènes historiques', or in the poet's intuitive manner favoured by Hugo: for Dumas, the reign of Henri III is a mere pretext, giving an opportunity for picturesque sets such as the astrologer Ruggieri's *cabinet de travail*, colourful costumes *à l'antique*, or allusive references to the most banal *idées reçues* about the life of the times (thus when 'M. Ronsard' sends some newly-composed verses to the Duchesse de Guise, these inevitably turn out to be the ode 'Mignonne, allons voir si la rose…', in spite of a gap of over twenty years between the composition of this poem and the events of the play). Altogether, this is historical drama at its most superficial: it is no more than 'comic-strip' history, such flesh and blood as there is being supplied by the conjugal drama in the foreground. Though even here, the characters are the two-dimensional stereotypes of melodrama, and the situations— the effects of suspense and surprise, the *coups de théâtre* by which Dumas liked to conclude his acts, the sensational climax in which the Duchesse de Guise thrusts her arm, in place of an iron bolt, through the rings of the door to keep her husband out while her lover tries to escape—these situations determine the development of character, not the other way round.

As for Dumas's prose style, to quote A. Brun:

> Un style dans le théâtre de Dumas père, le terme n'est guère de mise, disons une *manière*… Par son insouciance de la beauté expressive, il contribue à rejeter le drame, ou à maintenir le mélodrame, en dehors de la littérature.[14]

Dumas's dialogue is a second-hand amalgam of elements drawn from Diderot, from Pixérécourt and from other predecessors, in which the featureless banality of the 'style de base' is relieved from time to time by excessive use of 'le style haletant', crudely emphatic writing to point an emotional crisis, or the obtrusive introduction of archaic or technical terms. The only innovation, says Brun ironically, was "d'avoir fait applaudir ce langage par les habitués du Théâtre-Français, sanctuaire du style tragique"[15]—though it should be remembered that for sixty years or more the Théâtre-Français had been accepting, alongside traditional tragedy, the 'drames' of Diderot and others which from a stylistic point of view deserve very similar strictures. And even though for Mlle Mars, who played the Duchesse de Guise, the melodramatic mixture of commonplaces and sensationalism represented a considerable derogation from the nobility of tragedy, she is reported to have been much happier with *Henri III* than she was to be with *Hernani* the following year. Dumas's sense of theatre was a real compensation for the banality of his style, and even the mediocrity of his prose was safer than Hugo's alexandrines with their bizarre and provocative imagery.

Napoléon Bonaparte was one of the few Romantic plays to be staged at the Odéon. Harel, the dynamic *entrepreneur* who took over the direction of this theatre in April 1829, was well disposed to the new drama, and keen to attract, or to commission, suitable plays for his mistress Mlle George—who was herself much more favourably disposed than her rival, Mlle Mars, at the Français. *Christine*, which had been fairly successful, and Musset's *La Nuit vénitienne* (December 1830), which was an utter failure, were followed by *Napoléon Bonaparte* in January 1831; then came Vigny's *La Maréchale d'Ancre* (June 1831) and Dumas's *Charles VII* in October of the same year. But various factors—difficulties over the government subsidy, the hostility of the press, the unsatisfactory geographical location of the Odéon on the left Bank—made Harel desirous of finding a theatre on the fashionable boulevards, and at the beginning of December 1831, he was able to take over the Porte-Saint-Martin. His lease of the Odéon expired in April 1832, and for several years after this, no satisfactory permanent arrangement was found for the administration of this theatre. At all events, whereas it had appeared to provide the Romantic playwrights with the outlet they needed, the Odéon abruptly ceased to be a viable proposition, and throughout the middle years of the 1830s it was the Porte-Saint-Martin which, apart from occasional renewed attempts to conquer the Théâtre-Français, had to provide the regular home for Romantic drama.

One of the faults critics found with the Odéon was that it was an excessively large theatre, better suited to spectacle than to more intimate drama (indeed, one of the last productions put on there under Harel's management, in March 1832, featured a celebrated elephant, Kiouny); and it is perhaps this that leads both M. Descotes and Dr. Baldick to describe *Napoléon Bonaparte* as spectacular entertainment rather than literary drama[16]. It may well be that Harel's showmanship and flair for publicity did surround the play with a good deal of adventitious glamour: other managers had been quick to profit from the relaxation of censorship after the July Revolution by putting on plays about Napoleon, and Harel, in commissioning a play from Dumas which could compete with these, spared neither money nor effort on publicity and presentation. But to dismiss *Napoléon Bonaparte* as 'pageant' is to overlook the considerable interest it offers. For the play is a real exception among Dumas's historical dramas: far more than *Henri III* or *La Tour de Nesle*, it reflects an intelligent awareness of the problems of presenting history on the stage, and instead of merely using historical period as a superficial setting for a melodramatic plot, here Dumas has preferred to adopt the methods of Mérimée and the other authors of 'scènes historiques', and to construct a series of independent *tableaux*. These episodic scenes are linked by the character of Napoleon; but if the play differs in this from, say, *La Jaquerie*, in other respects it represents a complete break with conventional dramatic composition, and with its six acts and twenty-three *tableaux* it can be seen as an important step towards the 'epic' construction of Brecht's historical plays, or at least towards the episodic treatment of history shown in such plays of our own time as Anouilh's *Becket* or Robert Bolt's *A Man for all Seasons*. M. Descotes writes, as if indicating a serious defect: "Le seul rôle de la pièce est celui de Napoléon"[17]—but given the kind of historical play that Dumas has chosen to write, it would surely have been wrong to try to create 'characters' in the conventional sense; a similar remark could after all be made about Brecht's *Galileo*. The most important role alongside that of Napoleon is that of a totally fictitious character, L'Espion, pardoned by Napoleon in Act I, and reappearing throughout the play in various guises to show his devotion to the Emperor. Again, Descotes is critical:

> Le personnage n'est pas un caractère, même pas un symbole de la fidélité. Il n'est qu'un moyen dramatique, le lien entre les différentes scènes[18]

—but granted that it is a "moyen dramatique", we should surely recognize it as a highly imaginative one, a successful attempt to impose on the historical material a non-naturalistic pattern[19].

Napoléon Bonaparte is by no means a great play. Its success at the time was largely due to lavish productions and striking scenic effects (the crossing of the Beresina, the burning of Moscow), and also no doubt to the playing of Frédérick

Lemaître—although the part was outside his normal range, and the historical Napoleon inhibited the actor's idiosyncratic manner. But as historical drama, it is in quite a different class from others of its time; and for a play which was in certain respects so much in advance of its age, it has been strangely underestimated by modern critics[20].

Dumas's next historical drama in prose, *La Tour de Nesle*, was produced by Harel at the Porte-Saint-Martin in May 1832[21]. Written to provide another vehicle for Frédérick Lemaître, it certainly contained a role more suited to his bizarre genius, but in the event it was not Frédérick who created the part; when he left Paris during the cholera epidemic, to take his family— and also himself—to a place of safety, Harel and Mlle George took the opportunity to relieve him of the part. Frédérick was furious, Dumas indignant, but it was Bocage who created the role of Buridan—with less *panache*, but more *pathétique*—no doubt to the satisfaction of Mlle George, who thus had less competition to fear than she would have faced playing with Frédérick Lemaître.

The plot of this sensational melodrama is one of the most scabrous of any Romantic play, featuring the sexual orgies and murders attributed by legend to Marguerite de Bourgogne, wife of Louis X, and her sisters. Buridan, the hero, is one of the strangers enticed to the Tour de Nesle to take part in a nocturnal orgy, but he escapes, avoiding the outcome regularly prescribed by Marguerite: to be killed and thrown into the Seine. Buridan blackmails the Queen into making him prime minister, and the remainder of the preposterous plot is taken up with her attempts to destroy him, complicated by her love for a young captain, Gaultier, who proves to be the survivor of twins born to her in her extreme youth. Buridan had been their father, and the other twin has already perished as a victim of one of her orgies at the Tour de Nesle. Gaultier is finally killed by her orders, in mistake for Buridan, and he dies cursing his mother, as Marguerite and Buridan are arrested by the forces of justice.

Characterization is non-existent: Marguerite and Buridan exist merely as the sum total of their actions, and there is no attempt to establish plausible motive, or to show the working of their minds. Dialogue, indeed, is rudimentary; and the remarks made about *Henri III* apply with even more force here, where the mixture of banality and heavy emphasis is cruder still:

> — Une croix rouge? une croix au bras gauche? une croix pareille à tous deux? Oh! dis que ce n'était pas une croix que tu leur as faite, dis que ce n'est pas au bras gauche, dis que c'était un autre signe...
>
> — C'était une croix et pas autre chose; c'était au bras gauche et pas autre part.
>
> — Oh! malheur! malheur! mes enfants! Philippe! Gaultier! L'un mort, l'autre près de mourir!... tous deux assassinés, l'un par elle, l'autre par moi! justice de Dieu!... (V, i)

These are the stylized ejaculations of the comic-strip cartoon, with none of the genuine expressiveness of literary drama. Nevertheless, the role of Buridan, sombre and fatalistic, had enough scope for an actor to be able to mould it convincingly into a coherent whole; and Frédérick would doubtless have added it to his series of striking creations. In fact, the play had a long and successful run, and in September Bocage withdrew, giving way to Frédérick, whose interpretation is said to have corresponded more nearly to the author's intentions. But *La Tour de Nesle* illustrates Dumas's theatre at its most melodramatic and most ephemeral: the characters in the text are mere empty shells, waiting to be filled out by the stylized playing of a Frédérick, a Bocage, or a Mlle George. All that the dramatist himself contributes is the crude stimulus of contrived situations, and the play is devoid of any lasting quality[22].

Of the next play which falls to be considered, *Catherine Howard*, Dumas wrote in his Preface:

> Il m'a semblé qu'il était permis à l'homme qui avait fait du drame d'exception avec *Antony*, du drame politique avec *Richard Darlington*, du drame d'imagination avec *La Tour de Nesle*, du drame de circonstance avec *Napoléon Bonaparte*, du drame de mœurs avec *Angèle*, enfin du drame historique avec *Henri III*, *Christine* et *Charles VII*, de faire du drame extra-historique avec *Catherine Howard*.

Whatever absolute validity such categories may possess, it is difficult to accept this classification of Dumas's own historical dramas. If *Catherine Howard* ranks as a "drame extra-historique" on the grounds that it is "une œuvre d'imagination procréée par ma fantaisie: Henri VIII n'a été pour moi qu'un clou auquel j'ai attaché mon tableau", the same could also be said of *Henri III* and *Charles VII*; the only genuine 'historical' dramas so far written had been *Napoléon Bonaparte* and (possibly) *Christine*.

Catherine Howard (Porte-Saint-Martin, June 1834) is one of a number of plays written from 1833 onwards for Dumas's current mistress, and later wife, Ida Ferrier. She had stepped in and replaced Juliette Drouet when the latter had failed in *Marie Tudor*, and she had also played with some success in Dumas's *Angèle*; but the role of Catherine, calling as it did for the stylized portrayal of remorse and terror in the manner of the gothic melodrama, was really outside her range. Although the reviewers were severe in their criticism both of Mlle Ida and of Lockroy, who played opposite her, the play had a satisfactory run. But this time Dumas had produced a text without any pretensions, accumulating all the clichés of melodrama for the entertainment of a not very discriminating public. Lord Ethelwood, who has secretly married Catherine Howard, learns that Henry VIII has seen her and wants to marry her. He administers a sleeping-draught to her, and convinces the King of her death; but when his refusal to marry the King's sister, Marguerite, leads to his disgrace, the only solution is for him to feign death in his turn. However, the ambitious Catherine throws away the key to his tomb, and marries the King. Ethelwood, released by Marguerite, brings about Catherine's death for suspected adultery, himself taking the executioner's place when the latter is bribed by Catherine to defect. Whatever basis history provides for any of this material—Catherine's short-lived marriage, trial and execution for adultery are all historically true (and Ethelwood "duc de Dierham" is presumably based at one or two removes on the real Francis Dereham)[23]—this is merely a pretext for the gothic sensationalism of the double living entombment, the surprise resurrection of the husband believed dead, and the crowning horror of the husband turned executioner. This is historical drama at its nadir: the clichés of melodrama are unrelieved by any distinctive qualities of character or dialogue, and the historical setting is selected for the most meretricious reasons.

After *Catherine Howard*, Dumas's prodigious rate of production for the theatre—he had had eleven plays performed in less than five years—slackened appreciably; and in particular, he wrote no more historical melodramas in prose for a number of years. Apart from plays on modern subjects—*Kean* (1836), *Paul Jones* (1838)—we have seen that he was tempted by a subject from Roman history in *Caligula* (1837) and that he wrote another historical drama in verse, *L'Alchimiste*, in 1839; other plays calling for a more fanciful handling of material were *Don Juan de Marana*, a *mystère* written in a mixture of prose and verse (1836), and *Piquillo*, an *opéra-comique* written together with Nerval, also in a Spanish setting (1837). The next real historical drama in prose was his *Lorenzino* (Théâtre-Français, February 1842)[24], chiefly notable because it treated the same subject as Musset's *Lorenzaccio*, which had been published in 1834, but had not of course been performed. Though Dumas's version aims much higher than for instance a play like *Catherine Howard* had done, it suffers considerably by comparison with Musset's play. Lorenzino possesses some of the enigmatic quality of Musset's hero, but his character has little depth, and he is more simply resolute and dynamic than Lorenzaccio. The construction of the play is skilful, and the dénouement (the suicide by poison of Luisa Strozzi, who doubts Lorenzo's love for her at the crucial moment, and believes she is being given up to the Duke) is effective in theatrical terms; but all is clear-cut, unsubtle, self-sufficient action, and the extra metaphysical dimension, which makes Musset's play such a masterpiece in spite of its shapeless structure, is completely lacking.

By now, Dumas had embarked on his prolific career as a historical novelist, in collaboration with Auguste Maquet and others; and from the middle 1840s onwards, the most successful of these novels were regularly turned into dramatic form, usually also with Maquet's help (for instance *Les Mousquetaires*, at the Ambigu-Comique, October 1845). In 1847 Dumas belatedly achieved what both he and Hugo had hoped to obtain at the Renaissance ten years earlier: he became director of his own theatre, the Théâtre-Historique, which gave further impetus to the staging of adaptations of his novels: *La Reine Margot* (February 1847)[25], *Le Chevalier de Maison-Rouge* (August 1847), *Monte-Cristo* (February 1848), *Les Girondins* (April 1848),

La Jeunesse des Mousquetaires (February 1849) and others were
put on there. This spectacular form of historical melodrama,
which was to provide Dumas's principal contribution to the
Parisian theatre for the rest of his career, exploited the features
we have already noted: fast-moving action; situations controlling characters rather than the other way round; attention
to the superficial trivia of historical and local colour. The plays
which result from this formula are popular adventure-
melodramas rather than genuine historical plays. If the true
historical play is one which convinces the spectator or reader
that the events portrayed were the unique product of a certain
combination of time and place, there must be few indeed of
Dumas's plays which satisfy this condition: *Caligula*, perhaps, or
Napoléon Bonaparte. For the rest, the key to his formula is given
in this passage:

> Je commence par combiner une fable; je tâche de la faire
> romanesque, tendre, dramatique..., je cherche dans l'histoire
> un cadre où la mettre, et jamais il ne m'est arrivé que
> l'histoire ne m'ait fourni ce cadre, si exact et si bien approprié
> au sujet, qu'il semble que ce soit, non le cadre qui ait été fait
> pour le tableau, mais le tableau pour le cadre.[26]

Even if the events of his plays are taken from a documentary
source[27], the historical specificness of the subject makes less of
an impression on the spectator than the generalizing, *passe-
partout* quality of the romanesque invention. We have had
occasion to make the comparison between Pixérécourt's melodramas and the early popular films: Dumas's historical melodramas may similarly be seen to correspond to the popular
historical adventure film in the cinema of more recent years,
and Mélingue, the handsome, sympathetic actor for whom
Dumas wrote such parts as Henri de Navarre in *La Reine
Margot* or Lorin in *Le Chevalier de Maison-Rouge*, was very much
the Errol Flynn of his day[28].

(iii) 'La Maréchale d'Ancre'

"AVEC *La Maréchale d'Ancre*, j'essayai de faire lire une page
d'histoire sur le théâtre." Vigny's approach to historical drama
was much more erudite than that of his contemporaries:

explanatory footnotes are attached to the text, and the introductory comments on his characters are careful and scholarly. If
this suggests a close affinity with the 'scènes historiques', the
Preface to *La Maréchale d'Ancre* reminds us that Vigny the
dramatist was still Vigny the poet and thinker. Thus, the playwright's purpose was not merely to re-create the complex reality
of the events leading up to Concini's death, but to show behind
the detailed historical relationship of cause and effect the
'philosophical' workings of Justice and Retribution. Accepting
the view that Concini had been implicated in the assassination
of Henri IV, Vigny sees the favourite's own assassination as the
necessary and fitting consequence, and to reinforce this point he
makes Concini die on the very spot on which Ravaillac had
killed the king:

> La minorité de Louis XIII finit comme elle avait commencé
> par un assassinat. Concini et la Galigaï régnèrent entre ces
> deux crimes. Le second m'a semblé être l'expiation du
> premier; et, pour le faire voir à tous les yeux, j'ai ramené au
> même lieu le pistolet de Vitry et le couteau de Ravaillac,
> instruments de l'élévation et de la chute du maréchal d'Ancre,
> pensant que, si l'art est une fable, il doit être une fable
> philosophique.

One is reminded of Aristotle's example of the Statue of Mitys in
the *Poetics*: it is such features as the 'meaningful coincidence'
which transform the bare record of historical events into a
poetic, or philosophical, commentary on those events.

La Maréchale d'Ancre stands almost on its own among the
historical dramas of the period. It offers a responsible version of
the political events of an important moment in French history,
and neither subordinates these historical events to the personal
tragedy of a single protagonist (as does *Lorenzaccio*), nor uses
them as the backcloth to an essentially domestic drama (as
happens in *Henri III* or *Charles VII*). The episode of the minority
of Louis XIII, with the Queen Mother dominated by the
Concinis and the Court divided by warring factions, lends itself
well to this sort of drama. In such an atmosphere of intrigue and
conspiracy, private passions (the vendetta between Borgia and
Concini), whether authentic or not, can provide the motive

force of the plot without appearing either to distort or to
trivialize the course of history; and since Vigny's approach is
unusually objective—for *La Maréchale* is a play without a sympathetic character—we are poles apart from Dumas's type of
melodrama in which the ambiguity and complexity of historical
motivation are replaced by the over-simplified schema of a
black-and-white characterization.

Even the leading role, that of the Maréchale, is constructed
much more 'from the outside' than is usual, with the result that
we are not led to identify with her, but look on dispassionately as
she is brought to book along with her husband. It is clear that
Concini himself is far more guilty, but we are never allowed to
develop a genuine sympathy for any of these characters: if there
is any identification at all on the spectator's part, it is perhaps
with the people of Paris, represented by the honest bourgeois
Picard, for it is they who are the permanent victims of the
intrigues and rivalries of their betters.

Though the play was produced at the Odéon in June 1831
(where it was moderately successful, with a run of 30 performances), it had been written, with Marie Dorval in mind,
for production at the Porte-Saint-Martin, where Vigny's
mistress was currently engaged; however, the fact that *Marion
de Lorme*, set in the same period, had already been accepted at
the Porte-Saint-Martin (though production was to be deferred
until August) apparently persuaded Vigny to choose another
theatre. He therefore offered it to Harel at the Odéon, where the
Maréchale was played by Mlle George, Concini by Frédérick,
and Borgia by Ligier. Mlle George's role suited her queenly
bearing, and the interplay between the 'masculine' political
activities of the Maréchale, her maternal feelings, and her re-
awakened love for Borgia, gave her plenty of scope to display
her emotional range. Ligier managed to bring to the part of
Borgia some of the sombre Romantic fatalism that was later to
serve him in the role of Triboulet; as for Frédérick, his role
hardly allowed him enough scope for his talents: Concini was
too much the villain, quite lacking in that Romantic *panache*
which was the actor's speciality.

Vigny's style is certainly that of an author with literary pretensions—but too obviously so; M. Brun, contrasting his "style
manifestement soigné" with "le laisser-aller banal et plat

d'Alexandre Dumas"[29], is equally critical of its theatrical effectiveness. Too often the speech of Vigny's characters possesses neither the appearance of spontaneity conveyed by Dumas's dialogue at its best nor the different, but theatrically just as successful, dynamism of some of Hugo's prose rhythms; it suggests instead merely an over-careful regard for literary effect:

> ... Je veux sa mort, je veux sa mort, parce qu'il m'a ôté la vie en m'ôtant ta main. J'aime tous ses ennemis et je hais tous ses amis. J'ai épousé toutes les haines qu'il a soulevées, j'ai adopté toutes les vengeances, justes ou non, les premières venues. Mais vous, je veux vous sauver, parce que vous vous êtes souvenue de moi. Cela m'a touché. (III, iii)

Perhaps the most striking example of the inadequacy of Vigny's dialogue from the point of view of theatrical effect is provided by the closing lines. The Maréchale's false confession: "Je me confesse criminelle de lèse-majesté divine et humaine, et coupable de magie" is followed by Luynes's exclamation of triumph: "Brûlée!", by Vitry's "Messieurs, allons faire notre cour à sa Majesté le roi Louis treizième", and the play ends with Picard's enigmatic "Et nous?". The whole is too cryptic, and it is difficult to imagine that even with the additional emphasis of action and movement supplied by a producer, this ending could be anything other than a weak anti-climax.

It is a matter of speculation why Vigny chose to write *La Maréchale d'Ancre* in prose, rather than follow Hugo's lead and use the alexandrine. M. Descotes suggests that this may have resulted from the fact that the play was written for Marie Dorval, who as we have seen was a good deal happier with prose than with verse. It is difficult to agree with M. Descotes, however, that "en revenant à la prose, le drame se rapprochait dangereusement du mélodrame"[30]: with Dumas's historical plays, as we have seen, this is abundantly true, but surely not in the case of *La Maréchale d'Ancre*. Estève, also with reference to this play, similarly writes of "une action dont les péripéties semblent empruntées au plus noir mélodrame"[31]—but this view too seems difficult to accept. On the contrary, Vigny's play would have been better theatre—and not only in the superficial, almost pejorative, sense of the term—if he had been able to put into it some of the crude vigour of Dumas's melodramas. In dialogue, in structure, and in characterization, Vigny shows himself to be a man of letters rather than a man of the theatre: the search for contrived literary effects is too obvious; the composition is amateurish besides Dumas's skilled professionalism; and the characterization is over-subtle, lacking true dramatic relief. Far from suggesting melodrama, indeed, *La Maréchale d'Ancre* suggests a novelist's approach to the theatre; and while it represents an honourable attempt at genuine historical drama, of all the plays by the major Romantic playwrights it remains nearest to the formula—the faults as well as the virtues—of the 'scènes historiques' of the 1820s.

Notes to Chapter Six

1. Nebout, *op. cit.*, pp. 2–3.
2. The handlists published by C. B. Wicks (*The Parisian Stage, Part II (1816–30)*, Alabama, 1953) and by C. B. Wicks and J. W. Schweitzer (*The Parisian Stage, Part III (1831–50)*, Alabama, 1961) record more titles (34) under Dumas's name for the period 1841–50 than for the period 1826–40 (29).
3. Forty-two for the period after 1830, against sixteen for the previous period (see Wicks, *op. cit.*, and Wicks and Schweitzer, *op. cit.*).
4. Dumas's other verse plays included *Hamlet, prince de Danemarck*, adapted from Shakespeare's play in collaboration with Paul Meurice and performed at the Théâtre-Historique in December 1847, and *L'Orestie*, "imitée de l'antique", put on at the Porte-Saint-Martin in January 1856. Dumas's *Hamlet*, though in places a faithful and effective translation, is distinguished by a larger part being given to the Ghost, and by Hamlet remaining alive at the end of the play.
5. In fact, the play contains, alongside the personal drama of Bérengère, Savoisy and Yaqoub, a secondary plot illustrating the episodic structure of the 'historical chronicle'; this shows the King's relations with his people and his awakening to his responsibilities in a time of crisis.
6. Among the features which contributed to the success of the play was the visual effect of the stage décor. No doubt the choice of a single set for all five acts enabled more care to be given to the

evocation of the mediaeval setting: "Une salle gothique. Au fond, une porte ogive donnant sur une cour, entre deux croisées à vitraux coloriés. A droite du spectateur, une porte masquée par une tapisserie. A gauche, une grande cheminée; une autre porte masquée aussi par une tapisserie et donnant dans la chambre d'honneur. De chaque côté des croisées et entre les portes, des panoplies naturelles. Près de la cheminée, un prie-Dieu" (*Théâtre complet, ed. cit.*, II, p. 73); but Harel, for his part, took full advantage of the opportunity for detailed realism, borrowing suits of armour from the Musée d'Artillerie and introducing "tout un équipage de vénerie avec ses oiseaux de proie et ses chiens" (Allevy, *op. cit.*, p. 116).

7. Cf. M. Senelier, *Gérard de Nerval: essai de bibliographie*, Paris, 1959, p. 101.

8. Compare the much greater subtlety of Camus's portrait of Caligula in his play of the same name (1945).

9. These lines, anticipating the staging of the Triumphal March in *Aïda*, suggest an affinity with opera rather different from the one we have examined in the case of Hugo's plays. In practice, Dumas was forced to forgo the horses (cf. Descotes, *Le Drame . . .*, p. 313).

10. Quoted by S. Chevalley and F. Bassan, *Alexandre Dumas père et la Comédie-Française*, Paris, 1972, p. 98.

11. *Ibid.*, pp. 94–95.

12. For a consideration of the treatment of the Faust theme in this play, see C. Dédéyan, *Gérard de Nerval et l'Allemagne*, Paris, 1957–59, II, pp. 436–443.

13. Contemporary critics were generally uncomplimentary—one of them, Jules Janin, to the extent that Dumas challenged him to a duel; see Chevalley and Bassan, *op. cit.*, pp. 93–99. An exception is Théophile Gautier, who in an article on Dumas in 1841 perceptively referred to *Caligula* as "une de ses meilleures pièces injustement tombée" (*Les Maîtres du théâtre français*, ed. A. Britsch, Paris, 1929, p. 219). *Caligula* was revived in 1963 for an open-air production at the Festival de Marvejols.

14. A. Brun, *Deux Proses de théâtre*, Gap, 1954, p. 23.

15. *Ibid.*, p. 25.

16. "Le *Napoléon Bonaparte* n'est pas une œuvre littéraire... La soirée du 11 janvier 1831 n'eut que de lointains rapports avec l'art dramatique" (Descotes, *Le Drame . . .*, pp. 175, 176); "Perhaps 'Play' is not the right word to apply to *Napoléon Bonaparte*, for . . . it was rather an immense historical pageant" (Baldick, *op. cit.*, p. 89).

17. *Le Drame* . . ., p. 177.
18. *Ibid.*
19. Cf. the character of the Common Man in Bolt's *A Man for All Seasons*.
20. Dumas was to return to the 'Napoleonic legend' almost twenty years later with his 'drame militaire' *La Barrière de Clichy* (Théâtre National, April 1851). In it, Napoleon is shown returning from Elba, bringing liberty back to his people: and in an interesting 'Post-scriptum' Dumas justifies putting into the Emperor's mouth "des pensées de liberté qu'il n'avait pas dans le cœur" with the argument that "le théâtre n'est pas un cours d'histoire, mais une tribune par laquelle le poète répand et propage ses propres idées". Technically, the play is much less interesting than *Napoléon Bonaparte*: it accumulates all the sentimental clichés of patriotic melodrama.
21. *La Tour de Nesle* was one of the first examples of collaboration between Dumas and another playwright. In this case the 'collaboration' consisted in Dumas being invited by Harel to undertake the complete rewriting of a MS submitted by Gaillardet; he accepted, on condition Gaillardet received the full author's dues, and Gaillardet's name alone appeared on the posters. In spite of this, there was a protracted scandal, which ended in a duel between the two authors. For Dumas's vivid account of his relations with Gaillardet—deliberately exacerbated by Harel, in the interests of greater publicity for the play —see *Mes Mémoires*, ed. P. Josserand, Paris, V, 1968, pp. 119–170.
22. For a detailed analysis of *La Tour de Nesle*, and a perceptive appreciation of the nature of Dumas's 'drame populaire de cape et d'épée', see H. Parigot, *Le Drame d'Alexandre Dumas: étude dramatique, sociale et littéraire*, Paris, 1899, pp. 252–282.
23. Dumas tells us that his play, adapted from a contemporary novel, was first written in verse as *Édith aux longs cheveux*, rejected by the Théâtre-Français, then re-written (with a different ending, suggested by Mlle Mars) and arbitrarily transposed into the setting of Henry VIII's reign (*Mes Mémoires, ed. cit.*, V, pp. 104–111).
24. *Mlle de Belle-Isle*, for instance, produced at the Théâtre-Français in April 1839, although labelled 'drame', is really a cynical domestic comedy. Set in the early eighteenth century, it has some of the characteristics of *Paul Jones*, but with fewer Romantic clichés: it is probably nearest in spirit to Scribe's comedies like *Le Verre d'eau*.

25. See Gautier's entertaining—and indulgent—account of the opening of the Théâtre-Historique with this play (*Les Maîtres du théâtre français*, ed. cit., pp. 227–233).
26. Quoted by Parigot, *op. cit.*, p. 243.
27. Cf. Parigot's account of the documentary sources of *Le Chevalier de Maison-Rouge*, *op. cit.*, pp. 243ff.
28. For a comparison between Mélingue and the great Romantic actors of the 'first wave', Frédérick and Bocage, see Descotes, *Le Drame* . . . , pp. 337–339.
29. *Op. cit.*, p. 34.
30. *Le Drame* . . . , p. 214.
31. E. Estève, *Alfred de Vigny, sa pensée et son art*, Paris, 1923, p. 185.

7 Hugo's Prose Dramas

(i) 'Lucrèce Borgia'

Lucrèce Borgia, Hugo's first prose play since the early *Amy Robsart*, was performed at the Porte-Saint-Martin in February 1833. The Preface draws attention to the close link between this play and *Le Roi s'amuse*, acknowledging that the character of Lucrèce, like that of Triboulet, is based on an *a priori* application of the *sublime/grotesque* antithesis:

> Prenez la difformité morale la plus hideuse, la plus repoussante, la plus complète; placez-la là où elle ressort le mieux, dans le cœur d'une femme, avec toutes les conditions de beauté physique et de grandeur royale, qui donnent de la saillie au crime; et maintenant mêlez à toute cette difformité morale un sentiment pur, le plus pur que la femme puisse éprouver, le sentiment maternel; dans votre monstre, mettez une mère; et le monstre intéressera, et le monstre fera pleurer, et cette créature qui faisait peur fera pitié, et cette âme difforme deviendra presque belle à vos yeux.

Thus, "la paternité sanctifiant la difformité physique, voilà *Le Roi s'amuse*; la maternité purifiant la difformité morale, voilà *Lucrèce Borgia*". Lucrèce in fact stands, as a dramatic creation, somewhere between Triboulet and Marion de Lorme. Though the monstrous nature of her "difformité"—the crimes of the legendary poisoner—makes her less humanly sympathetic than Marion, the antithesis is less contrived than in the case of Triboulet: the two elements do not strike us as being incompatible, and they remain in effective contrast throughout the play (whereas with Triboulet, as we have seen, although his *physical* deformity is of course a permanent feature, the *moral* depravity, which is much more important, disappears at the end of Act I to leave the field clear for the idealized sentiment of paternal love).

There is another obvious source for *Lucrèce Borgia*, besides the link with *Le Roi s'amuse* and with the theoretical programme set out in the *Préface de Cromwell*. Reminiscences of *La Tour de Nesle*, produced nine months earlier, and one of the great successes of Romantic drama so far, are much too close to be coincidental; and it seems clear that Hugo, whether entirely deliberately or not, was copying certain features of Dumas's successful formula. As a result, there is a close parallelism of plot. The central mother/son relationship is essentially similar: a relationship of which the son in both cases remains in ignorance until the closing lines of the play; though the fact that Marguerite does not learn until the end of the play that Gaultier, whom she loves, is her son, gives *La Tour de Nesle* the added spice of the incest-motif, whereas Lucrèce has always known the identity of Gennaro, and has watched over his fortunes from a distance. The dénouements, though not identical, follow a similar pattern: Gaultier is killed in an ambush intended for Buridan, his father, and dies cursing his mother, while Gennaro, cursing Lucrèce Borgia (whom he does not yet know as his mother), kills her to avenge his dead friends; Marguerite's "Malheureux, malheureux! je suis ta mère" matches the "Gennaro, je suis ta mère" of the dying Lucrèce. Various subsidiary features, too, bear a striking resemblance: Gennaro and Buridan are both unknown adventurers; the 'frères d'armes' Philippe and Buridan correspond to a similar pair in Gennaro and Maffio; the faithful servant Gubetta matches the discreet and faithful Orsini; and even the Tiber, at the beginning of Hugo's play, is given a role similar to that of the Seine in *La Tour de Nesle*[1].

The role of Lucrèce was conceived by Hugo for Mlle George, who had recently scored such a triumph as the "Messaline bourguignonne". *Lucrèce Borgia* offered her the same blend of violent passion and elegiac remorse as Dumas's heroine had done; and both Dumas and Hugo succeeded far better than had Vigny, when creating the not dissimilar role of the Maréchale d'Ancre, in capturing that indefinable quality which allows a stage character to come to life. As for Frédérick's role of Gennaro, though a relatively modest part, this suited Frédérick's talent, providing an eminently Romantic mixture of action and brooding mystery. The combination of Frédérick and Mlle George thoroughly satisfied Hugo:

> M. Frédérick a réalisé avec génie le Gennaro que l'auteur avait rêvé. M. Frédérick est élégant et familier, il est plein de fatalité et plein de grâce, il est redoutable et doux; il est enfant et il est homme; il charme et il épouvante; il est modeste, sévère et terrible. Mademoiselle George réunit également au degré le plus rare les qualités diverses et quelquefois même opposées que son rôle exige... Elle fait applaudir et elle fait pleurer. Elle est sublime comme Hécube et touchante comme Desdémona.[2]

Indeed, on this occasion he had every reason to be satisfied with his choice of the Porte-Saint-Martin:

> Il n'est pas de troupe à Paris qui comprenne mieux que celle de la Porte-Saint-Martin la mystérieuse loi de perspective suivant laquelle doit se mouvoir et s'étager au théâtre ce groupe de personnages passionnés ou ironiques qui noue et dénoue un drame.[3]

The play had a successful run of two months, but it was taken off while still a commercial success, and Hugo was no doubt justified in suspecting collusion between Harel and Frédérick, by now tired of playing a secondary role, for the play which replaced *Lucrèce Borgia* was one which had provided the actor with one of his early triumphs, *L'Auberge des Adrets*[4]. In fact, Harel later admitted that "le plus grand succès d'argent obtenu sous mon administration est celui de *Lucrèce Borgia*"[5], and this was probably the high point of Hugo's relations with the world of the theatre.

It would be only reasonable, however, to consider what concessions to popular taste Hugo had had to make in order to achieve this kind of success at the Porte-Saint-Martin. Had the playwright been forced to lower his sights in writing a prose drama for a boulevard theatre, or is the formula still the same as that of the verse plays which had preceded *Lucrèce Borgia*? Certain scenes, it is true, do seem to betray more clearly their affinity with melodrama: the sequence in Act III, for instance, has a markedly gothic inspiration, with its procession of hooded monks chanting the mass for the dead, and the sudden disclosure of the row of open coffins. The exposition is unashamedly artificial:

> Savez-vous, madame, que je ne vous comprends plus, et que, depuis quelque temps, vous êtes devenue indéchiffrable pour moi? Il y a un mois, votre Altesse annonce qu'elle part pour Spolète, prend congé de monseigneur Alphonse d'Este, votre mari, qui a, du reste, la bonhomie d'être amoureux de vous comme un tourtereau et jaloux comme un tigre; votre Altesse donc quitte Ferrare, et s'en vient secrètement à Venise, presque sans suite, affublée d'un faux nom napolitain, et moi d'un faux nom espagnol. Arrivée à Venise, votre Altesse se sépare de moi, et m'ordonne de ne pas la connaître... (I, iii)

And the scenic effects generally are perhaps cruder than those of the verse plays: masks and disguises abound; there is much 'business' with poison and antidote; and such *coups de théâtre* as Gennaro's "Il en faut un sixième, madame!" (III, ii) as he steps out of the shadows to take his place by the side of his five friends, poisoned by Lucrèce at supper, and to claim an extra coffin, are worthy of Dumas at his best[6].

But if some contemporaries deplored these melodramatic excesses:

> M. Victor Hugo est trop juste pour ne pas nous permettre en finissant de regretter ce temps de chasteté de l'art et de virginité du public, où on sortait plus effrayé de ce simple vers:
>> Elle a fait expirer un esclave à mes yeux,
> que de ces sept cadavres empoisonnés et de ces pompes funèbres[7]

—there were others who situated the play in a different tradition, and stressed similarities between *Lucrèce Borgia* and Voltaire's tragedies *Mérope* and *Sémiramis*[8]. The following comment by Gautier probably does justice to the two points of view:

> En 1833, ivres de lyrisme, fous de poésie, nous étions moins sensibles au drame et à la situation scénique; mais si la

pièce alla aux nues, c'est peut-être justement qu'elle plaisait aux romantiques par sa couleur et aux classiques par la construction régulière qu'ils y trouvaient.[9]

As for Hugo's prose dialogue, this is marked neither by the banality of a Dumas nor by the scholarly effort of a Vigny. As one would expect from the style of his other prose works, whether imaginative, theoretical or polemical, it is a 'style à effets'—effects which must be presumed to have succeeded in the theatre. Even where the dialogue fails to ring true to the reader, forced to rely on the printed page—for instance in the much praised passage:

— Ah! prenez garde à vous, don Alphonse de Ferrare, mon quatrième mari!

— Oh! ne faites pas la terrible, madame! Sur mon âme je ne vous crains pas! Je sais vos allures. Je ne me laisserai pas empoisonner comme votre premier mari, ce pauvre gentil-homme d'Espagne dont je ne sais plus le nom, ni vous non plus! Je ne me laisserai pas chasser comme votre second mari, Jean Sforza, seigneur de Pessaro, cet imbécile! Je ne me laisserai pas tuer à coups de pique, sur n'importe quel escalier, comme le troisième, don Alphonse d'Aragon, faible enfant dont le sang n'a guère plus taché les dalles que de l'eau pure! Tout beau! Moi je suis homme, madame. Le nom d'Hercule est souvent porté dans ma famille. Par le ciel! j'ai des soldats plein ma ville et plein ma seigneurie, et j'en suis un moi-même, et je n'ai point encore vendu, comme ce pauvre roi de Naples, mes bons canons d'artillerie au pape, votre saint père! (II, iv)

—it has a crude vigour, and above all a clear-cut rhetorical structure which, if they cannot disguise the absurdity or the banality of much of the content, at least enabled Hugo to impose this melodramatic material on a theatre audience. The same repetition, balance and antithesis that lend force to the argument of his Prefaces recur throughout his prose dialogue, at any moment of heightened tension—together with that favourite device of the rhetorician, the ternary phrase, which in its various forms occurs so frequently as to become a veritable obsession. Normally used to give urgency, poignancy or argumentative emphasis to the utterances of a principal character:

> Gubetta! Gubetta! S'il y avait aujourd'hui en Italie, dans
> cette fatale et criminelle Italie, un cœur noble et pur, un
> cœur plein de hautes et de mâles vertus, un cœur d'ange sous
> une cuirasse de soldat; s'il ne me restait, à moi, pauvre
> femme, haïe, méprisée, abhorrée, maudite des hommes,
> damnée du ciel, misérable toute-puissante que je suis; s'il ne
> me restait, dans l'état de détresse où mon âme agonise
> douloureusement, qu'une idée, qu'une espérance, qu'une
> ressource, celle de mériter et d'obtenir avant ma mort une
> petite place, Gubetta, un peu de tendresse, un peu d'estime
> dans ce cœur si fier et si pur; si je n'avais d'autre pensée que
> l'ambition de le sentir battre un jour joyeusement et libre-
> ment sur le mien; comprendrais-tu alors, Gubetta, pourquoi
> j'ai hâte de racheter mon passé, de laver ma renommée,
> d'effacer les taches de toutes sortes que j'ai partout sur moi,
> et de changer en une idée de gloire, de pénitence et de vertu,
> l'idée infâme et sanglante que l'Italie attache à mon nom?
> (I, iii)

—the ternary structure becomes so habitual that we find it adopted quite mechanically, and without much obvious point, by other speakers:

> Vous avez métamorphosé votre nom, vous avez métamor-
> phosé votre habit, à présent vous métamorphosez votre
> âme. (I, iii)

This may perhaps not seem very far removed from the sort of over-emphatic dialogue that we have remarked on in the case of Pixérécourt's characters; and it is certainly a feature that the reader tends to find irritating on the printed page. However, it is not difficult to recognize in such features the idiosyncratic touch which distinguished Hugo's dialogue from that of the unambitious Dumas and the over-fastidious Vigny; and it was surely this that was appreciated by the spectators at the Porte-Saint-Martin:

> La Porte-Saint-Martin, voilà le vrai pays de l'art moderne!...
> Placée précisément au point d'intersection de ce qu'on

appelle le monde, son public mélange en soi l'intelligence des classes instruites et la sincérité de la foule, dans la proportion nécessaire pour que la pédanterie et la naïveté se corrigent l'une par l'autre.[10]

With a talented company and a director possessing a marked flair for showmanship, the Porte-Saint-Martin may seem to us to have offered Hugo (as well as Dumas) just the theatre he needed. But as will be seen, the clash of strong personalities was such as to make a stable relationship between Harel and Hugo impossible.

(ii) 'Marie Tudor'

IT was during the preliminary stages of rehearsals for *Lucrèce Borgia* that Hugo's attention was first caught by an actress newly engaged at the Porte-Saint-Martin. Though his first contact with Juliette Drouet gave little promise of their lifelong relationship[11], Hugo was soon won over to the extent of writing some extra lines of dialogue for the small part of the Princess Negroni that she was to play. By the time of Hugo's next play, *Marie Tudor* (also produced at the Porte-Saint-Martin, in November 1833), their liaison was well established, and alongside the central role of the Queen, again written for Mlle George, the new play included a substantial part, that of Jane, the Queen's rival in love, written for Juliette. Hugo's error of judgement in encouraging his mistress to take on a part which was well beyond her capabilities was one of the things which, during the rehearsals and production of *Marie Tudor*, helped to bring his relations with Harel near to breaking-point (they had already once been on the point of fighting a duel, during the run of *Lucrèce Borgia*[12]). In this particular instance, Harel had the foresight to have an understudy standing by; and indeed, after Juliette's lamentable failure in the opening performance, it was diplomatically announced that she had had a "serious indisposition", and she was relieved of her part in favour of Ida Ferrier.

This was not the only conflict of personalities: Hugo's protection of Juliette gave rise to jealousy on the part both of Mlle George and of Bocage, who was to play Gilbert. Hugo could not afford to risk losing his Queen, but the dispute which

ensued with Bocage led to the part being taken from this actor
and offered to Lockroy (who had been Dumas's Gaultier in *La
Tour de Nesle*). As a result of all this, even before the first performance of *Marie Tudor*, Harel was already planning to let
Hugo down and switch his allegiance to Dumas, and even went
so far as to print playbills with the title of Hugo's play in
smaller letters than that of Dumas's *Angèle*, which was to follow
it. In spite of these manoeuvres, and of the customary hostility
on the part of the press, *Marie Tudor* was quite well received,
and "eut un nombre de représentations plus qu'honorable"[13].
But it was clear that further collaboration between Hugo and
the Porte-Saint-Martin was out of the question, and by mutual
agreement the contract obliging Hugo to offer his next play to
Harel was cancelled[14].

Whatever concessions Hugo had had to make to a boulevard
audience in *Lucrèce Borgia*, that play had still been the work of a
poet. The central character had been a recognizable product of
the visionary's intuitive recognition, beneath the outward
surface of life, of those contrasts and conflicts which, for him,
formed the essence of poetic drama; and if we find it impossible
to identify with Lucrèce in the way that we do with Hernani or
Marion, nevertheless the horror that this character evokes is not
entirely without an accompanying element of pathos. Altogether, therefore, it is possible to understand, even if not to
share, the view of those contemporaries for whom the prose of
Lucrèce Borgia succeeded in carrying Romantic tragedy to the
same heights as Hugo's verse plays[15]. But with *Marie Tudor*, one
cannot but feel that Hugo has set his sights much lower, for the
level of artistic achievement is unquestionably inferior.

That *Marie Tudor* is a travesty of historical fact should not
surprise us; this is a feature of the play, in any case, to which
French readers and spectators might be expected to be less
sensitive than English. For what it is worth, however, the
portrait of Mary Tudor here given, with her scandalous
attachment to an Italian favourite, is at variance with every
account of her that has come down from contemporary sources;
Fabiano Fabiani is a product of Hugo's imagination, as are
Jane, the humble orphan girl whom he has seduced (he is
aware, though she is not, that she is the daughter of the dead
Lord Talbot, whose wealth and estates have been conferred on

him) and Gilbert, the simple, loyal man of the people who loves
Jane and wins her love. In other words, the plot is a gratuitous
creation of the author's fancy, and the impressive list of documentary sources Hugo gives in the 'Notes' to the 1837 Brussels
edition of the play is pure window-dressing. At best, one might
perhaps attempt to make out a case for a more diffuse sort of
historical 'colour' in default of accuracy as regards detail[16]. But
even here, comparison with any of Hugo's other plays is to
the disadvantage of *Marie Tudor*: place-names, family-names,
customs of nobility and people are all, if not the product of, at
least likely to have been distorted by, the author's fantasy.

Nor is the lack of historical verisimilitude redeemed by any
essential poetic quality possessed by the protagonists, deriving
from Hugo's characteristic *sublime/grotesque* antithesis. Whereas
this had been true even with Lucrèce, who had carried conviction as an imaginative creation, such compensation is lacking in
Marie; if she represents the familiar Hugolian antithesis at all,
it is only very feebly. There is no relief given to the character by
this or any other means: she is a two-dimensional villain of
melodrama, posturing and ranting in a most gratuitous manner,
with little attempt to make her actions plausible. Fabiani is
likewise taken straight from the tradition of melodrama, with
asides to the audience ("Il importe qu'il rentre chez lui et qu'il
cherche querelle à Jane, cela donnera à mes gens temps
d'arriver" ... "Il ne faut pas que le soleil de demain se lève
pour cet homme" (I, vii)) and other sinister touches under-
scoring this portrait of unrelieved black. Gilbert, on the other
hand, with his self-effacing devotion to Jane, is possibly over-
idealized in the other direction; and the only character at all
nuancé is that of Jane. Her weakness is plausible (though since
Fabiani is so openly evil whenever he appears during the play,
we do not find it easy to believe in the subtler blandishments by
which he has managed to overcome her virtue), and she is a
pathetic portrait of human frailty. But Jane is a passive character, and the action which goes on around her is a thoroughly
melodramatic clash between black and white.

The action is supported, too, by the subsidiary trappings of
the popular genre: the romanesque story of Jane's origins,
brought to Gilbert as a baby by an unknown man, with a note
written in blood pinned to her clothes: "Ayez pitié de Jane";

the equally romanesque secret of her true birth, revealed by a
mysterious omniscient Jew; the string of coincidences by which
Fabiani is trapped; and above all the figure of Simon Renard,
the Emperor's envoy, manipulating the other characters right
up to his curtain-line. The Queen and Jane, in a scene of high
dramatic tension, are waiting for proof of the identity of the
man who has gone to the scaffold, when Renard enters, leading
Gilbert by the hand (there is no explanation of how he has
saved Gilbert and substituted Fabiani):

La Reine: Et Fabiano?

Simon Renard: Mort.

La Reine: Mort?... Mort! Qui a osé?...

Simon Renard: Moi. J'ai sauvé la reine et l'Angleterre.

Finally, the language is for the most part devoid of poetic
suggestiveness; instead, we have the same rhetorical excesses as
in *Lucrèce Borgia*, but in a much cruder form. The harsh,
strident tirades of the Queen alienate all sympathy:

Ah! tu le prends ainsi! Ah! je suis bonne et douce, et je
pleure avec toi, et voilà que tu deviens folle et furieuse! Ah!
mon amour est aussi grand que le tien, et ma main est plus
forte que la tienne. Tu ne bougeras pas. Ah! ton amant!
Que m'importe ton amant? Est-ce que toutes les filles
d'Angleterre vont venir me demander compte de leurs
amants, maintenant? Pardieu! je sauve le mien comme je
peux et au dépens de qui se trouve là. Veillez sur les vôtres!
(III (2), ii)

Even Jane's outbursts follow too mechanically the predictable
rhythms of Hugo's 'style à effets':

Madame, par pitié! madame, au nom du ciel! madame, par
votre couronne, par votre mère, par les anges! Gilbert!
Gilbert! cela me rend folle! Madame, sauvez Gilbert! cet
homme, c'est ma vie; cet homme, c'est mon mari; cet
homme... je viens de vous dire qu'il a tout fait pour moi,
qu'il m'a élevée, qu'il m'a adoptée, qu'il a remplacé près de
mon berceau mon père qui est mort pour votre mère... (*ibid.*)

—and the only exception is the sudden revelation by Gilbert of a depth of feeling that impresses by its eloquent simplicity:

> ... Si on m'avait dit il y a un mois: Jane, votre Jane sans tache, votre Jane si pure, votre amour, votre orgueil, votre lys, votre trésor, Jane se donnera à un autre; en voudrez-vous après? — j'aurais dit: Non, je n'en voudrai pas! plutôt mille fois la mort pour elle et pour moi! Et j'aurais foulé sous mes pieds celui qui m'eût parlé ainsi. — Eh bien! si, j'en veux! — Aujourd'hui, vois-tu bien, Jane n'est plus la Jane sans tache qui avait mon admiration, la Jane dont je n'osais à peine effleurer le front de mes lèvres, Jane s'est donnée à un autre, à un misérable, je le sais, eh bien, c'est égal, je l'aime! J'ai le cœur brisé, mais je l'aime! Je baiserais le bas de sa robe, et je lui demanderais pardon si elle voulait de moi...
> (III (1), i)

This scene, and Gilbert's scene with Jane (III (1), vii)—though the latter is spoiled in places by rhetorical over-emphasis—carry genuine conviction, particularly after the hollow posturing of the scenes between Marie and Fabiani.

It is these scenes—Gilbert's quasi-monologue, and the scenes *à deux* between the Queen and Fabiani, Gilbert and Jane, and Jane and the Queen—which offered Hugo his only chance of redeeming the melodramatic excesses of his plot and the crudity of his characterization. In his verse dramas, as we have seen, such scenes are handled in an 'operatic' manner like solos and duets, exploiting the emotional potential in a highly figurative, imaginative style—a style which, at the same time as it transcends the banalities of prose, helps us to transcend the absurdities of the plot. Here, no such compensating factor exists; and the static moments which call for imaginative treatment by Hugo the poet are instead handled for the most part with the insensitive bombast and the crude bathos of melodramatic prose.

(iii) 'Angelo'

THE third and last of Hugo's group of prose dramas, *Angelo, tyran de Padoue*, was staged at the Théâtre-Français in April 1835. In the Preface, the playwright develops the idea animating his play;

Mettre en présence, dans une action toute résultante du cœur, deux graves et douloureuses figures, la femme dans la société, la femme hors de la société; c'est-à-dire, en deux types vivants, toutes les femmes, toute la femme...

In other words, if *sublime/grotesque* antithesis within a single character still finds expression here in the courtesan Tisbe, this play depends much more on opposition between two contrasting characters, those of Tisbe and Catarina. Descotes assures us that the part of Catarina, "une autre Jane", was originally conceived for Juliette Drouet[17]; but by the time the play was completed, and accepted by the Théâtre-Français, it was an essential feature of the agreement that the two parts should be played by the real-life rivals Dorval and Mlle Mars. While Mlle Mars was now in her mid-fifties, and had been a *sociétaire* since 1799, Marie Dorval had been admitted to the Théâtre-Français only in 1834, fresh from her triumphs at the Porte-Saint-Martin. She had scored a great success in *Chatterton*, but in the face of much opposition from conservative colleagues and journalists. Mlle Mars's campaign against her had begun during the run of *Chatterton*; and rehearsals and performances of *Angelo* were marked by jealousy and resentment frequently translated into acts of malice. Mlle Mars herself, as befitted her seniority, had been offered the choice between the two roles, and it may well be, as Mme Hugo suggests, that the choice she made was dictated by a desire to deprive Dorval of the one she thought more suited to her rival's talents:

Catarina, mariée, chaste, convenait à merveille au talent honnête et décent de Mlle Mars; mais la Tisbe, fille des rues, violente, déréglée, semblait faite pour le talent bohème et libre de Mme Dorval. Mlle Mars préféra donc la Tisbe.[18]

Whatever we may think of Mme Hugo's opinion of the two roles, and of Mars's likely motivation, it seems nevertheless to be the case that of the two, that of Catarina contains more features of 'le style Dorval', that familiar, prosaic style in which declamatory rhetoric is replaced by intimate apostrophe:

Vois-tu, il ne faut pas t'étonner si je n'ai pas tout de suite sauté à ton cou, c'est que j'ai été saisie. O Dieu, quand j'ai entendu ta voix, je ne puis pas te dire, je ne savais plus où j'étais. Voyons, assieds-toi là, tu sais, comme autrefois... (II, iv)

Though Tisbe's manner also contains such moments:

> Oh! c'est que je suis jalouse de toi, moi, vois-tu? mais jalouse... (I, ii)

her role covers a much wider range, and contains at the other extreme passages of genuine tragic exaltation. Indeed, the opposition between the two characters, "la femme dans la société" and "la femme hors de la société", however strongly it may have been present in the author's mind, does not come across precisely in these terms in the play itself. As Nebout perceptively remarks:

> Le défaut dans ces créations de courtisanes vertueuses, c'est que le poète ne montre pas assez la courtisane pour que son personnage ait deux faces... On nous fera avouer facilement que des courtisanes comme Tisbe sont bien intéressantes et dignes d'être aimées; mais nous nierons que des femmes comme Tisbe soient, puissent être des courtisanes... Le caractère de Tisbe est un caractère tragique quelconque, affublé d'une robe de courtisane.[19]

In the case of Marion de Lorme, or of Dumas *fils*'s Marguerite Gautier, we are made sufficiently aware of the conventions of the society portrayed for the equivocal position of the kept woman, on which both dramas depend, to be meaningful; here, on the other hand, Hugo has neglected to make Tisbe's social position really clear, so that her tirade:

> Ce que c'est que ceci, Madame? C'est une comédienne, une fille de théâtre, une baladine, comme vous nous appelez, qui tient dans ses mains, je viens de vous le dire, une grande dame, une femme mariée, une femme respectée, une vertu! qui la tient dans ses mains, dans ses ongles, dans ses dents! qui peut en faire ce qu'elle voudra de cette grande dame, de cette bonne renommée dorée, et qui va la déchirer, la mettre

en pièces, la mettre en lambeaux, la mettre en morceaux!...
(II, v)

seems to be lacking in credibility. It may perhaps not be of
great importance that the sociological reference of the play
misfires in this way: the sharp contrast between the two female
characters still comes across strongly in purely dramatic terms.
But it does mean that the claim Hugo makes in his Preface
loses much of its specific force, for it is in respect of *Angelo* that
the playwright makes his most stirring appeal, if not for *littérature engagée*, at least for a form of drama with a strong moral,
or didactic, element:

> On ne saurait trop le redire, pour quiconque a médité sur les
> besoins de la société, auxquels doivent toujours correspondre
> les tentatives de l'art, aujourd'hui, plus que jamais, le
> théâtre est un lieu d'enseignement. Le drame, comme l'auteur
> de cet ouvrage voudrait le faire, et comme le pourrait faire
> un homme de génie, doit donner à la foule une philosophie,
> aux idées une formule, à la poésie des muscles, du sang et de
> la vie, à ceux qui pensent une explication désintéressée, aux
> âmes altérées un breuvage, aux plaies secrètes un baume, à
> chacun un conseil, à tous une loi. [20]

In many ways, this was potentially the best of the three prose
plays. It has a much simpler plot, which concentrates on a
simple pattern of basic human relationships. Catarina and
Rodolfo have loved each other several years earlier, before
Catarina was forced to marry the *podesta* Angelo of Padua; they
have recently met again secretly, but Rodolfo is now loved by
the passionately jealous Tisbe, who is the official mistress of
Angelo. Here we have a pattern which can be expressed by the
same formula as many a seventeenth-century tragedy, including
most notably Racine's *Phèdre*: A loves B, who loves C, who loves
and is loved by D. Given that the B of this formula is a strong,
passionate character (and this is the case with Tisbe just as
much as with Phèdre), the constituents of violent drama stand
prepared, waiting for the catalyst. It is true that in Hugo's play
the catalyst is a rather melodramatic villain, Homodei, who
has discovered the relationship between Catarina and Rodolfo,

and who informs Tisbe in order to destroy the lovers; while the means of vengeance and summary punishment employed by Angelo are further features resembling the stock trappings of melodrama. Nevertheless, these melodramatic accessories can be said to be largely justified by the political situation in Padua, a police state controlled by the despotic Angelo, who is himself subject to the arbitrary power of the Council of Ten at Venice, represented by sinister agents such as Homodei. And in any case, the central relationships between the four characters are what matters; these are strong enough to outweigh subsidiary features of plot, and the latter serve merely to create suspense and tension, as we await what seems the inevitable outcome of a convincingly human drama.

More than either *Lucrèce Borgia* or *Marie Tudor*, therefore, *Angelo* makes us wonder why Hugo should have chosen to write some of his plays in prose. Here, characterization is plausible, and the dramatic force of the opposition between Catarina and Tisbe is quite impressive; there is little of the obtrusive gimmickry that we find in some of Hugo's other plays; and all that is lacking, to produce a Romantic tragedy of the same stature as *Hernani* or *Marion de Lorme*, is dramatic verse with the same degree of inspiration, the same imaginative power, that Hugo had achieved in these two plays.

The last scene of *Angelo* in particular seems ready-made for the 'operatic' treatment characteristic of Hugo's verse dramas. Tisbe has saved Catarina from her husband's revenge (having herself set the train of events in motion, she desists when she recognizes Catarina as the daughter of the noblewoman who had saved the life of her mother), and has made it possible for the lovers to flee together. Catarina has been given a sleeping-draught instead of the poison Angelo intended, and she is now lying on Tisbe's bed, with the curtains drawn; we know that she is due to regain consciousness at any moment. Rodolfo, however, does not share our knowledge: he thinks that Tisbe has been instrumental in bringing about Catarina's death, and comes to upbraid her with her treachery. Mortified by his scorn, Tisbe does not seek to enlighten him, but instead taunts him, deliberately inviting him to kill her. No sooner has he stabbed her than Catarina wakes, and Tisbe, her sacrifice now complete, dies in the arms of the man whom she has forced to kill her because he will not return her love. This could have been a tragic dénouement as sublime as any Hugo wrote: instead, it remains quite unmoving, not because the motivation of the characters' actions is not plausible, but because of the utter banality of the dialogue.

"Du sublime au ridicule il n'y a qu'un pas": we have examined scenes in Hugo's verse dramas in which a bizarre situation is redeemed by the imaginative quality of the writing; here is the negative proof of the same axiom, for from the moment of Rodolfo's entry there is a bathetic incongruity between the solemnity of the situation and the triviality and familiarity of what the characters say:

> D'où venez-vous? De quoi êtes-vous pâle? Qu'avez-vous fait aujourd'hui, dites? Qu'est-ce que ces mains-là ont fait, dites? où avez-vous passé les exécrables heures de cette journée, dites? Non, ne le dites pas. Je vais le dire. Ne répondez pas, ne niez pas, n'inventez pas, ne mentez pas. Je sais tout! Je sais tout, vous dis-je! Vous voyez bien que je sais tout, madame... (III (2), iii)

It would be pointless to repeat here the thorough analysis of the language of *Angelo* carried out by Brun[21]; but a careful reading of the three plays certainly supports this author's observation that Hugo, "loin de renouveler ses procédés, les accuse, les aggrave par accumulations massives, les emploie avec une continuité systématique"[22]. Language hardly varies from one character to another; there are very few images; and the vocabulary has none of the rich and colourful quality we associate with Hugo. The impact of the dialogue depends almost entirely on the phrasing: it is the same rhetorical manner, adapted from his non-dramatic works, that we have studied in the case of *Lucrèce Borgia* and *Marie Tudor*, but here used with even less discrimination.

It is perhaps not too difficult to account for the fact that the two preceding plays were written in prose. Both had been written for the Porte-Saint-Martin after Hugo's quarrel with the Théâtre-Français over *Le Roi s'amuse*, and in the words of P. and V. Glachant: "il ne pouvait songer à donner des vers au public ordinaire de ce théâtre"[23]. Admittedly, *Marion de*

Lorme had been staged at the same theatre, but as we have argued above, this had been an unfortunate error on Hugo's part. Now, when he had decided to try his fortunes at the Théâtre-Français again, to have written *Angelo* in prose seems to have been another glaring error of judgement. If the Glachants are correct in suggesting that this was a matter of doctrinaire decision:

> Il s'agissait de conquérir au romantisme, non plus le *public*, mais le *peuple*. C'est sur cette antithèse que se clôt la Préface d'*Angelo*. A nulle époque, Hugo ne fut plus préoccupé de ce qu'il appelait la *vertu éducatrice* du théâtre. Il fallait une scène-tribune pour ces drames-enseignements. Et comment prendre de l'influence sur ce public — ou plutôt sur ce peuple — en lui servant des couplets lyriques, trop fins et délicats pour son entendement?[24]

we must regretfully conclude that it was a decision that was hardly justified by the results. As an example of 'drame-enseignement', *Angelo* completely fails to impress; and by writing it in prose, Hugo threw away the chance of creating another powerful lyrical tragedy in verse.

(iv) Summary

PROSE drama, or melodrama? Hugo's contemporaries were already exercised by the problem of distinguishing between the two genres. Does such a distinction really exist, or was Hugo's dramatic formula, deprived of the adventitious prestige of the alexandrine, no different from that of Pixérécourt? The dramatist Ponsard makes a careful attempt to define the two genres, in the following terms:

> J'appellerai *drame* toute pièce qui se préoccupera surtout de représenter des caractères, de développer des passions, ou de résumer l'esprit et les mœurs d'un siècle, en les personnifiant dans les grands hommes de l'époque, et qui subordonnera l'intrigue à cette idée dominante. Toute pièce, au contraire, qui ne cherchera qu'à étonner et émouvoir le spectateur, par la succession rapide des aventures et l'imprévu des péripéties, sera un *mélodrame*. Chacune de ces œuvres a ses lois particulières, qu'il est nécessaire d'observer.

P. and V. Glachant, quoting this passage with approval, are in no doubt that the three plays of the middle 1830s qualify for the label of 'mélodrame' rather than for that of 'drame'; and they go on to trace Hugo's fondness for this popular genre back to the impressions left on the nine-year-old boy by seven consecutive visits to Pixérécourt's *Ruines de Babylone*, performed by an itinerant troupe at Bayonne[25]. The early *Inez de Castro*, as well as *Amy Robsart*, are very much in Pixérécourt's manner; and when circumstances forced him to turn to the Porte-Saint-Martin in 1833, it was only natural for him to recognize and to adopt "les enfants abandonnés de son génie naissant"[26].

This is an over-simplification, if only because it takes no account of Hugo's intentions. For between *Inez de Castro* and *Amy Robsart* on the one hand, and the prose plays of the 1830s on the other, had come the *Préface de Cromwell*; and there seems to be no doubt that the formula for Romantic drama there established, which agrees with Ponsard's definition in subordinating melodramatic trappings of plot to what the latter calls "caractères, ...passions, ...l'esprit et les mœurs d'un siècle", is a guide to the playwright's intentions in writing the prose plays as well as those in verse.

Dumas, it will be remembered, was to make a frank admission with regard to the relationship between subject and setting in his historical plays ("Je commence par combiner une fable..."[27]); and it is likely that, if pressed, Hugo too would have had to admit that in some cases 'tableau' took priority over 'cadre'. But whereas for Dumas it is the 'fable'—plot for plot's sake—which constitutes the 'tableau', what counts for Hugo is the portrayal of character according to a philosophical formula. Thus in plays like *Lucrèce Borgia* or *Marie Tudor* we are even less concerned than we are in a Dumas play with the specificness of the given historical situation: however much Hugo may assure us of the contrary by reference to documentary 'sources', the historical setting is there merely to give tangible embodiment to a character preconceived in the abstract according to the laws of the Hugolian dialectic. *Lucrèce Borgia* perhaps illustrates more clearly than any other of his plays the way in which this dialectic operates, in order to bring about the inevitable catastrophe. The construction of this play is classical, in that the two antithetical terms of Hugo's formula, 'la difformité' and 'la maternité', can no longer exist in a state of equilibrium: the only synthesis possible is a destructive one. This tragic resolution is the *quod erat demonstrandum* of Hugo's drama; but whether each case works out in practice as sublime tragedy or something nearer to the bathos of melodrama depends on various ancillary features, and above all on literary style.

The verse dramas, even at their most melodramatic (in *Ruy Blas* and in *Le Roi s'amuse*), contain compensating factors in the shape of lyrical passages whose imaginative quality enables us to forget the crudity of the dramatic contrivances; while Hugo's best plays, *Hernani* and *Marion de Lorme*, build up to such an intensity of genuine feeling that we cease to protest at the melodramatic nature of some of the features we have encountered on the way to the tragic dénouement. We have seen that the style of the prose plays does not succeed in reproducing the imaginative, lyrical qualities of the verse dramas: imagery is too rare, vocabulary too functional, and Hugo comes to rely almost exclusively (this is a tendency which becomes more pronounced in *Angelo*) on the repetitive rhythms of a literary prose that he had developed in his novels, essays and prefaces. At best this gives a crude, synthetic vigour to his dialogue; at worst it is a means of reinforcing its banality. Though it would hardly be true to say that the choice of a cruder linguistic vehicle impairs the primacy of character (the 'caractères' and 'passions' of Ponsard's formula) over plot, it does mean that in the prose plays characterization is much less subtle, and more reminiscent of the black-and-white delineation of melodrama.

There remains one other distinguishing feature, not specifically formulated by Ponsard, but which seems to be implicit in his definition: that is, the presence in genuine Romantic drama of an animating ideology, of that philosophical impulse whose importance Hugo stresses in the Preface to *Angelo*:

Laissez-vous charmer par le drame, mais que la leçon soit dedans, et qu'on puisse toujours l'y retrouver quand on voudra disséquer cette belle chose vivante, si ravissante, si poétique, si passionnée, si magnifiquement vêtue d'or, de soie et de velours. Dans le beau drame, il doit toujours y avoir une idée sévère, comme dans la plus belle femme il y a un squelette.

In spite of the grandiloquence that Hugo devotes, from the *Préface de Cromwell* onwards, to proclaiming the 'philosophical' content of his theatre, this is the vaguest, and least convincing, of his claims. Not that there is not a valid distinction to be drawn on the grounds of thought-content between melodrama and Romantic drama of more serious literary pretensions: this is probably, in the final analysis, the most important distinction, subsuming all the others. But it is important to be very clear what we mean by the 'philosophical' content of Hugo's dramas. If we mean that they have something of the capacity of all serious art to stimulate reflection in the mind of the reader or spectator, to offer us new insights, or to develop our awareness of the world about us, that is one thing; but to claim, as Hugo himself does in the Preface to *Ruy Blas*, that his plays contain a specific historical lesson, or as he does in the Prefaces to *Marie Tudor* and *Angelo*, that they offer a positive moral philosophy, is something quite different. The thought-content of these plays which matters is the fruit of the intuitive insights of Hugo the poet, not of the deliberations of a systematic thinker. It follows that the greater the imaginative power of the writing, the more capable Hugo's plays are of inducing reflective thought in reader or spectator; while paradoxically *Angelo*, the play on which Hugo bases his most forthright claim for the theatre as a 'lieu d'enseignement', has least to offer. For a more effective interpretation of the notion of didactic theatre during this period, we must look to dramatists other than Hugo.

Notes to Chapter Seven

1. For further aspects of the comparison between the two plays, see Descotes, *Le Drame . . .* , pp. 247–248.
2. *Note* published with the first edition of the play in 1833.
3. *Ibid.*
4. See Baldick, *op. cit.*, p. 123.
5. In a letter of November 1841, quoted by Sleumer, *op. cit.*, p. 149.
6. The parodists had a field-day with *Lucrèce Borgia*; cf. *L'Ogresse Gorgia*, and *Tigresse Mort-aux-rats, ou Poison et contrepoison, médecine en quatre doses et en vers*, both of which appeared within three weeks of Hugo's play itself.

7. H. Rolle in *Le National*, 7.ii.1833, quoted by Sleumer, *op. cit.*, p. 149. The quotation is from Racine's *Britannicus* (IV, iv).

8. Saint-Marc Girardin, quoted by Sleumer, *ibid.*, p. 151.

9. Quoted by Berret, *op. cit.*, p. 311.

10. A. Vacquerie, quoted by P. and V. Glachant, *Le Théâtre de V. Hugo: les drames en prose*, Paris, 1903, p. 1.

11. On learning that Juliette had rejected the costume designed for her in favour of a dress of more *décolleté* fashion, Hugo is said to have remarked: "Que voulez-vous? Je ne puis empêcher cette pauvre fille de montrer sa marchandise" (quoted by Descotes, *Le Drame . . .*, p. 250).

12. *Victor Hugo raconté . . .*, II, pp. 352–354.

13. *Ibid.*, p. 362.

14. He had had to enter into this agreement for a third prose drama, in order to force the parsimonious Harel to stage *Marie Tudor* with sufficient attention to spectacle.

15. Cf. the comments of Janin, Gautier and Banville quoted by Brun, *op. cit.*, pp. 43, 52.

16. "[Hugo] was not scrupulous with historical fact, but extremely so with the spirit of a historical period", *Marie Tudor*, ed. R. E. Palmer, London, 1961, p. 23.

17. *Le Drame . . .*, p. 285.

18. *Victor Hugo raconté . . .*, II, p. 364.

19. *Op. cit.*, p. 192.

20. It seems at least possible that this defence of didacticism in the theatre was a rejoinder to Vigny's veiled attack on the amorality of Romantic drama in his 'Dernière Nuit de travail'. See p. 268.

21. *Op. cit.*, pp. 48–52.

22. *Ibid.*, p. 48.

23. *Le Théâtre de V. Hugo: prose*, p. 6.

24. *Ibid.*

25. See also R. Fargher, *art. cit.*, pp. 297–299.

26. *Le Théâtre de V. Hugo: prose*, pp. 9, 31–36.

27. See p. 217.

8 'Le drame moderne' in the Romantic Period

(i) Dumas and 'Antony'

WHILE the kinds of play we have studied so far—the verse drama, and the historical drama in prose—are what is generally first brought to mind by the term 'Romantic drama' today, they are nevertheless quite unrepresentative of the total dramatic output of the period. The majority of plays produced at the time would almost certainly fall under the heading of 'drame moderne'—that is, prose plays with a contemporary setting; and if we turn our attention to these, the problem we have just faced in the previous chapter now confronts us in another form. For this broad category embraces traditional comedy of manners, vaudeville, and melodrama, as well as the select handful of plays which critical tradition accepts as a genuine variety of 'Romantic drama'. What are the criteria by which this selection is made? Would it be too simple to say that the Romantic dramas in this category are those plays on modern subjects written by authors who qualify as 'Romantic' writers, and whom we have already treated as such in another context— those authors, in other words, who were the self-proclaimed spearhead of the Romantic assault on the Parisian theatre? In practice, this is what it amounts to; though here again, a formula such as Ponsard's will enable us to support this arbitrary selection by reference to a theoretical distinction between 'mélodrame' and 'drame romantique'. Certainly, the plays which fall to be considered in this chapter not only subordinate the 'aventures' and 'péripéties' of Ponsard's formula to the portrayal of 'caractères' and 'passions', but also possess the 'idée dominante' he regards as necessary. They are plays which appealed to audiences of the time because they made a valid statement, in striking artistic form, about moral and social issues which were of topical interest: issues on which the ideas of the young Romantic writers, artists and thinkers were significantly opposed to those of the majority of their contemporaries.

In spite of Hugo's brushes with the censorship over *Marion de Lorme* and *Le Roi s'amuse*, and the occasional detail such as the reflection of the Napoleonic legend that some commentators have claimed to see in both *Cromwell* and *Hernani*, it could hardly be maintained that the historical dramas so far considered reflect contemporary social and political issues to any important degree. And although Hernani, Didier and Ruy Blas, each in his own way, embody various aspects of the Romantic hero, the literary antecedents of these characters are clearly far more important than any sociological significance they might have. Dumas's earliest plays, too, *Henri III*, *Christine* and *Napoléon Bonaparte*, had seemed to be chiefly inspired by a mixture of personal ambition and professional opportunism, and the degree of his commitment to militant Romanticism, on the evidence of these three plays, must have seemed very doubtful. Even in *Napoléon Bonaparte*, which had closed with the Emperor's death less than ten years before the writing of the play, the subject is treated with a remarkable degree of objectivity, in the manner of an episode from past history, rather than as a vehicle for ideological propaganda.

It is Parigot's thesis that "le drame historique et le drame moderne sont les deux faces d'une même conception". While it may be partly true that both represent a response "aux mêmes aspirations d'une même époque", the following passage surely blurs the very real differences between the two genres:

A l'origine de l'un et de l'autre, deux monologues, celui d'Hamlet et celui de Figaro, l'un qui restitue à la *thèse* ses droits sur la scène, l'autre d'où le théâtre social découle comme d'une source vive. La peinture des milieux diffère; mais le procédé de couleur est le même... L'homme qui avait commencé par *Henri III* devait écrire *Antony*.[1]

Not only does this argument over-emphasize the ideological or propagandist content of the historical dramas of the Romantic period, it also undervalues the topicality, and the genuine realism, of those plays which, at the same time, adopt the manner of 'drame bourgeois' and look back to the theories of

Diderot. In the case of *Antony*, Parigot himself has shown very clearly what a close relationship existed between the play and its autobiographical background—even if that background of 'fact' was in its turn very largely influenced by literary models. In reality, the young Dumas's affair with Mélanie Waldor was banal enough: on his side at least, it was one of a long series of such affairs, which hardly engaged his whole personality; and the account of the astute lover taking advantage of having a friend in the War Office, in order to keep the cuckolded husband posted far away from Paris and deprive him of leave, suggests vaudeville rather than Romantic drama. But the lovers corresponded, and Parigot's detailed analysis of forty-seven letters from Dumas to Mélanie (who was herself a poetess and bluestocking) shows very clearly how in the aftermath of Werther and the Byronic heroes, even the most matter-of-fact of seductions was based on the accepted literary models. Dumas, in Parigot's felicitous phrase, "ne sépara jamais nettement la chambre à coucher du laboratoire"[2], and the epistolary exchange was a self-conscious stylistic exercise in preparation for the writing of the play.

Completed in 1830, *Antony* was first offered to the Théâtre-Français; but the administrative crisis in this theatre had combined with a lukewarm attitude on the part of Firmin and Mlle Mars, for whom the roles of Antony and Adèle were intended, to delay rehearsals and introduce a variety of hindrances, until finally, in the spring of 1831, Dumas was driven to withdraw his play and offer it to the Porte-Saint-Martin. It will be remembered that it was at this very time that Hugo withdrew *Marion de Lorme*: the ostensible reason was fear of the reintroduction of censorship at the Théâtre-Français, but disillusionment with the attitudes there—those of both actors and administration—was certainly a relevant factor in Hugo's case as well; and the following comment by Vigny gives a clear indication of the unfavourable state of the Théâtre-Français from the point of view of an aspiring Romantic playwright:

Je ne vous dirai qu'une chose du premier Théâtre-Français, c'est qu'il est le dernier. Il doit cela à ses dissensions intestines, il porte la peine de ses haines d'acteur à acteur, de sociétaire à sociétaire, des intrigues inouïes des comédiens contre les pièces même qu'ils jouaient et qui les alimentaient; ils mordaient le sein de leur nourrice: à présent, ce sein n'a plus de lait.[3]

There can be little doubt that *Antony* was one play which benefited from the move from the Théâtre-Français to the boulevard. For the playing of the two leading roles by Marie Dorval and Bocage was not only much more sympathetic than their interpretation by Mlle Mars and Firmin could ever have been, but was so entirely suited to the spirit of the play that *Antony* became one of the great successes of the Romantic decade. Gautier's account of the first night deserves to stand alongside that of the première of *Hernani* as an outstanding expression of the nostalgia of his generation for the heroic days of their youth:

> Ce que fut la soirée, aucune exagération ne saurait le rendre. La salle était vraiment en délire; on applaudissait, on sanglotait, on pleurait, on criait. La passion brûlante de la pièce avait incendié tous les cœurs. Les jeunes femmes adoraient Antony; les jeunes gens se seraient brûlé la cervelle pour Adèle d'Hervey. L'amour moderne se trouvait admirablement figuré par ce groupe, auquel Bocage et Mme Dorval donnaient une intensité de vie extraordinaire; Bocage l'homme fatal, Mme Dorval la faible femme par excellence!... Jamais identification d'un acteur et d'un rôle ne fut plus complète: Bocage était véritablement Antony, et Adèle d'Hervey ne pouvait se détacher de Mme Dorval.[4]

Dumas's own *Mémoires* fill in the details of the memorable scene: the prolonged, frenzied applause at the end of Act IV, prompting his offer of a bribe to the *machinistes* if they could complete the change of scenery before the tumult died down, and the final delirium in which the author was mobbed as he went up on stage to take a curtain-call, and his coat pulled from his back and torn to shreds by playgoers eager for a memento of the great occasion[5].

Antony was brought back regularly through the 1830s and 40s; there was a *reprise* at the Théâtre Cluny in 1867 (inspiring Gautier's nostalgic piece), and a notable one at the Odéon in 1884, which gave rise to a highly appreciative *feuilleton* by

Sarcey. But it must now be several decades since *Antony* was revived, and this play, which more than any other had embodied for contemporaries the living spirit of Romantic passion, has long been confined to the inanimate black-and-white of the printed page. How does it read today, nearly 150 years after the event?

In fact, it stands up to the test remarkably well: the reader has little difficulty in visualizing the play as staged, and in recognizing its effectiveness in theatrical terms. This is partly due to the economy—or, to use Sarcey's term, the 'rapidity'—of the dramatic movement: the swift *entrée en matière*, the rigorous exclusion of everything irrelevant, the masterly dénouement:

> De tous les dénouements passés et présents et même peut-être futurs, celui d'*Antony* nous avait semblé le plus éclatant, le plus inattendu, le plus logique, le plus rapide: une trouvaille de génie.[6]

But it would be wrong to overlook the contribution made by the quality of the writing. Though it is true that there are passages in which the accumulation of Romantic clichés produces amusement or irritation rather than emotional involvement, we must remember that some of these phrases—"Je le reconnais bien à ces idées d'amour et de mort constamment mêlées"; "Si vous vouliez un amour ordinaire, il fallait vous faire aimer par un homme heureux"; "Hésiter devant un nouveau crime?... Perdre mon âme pour si peu? Satan en rirait"—must have had a very different resonance for the spectators of 1831. In any case, if Antony himself is the 'être d'exception', the fatalistic hero beloved of Romantic literature, it is principally through the portrayal of Adèle that the play carries conviction. And Adèle must have represented not a few women of her day: married, after a brief, intense love-affair with the mysterious Antony, to a man whom she respects but does not love, now that Antony comes back into her life she is torn between the claims of 'passion' and 'vertu'; a banal situation, in all conscience, and the fact that her suffering is so credible, and that she makes such a strong appeal to our sympathy, is a tribute to the sincerity of Dumas's writing. The role of Adèle is not overwritten; and 'le style Dorval', which as we have seen was to produce a jarring note in Hugo's historical dramas, here contributes to the portrayal of the heroine's dilemma in terms of a contemporary sensibility:

> Des soupçons! oui, oui, c'est cela...   Oh! mais je suis perdue, moi!...   Sauvez-moi, vous...   Mais n'avez-vous rien résolu?... Vous le saviez avant moi, vous aviez le temps de chercher... Moi, moi...   vous voyez bien que j'ai la tête renversée.
> (V, iii)

On all counts, *Antony* must rank as one of the most distinguished of 'drames bourgeois'. It is not, of course, a pure slice of life, but a striking example of theatrical artifice. Dumas certainly makes use here, as elsewhere, of effects that we conventionally term 'melodramatic'; however, to label the play a melodrama on this account would be a misuse of the term. For the *coups de théâtre* are here not an end in themselves: they are integrated into the totality of the play's conception. The point is perceptively made by a recent editor of Pixérécourt:

> Il n'existe aucun rapport...   entre *Cœlina* et *Antony*, bien que tous les deux soient des drames bourgeois. Malgré tous les défauts d'*Antony* — et ils sont nombreux —, malgré tous les éléments mélodramatiques de cette pièce, si on la compare à *Cœlina* il faut reconnaître qu'elle excelle par la simplicité de sa conception, la logique intérieure de son intrigue, la plausibilité de sa caractérisation et la verve de son dialogue.[7]

The three most striking *coups de théâtre* are those which close Acts I, III and V. In the first Act, Adèle has obeyed the call of duty: she writes a letter in reply to Antony's note, and is leaving the house to avoid meeting him; but her horses bolt, and are stopped by the heroic action of a stranger, who is brought in injured. This is of course Antony, and Adèle insists that he cannot stay without compromising her, once he is out of danger:

ANTONY: *déchirant l'appareil de sa blessure et de sa saignée:* Une excuse, ne faut-il que cela?

ADÈLE: Dieu! Oh! le malheureux! il a déchiré l'appareil... Du sang! mon Dieu! du sang! (*Elle sonne.*) Au secours!...   Ce

sang ne s'arrêtera-t-il pas?... Il pâlit!... ses yeux se
ferment...

ANTONY: *retombant presque évanoui sur le sofa :* Et maintenant je
resterai, n'est-ce pas?

In Act III, Adèle, having confessed her love for Antony, has
fled to join her husband at Strasbourg. Antony has overtaken
her, arrived at a staging-inn, and sent on the only available
horses. Adèle, though apprehensive, has no choice but to break
her journey, and the only two rooms in the inn have a com-
municating balcony:

> (*Elle rentre dans le cabinet et ferme la porte. Antony paraît sur le
> balcon, derrière la fenêtre, casse un carreau, passe son bras, ouvre
> l'espagnolette, entre vivement, et va mettre le verrou à la porte...*)
>
> ADÈLE: *sortant du cabinet :* Du bruit... Un homme!... Ah!...
>
> ANTONY: Silence!... (*La prenant dans ses bras et lui mettant un
> mouchoir sur la bouche.*) C'est moi!... moi, Antony!... (*Il
> l'entraîne dans le cabinet.*)

Finally, in Act V, with Colonel d'Hervey battering at the door,
and Adèle imploring "une mort qui sauverait [ma] réputa-
tion", Antony takes her in his arms and stabs her, greeting her
husband with the famous line: "Oui, morte! Elle me résistait,
je l'ai assassinée!"

'Melodramatic' these curtain-lines may be, but this is not
melodrama. All three of these sensational gestures by the hero
exhibit the same Romantic *panache*, but it is not a case of sensation for the sake of sensation: here, as elsewhere, his behaviour
is determined by coherent, plausible characterization. Whether
one identifies with his self-centred fatalism, as the embryonic
Byrons in the audience of 1831 no doubt did, or whether one
looks on him with greater detachment, as a pathological case of
someone compulsively acting out an artificial pose, Antony
represents a daemonic, destructive force, and these impulsive
acts are wholly in character.

Alongside these highly theatrical moments, the play contains
some admirable scenes depicting the milieu to which Adèle
belongs. Act IV is particularly praiseworthy in this respect: as

the conversation about literature in the fashionable salon of the Vicomtesse de Lacy develops into a debate on the rival claims of historical drama and 'drame moderne', the playwright achieves several things at once. He gives us a naturalistic portrait of the society of which his heroine is a member; he integrates into his play a skilful *plaidoyer* for the genre to which it belongs; he unobtrusively advances his plot, as the spiteful innuendos of the prudish Mme de Camps:

> Puis, s'ils doutaient, vous pourriez leur donner la preuve que ces passions existent véritablement dans la société. Il y a encore des amours profondes qu'une absence de trois ans ne peut éteindre, des chevaliers mystérieux qui sauvent la vie à la dame de leurs pensées, des femmes vertueuses qui fuient leur amant, et, comme le mélange du naturel et du sublime est à la mode, des scènes qui n'en sont que plus dramatiques pour s'être passées dans une chambre d'auberge... (IV, vi)

bring home to Adèle the enormity of her offence against the social law; and finally he makes us think about the thesis that he is concerned to present to us in the play.

In a general sense, *Antony* is a play of ideas because it calls into question the bourgeois morality of respectability and outward appearances. Adèle has offended against the conventions of this morality, but she remains an 'honnête femme'; we have no difficulty in accepting her as such, and she retains our sympathy by comparison, not only with the malicious Mme de Camps, but also with the flighty, empty-headed Vicomtesse, who flits from one enthusiasm to another, depending on the vocation of her current protégé. There is never any doubt of the heroine's authenticity—to use a modern term—by the side of the other representatives of this society whose care is all for appearances; and contemporary spectators must have been led to reflect, as is the modern reader, that the integrity of the individual personality is worth more than conventional 'virtue', if the latter merely consists of lip-service to a social code.

But more specifically, the play propounds a positive thesis with regard to the position of the illegitimate in the society of Dumas's day: a thesis all the more eloquently presented in that it is not argued directly by a *raisonneur*, but is allowed to emerge indirectly as Adèle, suddenly guessing the key to Antony's mysterious behaviour, intuitively shares his humiliation in the face of the Vicomtesse's insensitivity:

> ADÈLE: *avec expression:* Oh! si je n'avais pas eu d'enfants... j'aurais voulu adopter un de ces orphelins...
>
> ANTONY: Orphelins!... que vous êtes bonne!...
>
> LA VICOMTESSE: Eh bien, vous auriez eu tort: là, ils passent leur vie avec des gens de leur espèce. (II, iv)

The anti-social posturings of this particular Romantic hero are explained, if not fully justified, by the ostracism that society has invoked against those who have no name, no *état civil*:

> Ainsi, vous le voyez, l'anathème est prononcé... Il faut que le malheureux reste malheureux; pour lui, Dieu n'a pas de regard, et les hommes de pitié... (*ibid.*)

Indeed, compared both with Diderot's *Le Fils naturel* and Dumas *fils*'s play of the same name—neither of which lives up to the claim suggested by this title, to be judged as a serious 'pièce à thèse' on the subject of illegitimacy—*Antony* succeeds in marrying thesis and plot in a stimulating challenge to the prejudices of society.

One of the most interesting contemporary comments on Dumas's play is Vigny's 'Une Lettre sur le théâtre à propos d'*Antony*', which appeared in the *Revue des Deux Mondes* later in 1831. Though he appreciates both the documentary realism of the play and the moral force of its thesis, Vigny is very wide of the mark with regard to the author's intentions, and the impact on the public, in his analysis of this thesis. Defending the play against an "accusation presque générale d'immoralité", he argues that Antony himself embodies a salutary warning:

> Je crois ce drame médité dans un but d'utilité morale et même religieuse. Je le comprends comme une satire de notre siècle et de notre année même, portant à l'aversion, à l'horreur même de l'athéisme, du matérialisme, de l'égoïsme, de la présomption, de la domination orgueilleuse de la force publique sur la faiblesse; tout cela personnifié artistement dans le rôle original d'Antony.[8]

The hero's "fureur de bâtardise", according to Vigny, is "un peu trop philosophique pour l'indulgente année 1831"[9]; and far from seeing Antony's anti-social activities as in any way justified by the cruel prejudices of society, the austere moralist is as pitiless as society itself in condemning his individualistic ideology:

> Le nombre est incalculable d'hommes blasés, durs et altiers qui…, pour arracher des succès d'amour-propre à des êtres facilement intimidés et éblouis, s'inventent des malheurs mystérieux et le plus byroniens possible… Les garnisons regorgent d'exemples pareils: il était bon d'en faire une grande satire, l'auteur d'*Antony* vient de la donner avec un grand bonheur et une égale habileté; il ne peut pas avoir eu d'autre but, et c'est dans ce sens seulement qu'on doit et qu'on peut louer son œuvre. Antony est un type effrayant, et il est utile par cela même.[10]

It is ironical indeed that this misguided and misleading interpretation should have come from the pen of one who in a few years' time was to be the creator of the equally self-indulgent Chatterton.

Far from our predominant feeling at the end of the play being one of horror and righteous indignation, I think it is true to say that Dumas has persuaded us into a position in which our moral judgement is suspended. Not only Adèle as innocent victim, but the ill-fated couple of Adèle and Antony, succeed in claiming our sympathy; and if it is perhaps less easy to be moved by reading Dumas's prose than is the case with Hugo's alexandrines in *Hernani* or *Marion de Lorme*, nevertheless it is by no means impossible to imagine what must have been the emotional impact of this text in the theatre, as interpreted by Bocage and Marie Dorval, and to recognize that the author deserves credit not only for a cogent 'pièce à thèse', but also for a moving example of 'tragédie bourgeoise'.

(ii) '*Richard Darlington*', '*Kean*' and other plays

Richard Darlington was produced in December 1831, during the brief period when Harel was in charge of both the Odéon and the Porte-Saint-Martin theatres. It was evidently a play for boulevard audiences, so it was put on at the Porte-Saint-Martin, but it was decided to employ the Odéon troupe, with Frédérick Lemaître in the name part. The subject had been offered to Dumas by a pair of boulevard dramatists, Beudin and Goubaux, and *Richard Darlington* became the first instance of successful collaboration in Dumas's career. The whole play was in fact rewritten round the central character with Frédérick in mind, and not only was the play tremendously successful with the audiences at the Porte-Saint-Martin, but this was hailed as one of Frédérick's outstanding performances, memorable for its ruthless brutality.

In this case, there can be no doubt of the appropriateness of the label 'melodrama'. Characters are crudely divided into good and bad, and there is an accumulation of sensational *coups de théâtre*. If there is anything in common between *Antony* and *Richard Darlington*, the latter stands in a relationship of melodramatic parody to the earlier play. Richard has all, and more, of the daemonic destructive force of Antony, with none of the latter's saving idealism, nothing resembling his genuine love for Adèle. He is a cold, callous egoist who uses women, and marriage, as instruments to serve his ambition; and when Jenny, whom he has married for political reasons, stands in the way of a more advantageous marriage, he pushes her off a balcony to her death (a motif which appears to be borrowed, via *Amy Robsart* perhaps, from Scott's *Kenilworth*, just as the events in the Prologue, in which a young girl arrives at night, accompanied by a mysterious stranger and fleeing from her father, at Darlington "dans le Northumberland", where she gives birth to a child, are based on an episode from *The Surgeon's Daughter*[11]). As regards language, Dumas was quite content here to adopt the cliché-ridden style of Pixérécourt: the sensationalism of the subject is emphasized by the cries of "Malédiction!", "Mort et damnation!" and the like which punctuate the dialogue. Above all, this play remains wedded to the formula of melodrama, rather than aspiring to 'drame moderne' of a more ambitious nature, because the author neglects the opportunity to make of his hero anything more than a stereotype, and because plausibility of character is subordinated to plot.

The germ of a social thesis might certainly be found in the subject: not only is Richard a foundling without a family, but

9 'Chatterton', by H. Wallis:

Cut is the branch that might have grown full straight;
Burned is Apollo's laurel bough

Tate Gallery, London

10   Mlle George as Lucrèce Borgia

it is his father's status, as public hangman, which has prevented him from marrying Richard's mother and which finally shatters Richard's own ambitions. However, these facts are exploited to produce plot-interest, not food for thought; and of all Dumas's plays on modern subjects, *Richard Darlington* is the one that most tends to blur the distinction between Romantic drama and 'mélodrame'.

The tone and atmosphere of *Antony*, if not the social thesis, are to be found again in *Teresa* (February 1832). Indeed, the play is a sort of '*Antony* à rebours', since of the pair of adulterous lovers, this time it is Teresa herself who is the more forceful character, moved by the same Romantic dynamism, while Arthur remains the passive partner. The two have have had a passionate love-affair in Naples, and have had to part, before the play opens; Arthur is on the point of marrying Amélie, the daughter of his benefactor Delaunay, when the latter returns home to Paris from Italy with his new wife—who is of course Teresa. We may smile at this coincidence, and it is true that in a domestic setting such contrivances seem more obtrusive than in the poetic world of classical tragedy; but once these *données* have been established, the working-out of the plot has the simple inevitability that we associate with Racine. The lovers' adultery is discovered, and Teresa's suicide, prompted by a mixture of frustrated passion and remorse, possesses something at least of the logical necessity of Phèdre's end. There is no attempt to excuse or justify illicit love by an appeal to sociological arguments: the characters are victims of "la fatalité de la passion", and rather than a 'drame moderne' which makes use of particular social setting in order to indoctrinate the spectator, *Teresa* may be said to exemplify a more traditional sort of romantic tragedy, which in this instance happens to be in modern dress.

The circumstances of its staging tend to reinforce the impression that this play stands somewhat apart from the other 'drames modernes' to be discussed in this chapter. On this occasion, Dumas moved away from the Porte-Saint-Martin, and after some difficulty in finding a theatre, fell back on the Salle Ventadour, the home of the Opéra-Comique. Bocage, it is true, left Harel's troupe in order to play in *Teresa*—choosing, instead of the part of Arthur, that of the elderly colonel

Delaunay. Teresa, a role which was ready-made for Marie Dorval, was played by Mme Moreau-Sainti, an actress of conventional training, who had no experience of Romantic drama; Arthur, by the young Laferrière. From the point of view of the relationships between the Romantic dramatists and the professional theatre, the most important thing about *Teresa* was that it marked the beginning of the playwright's liaison with Ida Ferrier, who was given the part of Amélie, a 'rôle sacrifié', like that of Jenny in *Richard Darlington*. Ida was an actress of no outstanding talent, but Dumas was now regularly to write a part for her in each new play; and her rivalry with Juliette Drouet, as we have seen, was to have some importance in helping to determine the fortunes of Romantic drama in the middle 1830s. In fact, the part Dumas created for Ida in the play which marked his return to the Porte-Saint-Martin, *La Tour de Nesle*, became a casualty of the intrigues which always surrounded Harel's productions, and had to be cut before the play reached the stage; but in the dramatist's next modern play, *Angèle* (Porte-Saint-Martin, December 1833), Ida was given the female lead, opposite Bocage.

The plot of *Angèle* is thoroughly derivative. The hero, Alfred d'Alvimar, is another ruthless egoist like Richard Darlington, who seeks advancement by means of his relations with women: indeed, the play was originally to have been called *L'Échelle de femmes*. There is a resemblance to *Teresa* in that the hero deserts daughter for mother, and like *Richard Darlington* the play includes a clandestine illegitimate birth. The fifteen-year-old *ingénue* Angèle has been deliberately seduced so that d'Alvimar can be sure of marrying her for her money, but when her mother appears to offer better prospects, she is callously abandoned just as she gives birth to her child. However, whereas the dénouement of *Richard Darlington* had allowed the hero to get away with murder, the lesser crimes of Alfred d'Alvimar meet with retribution in the shape of Henri Müller, a consumptive painter who has long harboured a hopeless love for Angèle: he kills Alfred in a duel, marries Angèle and recognizes her child.

Parigot has some excellent pages on *Angèle*[12], showing how its theme prefigures that of many social dramas of the second half of the century, of which the best known example is perhaps the

Denise (1885) of Dumas *fils*. The theme of the calculating seducer using his conquests to further his social ambition or his career must evidently have possessed considerable topicality throughout the period, and *Angèle* is in the vanguard of the movement towards social realism in the nineteenth-century theatre: Alfred d'Alvimar is a product of his times, during which the dramatic reversals of fortune in 1815 and 1830 help to account for, if they do not excuse, a certain cynical opportunism. But what the play does not pretend to be is a 'pièce à thèse'. To the extent that plays like *Teresa* or *Angèle* convey a message (and the same is true of *Richard Darlington* inasmuch as the hero's ambitions are finally thwarted, even if he is allowed to escape the law), this is no more than a comfortable reinforcement of existing moral attitudes: scoundrels like Alfred may exist, but there is a divine justice which protects the social morality on which the life of the community is based. In *Antony*, however, Dumas had set out, not to bolster up the moral convictions of his contemporaries, but to shock them out of their prejudices; and in *Kean*, his next play in a modern setting, he again uses the theatre to put forward a thesis which challenges the complacent prejudices of a bourgeois society.

Kean, ou Désordre et génie (August 1836) is surely one of the most original plays produced during the Romantic period. In our own day it has acquired a new, and in a way accidental, interest by virtue of Sartre's adaptation, first performed in Paris in 1954 and more recently presented with great success (in English translation) in this country; but while a comparison of the two texts will probably lead most readers to conclude that Sartre has improved on Dumas, at any rate from the point of view of a twentieth-century audience, the adaptation is itself a tribute to the quality of the original, and to the theatrically imaginative way in which Dumas had treated the subject[13].

The great Edmund Kean had died in 1833. He had become a legend during his lifetime, and French audiences had had the opportunity in 1827 to measure the difference between the conventional, traditional acting style of the Théâtre-Français and the uninhibited, dynamic manner of Kean in particular among the visiting English players. But the legend was not limited to the great actor's professional achievements, and his capacity for wine, his debts and his sexual exploits were the subject of extravagant anecdote. In Paris, Frédérick Lemaître, now in his mid-thirties and at the height of his reputation, was beginning to be the subject of a similar legend, based as much on his expansive way of life as on his flamboyant acting. In spite of a contrast in physique—Kean had been short and stocky, while Frédérick was an imposing figure—connoisseurs saw a remarkable resemblance between the two men. Dumas's incarnation of the Romantic idea of unruly genius was a role tailor-made for Frédérick, and the play was therefore staged at a small theatre, the Variétés, where the actor was currently under contract[14]; Ida Ferrier was given the part of the young heiress Anna Damby, who throws herself at Kean's head and succeeds in rescuing him from the disastrous consequences of an affair with the Danish ambassador's wife, on which he has embarked out of rivalry with the Prince of Wales. While Ida scored a considerable personal success, the reception given to Frédérick himself was mixed. The press was rather reserved (perhaps because Dumas had taken the opportunity to give Kean several tirades against professional critics), but the *aficionados* showed their usual enthusiastic appreciation of his virtuoso performance, and many contemporary tributes are extant to the perfect matching of actor and part[15].

Whether or not we can accept a Kean whose friendship is sought by princes of the blood and ambassadors (and his love by ambassadors' wives), at the same time as he resorts for his drinking orgies to a dockland tavern frequented by common sailors, the representation of the various milieux in which the action takes place is recognizably in the tradition of realistic social drama, and we are given a vivid, if impressionistic, picture of backstage life and of fashionable English *mœurs* in the early nineteenth century. However, the notion of "désordre et génie" is clearly an *a priori* formula, not unlike the Hugolian antithesis—and to this extent characterization, as regards the central figure at any rate, is even more demonstrably unrealistic than in the case of Antony or Richard Darlington. The larger-than-life portrayal of Kean himself, symbolizing the abstract concept of Genius, completely dominates the play. Of the forty scenes following his first entry in Act I scene v, he is present in thirty, the rest being nearly all short linking scenes; he holds the centre of the stage virtually the whole time, and the role con-

tains some remarkable virtuoso passages. One of these is the
long tirade against the vicious nobleman Lord Mewill, who has
tried to abduct Anna and who now refuses to fight a duel with
"un bateleur, un saltimbanque, un histrion"—a tirade in which
it is perhaps not too fanciful to perceive an echo of Mark
Antony's speech in *Julius Caesar*, with its refrain of "Brutus was
an honourable man":

> Oui, vous avez raison, il y a trop de distance entre nous. Lord
> Mewill est un homme honorable, tenant à l'une des premières
> familles d'Angleterre... de riche et vieille noblesse con-
> quérante... si je ne me trompe. Il est vrai que Lord Mewill
> a mangé la fortune de ses pères en jeux de cartes et de dés, en
> paris de coqs et en courses de chevaux; il est vrai que son
> blason est terni de la vapeur de sa vie débauchée, et de ses
> basses actions... et qu'au lieu de monter encore, il a
> descendu toujours. Tandis que le bateleur Kean est né sur le
> grabat du peuple, a été exposé sur la place publique, et,
> ayant commencé sans nom et sans fortune, s'est fait un nom
> égal au plus noble nom, et une fortune qui, du jour où il le
> voudra bien, peut rivaliser avec celle du prince royal... Cela
> n'empêche pas que Lord Mewill ne soit un homme hono-
> rable, et Kean un bateleur!... (III, xiv)

In another, at the climax of the play, Kean breaks off in the
middle of a scene from *Romeo and Juliet* to harangue the Prince
of Wales, who has provoked his jealousy by appearing in his box
with Éléna, the ambassador's wife:

> Qui est-ce qui m'appelle Roméo? qui est-ce qui croit que je
> joue ici le rôle de Roméo?... Je ne suis pas Roméo... Je
> suis Falstaff, le compagnon de débauches du prince royal
> d'Angleterre... A moi, mes braves camarades! à moi,
> Pons!... à moi, Peto!... à moi, Bardolph! à moi, Quickly
> l'hôtelière!... et versez, versez à pleins bords, que je boive à
> la santé du prince de Galles, le plus débauché, le plus indis-
> cret, le plus vaniteux de nous tous! A la santé du prince de
> Galles, à qui tout est bon, depuis la fille de taverne qui sert
> les matelots du port, jusqu'à la fille d'honneur qui jette le
> manteau royal aux épaules de sa mère! au prince de Galles,
> qui ne peut regarder une femme, vertueuse ou non, sans la
> perdre avec son regard! au prince de Galles, dont j'ai cru

être l'ami, et dont je ne suis que le jouet et le bouffon!... Ah!
prince royal, bien t'en prend d'être inviolable et sacré, je te le
jure!... car, sans cela, tu aurais affaire à Falstaff. (IV (2), i)

As we read the text of the play, "désordre" may seem more
in evidence than "génie"; but such was the reputation of his
interpreter that no doubt the genius of Dumas's Kean, in the
person of Frédérick, was readily taken for granted. For Sartre,
the character was to prove interesting because he saw in it a
study in growing self-awareness in the existentialist manner: as
a mere *acteur*, Kean lacks 'authenticité', however great his
talents, because he is trying to be like those of noble blood
whom he envies; and it is only when, under the influence of
Anna, he learns to accept the limitations of his condition and
discovers his real identity, that he can become truly great as a
comédien[16]. For the nineteenth-century playwright, however, the
great actor illustrated a simple Romantic stereotype: the artist
imprisoned in his genius, forced to prostitute his talents to a
society which patronizes him without either accepting him or
really understanding him. It would no doubt be wrong to give
too much weight to the thesis in *Kean*: Dumas's play certainly
does not possess anything like the didactic purpose which so
obviously animates *Chatterton*. But where Sartre's Kean, like his
Oreste, is a study of the central character coming to terms with
himself and discovering his freedom as an individual, Dumas's
hero remains, like Chatterton, the man of genius at odds with
a hostile society.

"*Kean* sonne le glas du drame romantique d'Alexandre
Dumas" writes Dr. Ubersfeld; "après *Kean*, Dumas continue à
écrire pour le théâtre, mais sans faire le moindre effort pour se
maintenir au niveau « littéraire »"[10]. The latter part of this
judgement is certainly too harsh: *Caligula* and *L'Alchimiste*, for
instance, are both written in alexandrines, and the former at
least has serious literary pretensions, even if critical opinion has
never been very kind to the play. But in general, the development that we have traced in an earlier chapter with regard to
Dumas's historical dramas can be paralleled in the case of his
plays on modern subjects: after *Kean*, there is little evidence of
anything that can be called positively Romantic. Instead, in a
play like *Paul Jones* (Panthéon, October 1838), we are merely

offered the mechanics of the well-made play. Characters are subordinated to situation, and the influence of melodrama is very evident in the black-and-white opposition, even if the gothic sensationalism of vintage melodrama is here somewhat subdued. Whatever its ephemeral theatrical appeal—it was played in a boulevard theatre, with no actors of distinction even by boulevard standards—such a play had nothing to recommend it to a later generation of spectators or readers. It is by no means worthless as entertainment, but one recognizes, even while enjoying the superficial excitement of the plot, that it is a second-hand collection of literary and dramatic clichés. By 1838, Dumas the literary entrepreneur had almost completely succeeded in stifling Dumas the Romantic playwright.

(iii) *Vigny and 'Chatterton'*

THOUGH most readers would no doubt agree that it has dated more than *Antony* or *Kean*, *Chatterton* was certainly, in the eyes of the playgoers of the Romantic generation, the most distinguished 'pièce à thèse' of its time; and the production of Vigny's play at the Théâtre-Français in February 1835 constitutes one of the major events in the history of Romantic drama.

The thesis it illustrates represents one particular form of an idea dear to the Romantic mind, and one which, as we have seen, was also to find expression in Dumas's *Kean*: that of the man of genius isolated from his fellow-men by his divine mission to enlighten and guide them. Lamartine's *Les Destinées de la poésie*, Hugo's recurrent portrayal of the poet as visionary or *mage*, embody this idea; Vigny himself had given early expression to it in the allegorical 'Moïse' (1822), and again in the 'Lettre à Lord * * *' which served as preface to his *More de Venise*. Here, he uses the image of a large clock-face, on which the imperceptible movement of the hour-hand symbolizes the slow progress of the mass of humanity, while that of the minute-hand, quite easily detectable, represents the more rapid advance of "les gens éclairés":

> ... Mais, au-dessus de ces deux aiguilles, il s'en trouve une bien autrement agile et dont l'œil suit difficilement les bonds; elle a vu soixante fois l'espace avant que la seconde y marche et que la troisième s'y traîne.

Jamais, non, jamais, je n'ai considéré cette aiguille des secondes, cette flèche si vive, si inquiète, si hardie et si émue à la fois, qui s'élance en avant et frémit comme du sentiment de son audace ou du plaisir de sa conquête sur le temps, jamais je ne l'ai considérée sans penser que le poète a toujours eu et doit avoir cette marche prompte au-devant des siècles et au delà de l'esprit général de sa nation, au delà même de sa partie la plus éclairée.

The notion of the poet, or artist, as a creature of superior intelligence and sensibility set apart from others by his vocation, was one that was bound to appeal to the enthusiastic young followers of these Romantic leaders: it flattered their self-esteem by marking them off from the common herd. The particular emphasis of Vigny's play, however, is that it not only portrays the artist being at odds with a hostile society—"l'homme spiritualiste étouffé par une société matérialiste"[18]—but preaches the duty of that society to support the artist by providing him with the conditions in which his genius can flourish.

The relationship between 'romantisme pur' and 'romantisme social' in the 1830s has been studied by several literary historians, who have shown how the aristocratic aestheticism of the 1820s gave way in many cases to a doctrinaire humanitarianism much more concerned with social and economic realities:

Dans l'ensemble, il est impossible de méconnaître que l'orientation générale de la littérature a été modifiée, et on peut croire que le romantisme pur, le romantisme de 1830, est près de sa fin et que ses jours sont comptés.[19]

It would perhaps be truer to say that the 1830s witnessed a polarization of attitudes. On the one hand, we can see a growth in the solidarity of writers, artists and musicians against the bourgeois, materialist society under Louis-Philippe—attitudes which were to produce the Flauberts and the Baudelaires of the next generation; but this is countered by the conversion of Hugo, George Sand, Lamartine and other writers to 'social Romanticism', and by the development of the ideas of Saint-Simon, Fourier and other theorists of early socialism which were to underlie the revolution of 1848. Vigny was an early

convert (through a doctor, Philippe Buchez, whom he met in
1828), and became an active supporter of the Saint-Simonian
cause. His *More de Venise* had been directly criticized by the
Saint-Simonian Boulland, who accused him of preferring 'pure'
literature to the realities of life:

> Disons-le, la tragédie, classique ou romantique, qu'elle soit
> prise, pour son sujet, dans la Grèce ou dans le moyen-âge,
> pour ses formes, dans Racine ou dans Shakespeare, la
> tragédie est morte. Elle ne répond plus à aucun besoin, à
> aucun but; il faut qu'elle disparaisse, qu'elle emporte avec
> elle son manteau, son poignard et sa coupe, pour faire place
> au drame, au drame bourgeois, avec notre habit du dix-
> neuvième siècle, notre oisiveté et notre égoïsme[20]

—and at the same time a poem in Sainte-Beuve's *Consolations*
urged Vigny to concern himself with the problems of his time:

> Méritez qu'on vous dise Apôtre en poésie.[21]

The poem 'Paris', written in January 1831 as a reply to this
challenge, proclaims the Saint-Simonian ideal of

> un Temple immense, universel
> Où l'homme n'offrira ni l'encens, ni le sel,
> Ni le sang, ni le pain, ni le vin, ni l'hostie,
> Mais son temps et sa vie en œuvre convertie,
> Mais son amour de tous, son abnégation,
> De lui, de l'héritage et de la nation;
> Seul, sans père et sans fils, soumis à la parole,
> L'union est son but et le travail son rôle,
> Et, selon celui-là qui parle après Jésus,
> Tous seront appelés et tous seront élus.

Stello (1832) and *Servitude et grandeur militaires* (1835) both convey
a message of sympathetic understanding of the position of
individuals isolated by social forces; but it is *Chatterton* which
illustrates most fully the Saint-Simonian influence on Vigny,
expressed through the medium of what would have been called,
a century later, 'littérature engagée'.

In *Stello*, the story of the suffering and suicide of Chatterton
had formed one of three episodic narratives (together with the

account of the last days of the young French poet Gilbert, and that of André Chénier's death) illustrating the theme of the novel as expounded by the Docteur Noir to the poet Stello: that is, the duty of the genius to follow the call of his inspiration, and to shun the active life of the world around him: "Seul et libre, accomplir sa mission"[22]. The story is narrated by the Docteur as an eye-witness, and in detail corresponds closely to the course the play was to follow three years later, though the thesis to which it is harnessed in the later work is significantly different. This thesis is set out, forcefully and expressively, in 'Dernière Nuit de travail, du 29 au 30 juin 1834', the foreword to the published text:

> La cause, c'est le martyre perpétuel et la perpétuelle immola-
> tion du Poète. La cause, c'est le droit qu'il aurait de vivre.
> La cause, c'est le pain qu'on ne lui donne pas. La cause,
> c'est la mort qu'il est forcé de se donner.

The man of genius marked out by destiny may force himself to deny his calling: he may become an 'homme de lettres', or even a 'grand écrivain'; but if he remains true to his vocation as 'poète' he may well find, like Chatterton, that suicide is the only way out of his dilemma. And for such desperate acts, the moral blame does not lie with the unfortunate victim, but with society:

> Eh! n'entendez-vous pas le bruit des pistolets solitaires? Leur
> explosion est bien plus éloquente que ma faible voix. N'enten-
> dez-vous pas ces jeunes désespérés qui demandent le pain
> quotidien, et dont personne ne paie le travail?... C'est au
> législateur à guérir cette plaie, l'une des plus vives et des plus
> profondes de notre corps social; c'est à lui qu'il appartient de
> réaliser dans le présent une partie des jugements meilleurs de
> l'avenir, en assurant quelques années d'existence seulement à
> tout homme qui aurait donné un seul gage du talent divin.
> Il ne lui faut que deux choses: la vie et la rêverie; le PAIN
> et le TEMPS.

Cases of suicide on the part of real-life Chattertons in the years leading up to 1834 are well documented[23]; however, not only did Vigny's thesis, despite the serious, high-minded philanthropy which inspired it, remain completely without effect on the social conscience of his contemporaries, but by a sad irony *Chatterton* was to give rise, as *Werther* had done before it, to a suicide-cult among the young victims of 'le mal du siècle'. In a well-known passage on Vigny's play, Gautier represents it as a topical response to an already widespread phenomenon:

> Lorsqu'on n'a pas traversé cette époque folle, ardente, surexcitée, mais généreuse, on ne peut se figurer à quel oubli de l'existence matérielle l'enivrement, ou si l'on veut l'infatua-tion de l'art poussa d'obscures et frêles victimes qui aimèrent mieux mourir que de renoncer à leur rêve. L'on entendait vraiment dans la nuit craquer la détonation des pistolets solitaires. Qu'on juge de l'effet que produisit dans un pareil milieu le *Chatterton* de M. Alfred de Vigny, auquel, si l'on veut le comprendre, il faut restituer l'atmosphère contempo-raine[24]

—but a chapter in Maigron's *Le Romantisme et les mœurs* brings together an impressive collection of evidence to show how the cult was itself stimulated by works of imaginative literature, with *Chatterton* occupying by far the most prominent place[25].

At first sight, *Chatterton* seems far removed from the kinds of Romantic drama whose evolution we have traced so far, and which all have in common the theatrical and the larger-than-life. Whether we think of Hugo's characters based on his anti-thetical formula, or of the extravagance of Dumas's characters and the sensationalism of his plots, all the plays of these two dramatists are marked by the same vitality and crude vigour; and even Vigny's *Maréchale d'Ancre* had possessed something of these same characteristics. Here, however, is a play which strikes us by its subdued, unsensational manner and the rela-tively static quality of its action; a play which seems to achieve its effects by understatement and by subtle suggestion, rather than by theatrical over-emphasis. And this contrast with the manner of his contemporaries is underlined by Vigny's pro-vocative lines from the last page of the 'Dernière Nuit de travail':

> Puisse [la forme d'art que j'ai créée] ne pas être renversée par l'assemblée qui la jugera dans six mois! avec elle périrait un

plaidoyer en faveur de quelques infortunés inconnus; mais je crois trop pour craindre beaucoup. Je crois surtout à l'avenir et au besoin universel de choses sérieuses; maintenant que l'amusement des yeux par des surprises enfantines fait sourire tout le monde au milieu même de ses grandes aventures, c'est, ce me semble, le temps du DRAME DE LA PENSÉE.

For it would be impossible to mistake the target at which the "amusement des yeux par des surprises enfantines" is aimed, or to fail to recognize the extent to which Vigny's new formula implies a conscious repudiation of what had come to be called 'Romantic' drama.

But just how great is Vigny's originality from the formal point of view? To what extent can he be said to have 'created' a new art-form as a vehicle for his thesis? As regards the structure of *Chatterton*, the analogy of Racinian drama has often been cited; and though this can be very misleading, the play does possess something approaching the simplicity and concentration of a tragedy like *Bérénice*. The unities of time and place are rigorously observed; and as for the unity of action, there are virtually no digressions at all from a central theme whose résumé in Vigny's own words:

C'est l'histoire d'un homme qui a écrit une lettre le matin, et qui attend la réponse jusqu'au soir; elle arrive, et le tue[26]

almost matches the brevity of the 'invitus invitam' formula which defines Racine's masterpiece. What does perhaps support Vigny's claim of originality is the wedding of this classical simplicity of structure to the setting and idiom of 'drame bourgeois'.

For not only does *Chatterton* represent the most conscientious attempt by a dramatist of the Romantic generation to exploit the medium of 'drame bourgeois'; it was arguably the most faithful application of the principles of this genre since Diderot himself had laid them down. The transposition in time and place, from the London of the 1770s to the stage of the Comédie-Française in 1835, is immaterial in this connection: this is pure domestic drama in the manner of Diderot, Sedaine and Beaumarchais. The *tableau* which Diderot had prescribed in place of the *coup de théâtre* is exemplified in the repeated grouping of Kitty Bell and her children for pathetic effect; John Bell, "homme de quarante-cinq à cinquante ans, vigoureux, rouge de visage, gonflé d'ale, de porter et de roastbeef, étalant dans sa démarche l'aplomb de sa richesse", illustrates the Diderot concept of *la condition* just as well as Sedaine's *philosophe*; while the remainder of the 'Caractères et costumes des rôles principaux', and the detailed realism of the initial stage-direction[27], are fully in the tradition of Beaumarchais and other practitioners of the 'drame'.

The concentration of its structure, and the simple realism of its setting, make of *Chatterton* a most effective illustration of the theories of 'drame bourgeois'. In view of the intensity of the focus on the central character's predicament, leading to the final catastrophe, the play might well have been a powerful example of domestic *tragedy*, were it not for certain Romantic clichés which make of Vigny's characters symbols rather than convincing individuals. This is true in large measure of Chatterton himself: indeed, Vigny confesses, at the end of the 'Dernière Nuit':

> Le Poète était tout pour moi; Chatterton n'était qu'un nom d'homme, et je viens d'écarter à dessein des faits exacts de sa vie pour ne prendre de sa destinée que ce qui la rend un exemple à jamais déplorable d'une noble misère.

The result is that, for the first two Acts at any rate, Chatterton remains a rather shadowy figure, and we are as mystified by the enigma of his origins and background as are John Bell and his wife. He lacks the credibility that might have been provided by even the most rudimentary *état civil*, and Lord Talbot and his friends seem to have a more rounded stage presence than the hero himself. The fact is that this youth of seventeen, whose experience of life has already turned him into a mature cynic, is a familiar figure in Romantic literature. "Ton cœur", says the elderly Quaker, "est pur et jeune comme celui de Rachel [Kitty Bell's six-year-old daughter], et ton esprit expérimenté est vieux comme le mien" (I, v); there is an unmistakable parallel here with the scene between the young Lorenzo and the much older Philippe Strozzi in Act III of Musset's *Lorenzaccio*. The death-wish, the feeling of being persecuted by a malevolent

fate: these are features that Vigny's hero shares with a whole
generation of other heroes; but as for those traits which are
intended to characterize him as an individual, Thomas
Chatterton, they remain vague and unconvincing.

It may well be that this follows inevitably from the nature of
Chatterton's calling. Whereas a king or a courtier—*a fortiori* the
banker or businessman of 'drame bourgeois'—can establish
credibility on stage by his actions, pure genius has to be taken
on trust. Wordsworth's "marvellous boy" may be acceptable
as a disembodied literary symbol of precocious genius; and the
figure of Chatterton may lend itself well enough to the idealization of Romantic iconography[28]; but in the theatre it is not easy
to endow something as elusive as artistic genius with the necessary flesh and blood. (This is a handicap from which Goethe's
Torquato Tasso also suffers.) As a result, we are forced to
modify our first impression: the precision of the setting, the close
attention given to the presentation of John Bell in particular,
are not matched by the way in which the central character is
handled; and of the two terms in Vigny's formula, there is no
doubt that the "société matérialiste" carries much more conviction in realist terms than the "homme spiritualiste". There
are various subsidiary features of the play which also seem to
derive from a tradition other than the 'genre sérieux'. In the
characterization of John Bell and Kitty—not only in their
attitudes towards Chatterton, but in the husband's bullying of
his wife, and his tyrannizing of his employees—we can see the
black-and-white characterization of melodrama; the Quaker,
"vieillard de quatre-vingts ans", represents a cliché dear to
Pixérécourt and others; while Kitty's death of a broken heart,
within minutes of Chatterton's, illustrates another convention
of popular sentimental literature.

However, it is the way in which Chatterton himself is presented which constitutes the most important challenge to the
traditions and conventions of the domestic genre; as a poet of
genius, Chatterton in a sense represents the quintessence of the
Romantic hero. How well does the character work on this
level? Does he achieve the same universality, and obtain from
the reader the same emotional response, as the heroes of Hugo's
poetic drama are able to achieve by means of their lyrical
exaltation? One might observe to begin with that Chatterton's

appeal, though perhaps more intense, is also more austere and exclusive than that of Hernani, Didier or Ruy Blas. In these cases—unquestionably the ones which make the strongest appeal to the spectator's sympathy—we are made to identify not so much with the individual character as with the pair of lovers whose ill-fortune produces the emotional crisis (and the same is true of Dumas's *Antony*). Chatterton, however, though a lover, is first and foremost a solitary, a fugitive from society; Kitty, too, discovers her love only during the last Act, and although she does finally express it in a characteristic 'mot Dorval': "Et si je vous aime, moi!", for the most part their relationship is a formal one based on timidity and mutual avoidance, and hardly seems the sort of thing to inspire a wholehearted emotional involvement on the audience's part.

However, *Chatterton* is the work of a poet; and what redeems the play, though perhaps to a lesser extent than with Hugo's verse plays, are the passages in which the poet-hero transcends the limitations of his immediate context in order to express the playwright's thoughts on topics of universal appeal. The most important scene from this point of view is Act III, scene i—a scene, as Brun suggests in a happy phrase, "qui rappelle Hamlet et annonce Lorenzaccio"[29]. This is a long soliloquy in which it is impossible not to detect, behind Chatterton hesitating before the decision to take his life, Vigny's own disillusion and despair at the role of the creative artist writing for the public of the 1830s:

Il faut, à cette heure, que ma volonté soit assez puissante pour saisir mon âme et l'emporter tour à tour dans le cadavre ressuscité des personnages que j'évoque et dans le fantôme de ceux que j'invente! Ou bien il faut que, devant Chatterton malade, devant Chatterton qui a froid, qui a faim, ma volonté fasse poser avec prétention un autre Chatterton, gracieusement paré pour l'amusement du public, et que celui-là soit décrit par l'autre; le troubadour par le mendiant. Voilà les deux poésies possibles, ça ne va pas plus loin que cela! Les divertir ou leur faire pitié; faire jouer de misérables poupées, ou l'être soi-même et faire trafic de cette singerie! Ouvrir son cœur pour le mettre en étalage sur un comptoir! S'il a des blessures, tant mieux! il a plus de prix; tant soit peu mutilé, on l'achète plus cher!

character together here and elsewhere, finally
...herence it had earlier seemed to lack[30], is not an
...d from outside by means of the 'realistic' details
...y biography, but rather—and again, the com-
...orenzaccio imposes itself—an inner conviction
...deriving from the playwright's own sincerity. This is the justification for the existence of *Chatterton* as a symbol of the poet
victimized by a hostile society: the experience is Vigny's own,
just as the language, with its images and its highly literary
rhythms, is the language of Vigny himself; one can see at once
how different is Chatterton's stylized expression of despair from
the banal effects of Hugo's or Dumas's prose dialogue:

> Oh! loin de moi, — loin de moi, je t'en supplie, décourage-
> ment glacé! mépris de moi-même, ne viens pas achever de
> me perdre! détourne-toi! détourne-toi! car, à présent, mon
> nom et ma demeure, tout est connu; et, si demain ce livre
> n'est pas achevé, je suis perdu! oui, perdu! sans espoir! —
> Arrêté, jugé, condamné! jeté en prison!
> O! dégradation! ô! honteux travail!

The dialogue of *Chatterton* is one example of dramatic prose
of the Romantic period analysed by Brun which earns his
unstinted admiration, among other things for its flexibility and
the way in which the different characters are reflected in their
speech: "l'application à une tragédie intime de ce que Molière
et les grands comiques font d'instinct"[31]. But if the more
detached readers of today are perhaps better able to appreciate
features such as this, what mattered for Vigny's contemporaries
was above all the Romantic fervour of the play. Essentially,
Chatterton is a poet's play for poets[32]: more than any other play
of the period, it depends on the audience sharing certain
assumptions with Vigny and his hero: an audience fired by the
same intransigent idealism, for whom the very thought of
compromise with bourgeois values was anathema. Where they
were swept along willingly to the emotional climax as Chatterton
opens the Lord Mayor's letter:

> Voilà le juge!... le bienfaiteur! voyons, qu'offre-t-il? *Il
> décachète la lettre, lit...* et s'écrie avec indignation: Une place de

premier valet de chambre dans sa maison!... Ah! pays damné! terre du dédain! sois maudite à jamais! *Prenant la fiole d'opium.* O mon âme, je t'avais vendue! je te rachète avec ceci (III, vii)

the reader of today is no doubt tempted to look at Chatterton through Beckford's eyes, and to see his offer as a genuine act of philanthropy. If the play retains for us today any of its power to persuade, it seems likely that for most modern readers this is due to the strength of the negative component of Vigny's thesis—the critical portrait of John Bell—rather than to the positive example provided by Chatterton himself. As a 'tragédie intime', and as an appeal to the social conscience of the audience, the play was too much of its time for it not to have dated; what survives is above all a keenly observed and faithfully recorded portrait of the self-made industrialist. Just as Sedaine's *philosophe* stands as a permanent embodiment of the social virtues of the Enlightenment, so Vigny's John Bell epitomizes in equally memorable form the less admirable characteristics of the Industrial Revolution.

The story of the production of *Chatterton* provides us with a further illustration of the difficulties encountered by all the Romantic writers in their personal relationships with the world of the theatre. The play was written quite openly as a vehicle for Marie Dorval—Descotes points out how the treatment of Chatterton's case in *Stello* has been modified in order to give greater prominence to the role of Kitty[33]—and in particular as a means of securing her entry to the Comédie-Française. It was finished in June 1834, and promptly turned down by the *comité de lecture*; reluctance to accept a play on the tendentious subject of suicide may have contributed to this decision, but it was largely inspired by enmity towards Dorval on the part of a coterie led by Mlle Mars. Jouslin, now director of the Comédie-Française, was well enough disposed towards Vigny and Marie Dorval, but the majority of the *comédiens* were hostile, and their opposition was overcome only by the intervention of the royal family. Even when Jouslin, fortified by this support, had decided to override the committee's rejection of the play, there was a further difficulty when Mlle Mars tried to insist on her prerogative and claim the role of Kitty. Finally

Ligier, who had played Borgia in *La Maréchale d'Ancre*, and who had hoped for the part of John Bell, handed in his resignation as *sociétaire* on being passed over. The play was rehearsed, therefore, in an unfavourable atmosphere of hostility and resentment directed against the playwright and the leading actress. The part of Chatterton was allocated to Geffroy, a young actor for whom this was his first major chance, though he had played small parts in *Hernani* as well as Ludovico in *Le More de Venise*; John Bell was played by Guiaud, an actor of no great reputation; while Joanny, who had played Othello and Ruy Gomez, and who of all the actors at the Salle Richelieu was the most sympathetic towards Romantic drama, was given a role of considerable importance in Vigny's eyes, that of the Quaker.

As the date of the first performance drew nearer, Vigny retreated further into his pessimism and misanthropy. He now affected to disdain success in the theatre:

Dans l'état actuel des théâtres, et tel qu'est le public, j'ai peu d'estime pour une pièce qui réussit, c'est signe de médiocrité; il faut au public quelque chose d'un peu grossier[34]

and even as regards literary success, the optimism of the closing page of the 'Dernière Nuit de travail' is belied in other passages from this period:

Je me méfie aussi d'un livre qui réussirait sur-le-champ et sans un an au moins d'intervalle pour que l'élite puisse y convertir la masse idiote.[35]

However, the outcome was far more favourable than he had dared to hope, and with characteristic sincerity he consigned to his diary at midnight on February 12th, immediately after the first performance, the following more charitable view of his fellow-men:

Chatterton a réussi. C'est alors que mes amis sont venus à moi en fondant en larmes. Ils balbutiaient des paroles sans suite, des cris: mon ami, mon ami. Ils ont souffert aussi ce martyre

que j'ai écrit. Un sentiment doux et triste remplit mon cœur
et des larmes inondent mes yeux malgré moi. Je pense aux
douleurs que nous fait éprouver une trop grande défiance de
la méchanceté de nos frères. J'ai des remords d'avoir mal
jugé... Quel bonheur! France! France! On peut donc te
parler gravement quand on est grave, et avec tristesse quand
on est mélancolique et que l'on a au fond du cœur un incurable dédain de soi-même et une pitié bienveillante de la
pauvre humanité.[36]

Contemporary comment suggests, nevertheless, that as a 'pièce
à thèse' at any rate, *Chatterton* was perhaps a case of caviare to
the general. The 'gravity' of Vigny's philosophical message may
have been to the taste of an intellectual élite, but what the
public at large relished was the *pathétique* of the domestic drama.
The 'larmoyant' tableau of Kitty and her two children, and
especially the *jeu de scène* devised by Dorval herself for her
death-scene—the famous 'dégringolade' as she collapsed at the
top of the specially-constructed flight of stairs, sliding down
with her back against the banister-rail and coming to rest at the
bottom—were obvious concessions to a more popular taste; but
more generally, the innocent purity of her maternal love
contrasting with the growing awareness of her guilty love for
Chatterton, and the sudden outburst of her feelings in the last
Act, leading to the pathetic climax of her death, gave ample
scope to an actress trained in the *boulevard* genres, and there is
abundant evidence of the success obtained by Marie Dorval
in this, one of her greatest roles[37]. Once again, for a really
evocative tribute we can turn to the mature Gautier, looking
back in 1857 on one of the most memorable moments of his
youth:

Jamais peut-être cette admirable actrice ne s'éleva si haut;
quelle grâce anglaise et timide elle y mettait! comme elle
ménageait maternellement les deux babies, purs inter-
médiaires d'un amour inavoué! Quelle douce charité
féminine elle dépliait envers ce grand enfant de génie mutiné
contre le sort! De quelle main légère elle tâchait de panser les
plaies de cet orgueil souffrant!... Et quel cri déchirant à la
fin, quel oubli, quel abandon lorsqu'elle roulait, foudroyé de
douleur, au bas de ces marches montées par élans convulsifs,

par saccades folles, presque à genoux, les pieds pris dans sa
robe, les bras tendus, l'âme projetée hors du corps qui ne
pouvait la suivre![38]

But the hostility of Mlle Mars and Ligier triumphed in the end:
Chatterton was taken off while still successful, to make room for
the revival of a classical tragedy[39].

There is no reason to doubt the sincerity of Vigny's thesis, or
his belief in 'le drame de la pensée'; and no reason to doubt
that the play spoke eloquently to those who were already
converted. But in the case of the wider public, it seems likely
that the thesis was better served by the reflective prose of
Stello; and that considered purely as a 'pièce à thèse', *Chatterton*
must have been largely ineffective. A comment made by Vigny
himself some years later may serve as a pointer to the ambi-
valence of the play in this respect:

Les sujets où le cœur l'emporte sur le cerveau doivent être
écrits en prose; ceux où l'imagination a plus de part que
l'émotion doivent être écrits en vers. Des vers vont rarement
au cœur et rarement ils font pleurer.[40]

Not that there can have been any question of writing *Chatterton*
in verse; but there is perhaps a certain unresolved tension in the
play between the two kinds of inspiration here envisaged. On
the one hand, the poet's visionary imagination—which produced *Stello* and *Servitude et grandeur militaires* as well as *Les
Destinées*—conceived of Chatterton as a symbol of the poet-
martyr, and the writing of this part frequently betrays the abstract nature of this inspiration. On the other hand, the
dramatist with an eye to the effect his play would have in the
theatre—to say nothing of the lover writing a star part for his
mistress—recognized that it was the familiar, the prosaic, that
would appeal most directly to an audience's emotions. That
Vigny succeeded in creating a theatrically viable character in
Kitty Bell we can see from our own reading of the text: that he
created a character superbly suited to the particular gifts of
Marie Dorval is equally certain from the evidence of Gautier
and others. But he did not succeed nearly as well in clothing an
abstract thesis in dramatic flesh and blood; and in this respect

the concept of 'le drame de la pensée' remained to be realized
by playwrights of later generations.

(iv) Balzac: from 'Vautrin' to 'Mercadet'

ANY consideration of the development of 'le drame moderne'
in the Romantic period would be incomplete which did not
include at least a brief mention of the dramatic efforts of
another outstanding literary figure of the time, even though he
is not generally regarded as a major dramatist. The fascination
that the contemporary theatre held for Balzac can be seen in
novels like *Splendeurs et misères des courtisanes*, which give such a
lively picture of the seamier side of the small, ephemeral
boulevard establishments; while as regards writing for the
theatre, it is well known that one of his earliest literary ventures
was a classical tragedy on the subject of Cromwell[41], and from
then onwards, and particularly during the latter part of his life,
he was constantly planning new dramatic works. It is true that
what he appears to have sought in the theatre was the chance of
quick financial return, rather than the artistic success at which
he aimed with his *Comédie humaine*, for he wrote to Mme Hanska
as early as 1835:

Cette effroyable production de livres... ne suffit pas. Il faut
en venir au théâtre, dont les revenus sont énormes comparés
à ceux que nous font les livres.[42]

It is also true, unfortunately, that his ventures into the theatre
were hardly more successful than those of the other great
nineteenth-century novelists, Flaubert, the Goncourts or Zola.
But he did complete half a dozen plays with a view to performance, any of which might well have caught the fancy of the
contemporary public; and it is not difficult to imagine that an
early success would have encouraged him to bring to fruition
many more of his ideas[43].

The first of this group of plays, *L'École des ménages*, is in many
ways the most striking, and Balzac's ill-luck in this instance was
perhaps the most undeserved. Completed in 1839, this play was
refused by the Renaissance theatre, and negotiations with the
Théâtre-Français also came to nothing; and in spite of two very
successful 'lectures de société', the author was so discouraged

that he made no further attempt to stage his play. A 'tragédie bourgeoise', *L'École des ménages* is a play to which the cliché 'fifty years ahead of its time' can be applied with every justification: when it was produced for the first time, by Antoine at the Odéon in 1910, it was hailed by more than one reviewer as a true precursor of the repertory of the Théâtre-Libre, and indeed Balzac's treatment of his subject looks beyond the manner of Dumas *fils* and Augier to that of Becque and Brieux. What is most interesting about the play as a reflection of the literary tastes of the 1830s is the way in which Balzac has expressed in dramatic form the themes and the atmosphere of the *Comédie humaine*; but the theatregoing public (or at any rate conservative theatre managements) were not yet ready to accept the formula which had already been successfully established in the novel. The play combines the subject of a middle-aged *père de famille*'s adulterous passion, reminiscent of that of Baron Hulot in *La Cousine Bette*, with a faithful and convincing portrayal of a middle-class shopkeeper's establishment such as we see in *César Birotteau* or *La Maison du Chat-qui-pelote*. The endeavours of Monsieur Gérard's family to defend their home against his fatal passion for a young employee culminate in his daughter's ruthless attempt to poison the intruder, and the shock of this crisis causes both lovers to lose their reason. The fifth Act, which shows the pathetic spectacle of them both living in the past, each refusing to recognize in the other the object of his or her deranged affections, is based on a clinical case reported to Balzac: it could easily have lent itself to sensational or melodramatic treatment, but it is in fact handled with a restraint and understatement which look forward to the style of Brieux's case-histories, and the effect is all the more striking. If anything in *L'École des ménages* deserves the label 'Romantic', it is the familiar Balzac theme of the destructive effect of the passions. But this is the creative hypothesis of a psychologist, not the thesis of a social propagandist, and Balzac's formula is far removed from that of those 'drames modernes' which were more characteristic of the period; of the plays considered in this chapter, only *Teresa* offers any resemblance in this respect.

When we turn to *Vautrin* (Porte-Saint-Martin, March 1840), the first of Balzac's plays to be performed, the resemblance to the author's novels may at first sight perhaps be more obvious, but it is much more superficial: here, the portrayal of the anti-social genius completely lacks the subtlety of his portrait in *Père Goriot* and *Splendeurs et misères des courtisanes*, and the play is no more than a melodramatic imbroglio. Indeed, the affinity with popular melodrama is a good deal stronger than that with the *Comédie humaine*—though in one important respect this is a case of melodrama 'à rebours', since it is the amoral criminals and outlaws who represent the positive values in the play. It is true that the young Raoul de Frescas, Vautrin's protégé (who corresponds to Eugène de Rastignac and Lucien de Rubempré in the novels), has remained untainted by the corruption around him; but he is hardly an active character, and in any case he is pre-pared to accept the benefits of Vautrin's dubious activities on his behalf. It is difficult, reading *Vautrin*, not to think of *L'Auberge des Adrets* and *Robert Macaire*, those burlesque melo-dramas with which Frédérick Lemaître had largely built his reputation by cocking a snook at all the established values of traditional morality and social convention. The former play had been produced at the Ambigu-Comique in 1823, and a *reprise* at the Porte-Saint-Martin in 1832 was followed by the production of *Robert Macaire* at the Folies-Dramatiques in June 1834[44]. Pixérécourt had protested against the debasing of the moral function of melodrama, but the admiration of Balzac, and later Flaubert, for the character of Macaire is well known. However, it is difficult to accept a modern editor's claim that "*L'Auberge des Adrets*... sans le savoir, se trouva être le premier drame romantique"[45]: even if Don César in *Ruy Blas*, as well as Vautrin in Balzac's play, owes something to Frédérick's earlier (and most memorable) creation, *L'Auberge des Adrets* (to say nothing of *Robert Macaire*) is shot though with a spirit of burlesque and parody which distinguishes it very clearly from genuine Romantic drama[46].

Vautrin is a feeble play, but once again Balzac was ill-served by circumstances, and hardly deserved the complete fiasco which occurred: "ce désastre que l'énergie du gouvernement a causé, mais que, dit-on, le fer d'un coiffeur aurait pu réparer"[47]. At the dress-rehearsal Frédérick, who played the part of Vautrin, assumed as one of his disguises (his appearance in seven different outfits was an obvious concession to popular taste) a costume, and in particular a wig, which bore a strong resemblance to those of Louis-Philippe. Far from taking action to avoid this provocation, Harel instructed the barber to accentuate it, with the result that Frédérick's appearance on the first night brought the house down. The Duc d'Orléans left the theatre, and reported the outrage to his father, and the next day further performances of the play were banned: Harel went bankrupt, and Balzac received another major setback in his theatrical ambitions.

Strictly speaking, the subject of his next attempt, *Les Ressources de Quinola* (Odéon, March 1842), lies outside the scope of this chapter, for this was a historical drama set in Renaissance Spain. However, it was another failure—well deserved this time—and can be passed over briefly. The theme, that of the inventor of genius centuries ahead of his time—"une immense comédie sur la lutte d'un homme de génie avec son siècle"[48]— has obvious affinities with some of the 'Études philosophiques' in the *Comédie humaine*; but the execution, somewhat on the lines of Scribe's historical comedies, was not on a level with the inspiration which had conceived the theme, and the triumph Balzac had dreamed of soon turned into another fiasco. The first performance was the most tumultuous Paris had seen for a long time, and the reaction of the critics was almost universally savage; though on this occasion it must be said that the author had invited trouble by the tactless ostentation of his advance publicity[49]. *Les Ressources de Quinola* ran for 19 performances, but the reception was hostile enough to convince Balzac that if he had any hope of success as a dramatist, it lay not in the Romantic type of historical drama which was now well out of favour, but in the field of contemporary social studies.

However, *Paméla Giraud* (Gaîté, September 1843) has far too much of the melodrama about it for it to rank as anything more than a mediocre 'comédie de mœurs': the characters are grouped in two camps, the good and the bad, and the eponymous heroine, a pale copy of her English namesake (Balzac was moved to write the play after reading Richardson's novel), survives every trial and finally sees her virtue rewarded. In spite of a tighter and more efficient construction than that of *Vautrin* or *Quinola*, this was another play to fall foul of the critics; and if Milatchitch's description: "une amère satire des mœurs d'une société"[50] is perhaps justified by Balzac's conception of his subject, both dialogue and characterization show only too clearly the limitations of his talent when it came to writing for the theatre.

Nevertheless, throughout the 1840s he continued to hope for success in the theatre as a means of stabilizing his financial position:

> Il faut que je fasse à la scène les mêmes efforts que j'ai faits *en livres*, en 1830. Il s'agit de trouver pour la Porte-Saint-Martin une *Peau de Chagrin*, pour l'Ambigu une *Eugénie Grandet*, pour les Français les *Treize*, pour les Variétés un *Père Goriot*.[51]

But there was to be a gap of nearly five years before the appearance of his next play, *La Marâtre* (Théâtre-Historique, May 1848)—a fact which may have some bearing on the marked improvement it shows compared with the previous efforts. This time Balzac's literary workmanship did much better justice to the inspiration behind the play, and with a run of about forty performances it was the only one of his plays to achieve even a moderate success during its author's lifetime. If his reaction was, as usual, wildly optimistic:

> Ce que je voulais, je l'ai obtenu... Je suis sûr de mon avenir et d'une fortune[52]

—nevertheless one can understand why discerning critics gave a much warmer welcome to *La Marâtre* than to Balzac's earlier plays, and why Sarcey was led to write, à propos of the 1859 revival:

> *La Marâtre*, quoi qu'on ait pu dire, n'est point un chef-d'œuvre: il s'en faut de beaucoup; elle est bien mieux que cela: elle est une révolution. Chapeau bas, s'il vous plaît; c'est le réalisme qui prend possession du théâtre.[53]

In retrospect, it is not difficult to recognize in it—as in *L'École des ménages*—one of the most notable of the plays in the realist-domestic genre which helped to bridge the gap between the 'drame bourgeois' of Diderot and the naturalist plays of Becque and the Théâtre-Libre. The particular characteristics of the *Comédie humaine* which this play succeeds in transferring to the stage are both in their way eminently Romantic: the concern for the details of local colour—in this instance the portrayal of the social hierarchy of small-town provincial life—and the taste for heightened action. In the novels, the scale on which the narrative is constructed, with scope for lengthy exposition and ample development, helps to reconcile these two conflicting characteristics, and we do not find the sensational events of, say, *La Cousine Bette* or *La Rabouilleuse* incompatible with the setting they are given; but in the five acts of a play there is no room for such preparation, and we may well feel that there is something incongruous in the speed with which the domestic drama rushes to its fatal conclusion, after a leisurely opening devoted to the portrayal of milieu.

The subject of *La Marâtre* bears a striking similarity to that of Dumas's *Teresa*: the jealous passion of Gertrude, married to a widowed Napoleonic general, for her former lover Ferdinand who now loves (and is loved by) Pauline, the general's daughter, leads to the death by suicide of the two frustrated lovers. Comparison of the two plays is not necessarily to Balzac's advantage, for if *La Marâtre* scores by the greater realism of its setting, Dumas's play is much more credible in terms of character and dialogue. Where Dumas had been content with the simple working-out of a fatalistic tragedy, Balzac's plot is full of complications and contrivances; the general is something of a caricature (foreshadowing those of Anouilh's *Ardèle*, *La Valse des toréadors* and *L'Hurluberlu*), and the confrontation of the two female rivals has a sensational quality that we recognize easily enough in Balzac's novels, but which is quite lacking in *Teresa*.

Mercadet, Balzac's last play, suggests the genre in which his talents as a dramatist might have developed most successfully; he himself wrote that it marked a return to "l'ancien genre des pièces à caractère"[54], though it might be more accurate to suggest that he has followed Diderot's precept and substituted 'conditions' for 'caractères'. In other words we have a detailed depiction of a specialist milieu—here, the dubious world of the financial speculator, with the Paris *bourse* as a background:

social satire, without the sensational catastrophe of *L'École des ménages* or *La Marâtre*. *Mercadet* is squarely in the tradition which runs from *Le Philosophe sans le savoir* to *Le Gendre de Monsieur Poirier*: social comedy with a conventional plot and a happy ending. It is the character of Mercadet himself that makes the play: he is a comic character in the traditional sense, sufficiently larger than life to be memorable; and the play is an excellent reminder of Balzac's gifts as a comic writer. Mercadet's "Je serai le Napoléon des affaires" (III, xvi) proclaims his affinity with César Birotteau and other would-be geniuses from the world of the novels; but his friend Verdelin's "Vivat Mercadetus, speculatorum imperator!" (*ibid.*) is an even clearer indication of his relationship with Molière's Mascarille. He is the arch-schemer, the eternal optimist—and the similarity of his situation to Balzac's own, as disaster follows disaster and bankruptcy threatens, is no doubt one reason for the sympathy with which Mercadet is treated by his creator: an indulgent irony very different from the merciless way in which Turcaret, for instance, had been lampooned by Lesage.

Under the title of *Le Faiseur*, *Mercadet* was read to the committee of the Comédie-Française in August 1848, and unanimously accepted. "Il y aura succès", wrote Balzac with his incurable optimism. "Je doutais de celui de *La Marâtre*; mais celui-ci est certain... C'est la porte de l'Académie enfoncée, surtout"[55]. Rehearsals began, but Balzac found himself obliged to depart for Russia before the opening night, whereupon the production was first delayed, then indefinitely postponed; and the play was finally withdrawn on Balzac's instructions, when the actors insisted on further alterations. Negotiations with other theatres came to nothing, and the play was still shelved at the time of Balzac's death in 1850. However, in 1851 the Gymnase put it on, in a shortened three-act version made from Balzac's original five acts by Adolphe Dennery. In this form it had a considerable success, both in 1851 and on the occasion of later revivals; and it is on this modified text that Balzac's reputation as a dramatist *manqué* has principally been based.

It is highly ironical that of the half-dozen plays completed and offered to theatre managers, the best two should be the ones which were to remain unperformed in Balzac's lifetime. Of those that were performed, only *La Marâtre* made any significant contribution to the history of French drama during the Romantic period: the other three have been saved from complete oblivion only by the fact that Balzac was their author. In his two bourgeois tragedies, *L'École des ménages* and *La Marâtre*, however, and especially in the vein of social comedy in *Mercadet*, Balzac showed how the peculiar blend of dynamic Romanticism and sober realism that he had developed in his most characteristic novels could be exploited in the theatre; and he went further than any playwright of his time towards creating a form of drama that could serve as a vehicle for the analysis of the forces motivating the behaviour of representative individuals in contemporary society. For various reasons— partly because he was slow in adapting himself to the exigencies of writing for the stage; partly because he was a victim, like all the Romantic dramatists, of the capricious judgement of managers and critics; above all, no doubt, because of his early death—he suggested the new realist drama rather than fully developed it. Something of what he attempted was to be achieved by Augier and Dumas *fils*; but its full realization had to wait for the naturalist drama of the end of the century.

Notes to Chapter Eight

1. *Op. cit.*, p. 284.
2. *Ibid.*, p. 295.
3. Quoted by Descotes, *Le Drame* . . . , pp. 147–148.
4. *Histoire du romantisme*, ed. *cit.*, p. 144.
5. *Ed. cit.*, IV, pp. 294–301.
6. *Op. cit.*, IV, p. 88.
7. *Cœlina*, ed. Perry, p. xix.
8. Vigny, *Le More de Venise, Journal d'un poète, Morceaux divers*, Paris (Nelson), n.d., p. 528.
9. D. O. Evans, *op. cit.*, pp. 160–161, refers to the "unanimity" of contemporary reviewers on this question of anachronism in *Antony*, and quotes the *Revue Encyclopédique*: "Où trouve-t-on aujourd'hui le préjugé de la naissance? Franchement, rien n'est plus commun que les « mésalliances »: il n'est point de parti... auquel un jeune homme ne puisse prétendre, s'il est instruit, bien élevé, et surtout s'il a 60 000 livres de rente ... je ne vois donc pas ce qui empêcherait Antony d'épouser Adèle".
10. Vigny, *Le More de Venise* . . . , p. 533.

11. For a detailed treatment of Dumas's borrowings from Scott, see Parigot, *op. cit.*, pp. 60–74.

12. *Op. cit.*, pp. 365–375.

13. It should not be forgotten that Dumas's play itself represents a revised version. The original, by one Théaulon, had failed to satisfy Frédérick Lemaître, as had a first re-writing by a colleague, Courcy, so Dumas had been called in.

14. This was because a coalition of managers, led by Harel, had imposed a boycott on him which effectively closed all the principal theatres to him for the time being.

15. See Descotes, *Le Drame* . . . , pp. 306–309.

16. Cf. Sartre, *Kean*, ed. D. J. Bradby, London, 1973, pp. 15–16. Dr. Bradby's edition gives the complete text of Dumas's *Kean* as an appendix to that of Sartre's version.

17. A. Ubersfeld, 'Désordre et génie' in *Europe*, nos. 490–491, February-March 1970, p. 119.

18. *Chatterton*, ed. L. Petroni, Bologna, 1962, p. 59.

19. A. Cassagne, *La Théorie de l'art pour l'art en France*, Paris, 1906, p. 71. See also H. J. Hunt, *Le Socialisme et le romantisme en France*, Oxford, 1935; D. O. Evans, *Social Romanticism in France, 1830–1848*, Oxford, 1951; L. Maigron, *Le Romantisme et les mœurs*, Paris, 1910.

20. *L'Organisateur*, 7.xi.1829; quoted by Evans, *Social Romanticism . . .*, p. 86.

21. XXVI, quoted by Evans, *ibid.*, p. 87.

22. *Stello*, édition définitive, Paris, n.d., p. 288.

23. One case which attracted particular attention was the suicide-pact of two young poets, Escousse and Lebras, in February 1832.

24. *Histoire du romantisme, ed. cit.*, p. 133.

25. Cf. '*Chatterton* et le chattertonisme', pp. 106–120; and see also 'Le Romantisme et le suicide', pp. 312–350.

26. *Chatterton, ed. cit.*, p. 58.

27. Another stage-direction, from the last scene of the play: "Il entre chez Chatterton et s'enferme avec lui. *On devine* des soupirs de Chatterton et des paroles d'encouragement du Quaker..." (*Ed. cit.*, p. 165; my italics) might well have been written by Diderot.

28. See Plate 9.

29. *Op. cit.*, p. 40.

30. Cf. Gautier's comment: "Chatterton, dès qu'il s'est décidé à mourir, redevient un homme et cesse d'être une abstraction", *Histoire du romantisme*, p. 138.

31. *Op. cit.*, p. 42.
32. Cf., for instance, Musset's sonnet, addressed to Vigny's hostile critics:

> Quand vous aurez prouvé, messieurs du journalisme,
> Que Chatterton eut tort de mourir ignoré,
> Qu'au Théâtre-Français on l'a défiguré,
> Quand vous aurez crié sept fois à l'athéisme,
>
> Sept fois au contre-sens et sept fois au sophisme,
> Vous n'aurez pas prouvé que je n'ai pas pleuré,
> Et si mes pleurs ont tort devant le pédantisme,
> Savez-vous, moucherons, ce que je vous dirai?
>
> Je vous dirai, sachez que les larmes humaines
> Ressemblent en grandeur aux flots de l'Océan;
> On n'en fait rien de bon en les analysant;
>
> Quand vous en puiseriez deux tonnes toutes pleines,
> En les faisant sécher, vous n'en auriez demain
> Qu'un méchant grain de sel dans le creux de la main.

Correspondance d'Alfred de Musset, ed. L. Séché, Paris, 1907, pp. 126–127.
33. *Le Drame* . . . , pp. 276–277.
34. *Journal d'un poète* in *Le More de Venise* . . . , p. 268.
35. *Ibid.*, p. 269.
36. *Ibid.*, p. 273.
37. Cf. Descotes, *Le Drame* . . . , pp. 281–282.
38. *Histoire du romantisme*, pp. 138–139.
39. Cf. Descotes, *Le Drame* . . . , pp. 282–283; M. Carlson, *The French Stage in the Nineteenth Century*, Metuchen, N.J., 1972, pp. 70–71.
40. Quoted by Brun, *op. cit.*, p. 42.
41. Written in 1819, and first published in D. Z. Milatchitch, *Le Théâtre inédit de Honoré de Balzac*, Paris, 1930.
42. Letter of 23.viii.1835 (*Lettres à Madame Hanska*, ed. R. Pierrot, Paris, 1967, I, p. 354).
43. Milatchitch, *op. cit.*, discusses no less than forty-one 'pièces projetées' as well as fifteen 'pièces ébauchées' and three complete texts of hitherto unpublished plays (in addition to *Cromwell*, these are two melodramas, *Le Nègre* and *Le Corse*). See also the edition of Balzac, *Théâtre*, ed. R. Guise, 3 vols., Paris, 1969–71.

44. Cf. the critical edition of these two plays by C. Cœuré, Grenoble, 1966.

45. *Ibid.*, p. 13.

46. See R. Baldick, *op. cit.*, ch. x.

47. Preface.

48. Letter to Madame Hanska, 5.i.1842.

49. See D. Z. Milatchitch, *Le Théâtre de Honoré de Balzac*, Paris, 1930, pp. 125–134.

50. *Le Théâtre* . . . , p. 178.

51. Letter of 8.iii.1848, quoted by Milatchitch, *Le Théâtre* . . . , pp. 183–184.

52. Letter of 26.v.1848, quoted *ibid.*, p. 201.

53. *Op. cit.*, IV, pp. 192–193.

54. Letter to Laurent-Jan, 9.ii.1849.

55. Letter to Madame Hanska, 16.viii.1848, quoted by Milatchitch, *Le Théâtre* . . . , pp. 238–239.

9   Musset à l'école de Shakespeare

(i) 'La Nuit vénitienne'; 'André del Sarto'

AS has been seen in previous chapters, the individual fortunes of Hugo, Dumas and Vigny as dramatists were continuously interwoven—if not interdependent—during the late 1820s and the early 1830s. Starting out with the enthusiastic idealism of all young Romantics, they had made common cause together until the strain of working in an atmosphere beset by the rivalries of managers and actresses, and the hostility of actors and critics, so accentuated the differences of temperament and personality, that by 1836 or so their precarious unity was thoroughly exploded.

The fourth member of the quartet of major Romantic dramatists, Alfred de Musset, stands on his own. To begin with, he was much younger: born in 1810 (whereas Hugo and Dumas were born in 1802, and Vigny in 1797), he was more of an age with Gautier and Nerval; only nineteen at the time of the battle of *Hernani*, he took part in the most spectacular occasions of Romantic drama as spectator rather than as protagonist. Secondly, from his earliest, precocious literary essays onwards there was always something equivocal in Musset's attitudes towards Romantic ideas and fashions: if on the one hand certain writings (the four 'Nuits', for example) seem to express the very essence of Romantic idealism, on the other hand he was capable at times of debunking that idealism with a characteristic irony (e.g. 'Ballade à la lune', 'Namouna'). And finally, Musset's initial contact with the professional theatre was so profoundly discouraging that the great majority of his plays were to be written in a sort of splendid isolation, uncontaminated by the compromises and concessions that his fellow-dramatists, seeking to satisfy the demands of managers and mistresses, were constantly compelled to make.

11 (a) 'Costume de Mme Dorval,
rôle de Catarina'

(b) 'Costume de Mlle Mars,
rôle de Tisbé'

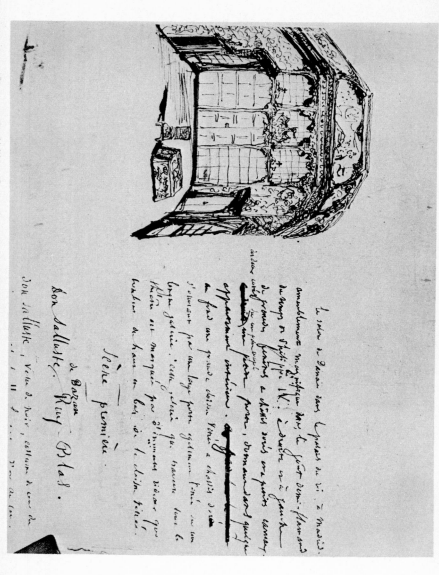

It is not altogether easy to know where to draw the line, in dealing with Musset's early writings, between the dramatic and the non-dramatic. The volume *Contes d'Espagne et d'Italie* of 1830 contained among its 'contes' one piece, 'Les Marrons du feu', which is wholly in dialogue form, and of which its author says ironically in his Prologue: "c'est une comédie... digne de Molière". In fact, in its nine brief scenes it contains two violent deaths, and reads very much like a parody of the more sensational of Mérimée's Clara Gazul pieces, which many scholars insist were themselves written as parodies. There is no attempt at convincing motivation of the characters' actions; the plot is manifestly absurd; and the only saving grace is provided by a few felicitous couplets which must have suggested to readers that if the young Musset had any dramatic gifts, these would be likely to find expression in the sort of exuberant verbal play that had already distinguished *Cromwell* and *Hernani*.

'Les Marrons du feu' represents a pastiche of a certain poetic style, rather than genuine dramatic creation, and it is not normally regarded as forming part of Musset's dramatic writings[1]. However, Musset's début in the theatre followed hard on the heels of his début in other literary fields (he had had his first poems published as a student of seventeen, and his free translation of de Quincey's *Opium Eater* was published in 1828, before his eighteenth birthday). His first real dramatic work, *La Quittance du diable*, was composed when he was still only nineteen, and accepted for performance at the Théâtre des Nouveautés: the failure of his second venture, *La Nuit vénitienne*, at the Odéon in December 1830 is said to have been the reason for its non-performance[2].

La Quittance du diable is a one-act play in three *tableaux*, based on 'Wandering Willie's Tale' from Scott's *Redgauntlet*. It accumulates a wealth of Romantic clichés, paying tribute to Scott's mediaevalism as well as to contemporary interest in the occult. Characterization, dialogue and plot are all mediocre, and it is only the fact that it is by the author of *Lorenzaccio* and *On ne badine pas avec l'amour* that makes *La Quittance du diable* more noteworthy than hundreds of similar trifles composed at the time. As it is, it is difficult to discern any connection of theme or style with Musset's later plays.

This is certainly not true of *La Nuit vénitienne*; Musset's second

play is a much subtler, altogether much more characteristic
piece of work, in which the Romantic theme of a disappointed
lover's despair and violent revenge is handled with delicate
irony. Razetta, a young Venetian, loves Laurette, who has
returned his love, but is now to be married for reasons of state
to a German prince whom she has never seen. As the Prince is
due to arrive, Razetta in vain asks her to elope with him, then
sends her a dagger, threatening to take his own life if by a given
hour she has not killed the Prince and come to join him. The
Prince arrives, and by his charm and civilized behaviour succeeds in winning the esteem of his bride and showing her how
to treat Razetta's melodramatic posturing. The hour strikes, and
instead of suicide the disappointed lover accepts the invitation
of a passing gondola-full of pleasure-seekers, to join them in
a night's revelry. If the Romantic convention is exploded—for
the triangle formed by Razetta, Laurette and the Prince
d'Eysenach corresponds, for instance, to that formed by
Antony, Adèle and Colonel d'Hervey—the dénouement makes
use of a contrivance just as artificial, in that the state marriage
of two strangers turns out to be a marriage based on love. But
plot is unimportant: what matters are the attitudes of the
characters, and in the long central scene between Laurette and
the Prince, Musset creates an atmosphere that, instead of being
'Romantic' in the sense of the literary fashion current at the
time, belongs to a perennial tradition of 'romantic' comedy—an
atmosphere of fantasy, in which idealized characters can discuss
with a considerable degree of psychological realism the affairs
of the heart. It is the world of *Twelfth Night* or *As You Like It*,
of *Le Jeu de l'amour et du hasard*, and in our own day of a play like
Anouilh's *Léocadia*; a world to which we shall frequently be
introduced in Musset's theatre. As regards prose style, Musset's
affinity with Marivaux in this connection has often been noted,
and indeed the debt to Marivaux can be seen in *La Nuit vénitienne*; but what distinguishes Musset's dialogue already in this
play, rather than a genuine *marivaudage*, is an idiosyncratic use
of sustained imagery that is to be found again in the *comédies* and
proverbes as well as in *Lorenzaccio*:

Vous êtes bien jeune, madame; et moi aussi. Cependant,
comme les romans ne sont pas défendus, non plus que les

comédies, les tragédies, les nouvelles, les histoires et les mémoires, je puis vous apprendre ce qu'ils m'ont appris. Dans tout morceau d'ensemble, il y a une introduction, un thème, deux ou trois variations, un andante et un presto. A l'introduction vous voyez les musiciens encore mal se répondre, chercher à s'unir, se consulter, s'essayer, se mesurer; le thème les met d'accord; tous se taisent ou murmurent faiblement, tandis qu'une voix harmonieuse les domine; je ne crois pas nécessaire de faire l'application de cette parabole. Les variations sont plus ou moins longues, selon ce que la pensée éprouve: mollesse ou fatigue. Ici, sans contredit, commence le chef-d'œuvre; l'andante, les yeux humides de pleurs, s'avance lentement, les mains s'unissent; c'est le romanesque, les grands serments, les petites promesses, les attendrissements, la mélancolie. — Peu à peu tout s'arrange; l'amant ne doute plus du cœur de sa maîtresse; la joie renaît, le bonheur par conséquent: la bénédiction apostolique et romaine doit trouver ici sa place; car, sans cela, le presto survenant... Vous souriez? (sc. ii)

Unfortunately, the irony and detachment which are so attractive to a modern reader, and which suggest a remarkable sophistication in a youth of nineteen, quite failed to impress Musset's contemporaries. Public and critics united in condemning the play: the plot as gratuitous, the dialogue as obscure; and the reception it received at its two performances was disastrous. The play had been specially commissioned by Harel for the Odéon, and the young author was in high hopes of a successful start to his career in the theatre. The setback was so wounding to his pride and sensitivity that for another seventeen years he was completely absent from the Paris stage; and even when one of Musset's plays was performed again in 1847, this was *Un Caprice*, written, like the great majority of his plays, as 'armchair drama', and already published ten years earlier: it was not until 1849, with *Louison* and *On ne saurait penser à tout*, that he began again to write directly for the theatre. "Qui peut dire où en serait le théâtre aujourd'hui", wrote his brother Paul in 1877, "si une poignée de Béotiens n'en eût écarté pendant tant d'années le seul écrivain capable d'arrêter la décadence de l'art dramatique?"[3]. The opinion is naturally a biased one; perhaps it would be fairer to Musset's contemporaries in the theatre if one were to call him the playwright capable of making the most

imaginative use of the new freedom already being exploited
with at least partial success by others. At all events, here was a
young writer who was determined not to compromise with his
artistic integrity in order to win the favour of commercially-
minded managers, hostile critics, or a capricious public.

André del Sarto in many ways represents the quintessence of
Romanticism in the theatre. Set, as *Lorenzaccio* was to be, in an
Italian Renaissance milieu, it portrays three principal characters, each of whom sacrifices honour and duty to love: the
triangular relationship between André, his wife Lucrèce and his
friend Cordiani strangely prefigures, as Philippe Van Tieghem
points out[4], the real-life relationship between Musset, George
Sand and Pagello which was to terminate the lovers' Venetian
idyll in 1834. Cordiani justifies his betrayal of his friend in a
typically Romantic appeal to the overriding rights of passion:

> Depuis un an que je la vois tous les jours, je lui parle, et elle
> me répond; je fais un geste, et elle me comprend. Elle se met
> au clavecin, elle chante, et moi, les lèvres entr'ouvertes, je
> regarde une longue larme tomber en silence sur mes bras
> nus. Et de quel droit ne serait-elle pas à moi?
>
> — De quel droit?
>
> — Silence! j'aime et je suis aimé. Je ne veux rien analyser,
> rien savoir; il n'y a d'heureux que les enfants qui cueillent
> un fruit et le portent à leurs lèvres sans penser à autre chose,
> sinon qu'ils l'aiment et qu'il est à portée de leurs mains (I, i)

—while even André himself, although his love for Lucrèce has
the sanction of marriage, has been so enslaved by his passion
that he has misappropriated money entrusted to him by the
King of France, and has betrayed his integrity as an artist. A
passionate violence, conventionally associated with the Renaissance, runs through the play: we have the wounding, then the
murder, of a faithful servant of André's by the desperate
Cordiani; a duel, in which Cordiani himself is wounded; and
the dénouement, in which André takes poison, having sent this
message after the fugitive lovers:

> Pourquoi fuyez-vous si vite? la veuve d'André del Sarto peut
> épouser Cordiani. (III, ii)

The language, although less idiosyncratic than the passage quoted from *La Nuit vénitienne*, does contain some of the imagery which is to be characteristic of Musset's later theatre:

> Je la tenais embrassée durant les longues nuits d'été, sur mon balcon gothique. Je voyais tomber en silence les étoiles des mondes détruits. Qu'est-ce que la gloire? m'écriais-je; qu'est-ce que l'ambition? Hélas! l'homme tend à la nature une coupe aussi large et aussi vide qu'elle. Elle n'y laisse tomber qu'une goutte de sa rosée; mais cette goutte est l'amour, c'est une larme de ses yeux, la seule qu'elle ait versée sur cette terre pour la consoler d'être sortie de ses mains. (*ibid.*)

But such passages are hardly integrated into the atmospheric mood of the play as a whole, which is too close to that of a melodrama. Altogether, *André del Sarto* remains very slight. Apart from the central figure, the rest of the characters are stereotypes of the devoted comrade, the faithless friend, the unfaithful wife, or the loyal servant; and Musset has succeeded in showing originality and insight only in André himself, the character which is in many ways a self-portrait. Talented but unstable, forgiving towards others but haunted by consciousness of his own guilt, he is driven to take his life as much as anything else by a *taedium vitae* that has in it more than a touch of the Romantic *mal du siècle*.

Published in the *Revue des Deux Mondes* in April 1833, *André del Sarto* apparently attracted no notice at the time. After the success of *Un Caprice* in 1847, it was one of the first of Musset's plays to be performed (Théâtre-Français, November 1848), but once more it failed to make much impact. For the *reprise* at the Odéon in 1850, the play was considerably modified: not only to make it more stageworthy (the new version was re-cast in two acts, instead of three), but also in order to satisfy the moral censorship of the new régime. André's pardon of the adulterous lovers, and his death which enabled them to marry, were now seen as an encouragement to Romantic licence; in the new version, although this still ends with André's death, Cordiani too dies as a result of their duel: a singular victory for the new morality, and a forecast of things to come.

(ii) 'Lorenzaccio'

THE early dramatic essays so far considered, with their colourful, lively picture of an Italy that owed more to fancy than to fact, certainly provide one important source when we come to study the origins of *Lorenzaccio*. There is a more tangible source, however, which links Musset's masterpiece with those sober, over-academic attempts to re-create the fabric of the past that we have examined in an earlier chapter. This is George Sand's 'scène historique', *Une Conspiration en 1537*, which probably dates from 1831 or 1832, and is thought to have been written with a view to publication in the *Revue de Paris*[5]. An excellent example of the formula as defined by Vitet: "des faits historiques présentés sous la forme dramatique, mais sans la prétention d'en composer un drame", her text is based on, and closely follows, Varchi's sixteenth-century chronicle of the same events in his *Storia fiorentina*[6].

Varchi's history was commissioned by Cosmo de Medici (the Côme de Médicis who appears in Act V of Musset's play), but in spite of its 'official' character, this is no black-and-white account, whitewashing Duke Alexander and vilifying his enemies. The treatment of the relationships between the various republicans shows considerable psychological subtlety; and with regard to Lorenzo's reasons for killing the Duke, Varchi lists some of those alleged by contemporaries—personal ambition, family honour, patriotic idealism, temperamental instability, and a warped moral sense—and prudently refrains from drawing any conclusions other than that his motivation must have been very complex[7].

George Sand's text provides a most interesting half-way stage between historical document and theatrically viable drama. As Dimoff has shown, *Une Conspiration en 1537* remains faithful to Varchi—or to certain other historians with whom the author supplemented the latter's account—in nearly every detail; even the error in the title, for instance (Alexander was in fact murdered in 1536) is copied from Moreri[8]—but the historian's inconclusive treatment of Lorenzo's motivation is replaced by the creative artist's delineation of a coherent, if sketchy, character. George Sand has confined her selection of events to the crisis, and treated this in the space of a few hours; her approach gives the central character a prominence, and endows the material with a conventional dramatic shape, that one would look for in vain in most 'scènes historiques'. Partly for this reason, no doubt, her Lorenzo is a simpler and more straightforward conception, compared with Musset's Lorenzaccio: the ambiguity attaching to his past behaviour is resolved, as soon as the principal action begins in scene iii with the preparations for the Duke's murder, while the fact that *Une Conspiration en 1537* ends abruptly with Lorenzo's escape to safety once the murder has been committed, gives this deed a much more positive character than it has in Musset's play.

The liaison between Musset and George Sand began in July 1833. There is no reason to think that Musset had shown any previous interest in the subject of Lorenzo de Medici, and every reason to believe that even the earliest of the plans for *Lorenzaccio*[9] was based on the text of *Une Conspiration en 1537*. The extent to which the play was written before the Italian visit (December 1833—March 1834); how much was written in Italy (the lovers stayed briefly in Florence before going on to Venice); and the amount of writing, as distinct from arranging of material, that remained to be done after the separation and Musset's return home: these points remain obscure, but it seems that by the middle of May 1834 the poet was able to speak of the play as complete, and it was published by August of the same year.

Dimoff's analysis[10] indicates the way in which Musset must have set about filling out the framework provided by his mistress's 'scène historique'. The subsidiary episodes of the liaison between the Duke and the Marquise Cibo, and the death of Louise Strozzi, were taken from passages in Varchi that had not been used by George Sand; and on this additional material all of the Cibo and Strozzi scenes, which contribute so much to the atmosphere as well as to the action of Musset's play, were based. The study of the three surviving plans enables one to see how this filling out of *Une Conspiration* took place, and reveals the interesting fact that in the two scenes taken over most closely from George Sand (the 'scène de l'épée' and the 'scène des républicains devant le duc') his second and third plans are much closer to the original than the first, in which he had evidently been tempted to show a greater measure of independence. The rest of the creative work, from this preliminary point onwards, remains undocumented: the third draft contains a mere twenty-four scenes, against the thirty-nine[11] of the finished play, and it is not possible to say in what stages this further work of enrichment and amplification was undertaken. With regard to the debt to George Sand, however, the evidence is perfectly clear, not only that *Une Conspiration en 1537* provided Musset with his starting-point, but that he owed to this "indiscutable collaboration", as Dimoff calls it, a good deal of the character of the finished work:

> Il a traité cette pièce comme il eût fait d'une première ébauche de son futur drame, s'évertuant sans doute à la remanier, à l'étoffer, à la perfectionner, mais aussi conservant telles quelles, ou à peu près, les parties qu'il estimait bien venues. Ainsi y a-t-il, dans *Lorenzaccio*, quelques passages de la seule invention de George Sand, d'autres, de beaucoup les plus nombreux, de la seule invention d'Alfred de Musset, d'autres enfin qu'on serait fort embarrassé d'attribuer à l'un des deux écrivains, parce que tous deux ont concouru, dans une proportion d'ailleurs variable, à les faire ce qu'ils sont.[12]

The origins of *Lorenzaccio* could therefore not be more different from those of most other Romantic dramas on historical subjects. Dumas, as we have seen, was to be quite open in confessing that for him 'le cadre' was a secondary consideration, and that 'la fable' always came first; while Hugo, for his part, frequently went to considerable lengths to mask his own not very dissimilar practice by a display of totally irrelevant historical scholarship. *Lorenzaccio*, on the other hand, stands in a close and responsible relationship, via George Sand's *Conspiration*, to a Renaissance chronicle, itself a responsible and authoritative account of the events it narrates. The result is that the play possesses a historical authenticity that one finds nowhere else in the field of Romantic historical drama, with the single exception of *La Maréchale d'Ancre*; but while Vigny's play remains very much an academic exercise, *Lorenzaccio* combines this responsible approach towards history with a poet's insight and a dramatist's skill.

The resultant formula, satisfying a demand which, as we have seen, had been voiced from the middle of the eighteenth

century onwards by Hénault and others, is one of the characteristics of *Lorenzaccio* that have earned for it the label
'Shakespearean'. The first feature which suggests comparison
with the English playwright's technique is naturally the
amplitude of Musset's drama. The mere number of scenes gives
some idea of this; but in fact this figure, thirty-nine, does no
more than denote an equivalent number of changes of setting,
and if Musset had followed the practice of French classical
dramatists and indicated a new 'scene' at each entrance or exit
of a character, the total would have been far greater[13]. For
instance, the six scenes of Act I would have to be counted as
sixteen at least, in order to take note of even the principal
comings and goings of characters during this Act; while a scene
like V, v is made up of two encounters between separate groups
of characters, and liaison between the two halves is entirely
lacking. This is of course very much in Shakespeare's own
manner, and it was presumably this feature more than any
other which deterred producers from tackling *Lorenzaccio* for
another half-century after the successful staging of some of his
other plays. With a structure as episodic as this, it becomes
impossible to talk of 'plot' and 'sub-plot'; and the unity of
Lorenzaccio, from the structural point of view, is that which is
conferred by the historical material provided by Musset's
source. This is a chronicle play about the fortunes of a particular
community at a given moment in history; and the 'fortunes' of
Florence are interpreted with a breadth unknown before in
French drama (with the possible exception of *Cromwell*).

While conventional unity of place has of course gone by the
board, the diversity of successive locations in and around
Florence has the cumulative effect of creating, from the
multiple aspects of the life of the city that are evoked by the
playwright, a different sort of unity: even the three or four
scenes that are set away from Florence itself do not destroy this
effect, since the dialogue of the exiles is completely taken up
with the fortunes of Florence. At any rate, this illusion of the
'personality' of the city of Florence is something which is
powerfully present for the reader of the play; it is obvious,
however, that Musset's technique would have put too great a
strain on nineteenth-century ideas about *mise en scène*, and that
to be carried out as the author envisaged it, the staging of

Lorenzaccio would have entailed either a reversion to the symbolic *décor simultané* of the pre-classical theatre, or else the anticipation of the resources of twentieth-century stage design. At all events, it was quite unsuited to the detailed naturalism of the nineteenth-century representational tradition—whereas Hugo's standard practice, for all its breach with unity of place, remained well within that tradition. *Hernani*, for instance, calls for the creation of five naturalistic sets, each of which remains undisturbed for a complete act (and it is interesting to note that when *Lorenzaccio* was finally produced in 1896, precisely the same effect was achieved in Armand d'Artois's adaptation by regrouping the material as follows: Act I a street-scene; Act II 'au palais des Soderini'; Act III 'au palais des Strozzi'; Act IV 'au palais du Duc'; Act V 'la chambre à coucher de Lorenzo').[14]

Another recognizably 'Shakespearean' feature is the effect produced by the social 'spread' of the characters. The picture we are given of Florence may be less rich than that of Verona in *Romeo and Juliet*, where not only the principal members of the feuding families are shown, but also their friends and servants, as well as representatives of the neutral, or uncommitted, citizens; nevertheless, the influence of Shakespeare is surely to be seen in the roles of the Orfèvre and the Marchand de Soieries, the Écoliers, and the Bourgeois and his wife in Act I, scene ii, and in the conversation between the merchants and their customers in Act I, scene v; in the introduction of such minor characters as Maffio or Tebaldeo, or the banquet scene with the forty members of the Strozzi family; and in Act V, scene v, which brings back the Orfèvre and the Marchand, as well as introducing the Strozzi and the Salviati children with their tutors. No longer is the political unrest of an oppressed community deemed to be adequately represented by the portrayal of a handful of conspirators and their confidants; Musset is at pains to indicate, to an extent not previously tried by any French dramatist, the involvement of ordinary people in the affairs of state[15].

Another way in which Musset's historical drama achieves its characteristic breadth concerns the author's treatment of all that comes under the head of 'local colour'. Local colour has often been seen as a positive achievement of the Romantic dramatists—though Corneille, for instance, had shown how much could be done, even within the formula of French classical tragedy, by concentrated reference to well-known features of the Roman way of life—but comparison with the practice of Hugo and Dumas shows at once how much more discreet, yet more penetrating, was Musset's handling of it. Musset, in fact, steered a middle course between the superficial manner of Dumas (which we have discussed in respect of *Henri III et sa cour*) and the pedantry of Vigny, whose *Maréchale d'Ancre* had been accompanied by footnotes addressed to the reader. Thus, one of the functions of the dialogue between the Orfèvre and the Marchand de Soieries (I, ii), or between the Marquise Cibo and the Cardinal (I, iii), is to establish the historical facts of the relationship between Florence and Rome, politics and the Church; and there is gradually built up a picture of a well-defined community, with its characteristic mixture of opulence and depravity, of corruption and republican idealism, of naive faith and amoral cynicism, which could only be sixteenth-century Florence. This detailed documentation of background is essential if we are to be given the impression of a dramatized version of a specific event, determined by unique conditions of time and place—and that, surely, is what we understand by a genuine historical drama.

But if it is by common consent the most distinguished of the historical dramas written at this period, *Lorenzaccio* is also without any doubt the most distinguished Romantic tragedy; and the majority of those who have applied the adjective 'Shakespearean' to Musset's play seem to have had in mind a comparison, not with the manner of the Histories, but with the treatment of the central character in a tragedy like *Hamlet*.

This comparison, it is true, has often been made on the superficial, and rather trivial, grounds of a close coincidence of subject-matter[16]: *Lorenzaccio*, like *Hamlet*, is the study of a man bringing himself to the point of killing a close relative, the ruler of the state, out of a sense of duty; and both heroes assume a mask of irresponsibility in order the better to achieve their objective[17]. But this is no more than an accidental resemblance; and it is Musset's sympathetic understanding of Shakespeare's *manner*, which led him to apply to the portrayal of his hero a technique totally opposed to that found in French classical tragedy, that constitutes his real debt to the English dramatist.

Where French playwrights from Corneille to Voltaire had
created a dilemma for their heroes which could be analysed in
terms of a dialectical confrontation of opposites[18], Musset
chooses the gradual approach, enabling the spectator to build
up a synthetic picture of Lorenzo's tragic situation from a
series of 'experimental' approximations[19]. Thus, the reader
coming to *Lorenzaccio* for the first time is as mystified as are the
other protagonists themselves by Lorenzo's behaviour throughout Acts I and II. His complicity in the abduction of Maffio's
sister; his apparent cowardice in the face of Sire Maurice's
insults; his flippant treatment of Tebaldeo's idealism; his
'betrayal' of Bindo and Venturi to the Duke: all this appears
completely enigmatic, and we have no other clue to his motives
than the conflicting reactions of the other characters: Philippe
Strozzi's disappointment, Marie's shame, the Duke's amused
contempt, and Pierre's undisguised hostility. There are occasional hints, at most, that Lorenzo is playing a part, and these
hints become a certainty in the first scene with Scoronconcolo
(III, i); but it is only in the long scene with Philippe that the
key to the enigma is given to us. Even then, this is a slow and
gradual revelation, as the scene (III, iii), placed at the structurally important mid-point of the play, itself hinges about a
decisive turning-point. Lorenzo has so far appeared to be a
detached commentator on the goings-on in Florence, himself
taking little active part in them; while the affairs of the Strozzi
family have been assuming increasing importance, and Philippe
himself has emerged as the one character with unchallenged
moral authority. At the beginning of this dialogue, it is still
Philippe who takes the initiative, and Lorenzo's response is
characteristically evasive to start with; but from the point at
which Philippe rises to leave, despairing of rousing Lorenzo to
action, the latter begins to declare himself, at first indirectly:

Il y a plusieurs démons, Philippe. Celui qui te tente en ce
moment n'est pas le moins à craindre de tous

—then with direct reference to his own predicament:

Prends-y garde, c'est un démon plus beau que Gabriel: la
liberté, la patrie, le bonheur des hommes, tous ces mots

résonnent à son approche comme les cordes d'une lyre; c'est le bruit des écailles d'argent de ses ailes flamboyantes. Les larmes de ses yeux fécondent la terre, et il tient à la main la palme des martyrs. Ses paroles épurent l'air autour de ses lèvres; son vol est si rapide que nul ne peut dire où il va. Prends-y garde! une fois dans ma vie, je l'ai vu traverser les cieux. J'étais courbé sur mes livres — le toucher de sa main a fait frémir mes cheveux comme une plume légère. Que je l'aie écouté ou non, n'en parlons plus.

It is as though the apocalyptic imagery of this speech breaks through some barrier, releasing Lorenzo from the laconic, prosaic manner that he has affected up to this point; and for the remainder of this scene, as he proceeds with his confession to Philippe, he continually has recourse to the aid of vigorous, colourful imagery to convey both his past exaltation and his present conviction of complete isolation from his fellow-men. Now it is done by a single striking metaphor:

Le vice a été pour moi un vêtement, maintenant il est collé à ma peau

—now by a brilliant development of a sustained image:

Ah! vous avez vécu tout seul, Philippe. Pareil à un fanal éclatant, vous êtes resté immobile au bord de l'océan des hommes, et vous avez regardé dans les eaux la réflexion de votre propre lumière. Du fond de votre solitude, vous trouviez l'océan magnifique sous le dais splendide des cieux. Vous ne comptiez pas chaque flot, vous ne jetiez pas la sonde; vous étiez plein de confiance dans l'ouvrage de Dieu. Mais moi, pendant ce temps-là, j'ai plongé — je me suis enfoncé dans cette mer houleuse de la vie; — j'en ai parcouru toutes les profondeurs, couvert de ma cloche de verre; — tandis que vous admiriez la surface, j'ai vu les débris des naufrages, les ossements et les Léviathans

—and now by reference to a continuing leitmotif, as Lorenzo casts himself in the role of a modern Brutus[20].

From this point onwards Lorenzo succeeds in establishing himself as the central and most important character, not only in terms of plot—we now know that his mask of debauch has been deliberately assumed in order to enable him to profit from the Duke's intimacy and assassinate him—but also in terms of dramatic interest; and the transformation of the character from the Lorenzo of Acts I and II (at best neutral from the point of view of the reader's sympathy, if not positively antipathetic) to a fully sympathetic figure with the undoubted stature of a tragic hero, is a remarkable *tour de force*. This depends almost entirely on the poetic quality of Musset's writing, for the second half of the play is punctuated by three major soliloquies on the hero's part (IV, iii; IV, v; IV, ix) which continue the self-analysis and revelation of motive that has been begun in Act III, scene iii.

The way in which these soliloquies work is very unlike the dialectical manner of the classical monologue, often clearly based on a thesis-antithesis-synthesis pattern. It is nearer to that of the Shakespearean soliloquy; indeed, Musset seems to have gone further than Shakespeare in contrasting two types of scene: those in which rapid, even perfunctory action is matched by a simple, functional prose style, and the static soliloquies (and other scenes devoted to reflection rather than action, such as III, iii), which are characterized by a poet's highly imaginative writing. The cumulative effect of the hero's soliloquies in *Lorenzaccio* is that by the time his deed is committed, we have been given a quite unusual insight into his state of mind. These are not the self-sufficient 'arias' of Hugo's verse drama, which take the plot-situation as the starting-point for an imaginative lyric development on a poetic theme of universal appeal: Lorenzo's soliloquies remain more closely related to dramatic situation, and their function is as it were to strip away successive layers of the character's consciousness, and progressively to reveal the essential Lorenzo. This is the way Musset's imagery works: it appeals to our imaginative sympathy, not to our rational understanding; for example in the long sequence of images at the beginning of the soliloquy in Act IV, scene v:

Par le ciel! quel homme de cire suis-je donc! Le Vice, comme la robe de Déjanire, s'est-il si profondément incorporé à mes fibres, que je ne puisse plus répondre de ma langue, et que l'air qui sort de mes lèvres me fasse ruffian malgré moi? J'allais corrompre Catherine. — Je crois que je corromprais ma mère, si mon cerveau le prenait à tâche; car Dieu sait quelle corde et quel arc les dieux ont tendus dans ma tête, et quelle force ont les flèches qui en partent. Si tous les hommes sont des parcelles d'un foyer immense, assurément l'être inconnu qui m'a pétri a laissé tomber un tison au lieu d'une étincelle dans ce corps faible et chancelant...

—or in this passage from Act IV, scene ix, in which Lorenzo's thoughts go from the dead Louise Strozzi to his own youth and innocence:

Pauvre Philippe! une fille belle comme le jour. Une seule fois, je me suis assis près d'elle sous le marronnier; ces petites mains blanches, comme cela travaillait! Que de journées j'ai passées, moi, assis sous les arbres! Ah! quelle tranquillité! quel horizon à Cafaggiuolo! Jeannette était jolie, la petite fille du concierge, en faisant sécher sa lessive. Comme elle chassait les chèvres qui venaient marcher sur son linge étendu sur le gazon! la chèvre blanche revenait toujours avec ses grandes pattes menues.

Despite the argumentative framework which gives coherence to such speeches, their purpose is not, like that of the classical soliloquy, moral justification by logical persuasion, nor yet a rational appeal to the spectator to identify himself with the hero's motivation. Rather it is an emotive appeal for sympathetic understanding of his unique predicament, from a character conscious of having reached an extreme limit of human experience. Hence the reliance on such features as exclamatory rhetoric; and hence above all the imagery by means of which, in a truly Shakespearean manner, Musset elevates the soul-searching of his hero into a poetic appeal to the reader's sensibility.

If we apply to *Lorenzaccio* the criterion of 'ambiguity' proposed by Camus for the identification of genuine tragedy[21], there would seem to be little difficulty in accepting the character of Lorenzo himself in these terms. The enigmatic quality of his actions in the first half of the play, and the equivocal relationship between the mask and the features beneath once his situation has been fully revealed, establish him as a truly tragic figure. In connection with the ambiguity of Musset's hero, H. S. Gochberg makes a good deal of play with the various names he is given by the other characters (Lorenzo, Lorenzaccio, Renzo, Renzino, Renzinaccio, Lorenzino, Lorenzetta):

> Even the proliferation of names is meaningful, for it is a way of posing the play's crucial problem, namely the identification of the hero and the attribution of motive to his actions.[22]

However, to speak of Lorenzo "playing at being Lorenzaccio" or of "the *dédoublement* and the role-playing associated with the Lorenzo–Lorenzaccio transformation"[23] is perhaps to fall into the trap of seeing Musset's hero as a second Hamlet, in conscious control of the disguise he has assumed as a mask for his secret purpose. For in Lorenzo's case we are asked to believe that he has *become* Lorenzaccio, and that the virtuous idealist and the depraved pander coexist in the same character. This is surely the grotesque/sublime antithesis of the *Préface de Cromwell* in its most compelling incarnation: not the crude juxtaposition of extremes that we find in Triboulet or Lucrèce Borgia, but something much subtler, nearer to the hauntingly human dualism of Baudelaire's 'Spleen et Idéal'. Even Lorenzo's original purpose was not entirely pure, as he tells Philippe:

> Les hommes ne m'avaient fait ni bien ni mal, mais j'étais bon, et, pour mon malheur éternel, j'ai voulu être grand. Il faut que je l'avoue, si la Providence m'a poussé à la résolution de tuer un tyran, quel qu'il fût, l'orgueil m'y a poussé aussi (III, iii)

—and now his former self has disappeared without trace: Dejanira's cloak has burnt itself into the flesh beneath, and the mask of evil is no longer a mask. The killing of Alexandre will not restore his own lost innocence, and he has no illusions left about its political outcome: all he can hope to achieve is to justify himself in the eyes of others, having destroyed himself in the process. In fact, if we experience any feeling of release at the end of the play, it is not at Alexandre's death, which merely marks the dramatic climax, but at Lorenzo's, which alone can restore some sense of the rightness of things[24].

When we turn to look at the principal characters surrounding the hero, it is perhaps natural that none of them should exhibit the same degree of ambiguity that he does. At first sight, indeed, it may seem as though they are divided, according to the formula of melodrama, into extremes of good and bad: the latter comprising the Duke and his courtiers, while the opposition consists of Lorenzo's family, the Strozzis, and the Marquise Cibo and her husband. However, while this opposition is real enough, it is hardly a case of a contrast of absolute black and white. None of the patriots, for instance, preserves an untarnished ideal: the Marquise, reflecting Lorenzo's own dilemma, sacrifices her virtue in a misguided attempt to influence the affairs of state by becoming the Duke's mistress; Philippe Strozzi remains detached and inactive in a situation which calls for action; while Pierre's hot-headedness leads him to insult his father and forfeit the spectator's sympathy. On the other side, however extreme the colours in which Alexandre is painted, the character as we see him is to some extent redeemed by the good-humoured tolerance he displays, and by his genuine affection for Lorenzo. It is true that the Duke's entourage contains minor characters like Salviati, whose evil nature is unrelieved—just as there is, opposed to them, a group of less prominent characters without any moral blemish: Lorenzo's mother, Catherine, the Marquis, Louise and Tebaldeo, all of whom are exploited, deceived or destroyed by others. But the only major figure who is utterly evil is the Cardinal Cibo (the soliloquy that he is given in Act II, scene iii has the opposite effect from those of Lorenzo: instead of revealing complexity of motivation, it stands out as an example of melodramatic confession by the villain of the piece): otherwise, the complexity of the action, and the general 'greyness' of the principal characters, adds without a doubt to the moral ambiguity of the play. Thus the episodic structure, the presentation of 'background', and the treatment of the two principal 'sub-plots' all work together with the way in which the central character is developed: the two aspects of the play—historical drama and tragedy—do not stand in opposition, but complement each other. Indeed, one can see that the composite tragedy of Florence underlines that of Lorenzo himself; the relationship between these two elements is well expressed as follows in a recent critical assessment of Musset's theatre:

The private anguish of Lorenzaccio is regularly interwoven with an anonymous urban complaint in a fugal pattern of restatement and counterpoint which shapes the theme in time without altering its integrity.[25]

The play was published in August 1834 in *Un Spectacle dans un fauteuil. Seconde Livraison, prose*, Volume I. There were further editions in 1840, 1848, 1850 and 1851; and in 1853 an edition of *Comédies et proverbes d'Alfred de Musset, seule édition complète, revue et corrigée par l'auteur*, Volume I of which contained a revised text of *Lorenzaccio*[26]. Various attempts to stage the play came to nothing throughout the second half of the century; in 1861, a proposal to put it on at the Odéon met with the following comment from the Imperial censor:

La discussion du droit d'assassiner un souverain dont les crimes et les iniquités crient vengeance, le meurtre même du prince par un de ses parents, type de dégradation et d'abrutissement, nous paraissent un spectacle dangereux à présenter au public.[27]

The first performance, therefore, took place at the Théâtre de la Renaissance in 1896. Sarah Bernhardt created the role of Lorenzo, but the public was not yet ready for the full impact of Musset's text: the version used was the adaptation by A. d'Artois which considerably toned down some of the provocative ideas of the play, as well as rearranging it to make it more 'acceptable' aesthetically[28]—and even then, the success of this first production was no more than "simplement raisonnable"[29].

Other adaptations were staged in 1926–27 (Monte Carlo and Paris, with Renée Falconetti as Lorenzo), 1927 (Comédie-Française: Marie-Thérèse Piérat as Lorenzo) and 1932 (Odéon, with Falconetti again playing Lorenzo); but the most notable productions of the play have been those which have taken place since the Second World War. Gaston Baty directed it in 1945 at the Théâtre Montparnasse, with Marguerite Jamois in the leading role, and Gérard Philipe at Avignon for the Théâtre National Populaire in 1952. When the director himself played Lorenzo on this latter occasion, it was the first major production in which the part had been undertaken by a male actor[30].

Though the size and complexity of the work will presumably always be a barrier to frequent performance, *Lorenzaccio* is now well established as a major work in the national repertory; and in the opinion of most connoisseurs there is no doubt of its acceptance as the most successful example of a Romantic drama not only from the reader's point of view, but also from the spectator's. Professor Affron concludes his study of Hugo's and Musset's dramas by remarking on the paradox that it is the plays not originally written for the theatre which now enjoy critical acclaim:

> Works written for the stage languish on bookshelves; the 'armchair theatre' is miraculously transplanted to the proscenium and thrives . . .[31]

With regard to Hugo's 'armchair theatre'—his later 'Théâtre en liberté'—such preference seems thoroughly perverse; but the case of *Lorenzaccio* is very different. Here, at long last, critical opinion has begun to give a masterpiece its due.

Notes to Chapter Nine

1. Cf., however, a rather solemn and laboured analysis in H. S. Gochberg, *Stage of Dreams: the Dramatic Art of Alfred de Musset*, Geneva, 1967, pp. 33–49.

2. The text of *La Quittance du diable* was first published by Maurice Allem in the *Revue Bleue* of May 1914.

3. Quoted by L. Lafoscade, *Le Théâtre d'Alfred de Musset*, Paris, 1901, p. 6.

4. *Musset, l'homme et l'œuvre*, Paris, 1944, pp. 59–60.

5. In fact, it was to remain unpublished until 1921. See P. Dimoff, *La Genèse de Lorenzaccio*, Paris, 1936, pp. xxii–xxxiii.

6. Dimoff's volume, which presents the text of Varchi as well as that of George Sand and of extant MS variants of *Lorenzaccio* itself, is an invaluable aid to a scholarly study of Musset's play.

7. See Dimoff, *op. cit.*, pp. xii–xiii, 57–58; Joyce Bromfield, *De Lorenzino de Médicis à Lorenzaccio*, Paris, 1972, pp. 44–50.

8. Dimoff, *op. cit.*, p. xxxi; see also Bromfield, *op. cit.*, pp. 139–143.

9. Dimoff, *op. cit.*, reproduces three such plans, as well as the text of two complete scenes not included in the published versions of the play.

10. *Op. cit.*, pp. xlvi ff.

11. While the first edition, and those published up to 1851, retained the thirty-nine scenes of the definitive MS, the 1853 edition, revised by Musset himself, suppressed the original Act V, scene vi. This revised text is the one reproduced by most modern editors.

12. *Op. cit.*, pp. vii, viii.

13. P. M. Levitt, *A Structural Approach to the Analysis of Drama*, The Hague, 1971, suggests as the most meaningful definition of *scene* "the unit of action marked off by the exit or entrance of a character" (p. 15).

14. It is also interesting to observe that Lafoscade, whose *Le Théâtre d'Alfred de Musset* appeared in 1901, writes of "toutes les suppressions et toutes les transformations auxquelles l'adaptateur *avait été obligé*" (p. 348; my italics).

15. The original Act V, scene vi, rejected in editions from 1853 onwards, also contributed to this 'Shakespearean' portrait of Florentine life by presenting a quarrel between students and soldiers.

16. Cf. for instance Lafoscade, *op. cit.*, pp. 81–82.

17. Lorenzo's conversation with Tebaldeo (II, ii) may be compared to Hamlet's in the scene with Polonius (II, ii).

18. This is true, though perhaps more subtly so, even in the case of Racine. Cf. Phèdre's "Sers ma fureur, Œnone, et non point ma raison"; or Titus's "Je puis faire les rois, je puis les déposer: / Cependant de mon cœur je ne puis disposer".

19. To use F. C. Green's term. Cf. *Minuet*, ch. ii, 'The Philosopher and the Dramatist'.

20. Another recurrent theme, or leitmotif, is the one expressed in the sexual imagery with which Lorenzo refers to his killing of the Duke. This act represents the consummation of a perverse sort of courtship: the rendezvous in Lorenzo's bedroom is more than once called a "wedding-night", and when Alexandre has bitten Lorenzo on the finger during the course of the assassination the wound is referred to as "cette bague sanglante, inestimable diamant" (IV, xi).

21. See above, p. 68.

22. *Op. cit.*, p. 170.

23. *Ibid.*, pp. 173, 174.

24. For a perceptive analysis of the ambiguity of Lorenzo's character, see R. Grimsley, 'The Character of Lorenzaccio', *French Studies*, XI, 1957, pp. 16–27.

25. Affron, *op. cit.*, p. 201.

26. See above, p. 308, note 11.
27. Quoted by Lafoscade, *op. cit.*, p. 353.
28. This version was published as *Lorenzaccio, drame mis à la scène, en cinq actes, par Armand d'Artois* (Paris, 1898).
29. Lafoscade, *op. cit.*, p. 348.
30. There had in fact been two performances at Bordeaux, with Jean Marchat as Lorenzo, in 1933, and Christian Casadesus had played the part with a touring company in the provinces in 1943. For a detailed analysis of stage performances of *Lorenzaccio*, see B. Masson, *Musset et le théâtre intérieur*, Paris, 1974, pp. 225–391.
31. *Op. cit.*, p. 228.

10 Musset's 'Armchair Theatre'

(i) The 'comédies'

THE volume in which *Lorenzaccio* was published in 1834 had been preceded by an earlier volume bearing the title *Un Spectacle dans un fauteuil*, which had appeared in December 1832. This had contained two poems in dramatic form, *La Coupe et les lèvres* and *A quoi rêvent les jeunes filles*, together with a narrative poem in mock-heroic vein, 'Namouna'. The first of these pieces is accompanied by a 'Dédicace': a brief manifesto, ironical in its manner but serious in intention, in which the young poet proclaims his independence of existing models:

> Je hais comme la mort l'état de plagiaire;
> Mon verre n'est pas grand, mais je bois dans mon verre

and the eclecticism of his subject-matter. There are two kinds of dramatist, says Musset:

> L'un, comme Calderon et comme Mérimée,
> Incruste un plomb brûlant sur la réalité,
> Découpe à son flambeau la silhouette humaine,
> En emporte le moule, et jette sur la scène
> Le plâtre de la vie avec sa nudité...
> L'autre, comme Racine et le divin Shakespeare,
> Monte sur le théâtre, une lampe à la main,
> Et de sa plume d'or ouvre le cœur humain.

If he has to choose between the two groups, the 'realists' and the 'dreamers', he will line himself up with the latter, and seek to adopt the Shakespearean manner, for

> Celui-là voit l'effet — et celui-ci la cause.

La Coupe et les lèvres, called a 'poème dramatique', shows the playwright almost completely emancipated from the contingencies of realism. It is true that scene-changes are indicated, but setting is of minimal importance; and rather than a coherent character, Frank, the hero, is a symbolic representation of the poet's own subjective mood—or at any rate of the fashionable Romantic clichés to which Musset here chose to subscribe. The comparison has been made with Goethe's *Faust*[1], but as far as form is concerned, if this analogy has any meaning at all, the affinities are with the abstract and philosophical *Faust, Part II* rather than with the more conventionally dramatic *Part I*. *La Coupe et les lèvres* is an immature work, holding out less promise of a dramatist's gifts than *La Nuit vénitienne* or *André del Sarto*. It would in any case be unrealistic to judge it as a play: the chief interest resides in the imagery Musset puts into the mouth of his hero, much of which anticipates that of *Lorenzaccio* and later plays[2].

A quoi rêvent les jeunes filles is called a 'comédie'. It is certainly easier to accept this as a dramatic work, though the indication of the play's setting: "où l'on voudra", suggests clearly enough that it is a product of a poet's fantasy rather than a work intended for the practical theatre. Again, the principal interest is to be found in the prefiguration of later comedies: not in the imagery this time, but in the easy handling of comic dialogue. Indeed, *A quoi rêvent les jeunes filles* can be seen as a lighthearted variant of Marivaux's characteristic theme of young love coming to self-knowledge; though Marivaux's keen psychological insight is replaced by the gratuitous invention of Musset's poetic fancy.

Whereas these texts, which had composed the verse *Spectacle dans un fauteuil* of 1832, were later incorporated in the author's *Premières poésies*, the prose works which constituted the 'Seconde Livraison' of 1834 (Volume I: *Lorenzaccio, Les Caprices de Marianne*; Volume II: *André del Sarto, Fantasio, On ne badine pas avec l'amour, La Nuit vénitienne*) were later to be republished in successive editions of the *Comédies et proverbes*. This provides us with a convenient means of distinguishing between 'dramatic poems' and works with a more genuinely dramatic character: if arbitrary, the distinction is at least one drawn by the author himself, and one that was largely confirmed by the fortunes of the latter group towards the end of Musset's life and after his death. *Un Caprice*, published in the *Revue des Deux Mondes* in June 1837, was performed in Russian at Saint-Petersburg in December of the same year; the French actress Mme Allan played in it in French in Saint-Petersburg in 1843, and on her return to Paris acted in its first performance at the Théâtre-Français in 1847. From this date onwards, theatre managers were eager to stage Musset's plays, and most of the 'comédies' and 'proverbes' were played in the period up to 1851, while as a result of this activity, *Louison* (Théâtre-Français, February 1849), *On ne saurait penser à tout* (Théâtre-Français, May 1849) and *Bettine* (Gymnase, October 1851) were to be written directly for stage performance.

The distinction between 'comédies' and 'proverbes' is not an easy one to establish. The latter label denotes a genre developed during the eighteenth century out of a 'jeu de société' not unlike the charade, which consisted of a short scene illustrating a proverbial saying that spectators were invited to identify. To cater for the popularity of this pastime, certain authors began writing, at first *canevas*, then complete texts; these were unpretentious sketches with minimal plot, little more than one-act conversation-pieces. Carmontelle, whose *Proverbes dramatiques* were published from 1768 to 1787, had been a friend of Musset's grandfather, who had kept up the habit of acting these sketches; and it is interesting to note that *La Coupe et les lèvres*, however far removed in mood and tone from the salon conversation-piece, had as its epigraph the proverb 'Entre la coupe et les lèvres, il reste encore de la place pour un malheur', of which its plot could be said to be an illustration. Of the plays published under the general title *Comédies et proverbes*, four have been given proverbial sayings as titles; however, this does not seem to be the most satisfactory criterion on which to base the distinction of genre: indeed, the subtitles given by Musset himself are sometimes in conflict with the title of a particular play[3]. For the purposes of this study it is proposed to treat under the heading of 'comédies' those plays (excluding *La Nuit vénitienne*, *André del Sarto* and *Lorenzaccio*) in which fantasy or imagination predominate, which have a more pronouncedly romanesque tone, or in which plot is more important; and to reserve the label 'proverbes' for those which belong to, or which tend towards, the genre of the realistic conversation-piece.

Even so, to assess the 'comédies' as a group of plays all show-ing a romanesque, imaginative attitude towards plot involves taking a very broad interpretation of the term 'comedy'. The mood of these plays varies considerably, and the conventional happy ending can by no means be taken for granted. Whereas a play like *La Quenouille de Barberine* presents a serene picture of conjugal love overcoming the threat of a would-be seducer, and *Le Chandelier*, albeit more cynical, ends with the victory of the sympathetic young lover over his older and more experienced rival, both *Les Caprices de Marianne* and *On ne badine pas avec l'amour* end with a death. Certainly in the earliest plays of this group, written in the years 1833–34, the Romantic tone im-parted by the poet's jaundiced view of life based on his own precocious experiences is stronger than any comic flavour attaching to the conventional setting, the caricatural presenta-tion of minor characters, or the occasional example of verbal virtuosity. *Les Caprices de Marianne* (published May 1833), *Fantasio* (January 1834) and *On ne badine pas avec l'amour* (July 1834) present an imaginary world not unlike the fantasy settings of Shakespeare's comedies, but at the centre of it we see the poet's *alter ego*, now a cynical misanthropist, now a defeated idealist. The clichés of *La Coupe et les lèvres* and *André del Sarto* have given way to a pessimism more persuasive, presumably because more intensely felt. Even where literary sources can be found for romanesque elements of plot, the central situations seem to have been chosen because of their conformity with episodes from the author's sentimental life. The writing of the last of these plays, *On ne badine pas avec l'amour*, was contemporary with that of *Lorenzaccio*. The extent to which the composition of a full-scale historical drama may have been responsible for a change in Musset's other writings for the theatre is impossible to determine, but it is a fact that after 1834 his comedies never again showed the same degree of subjective involvement; while the move towards a kind of comedy equally imaginative and 'Shakespearean' as regards setting, but lacking this introspec-tive, confessional quality (a type exemplified by *La Quenouille de Barberine*, *Carmosine* and *Bettine*) was to be followed in its turn by a move away from the world of the imagination towards the realistic portrayal of contemporary society; from a poet's theatre towards the documentary 'slice of life'.

In *Les Caprices de Marianne* the poet-hero, whom we have previously seen in Cordiani of *André del Sarto* and in Frank of *La Coupe et les lèvres* (and whom we shall see again transformed into Lorenzaccio), has been split into two contemporary parts, Octave the world-weary cynic and Cœlio the timid idealist. Cœlio loves Marianne, the wife of the elderly judge Claudio, but despairing of obtaining a hearing, he entrusts his suit to the experienced Octave. Marianne at first repulses him, but her profession of fidelity to her husband is a mere pretence, and she proves quite willing to embark on an affair with Octave. Octave, however, remains loyal to his friend, and sends Cœlio to the rendezvous. But Claudio's suspicions have been alerted, and hired assassins are waiting. Cœlio is killed, thinking he has been betrayed by Octave, and in the final scene Octave says farewell to the proud, selfish Marianne. Cœlio, the Romantic idealist, is dead:

> Cœlio était la bonne partie de moi-même; elle est remontée au ciel avec lui. C'était un homme d'un autre temps; il connaissait les plaisirs, et leur préférait la solitude; il savait combien les illusions sont trompeuses, et il préférait ses illusions à la réalité. Elle eût été heureuse, la femme qui l'eût aimé! (II, vi)

—and it is the cynic, tarnished by his contact with life, who survives:

> Je ne sais point aimer; Cœlio seul savait... Lui seul était capable d'un dévouement sans bornes; lui seul eût consacré sa vie entière à la femme qu'il aimait, aussi facilement qu'il aurait bravé la mort pour elle. Je ne suis qu'un débauché sans cœur; je n'estime point les femmes; l'amour que j'inspire est comme celui que je ressens, l'ivresse passagère d'un songe. Je ne sais pas les secrets qu'il savait. Ma gaieté est comme le masque d'un histrion; mon cœur est plus vieux qu'elle, mes sens blasés n'en veulent plus. (*ibid.*)

But Octave is just as much a product of his times as Cœlio; the imagery he uses: "l'ivresse passagère d'un songe", "le masque d'un histrion", "mon cœur est plus vieux . . ." has a familiar ring, and it was the fusing of these two complementary personifications of the author's poetic sensibility into the single character of Lorenzo that was to make the hero of *Lorenzaccio* such a powerful embodiment of that eminently Romantic concept, the synthesis of grotesque and sublime elements.

Genuinely comic elements are rare in this bitter-sweet comedy: they are limited to a few passages of *marivaudage* between Octave and Marianne, and of patterned repartee between Octave and Claudio; in any case, the ending, with the threat of broken faith and the destruction of an ideal, establishes a final mood that is anything but lighthearted. *Fantasio*, on the contrary, preserves the lighthearted tone, partly because the setting so clearly owed much more to imagination than to observation, and the characters are more clearly creatures of fancy; and partly because the subjective hero is here allowed to succeed in his altruistic attempt to help another sufferer. Fantasio takes the post of Court jester to avoid being imprisoned for debt, and is able to save the Princess Elsbeth from a political marriage to a man she cannot love. The play ends with a declaration of war, resulting from Fantasio's insult to the royal suitor, but this is of no consequence: the threat of war has neither more nor less reality than the rest of the fantasy plot. What does carry conviction is the Romantic introspection of Fantasio himself: a sort of Octave-figure, disillusioned by experience:

> L'amour n'existe plus, mon cher ami. La religion, sa nourrice, a les mamelles pendantes comme une vieille bourse au fond de laquelle il y a un gros sou. L'amour est une hostie qu'il faut briser en deux au fond d'un autel, et avaler ensemble dans un baiser; il n'y a plus d'autel, il n'y a plus d'amour. Vive la nature! il y a encore du vin (I, ii)

but endowed with enough of Musset's imaginative lyricism for us to be able to believe that the Cœlio in him is not completely dead:

> Regarde cette vieille ville enfumée; il n'y a pas de places, de rues, de ruelles où je n'aie rôdé trente fois; il n'y a pas de pavés où je n'aie traîné ces talons usés, pas de maisons où je ne sache quelle est la fille ou la vieille femme dont la tête stupide se dessine éternellement à la fenêtre; je ne saurais

faire un pas sans marcher sur mes pas d'hier; eh bien, mon
cher ami, cette ville n'est rien auprès de ma cervelle. Tous
les recoins m'en sont cent fois plus connus; toutes les rues,
tous les trous de mon imagination sont cent fois plus fatigués;
je m'y suis promené en cent fois plus de sens, dans cette
cervelle délabrée, moi son seul habitant! je m'y suis grisé
dans tous les cabarets; je m'y suis roulé comme un roi
absolu dans un carrosse doré; j'y ai trotté en bon bourgeois
sur une mule pacifique, et je n'ose seulement pas maintenant
y entrer comme un voleur, une lanterne sourde à la main.
(*ibid.*)

Once more the comparison with Lorenzo is inescapable. But the
comic gesture by which Fantasio chooses to rescue the Princess
Elsbeth—removing her ridiculous suitor's wig as the procession
passes beneath his balcony—could not be further removed from
the killing of Alexandre. Reality is not allowed to break in and
disturb the fantasy world created by the author and his poet-
hero; and this is the most reassuring, because the most escapist,
of all these early comedies.

With *On ne badine pas avec l'amour* we return to the bitter-sweet,
tragi-comic mood of *Les Caprices de Marianne*. Here, however, the
death with which the play concludes comes as even more of a
shock, for the alternation of serious and comic elements has been
more persistently maintained, as the scenes developing the
central relationship between the young hero and heroine,
Perdican and Camille, are framed by others showing the
grotesque behaviour of the puppet-like caricatures by whom
they are surrounded. Moreover, Rosette's death is the death
of an innocent, passive character. She is the victim of Perdican's
selfish whim, as he flirts with her in an attempt to rouse
Camille to jealousy; and dying of a broken heart as she overhears the two lovers finally confess their feeling for each other,
she pays the price no less than Perdican and Camille themselves, who learn too late not to trifle with love. Perdican is a
simple character: he knows he loves Camille, and acts as he
does towards Rosette because his feelings have been hurt.
Camille's is a more complex personality: disillusioned cynics in
the convent where she was brought up have taught her to
distrust men, and it is this vicarious 'experience' which combines with her selfish pride, and prevents her from yielding to

the evidence of her senses and acknowledging her love for her cousin. Perdican's eloquent appeal:

> Tous les hommes sont menteurs, inconstants, faux, bavards, hypocrites, orgueilleux et lâches, méprisables et sensuels; toutes les femmes sont perfides, artificieuses, vaniteuses, curieuses et dépravées; le monde n'est qu'un égout sans fond où les phoques les plus informes rampent et se tordent sur des montagnes de fange; mais il y a au monde une chose sainte et sublime, c'est l'union de deux de ces êtres si imparfaits et si affreux. On est souvent trompé en amour, souvent blessé et souvent malheureux; mais on aime, et quand on est sur le bord de sa tombe, on se retourne pour regarder en arrière, et on se dit: — J'ai souffert souvent, je me suis trompé quelquefois, mais j'ai aimé. C'est moi qui ai vécu, et non pas un être factice créé par mon orgueil et mon ennui (II, v)

too obviously indicates the poet speaking through his character: the words suggest a maturity of judgement which is belied by Perdican's behaviour towards Rosette. It is an appeal that could have been addressed by Octave to Marianne: Camille shows the same proud, independent spirit, which Musset sees as an invincible obstacle to true love. While the bitterness of the ending of *Les Caprices de Marianne* obviously cannot be attributed to the rupture with George Sand—this did not take place until the spring of 1834—that of *On ne badine pas avec l'amour*, and the role given to Camille in this play, must reflect the events that preceded its writing. It is clear that the experience at Venice intensified the analytical interest the author had already shown in the role of pride in the relationship between the sexes, and in the kind of female temperament illustrated in both these heroines, which he recognized in real life in George Sand. However, if the moral of the play seems to be primarily directed at Camille—and beyond her at George Sand, the Princess Belgiojoso and other women at whose hands Musset had suffered—it is by no means a one-sided verdict, and Perdican's final speeches leave his self-condemnation in no doubt:

> Je ne sais ce que j'éprouve; il me semble que mes mains sont couvertes de sang... Je vous supplie, mon Dieu! ne faites pas

de moi un meurtrier! Vous voyez ce qui se passe; nous
sommes deux enfants insensés, et nous avons joué avec la vie
et la mort; mais notre cœur est pur... (III, viii)

On ne badine pas avec l'amour marks the end of Musset's most
intense involvement with his characters; but even before this,
he had shown himself capable of sufficient detachment to be
able to create a heroine very different from the proud, self-
centred Marianne or Camille. The *ingénue* Elsbeth, the heroine
of *Fantasio*, ready to sacrifice herself for the welfare of others, is
only a sketch; nevertheless, she is the prototype of a series of
generous, sympathetic heroines who were to give to the remainder of Musset's comedies a very different character. *La
Quenouille de Barberine* (published August 1835) is the first of
these, but *Le Chandelier*, published slightly later (November
1835) may be seen as a transition between the subjective manner
of the earlier plays and the greater detachment of those which
follow.

Le Chandelier is said to be based on a precocious love-affair, in
which the young Musset had himself played the role assigned
to Fortunio in this play. Jacqueline, the heroine, might be said
to be an older and more experienced Marianne, who has settled
down to deceiving her husband with a series of lovers; the
current 'amant en titre', Clavaroche, explains to her that for
their protection they need a 'chandelier', the name given to a
third party, whose presence is deliberately encouraged in order
to divert a husband's suspicions. Although Fortunio himself
learns of the lovers' intentions, he is nevertheless prepared to
fit in with this plan, and to sacrifice himself, if he has to, for the
happiness of Jacqueline, whom he loves. This devotion earns its
reward, however: Jacqueline's eyes are opened to the shortcomings of the self-satisfied Clavaroche, and the play closes
with the pleasing spectacle of Fortunio turning the tables on his
rival. In one sense, *Le Chandelier* is a comedy with a moral,
though it would be wrong to take the moral too seriously: in
fact, the play is based on a dubious sort of morality, since we are
left to envisage at least the possibility of Fortunio himself becoming a Clavaroche in his turn. But whether moral or not, the
ending depends on the wishful thinking characteristic of
comedy: if indeed, as J. Sarment suggests, this is yet another

treatment of Musset's favourite theme, "le heurt douloureux de la naïveté d'un être jeune, amoureux au plus profond de lui-même, contre l'insensibilité d'un être averti et froid qui se joue de lui"[4], then experience tells us that the happy ending is less realistic than the final catastrophes of *Les Caprices de Marianne* or of *On ne badine pas avec l'amour*. A real-life Jacqueline would no doubt have continued to prefer the greater security of a liaison with Clavaroche, and would hardly have been capable of the change of heart which forces her to confess:

> Vous saviez que je mens, que je trompe, que je vous raille, et que je vous tue? vous saviez que j'aime Clavaroche et qu'il me fait faire tout ce qu'il veut? que je joue une comédie? que là, hier, je vous ai pris pour dupe? que je suis lâche et méprisable? que je vous expose à la mort par plaisir? Vous saviez tout, vous en étiez sûr? Eh bien! eh bien! qu'est-ce que vous savez maintenant?
>
> — Mais, Jacqueline, je crois... je sais...
>
> — Sais-tu que je t'aime, enfant que tu es? qu'il faut que tu me pardonnes ou que je meure; et que je te le demande à genoux? (III, iv)

If it were merely a question of the sympathetic lover scoring off the case-hardened roué, this would be a banal comedy, worlds apart from Musset's other plays. What preserves the peculiar tonality common to this group of plays is partly Jacqueline's conversion, partly the development given to Fortunio in the scenes in which he is contrasted with his more prosaic friends, in the exchanges with Clavaroche, and especially in a long soliloquy:

> Non, tant d'horreur n'est pas possible! Non, une femme ne saurait être une statue malfaisante, à la fois vivante et glacée! Non, quand je le verrais de mes yeux, quand je l'entendrais de sa bouche, je ne croirais pas à un pareil métier. Non, quand elle me souriait, elle ne m'aimait pas pour cela, mais elle souriait de voir que je l'aimais. Quand elle me tendait la main, elle ne me donnait pas son cœur, mais elle laissait le mien se donner. Quand elle me disait: « Je vous aime », elle voulait dire: « Aimez-moi ». Non, Jacqueline n'est pas méchante; il n'y a là ni calcul, ni

froideur. Elle ment, elle trompe, elle est femme; elle est
coquette, railleuse, joyeuse, audacieuse, mais non infâme,
non insensible. Ah! insensé, tu l'aimes! tu l'aimes! tu pries, tu
pleures, et elle se rit de toi! (II, ii)

This is another lyrical expression of faith in the love of man
for woman. It lacks the striking imagery of Perdican's 'profession
de foi', but its rhythms are the rhythms of a poet's prose: they
lift the subject-matter above the prosaic and the ordinary, and
it is this lyrical quality that constitutes the principal charm of
Le Chandelier, and that has made the play one of the most
popular 'levers de rideau' at the Comédie-Française in our own
day. Its first performance was in fact in 1848 at the Théâtre-
Historique; it was accepted by the Théâtre-Français in the
same year, but production there was delayed owing to difficulties with the censor over the alleged immorality of the play.

Le Chandelier is the last play in which Musset seems to have
drawn on his own experience; and already in *La Quenouille de
Barberine* he had adopted a very different manner. This time,
the happy ending of the comedy brings the triumph of conjugal
love, and a certain type of Romantic pose is mocked in the dis-
comfiture of the would-be seducer, Rosemberg. Rosemberg is
treated with the same sort of irony as Razetta of the early *La
Nuit vénitienne*: when he arrives at her castle, determined to profit
from her husband's absence, Barberine shuts him up in a
deserted wing of the building and sets him to spin flax in order
to earn his keep. *La Quenouille de Barberine* was inspired by the
same *novella* of Bandello's as Shakespeare's *Cymbeline* (to the plot
of which there is an explicit allusion in the 1851 version, re-
written for the stage). Not only is the Rosemberg–Barberine–
Ulric relationship analogous to that between Iachimo, Imogen
and Posthumus in Shakespeare's play, but the atmosphere of
La Quenouille de Barberine shows a more general affinity with that
of Shakespearean comedy, which had been absent from
Musset's theatre since *La Nuit vénitienne* and *Fantasio*. The setting
(in Bohemia at the court of the King of Hungary) recalls
Shakespeare's Illyria; there is an ironical detachment in
Musset's characterization which reminds us of Shakespeare's;
and overall, the play possesses an agreeable air of escapist
unreality, which marks a complete change from the introspec-

tive intensity of *Les Caprices de Marianne* and *On ne badine pas avec l'amour*.

In the version composed in 1851 for the Théâtre-Français the original two acts were expanded into three, a new principal character created, and much new dialogue added. Altogether, this was the most considerable re-writing undergone by any of Musset's plays; however, it is generally agreed that the original version has a freshness lacking in the later adaptation[5]. Indeed, this is true in general terms of all the cases in which Musset undertook expensive alterations to the text of his plays for purposes of performance: nowhere did the revised version improve on the inspiration of the original 'armchair comedy'[6].

Something of the romanesque, escapist quality of *La Quenouille de Barberine* is to be found in *Carmosine*, also taken from an Italian *novella*. Published in 1850 in *Le Constitutionnel*, this play was not performed until after the poet's death, in 1865. It is another piece remote from contemporary life, set this time in Palermo. Musset follows Boccaccio's account of a young girl whose unacknowledged love for the King of Sicily has led to her serious illness, and the despair of her family. At death's door, she is persuaded to disclose her secret to a troubadour who solicits the King on her behalf; she is visited by the Queen, who gives her wise, friendly counsel, and finally by the King, who marries her to the young man who loves her, and promises that he himself will always be her "chevalier servant". The comic element is provided by Ser Vespasiano, an absurd suitor who appears in each of the three acts, and by Carmosine's mother, who favours his suit; but the comic scenes are not prominent enough to prevail against the overall tone of gentle melancholy that characterizes this play. It is not quite the same 'bitter-sweet' formula that we have remarked on in the case of certain earlier comedies: there is no final catastrophe here, but rather a resigned acceptance of the rarity of reciprocated love, and of the necessity for compromise in human relationships. Of all Musset's comedies, this is perhaps the least stageworthy, and the least characteristic of his individual manner as a playwright: the interest lies in the fable, rather than in the characters, and the reader is better able than the spectator to appreciate the way in which the fable has been dramatized without entirely losing the distinctive romanesque quality of the Renaissance *novella*.

(*ii*) The '*proverbes*'

IN the letter-preface to the 1773 edition of his *Proverbes dramatiques*, Carmontelle had written:

> Il n'y a presque pas de comédie à laquelle on ne pût donner un proverbe pour titre, si l'on voulait. On dirait du *Joueur*, « promettre et tenir sont deux ». Du *Philosophe marié*, « un peu de honte est bientôt passé », etc.
>
> Un proverbe dramatique est donc une espèce de comédie, que l'on fait en inventant un sujet, ou en se servant de quelques traits, quelque historiette, etc. Le mot du proverbe doit être enveloppé dans l'action, de manière que si les spectateurs ne le devinent pas, il faut, lorsqu'on le leur dit, qu'ils s'écrient « ah! c'est vrai », comme lorsqu'on dit le mot d'une énigme que l'on n'a pas trouvé. [7]

In practice, the chosen proverb did not itself appear in the text of a Carmontelle *proverbe*: the published collection of these comedies lists the proverbs on which they are based as a key in an appendix to each volume; with Carmontelle, the element of the 'jeu de société' still had some importance. However, it seems that as the *proverbe* developed from an impromptu *jeu de société* into an accepted form of literary comedy, the importance of the conundrum element in its make-up, the puzzle to be solved by the spectators, was gradually subordinated to that of another feature: the dialogue, seen as the convincing reproduction of contemporary speech. Carmontelle was a painter by profession, and it has been suggested that his dramatic *proverbes* "offrent une galerie de caractères qui complètent pour ainsi dire ses portraits au crayon, et constituent une œuvre dont l'importance documentaire n'est point moindre" [8]. Carmontelle himself modestly claimed:

> Dans ces dialogues, je n'ai cherché à mettre que le ton de la conversation, et je ne me suis pas appliqué à faire de belles phrases... ainsi, ce n'est pas du style que vous trouverez ici, mais un grand désir d'avoir le ton de la vérité. [9]

This, then, was the genre that was taken up by Musset and other dramatists of the Romantic generation [10]: essentially a one-act comedy in prose, a sketch with the minimum of plot, providing a vehicle for the portrayal of the manners, and reproduction of the speech, of contemporary society. To give but one example of Carmontelle's own *proverbes*: *Le Veuf* portrays three male characters, two of whom succeed in persuading the third, a widower who claims that his grief is inconsolable, to go off with them to seek an evening's innocent distraction at the Opéra. The proverb illustrated is 'Il n'y a point d'éternelles douleurs', but the 'puzzle' interest is of the slightest, as is that of plot in a more general sense, and it is clear that any attraction that such a piece holds must reside in the way in which the author has captured the manners and the conversation of a particular society[11].

Before Musset embarked on his comedies in the manner of Carmontelle, there had been noteworthy contributions to the genre of the *proverbe* by two other leading Romantic dramatists: Dumas's *Le Mari de la veuve* had been performed at the Théâtre-Français in April 1832, and Vigny's *Quitte pour la peur* at the Opéra in May 1833. The former is entirely in the Carmontelle tradition, except that no actual proverb seems to be illustrated: it is a one-act prose comedy, set in "une maison de campagne aux environs de Paris". The plot concerns the enlightening of the hero Léon, a good young man at heart but with some of the vanity of the traditional *petit-maître* type, as to the true nature of his feelings. He has persuaded himself that he loves, not the young *ingénue* Pauline, but her aunt Mme de Vertpré, apparently a young widow, but whose husband proves to be still alive. As one would expect from Dumas, the plot, although simple, is neat and effective; but once again, it is the realistic portrait of a particular society that counts. The portrait is drawn with conviction, and *Le Mari de la veuve* is an interesting contribution to the genre of the *proverbe* as it came to be regarded in the 1830s: a comedy of manners with a genuine documentary value, and with a minimum of distortion due to exigencies of plot or characterization. Mme de Vertpré, the charming, accomplished heroine who teaches Léon his lesson, was played by Mlle Mars, Pauline by Mlle Anaïs, and the two male characters by Monrose and Menjaud.

Vigny's play differs from Dumas's most noticeably in that it portrays not contemporary society, but that of the *ancien régime*. Again, a simple plot, with a handful of characters, allows the author to paint a faithful, detailed portrait *en miniature* of the manners of a chosen social class; and the fact that Vigny is evidently more concerned with the portrayal of his characters from a moral point of view does not stand in the way of the credibility of the external portrait. In fact, *Quitte pour la peur* goes further than any other play of its time in examining a serious social problem that had been largely avoided by previous dramatists: the reign of Louis XVI was deliberately chosen as "une époque où régnaient à la fois le rigorisme du point d'honneur et la légèreté dans les mœurs", and it is the relationship between these two phenomena that interests Vigny. He portrays a young aristocratic couple, who have married purely as the result of a business transaction between their families, and who live apart, having in fact never met since their wedding-day: the Duc has a long-standing liaison with a Marquise, while his young wife has embarked on an affair with a Chevalier. She now finds herself pregnant, and is terrified of the reaction of the husband who is a complete stranger to her; however, the enlightened Duc, informed by the wise family doctor, visits her apartment, not to exact a vengeance to which he considers he has forfeited the right, but in order to preserve the family honour by 'officially' spending the night with his wife so that the proprieties shall be seen to have been observed. As Vigny says, "l'auteur a conclu pour une miséricorde qui ne manque peut-être pas de dignité"; and the Duchesse is "quitte pour la peur". This latter role, with its interesting blend of naivety, selfish indulgence, genuine remorse and apprehension, was created as a vehicle for Marie Dorval, at a time when determined attempts were being made, with the support of Hugo and Dumas, to secure her admission to the Théâtre-Français, "pour combattre le tenace préjugé selon lequel elle n'était pas capable de représenter d'autres héroïnes que celles du mélodrame"[12]. The Duc was played by Bocage. The one formal departure from the tradition developed by Carmontelle for the *proverbe* is that scene viii of this one-act play introduces a change of scene, as Dr. Tronchin visits Versailles to discuss the situation with the Duc; but there is no doubt that *Quitte pour la peur* represents a contribution to the same genre, however individual the purpose to which Vigny here adapts the *proverbe*.

The first play of Musset's which falls to be considered under this heading cannot itself be called a *proverbe*; though if *Il ne faut jurer de rien* (published in the *Revue des Deux Mondes* in July 1836) is compared with Musset's earlier comedies, it is not difficult to recognize the influence of the eighteenth-century genre. *On ne badine pas avec l'amour*, for instance, despite its proverb-title, had been set in a world of fantasy, and the characters surrounding Perdican and Camille had been pure caricatures; *Il ne faut jurer de rien*, however, presents a credible portrait of the manners of the wealthy upper-class society of Musset's day, and its plot illustrates very effectively the proverb which serves as its title (and recurs in the closing line of the play), as Valentin, the young dandy, sceptical about all romantic attachments and determined to prove his point by taking Lovelace as his model, is conquered by the innocent trust and naive charm of Cécile. In fact, only its form—in three acts, with a corresponding elaboration, if not complexity, of plot—prevents it from qualifying as a *proverbe*. The message is the same as that of *La Quenouille de Barberine*: pure, unselfish love is stronger than cynical libertinage; and it is difficult to accept the views of the editors of a recent edition of Musset's theatre that:

> [*Il ne faut jurer de rien*] marque, dans l'évolution de Musset comme auteur dramatique, un tournant décisif. Auparavant, et jusqu'au *Chandelier* inclus, le romantisme se mêle sans cesse à l'esprit hérité du xviiie siècle. A partir de 1836, au contraire, ce romantisme disparaît. Ni dans les sentiments, ni dans les idées, ni dans l'expression, on ne trouve désormais rien des élans qui animaient les personnages d'*On ne badine pas...*, ou de *Lorenzaccio*, voire de *Fantasio* ou du *Chandelier*.[13]

On the contrary, the lovers' exaltation in the final scene has a very familiar ring:

> Dis-moi: dans cette poussière de mondes, y en a-t-il un qui ne sache sa route, qui n'ait reçu sa mission avec la vie, et qui ne doive mourir en l'accomplissant? Pourquoi ce ciel immense n'est-il pas immobile? Dis-moi: s'il y a jamais eu un moment où tout fut créé, en vertu de quelle force ont-ils commencé à se mouvoir, ces mondes qui ne s'arrêteront jamais?
>
> — Par l'éternelle pensée.

— Par l'éternel amour. La main qui les suspend dans l'espace n'a écrit qu'un mot en lettres de feu. Ils vivent parce qu'ils se cherchent, et les soleils tomberaient en poussière si l'un d'entre eux cessait d'aimer.

In its imagery and its rhythms, such dialogue stands out as entirely different from the realistic transcription of everyday speech; and if we are at all disposed to think of *Il ne faut jurer de rien* as a *proverbe*, we must recognize that Musset has here extended the scope of this genre, to serve as a vehicle for an idealistic message, expressed in his highly individual kind of poetic prose.

Un Caprice (published in the *Revue des Deux Mondes* in June 1837) is by contrast a pure *proverbe* in the Carmontelle manner. It possesses none of the imaginative qualities that had characterized all Musset's theatre up to this point, in the form of setting, imagery or flights of poetic fantasy; it is in a single act, in a prose that convincingly suggests the faithful reproduction of genuine speech; and although it has not been given a proverbial saying for a title, the last line of the text contains a proverb, 'Un jeune curé fait les meilleurs sermons', which expresses in a nutshell the theme of the play. There are three characters: a recently-married couple, the Comte de Chavigny and his wife Mathilde, and a slightly older friend of Mathilde's, the widowed Mme de Léry. Chavigny, though he loves his wife, has been neglecting her; Mathilde confides in her friend, who with the delicacy, charm and wit that make her one of Musset's most attractive characters (she is said to have been modelled on his 'marraine' Mme Joubert) opens the husband's eyes to the danger of indulging in 'caprices' in marriage. Chavigny has accepted a purse embroidered for him by another woman, and in scene viii, which forms the climax of the play, Mme de Léry, by appearing to flirt with him, prevails on him to surrender the purse, and to accept another in exchange that she encourages him to think has been embroidered by herself; only when the exchange has been made does the Count learn that this was a task to which his wife had devoted her lonely evenings. If the affinity with the eighteenth-century *proverbe* tradition is this time very close indeed, we should perhaps not overlook the debt to Dumas, for not only had *Le Mari de la veuve* pointed the way in respect of the formal resemblance to Carmontelle's *proverbes*, but there is also a striking similarity of subject-matter between the two nineteenth-century plays. Both deal with the re-uniting of a temporarily estranged couple by the common-sense and ingenuity of a more experienced woman: Dumas's Mme de Vertpré has a good deal of the charm of Musset's Mme de Léry, and in both cases the young man, for all his good qualities, has something of the *petit-maître* about him. Indeed, the theme of both plays—if 'theme' is not too earnest a term for such essentially lighthearted pieces—may be said to be the same as that of Marivaux's *Le Petit-maître corrigé* of a hundred years earlier[14].

The historical importance of *Un Caprice* is considerable. This is the play which, translated into Russian within months of its appearance in the *Revue des Deux Mondes*, was performed at St. Petersburg, and thus eventually came to be the first of Musset's plays since *La Nuit vénitienne* to be staged in Paris (in November 1847 at the Théâtre-Français, where Musset's friend Buloz had just become Administrator). Since then, this has always been a favourite 'lever de rideau' with audiences at the Comédie-Française, where it has now reached the distinction of over a thousand performances. Another *proverbe* that has long been established as a curtain-raiser at the Comédie-Française is Musset's next play, *Il faut qu'une porte soit ouverte ou fermée* (published *Revue des Deux Mondes* November 1845; produced Théâtre-Français April 1848). This might be said to represent the genre in its quintessential form: a single long scene between two characters, it is a pure conversation-piece, and the fact that the conversation leads up to a declaration of love and a promise of marriage, while it gives a satisfying shape to the play, is really of secondary importance. It has been said that the two characters are recognizable versions, older and more mature, of Musset's earlier heroes and heroines, the Comte representing Perdican's ideal belief in love and the Marquise embodying something like Camille's obstinate pride; but this too is unimportant, compared with the overriding difference between on the one hand Perdican, Camille and Musset's other early heroes and heroines, products of a poet's imagination in settings of pure fantasy, and on the other these representatives of an urbane, sophisticated society in a setting whose documentary realism is never for a moment in doubt. And this difference is nowhere more evident than in the passage in which the Comte, taking his text as it were from Perdican's apologia, taxes the Marquise with scepticism and indifference:

> Si l'amour est une comédie, cette comédie, vieille comme le monde, sifflée ou non, est, au bout du compte, ce qu'on a encore trouvé de moins mauvais. Les rôles sont rebattus, j'y consens, mais, si la pièce ne valait rien, tout l'univers ne la saurait pas par cœur; — et je me trompe en disant qu'elle est vieille. Est-ce être vieux que d'être immortel?

The attitude may be the same; but the vocabulary, the rhythms, the tone, are prosaic and conversational, they no longer bear the imprint of the Romantic poet. More clearly here than anywhere else, Musset proclaims his debt to eighteenth-century comedy: the Comte and the Marquise are indulging in an elegant game of *marivaudage*. The key to the conversational style to which the eighteenth-century dramatist has given his name is to be found in M. Deloffre's observation: "Il n'est pas tant le secret d'un style que l'intuition du rôle joué par le langage dans le drame et dans la vie"[15]. In Marivaux's most characteristic dialogue, the verbal play is no mere superficial embellishment of the subject-matter, but is so intimate an expression of the relationship between the characters that these exchanges create the psychological development: the action grows out of the dialogue as it proceeds. The eighteenth-century *néologistes* had held the view that "les mots non seulement représentent les idées, mais ils les créent"[16]: this is demonstrably the case with Marivaux's own dialogue in the theatre, and it is in this sense that the term *marivaudage* can aptly be used of a play like *Il faut qu'une porte soit ouverte ou fermée*. Here, external 'plot' in a conventional sense is non-existent, and the dialogue creates its own subject-matter as it goes along. The Comte confesses towards the end of the play:

> Je conviendrai, tant que vous voudrez, que j'étais entré ici sans dessein; je ne comptais que vous voir en passant, témoin cette porte que j'ai ouverte trois fois pour m'en aller. La conversation que nous venons d'avoir, vos railleries, votre froideur même, m'ont entraîné plus loin qu'il ne fallait peut-être

—and we too are carried along irresistibly by the sophisticated badinage which has captured so well the accents of a civilized society with its ritual, its etiquette, and its serious pursuit of amusement.

The reception given to *Un Caprice* in November 1847 had been remarkably enthusiastic—Gautier had led the chorus of praise, declaring that since Marivaux's day, the Théâtre-Français had never staged anything "de si fin, de si délicat, de si doucement enjoué que ce chef-d'œuvre mignon"[17]—but this success in the theatre was not to be sustained. However, after the breakthrough with *Un Caprice*, several other plays were produced in quick succession—*Il faut qu'une porte soit ouverte ou fermée* (Théâtre-Français, April 1848), *Il ne faut jurer de rien* (Théâtre-Français, June 1848), *Le Chandelier* (Théâtre-Historique, August 1848), *André del Sarto* (Théâtre-Français, November 1848)—and Musset now felt encouraged to try once more writing for immediate stage production, with the result that two new plays were accepted by the Théâtre-Français.

The first of these, *Louison* (February 1849), is a verse play in two acts. It has been suggested that its plot derives from *Le Mariage de Figaro*, and indeed there is a very general resemblance in that both plays show a nobleman forsaking his wife and seeking to amuse himself with her maid. But whatever its source, *Louison* is a feeble play, and if it has an eighteenth-century analogue, this is to be found not in the wit and panache of Beaumarchais, but in the trite moralities of Voltaire's comedies such as *Nanine* or *Le Droit du seigneur*; the parallel is hardly flattering to Musset.

The second play to be written directly for the Théâtre-Français was *On ne saurait penser à tout* (May 1849). This marks a return to the one-act *proverbe* in prose—but it is a *proverbe* with a difference. Although not only the form but also the subject comes from Carmontelle—whose play *Le Distrait* has as its theme the proverb 'On ne saurait penser à tout'—Musset's adaptation has superimposed an extra comic dimension absent from the original. Carmontelle's play portrays a Marquis and a Comtesse, who are both so absent-minded that they never get to the point of discussing their marriage; in Musset's play, however, this simple sketch is filled out with the anxiety of a punctilious uncle of the Marquis's who is to accompany his absent-minded nephew on a diplomatic mission to congratulate a German Grand-Duchess on the birth of a child. In fact, Musset's Marquis and Comtesse, in spite of their *distraction*, do manage to reach an understanding, and the point of the proverb in his version is that it is the fussy uncle who is shown not to have thought of every eventuality, for just as everything seems in order for their departure news arrives that the Grand-Duchess has died in childbirth![18] Not only is Musset's play more highly organized from the point of view of plot than Car-montelle's original: it also departs from the formula of the *proverbe* as illustrated in *Un Caprice* and *Il faut qu'une porte soit ouverte ou fermée* by virtue of the concessions that are made to more conventional forms of comic writing. Both the Marquis and his uncle are pure caricatures—figures of fun like some of the supporting characters in Musset's early comedies (the Prince in *Fantasio*, or the *curé* and the tutor in *On ne badine pas avec l'amour*); and moreover, the use of such theatrical devices as the aside forms a striking contrast to the naturalistic technique of his other *proverbes*.

In June 1851, *Les Caprices de Marianne* was performed at the Théâtre-Français with a moderate success; but there is no indication that Musset was tempted to resume the formula of nearly twenty years earlier, and the only other play he was to write directly for stage production remains close to the realist manner of the *proverbes*. *Bettine* (Gymnase, October 1851) was a failure; this time Musset's disillusionment was complete, and during the last half-dozen years of his life he sought no further connection with the theatre: the one remaining work that he wrote in dramatic form, *L'Ane et le ruisseau*, remained unpublished and unperformed at his death. *Bettine* is set in Italy: the heroine is a rich opera-singer who is about to settle down and marry Baron Steinberg. He apparently loves her, but during the course of the one-act play we see him deceive her, tricking her of a large sum of money, and depart with another woman, while Bettine gratefully accepts the protection of a devoted admirer of long standing. The characterization is somewhat melodramatic: Steinberg is the bizarre and unpredictable lover, Bettine the artist with a volatile temperament, Stefani the loyal, dependable friend. In addition, the dialogue lacks Musset's early sparkle, and *Bettine* illustrates all too clearly how he had lost the lightness of touch that had earned comparison with Marivaux—the more so in that the dramatic framework of the play (the couple AB, with C as the outsider, gives way to the couple AC, B having shown his true feelings) is one that might well have attracted Marivaux himself.

In *L'Ane et le ruisseau* Musset finally returned to something like the manner of the pure *proverbe*. The setting is a fashionable salon, in which a quartet of characters act out the proverbial saying about the donkey who has to be tricked into crossing a stream. The Baron de Valbrun, a timid and hesitant lover, resists all the attempts of the Comtesse to bring him to the point of asking for her hand, and it is necessary for his friend the Marquis to lay a trap for him: nothing less than the belief that he has been deceived by his friend is sufficient to stir him to the necessary action. The plot is somewhat laboured, and the dialogue consequently lacks the subtlety of the best of Musset's *proverbes*: there are some effective scenes of *marivaudage* between the Marquis and the Comtesse's cousin Marguerite, but the scenes between the Comtesse and Valbrun show all too clearly that *marivaudage* depends on the cooperation of two participants: if one of the pair refuses to play the game, as the Baron does here, it cannot work. Nevertheless, the characters are successfully drawn, and altogether *L'Ane et le ruisseau* marks a welcome return to a manner of writing that had produced some of Musset's most successful work for the theatre.

The eighteenth-century affinities of this part of Musset's theatre—the source of the *proverbe* form in Carmontelle and other playwrights, the similarity between Musset's dialogue and that of Marivaux, the reflection of the social graces of the *ancien régime*—should not lead us into thinking that this was a backward-looking phenomenon, and that when Musset turned away from Romantic fashions in the theatre, it was to take refuge in outdated dramatic forms. On the contrary: there is a sense in which the *proverbe*, as a realistic transcription of contemporary manners and speech-habits, is more obviously forward-looking and progressive than anything else written by the playwrights of this generation. For while the work of Hugo, Dumas and Vigny in various ways all looks forward to the formally very traditional drama of the next generation, to the various forms of 'well-made play' which flourished in the Second Empire,

Musset's *proverbes* anticipate the reaction against these conventions in the name of Naturalism. In the 1880s Zola, Becque and Antoine were all to champion the theatrical ideal of the 'slice of life': the theory that drama should aim at unadorned, uncontrived documentary realism. In two at least of his one-act *proverbes*, *Un Caprice* and *Il faut qu'une porte soit ouverte ou fermée*, Musset had come nearer than any other dramatist of distinction to showing how this could be achieved[19].

Notes to Chapter Ten

1. Van Tieghem, *Musset, l'homme et l'œuvre*, p. 43.
2. For instance, the final image in the passage from *Lorenzaccio* quoted on p. 303 is suggested in the following lines:

    Esprits! si vous venez m'annoncer ma ruine,
    　　Pourquoi le Dieu qui me créa
    Fit-il, en m'animant, tomber sur ma poitrine
    　　L'étincelle divine
    　　Qui me consumera? (I, iii)
3. For instance, on first publication *On ne badine pas avec l'amour, Il ne faut jurer de rien, Faire sans dire* (a melodramatic fragment published in 1836), *Un Caprice, Il faut qu'une porte soit ouverte ou fermée* and *Carmosine* were labelled 'proverbes', while *On ne saurait penser à tout* appeared as a 'comédie'.
4. *Théâtre complet de Musset: texte établi et annoté par Philippe Van Tieghem; présentation par Jean Sarment* (Les Classiques Verts), Paris, 1948, p. 243.
5. Cf., for instance, A. Lebois, *Vues sur le théâtre de Musset*, Paris, 1966, pp. 158–159.
6. Cf. J. Sarment, *op. cit.*, *passim*.
7. Quoted by C. D. Brenner, *Le Développement du proverbe dramatique en France et sa vogue au xviiie siècle*, Berkeley, 1937, p. 16.
8. Brenner, *op. cit.*, p. 17.
9. Letter-preface, *ibid.*, p. 16.
10. Marjorie Shaw, 'Les Proverbes dramatiques de Carmontelle, Leclercq et Alfred de Musset', *Revue des Sciences Humaines*, XIII, 1959, pp. 56–76, stresses the role of Théodore Leclercq, who published *proverbes* between 1823 and 1833, in completing the change from an improvised genre to a more polished form of literary comedy.
11. J. H. Donnard, *Le Théâtre de Carmontelle*, Paris, 1967, p. 106,

points out that since the inclusion of Carmontelle in the repertory of the Comédie-Française in 1938, *Le Veuf* has been the most popular of his plays, with 91 performances to date.

12. Descotes, *Le Drame . . .* , p. 271.

13. *Théâtre complet*, ed. Van Tieghem and Sarment, p. 273.

14. Cf. the edition by F. Deloffre, Geneva–Lille, 1955, especially the Introduction, which contains a comprehensive survey of this social type.

15. *Marivaux et le marivaudage*, revised edition, Paris, 1967, p. 216.

16. A. François, *Histoire de la langue française*, ed. F. Brunot, VI (ii), Paris, 1933, p. 1280.

17. *La Presse*, 29.xi.1847.

18. For a comparison of the two versions, see Shaw, *art. cit.*, pp. 72ff.

19. Cf. S. M. Waxman, *Antoine and the Théâtre-Libre*, Cambridge (Mass.), 1926. ch. i.

11 Romanticism in Decline

(i) 'Les Burgraves' and after

THE 'failure' of *Les Burgraves* is one of the well-established commonplaces about French Romantic drama. Hugo's play, produced in March 1843 at the Théâtre-Français, is universally agreed to have been a resounding failure, and the author's consequent discouragement is invariably adduced as one of the principal causes of the demise of Romanticism in the theatre. On the face of it, the facts might appear not to support such a view, for the play ran for thirty-three performances, compared with thirty-nine and thirty-six respectively for the first runs of *Hernani* and *Angelo* at the same theatre, and thirty-seven for that of *Chatterton*. A total of over thirty performances was by no means negligible for this period: as we have seen, many plays by Hugo and his colleagues had been withdrawn after a much shorter run than this. Why then did the reception of *Les Burgraves* have such a decisive effect, and how did the play come to leave behind it such a catastrophic memory?[1]

To begin with, the number of performances is perhaps misleading: even if *Les Burgraves* did not fail outright, it seems that it never played to full or enthusiastic audiences, and Daumier's well-known cartoon showing a worried Hugo beside a poster advertising the play is accompanied by the following verse:

> Hugo, lorgnant les voûtes bleues,
> Au Seigneur demande tout bas
> Pourquoi les astres ont des queues
> Quand Les *Burgraves* n'en ont pas.[2]

Gautier's account of the first night—a social occasion of rare distinction—speaks of respectful rather than enthusiastic spectators[3]; and while he himself was capable of showing an

appreciation of the spirit of the play which was in keeping with
the author's intentions:

> C'est la plus énorme conception qui se soit produite à la
> scène depuis Eschyle[4]

—other critics were less generous, and even the most favourable
reviews were qualified by reservations about the melodramatic
character of the play[5].

As regards Hugo's relations with his actors, these followed a
familiar pattern. The play was completed in October 1842, and
although it had apparently been conceived with Frédérick
Lemaître and Dorval in mind, it was offered to the Théâtre-
Français. It was read to the *comité de lecture* in November, and
accepted with only one contrary vote; but casting difficulties
ensued, particularly over the role of the ninety-year-old
Guanhumara. Rachel did not show the interest Hugo seems to
have hoped for, and the part was given to Mlle Maxime, only
to be taken away from her during rehearsals (a law-suit
ensued, brought by the actress against Hugo and the theatre)
and offered to Mme Mélingue, who was brought in for the purpose from the Ambigu-Comique[6]. The other major parts were
played by Ligier (Barberousse), Beauvallet (Job), and Geffroy
(Otbert). As usual, Hugo proved himself very loyal towards his
actors; and as he had done in the case of *Ruy Blas*, his greatest
success, he went out of his way to publish an appreciation of the
performance of his leading players. Speaking of "cette belle
mise en scène des *Burgraves*, qui a fait tant d'honneur à la
Comédie-Française", he wrote that "jamais pièce n'a été
montée avec plus de soin et représentée avec plus d'ensemble";
and of Geffroy:

> M. Geffroy... a imprimé au personnage d'Otbert cette
> physionomie fatale que les poètes comme Shakespeare savent
> rêver et que les acteurs comme M. Geffroy savent réaliser.[7]

His friends were less complimentary, however, and according
to Frédérick and others, the mediocrity of the performance was
largely responsible for the play's lack of success[8].

This is not the whole of the story, though: in the five years
since *Ruy Blas*, Hugo's conception of poetic drama had undergone

a considerable change. In 1839, he had written four acts of a projected verse drama, *Les Jumeaux*, based on the story of the Man in the Iron Mask; this would have been a personal interpretation of historical subject-matter, very much in the manner of *Marion de Lorme*. It is not known why this project was abandoned: the extant draft contains some very effective dramatic writing[9]. But by the time of *Les Burgraves*, Hugo had moved towards a form of epic drama whose affinities are really less with the plays written during the 1830s than with the historical epic *La Légende des siècles*, the first two books of which were to be published in 1859. Even before this, the poet's imagination had begun to tend more and more towards the grandiose and the superhuman. The collection *Les Contemplations* for instance, whose composition spans the period from 1830 to 1855, reveals a steady progression from the intimate personal and domestic inspiration of the earlier years to that of the visionary 'Ce que dit la bouche d'ombre', in which the themes of suffering and expiation, the nature of evil, and human progress through metempsychosis are treated on a cosmic scale. *Les Burgraves* seeks to give expression to similar themes of retribution and expiation, and embodies the same belief in perfectibility and progress; and although the abstractions of the poet-philosopher are necessarily, in a dramatic work, clothed in human form, the symbolic, philosophical function of his characters remains paramount, and it is impossible to accept them in ordinary theatrical terms as credible dramatic protagonists.

The historical setting in which the events of the play are acted out was suggested by Hugo's visits to the Rhineland in 1838 and the two following years, during which he had been much impressed not only by the wild beauty of the region, but also by the legendary associations of the imposing ruins, a reminder of the titanic struggles for power of the early Middle Ages. The term 'titanic' is not used loosely: it is employed by Hugo himself, who regarded these conflicts in poetic, visionary terms:

Au temps d'Eschyle, la Thessalie était un lieu sinistre. Il y avait eu là autrefois des géants; il y avait là maintenant des fantômes...; pour Eschyle et ses contemporains,... c'était l'effrayant champ de bataille où les titans avaient lutté contre Jupiter.

Ce que la fable a inventé, l'histoire le reproduit, parfois.
Ainsi,... il y a aujourd'hui en Europe un lieu qui, toute
proportion gardée, est pour nous, au point de vue poétique,
ce qu'était la Thessalie pour Eschyle, c'est-à-dire un champ
de bataille mémorable et prodigieux... Là, en effet, il y a
six siècles, d'autres titans ont lutté contre un autre Jupiter.
Ces titans, ce sont les burgraves; ce Jupiter, c'est l'empereur
d'Allemagne.

Although he specifically rejects the 'visionary' quality lent by
poets to the Greek fables, and although he continues, in the
Preface to the play, to insist that "les titans sont des mythes,
les burgraves sont des hommes", nevertheless his manner
of treating the historical material is such as to reinforce the
mythical character of his subject-matter at the expense of
purely human values. The only attempt at anything like historical—or psychological—verisimilitude is in the portrayal of
the burgraves of the younger generation, led by the degenerate
Hatto: in one or two colourful scenes we see them carousing
to excess, and hear them boasting of pillage, plunder, and
injustice of every sort. But these robber-barons are merely the
background to the essential action of the play, which takes place
between Magnus, Hatto's father, Job, his grandfather, the
Emperor Frederick Barbarossa, and the aged hag Guanhumara,
once the beautiful Ginevra and the object of bitter rivalry
between the two brothers Frederick and Job. Job, who had
sixty years earlier committed fratricide in a fit of jealousy,
represents Expiation; Guanhumara represents Revenge; and
Barbarossa (who had after all survived his brother's murderous
attack), represents Forgiveness, as he emerges from his long vigil
to safeguard the wellbeing of the Empire and punish the last of
the burgraves. Even the young lovers, Regina and Otbert,
intended by Guanhumara to be the instruments of her revenge
on Job, are little more than abstractions representing on the one
hand Innocence, and on the other the knightly virtue of Honour.
If these identifications are not all as explicit as that offered in
Guanhumara's couplet:

Eh bien! je suis le meurtre et je suis la vengeance.
Je vais, fantôme aveugle, au but marqué d'avance;
Je suis la soif du sang (I, ix)

nevertheless all the major characters are conceived on *a priori*
lines as embodiments of abstract virtues or vices, and rather
than the ostensible working-out of a plot conceived in normal
human terms, what matters is the symbolic victory of Good
over Evil, as part of the "seul et immense mouvement d'ascen-
sion vers la lumière", as Hugo the thinker envisaged the process
of history[10].

It is not that the creation of a mythological world is unacceptable *per se*: one has only to look at the success of J. R.Tolkien's
Hobbitland, or of Mervyn Peake's Gormenghast, in our own
day. But such fantasies can more easily be realized in the novel,
or the epic poem, than in the theatre: the novelist's fantasy
world can be communicated by the imaginative quality of his
writing, and does not depend on visual manifestation, while the
necessity of tailoring the imaginary world to the scale of a three-
hour theatrical performance inevitably means that there is no
room fully to establish a mythological world with its own
coherent logic. The one example of a poet creating a mythological world in the theatre and successfully imposing it on a
modern audience is that of Richard Wagner; and Wagner's
achievement in the Ring cycle provides a most instructive
contrast with Hugo's experience in the case of *Les Burgraves*. In
fact, the central motifs of betrayal and revenge, forgiveness and
reconciliation are common to the two works (it is not without
interest that Gautier's notice of *Les Burgraves* anticipates the
comparison by referring to the *Nibelungenlied*) but whereas
Wagner's lyrical genius succeeds in arousing the spectator's
vital spiritual concern for these issues, in Hugo's epic drama
they remain empty abstractions. "To the true Wagnerian", it
has been said, "his characters . . . are real persons—be they
gods or mortals—with whom we love and hate, suffer or
rejoice"[11]. It would be difficult to make this claim for *Les
Burgraves*.

Partly, this is due to the mediocrity of the play's dramatic
invention: the plot is full of the sort of melodramatic clichés that
hostile critics have been ready to see in almost all of Hugo's
plays; but a more important reason is surely to be found in the
language of *Les Burgraves*. For whereas in the earlier verse plays,
even in the estimation of those most hostile to Romantic drama,
the banalities and the melodramatic contrivances had been

compensated for in some measure by passages of inspired lyrical writing, here such inspiration seems entirely lacking. Hugo's rhyming is now forced rather than inventive; his metaphors and similes are not so much imaginative as bizarre and arbitrary. For Gautier, Hugo's writing in *Les Burgraves* "annonçait le poète souverain":

A chaque instant, un vers magnifique, d'un grand coup de son aile d'aigle, vous enlève dans les plus hauts cieux de la poésie lyrique. C'est une variété de ton, une souplesse de rythme, une facilité de passer du tendre au terrible, du plus frais sourire à la plus profonde terreur, que nul écrivain n'a possédée au même degré.[12]

Such an appraisal appears indulgent to a degree; and Hugo seems to us to have committed the cardinal error of imposing on *Les Burgraves* the style that he was coming to adopt more and more for his non-dramatic writings. This style, full of historical and moral abstractions, of rhetorical figures such as personification and hyperbole, may conceivably be appropriate to the genre of the 'petite épopée' that Hugo was to exploit in the *Légende des siècles*; it is quite unsuited to a genre which depends above all on communication with a theatre audience by means of credible dramatic characters:

J'ai su juger les rois, je sais traquer les loups.
J'ai fait pendre les chefs des sept cités lombardes;
Albert l'Ours m'opposait dix mille hallebardes,
Je le brisai; mes pas sont dans tous les chemins;
J'ai démembré Henri le Lion de mes mains,
Arraché ses duchés, arraché ses provinces,
Puis avec ses débris j'ai fait quatorze princes;
Enfin j'ai, quarante ans, avec mes doigts d'airain,
Pierre à pierre émietté vos donjons dans le Rhin! (II, vi)

Hugo's last attempt to conquer the public of the Théâtre-Français failed, therefore, as much because of changes in his own approach to the theatre as because of the public's hostility towards Romanticism. It seems that in any case the general reaction was probably not one of hostility, but took the far more deadly form of indifference. And whatever the causes of this indifference, the effect of the play's reception on Hugo himself was certainly decisive: from 1843 onwards, he was to make no further attempt to impose himself on Parisian theatre audiences. By this time Vigny too had already given up the struggle, Musset had not yet returned to writing directly for the theatre, and Dumas was already busy turning his historical novels into popular melodramas of a thoroughly anodine character. As far as its major practitioners are concerned, therefore, the days of Romantic drama—that is, of plays with genuine literary aspirations, reflecting the mood and expressing the ideals of a whole generation of young writers and artists—were virtually at an end.

The few dates that still remain to be chronicled concern other poets and men of letters who in one way or another remained true to Romantic idealism and continued, in the late 1840s and into the 1850s, to express this idealism in works written for the theatre—works which, while they may have had little influence on the course of theatrical history, nevertheless occupy a modest place in the story of Romantic drama. Balzac, we have seen, alternated as a dramatist between the stylized presentation of a Romantically heightened reality and a formula which anticipated the more sober realism of a later generation; but Nerval, Gautier and Lamartine, however different their plays, all employ an unmistakable version of the Romantic idiom.

Of these writers, Gérard de Nerval made the most sustained and serious contribution to the drama of his day. We have seen that he collaborated with Dumas in the creation of the verse dramas *Caligula* and *L'Alchimiste*; and by the same token, Dumas also had a hand in the writing of Nerval's 'drame' *Léo Burckart*[13]. This play was first written for the Théâtre de la Renaissance under Joly, but was finally put on by Harel at the Porte-Saint-Martin in April 1839, after changes imposed by the censor[14]. The subject was a historical one: Léo Burckart corresponds to the German politician Kotzebue, and Frantz Lewald to the student Karl Sand who assassinated him in 1819. The setting is the same, that of political milieux in modern Germany; but the characters of the protagonists have been changed, as well as their names. Burckart is an idealized version of Kotzebue: an enlightened journalist with progressive ideas, he accepts the Duke's invitation to join the government as prime minister, and immediately has to face the necessity for compromise with his ideals in the name of practical politics. This is regarded as betrayal by the 'Young Germany' movement, and Frantz is chosen by lot to be his assassin. It is he who is the central figure of the play: his Hamlet-like hesitation, complicated by his former love for Burckart's wife Marguerite, ends with his refusal to kill, and his own suicide (whereas Karl Sand, his model, had tried unsuccessfully to shoot himself after killing Kotzebue). As well as being inspired by a near-contemporary *fait divers* and by the revolutionary ideals of post-Napoleonic Europe—and it was of course this provocative subject-matter which caused the censor to interest himself in the play—*Léo Burckart* shows the influence of Nerval's life-long obsession with the Faust theme (he published a translation of Goethe's work, and left an unfinished *Faust* of his own). Burckart is the idealist who succumbs to temptation (represented by the Duke, and more tangibly by the cynical Paulus), and like Goethe's hero he is redeemed by the force of true love represented by the Gretchen figure in the form of his wife Marguerite. There are textual reminiscences of Goethe, and also of Schiller: the conception of Frantz owes something to that of the latter's hero Karl Moor in *Die Räuber*. Nerval is of all the French dramatists of the period the one who reveals the biggest debt to the German drama of preceding generations, which had exerted such a strong influence on dramatic theory through Constant and other interpreters[15]. But Frantz is also a Romantic hero with echoes much nearer home. Just as much as Frank of *La Coupe et les lèvres*, Didier or Chatterton, he is a creation of the times that had produced Nerval himself, a reflection of a recognizably French *mal du siècle*:

Ce siècle, qui ne compte pas encore vingt années, s'est levé au milieu de l'orage et de l'incendie. La guerre rugissait autour de nos berceaux, et nos pères absents revenaient par instant nous presser sur leur sein, tantôt vainqueurs, tantôt vaincus et consternés! La passion politique, qui d'ordinaire est une passion de l'âge mûr, nous a pris, nous-mêmes avant l'âge de raison; et nous l'avons retrouvée plus tard encore dans l'étude et dans la famille et le jour où nos bras furent assez forts pour lever un fusil, la patrie nous jeta tout frémissants sous les pieds des chevaux, au milieu du choc des

armures. Oh! maintenant qu'un calme plat a succédé à tant
d'orageuses tourmentes, étonnez-vous que nous ayons peine à
nous remettre de ces efforts prématurés, et que nous n'ayons
plus à offrir aux femmes qu'une âme flétrie avant l'âge, et des
passions énervées déjà par le doute et le malheur. (I, ii)

It is difficult to imagine a modern playwright tackling the
theme of *Léo Burckart* without taking up a committed stance: one
thinks of Camus's treatment of a similar subject in *Les Justes*, or
Sartre's in *Les Mains sales*. But Nerval's purpose was explicitly
not to take sides in a debate between contemporary political
ideologies:

> Ce n'est ni Kotzebue, ni Sand, que j'ai voulu peindre, ni
> aucun personnage défini, seulement, j'ai toujours haï
> l'assassinat politique, qui n'amène jamais que le contraire
> du résultat qu'on en attend.[16]

Hippolyte Lucas, reviewing the play, paid tribute to his success
in this:

> L'auteur,... avec un art infini, a fait en sorte qu'on estime
> également le prince, Léo Burckart et les étudiants, malgré
> leur antagonisme constant.[17]

And indeed, the playwright has managed to imbue his play
with the conviction deriving from the treatment of serious
contemporary issues, without subordinating the humanity of
his characters to the exigencies of partisan propaganda.

The play had twenty-six performances; it was apparently
well received by the press; and altogether it hardly deserves the
neglect into which it has fallen. On the contrary, it is a notable
example of historical drama in a form strongly influenced by
the 'scène historique'—in particular the presentation of the
student societies shows the conscientious use of detailed documentation[18]—but nevertheless one that is theatrically viable.
To quote Jean Richer, in the article of 1948 in which he
attempted a rehabilitation of *Léo Burckart*:

> [Ce drame] nous semble l'une des meilleures pièces de
> l'époque romantique, et une adaptation respectueuse de

l'esprit du poète pourrait sans doute en être portée sur la scène contemporaine.[19]

In 1851 Nerval returned to the Faust legend, this time with two collaborators, Méry and Lopez. *L'Imagier de Harlem*, like the earlier *L'Alchimiste* and an unfinished 'drame', *Nicolas Flamel*, is set in the early Renaissance; but whereas in these earlier versions, as in the Faust legend itself, the search for the key to knowledge and power had been represented by the symbolic figure of the alchemist, now the hero is the inventor of printing. An idealist who wants to use his invention in the service of mankind, the impoverished Laurent Coster succumbs to temptation in the form of a series of incarnations of Satan. The first, the Comte de Bloksberg, uses the printing-press to make paper money, while in a later episode Machiavelli proposes to turn the printer's genius to his own profit by a strict control over the licence to publish. Coster forsakes his wife and daughter, but he is redeemed by their selfless love, and the play closes with Satan acknowledging defeat. The idiom chosen for *L'Imagier* is very different from that of *Léo Burckart*: the play is written in a mixture of verse and prose, and although there are certain awkwardnesses, particularly in expository passages, and although the prose dialogue occasionally lapses into banality, Nerval has been quite successful, particularly in the scenes written in verse, in creating a style capable of doing justice to the mythical quality of the legend. The construction is episodic, and perhaps shows the influence of Goethe's *Faust, Part II* in that Nerval and his collaborators have broken out of the confines of realism in their attempt to find a non-representational form suitable to the scenes of pure allegory. *L'Imagier de Harlem* is a poet's drama: it is not entirely successful, for there remains too great a mixture of styles. Nevertheless, whereas Goethe's *Part II*, however impressive, is an abstract philosophical poem, Nerval's play does not lose sight of the human appeal of the Faust theme, and the adaptation of the theme to the stage has been realized in dramatically effective terms. The play was produced at the Porte-Saint-Martin in December 1851, the part of Satan, in his seven embodiments, being played by Mélingue[20].

When we turn to Théophile Gautier, we find a writer with a life-long interest in the theatre, and a warm-hearted attachment to the fortunes of Romantic drama, though both of these were expressed most memorably in his personal relationships with Hugo and the other dramatists, and in the accounts he left of the first night of *Hernani* and similar historic occasions. In addition to this, however, Gautier was himself constantly tempted to write for the theatre; and while perhaps his best-known work consists of the libretti he wrote for such ballets as *Giselle* (1841, music by Adam) or *La Péri* (1843, music by Burgmuller), and his most typical the sort of light-hearted comedy represented by *Le Tricorne enchanté* (Variétés, April 1845), he did also try his hand at dramatic works more squarely in the tradition whose evolution we have been following.

In 1846, he published in the *Revue des Deux Mondes* an excellent example of the *proverbe*, *La Fausse Conversion, ou Bon Sang ne peut mentir*. While less subtle than the best of Musset's *proverbes*, this little play gives a pleasant documentary account of Parisian society manners under the *ancien régime*. Célinde, an opera singer, has fallen in love with Saint-Albin, a disciple of Rousseau, and leaves Paris to act out a Romantic idyll with her lover; but a month in the country is more than enough for both lovers, and in any case Saint-Albin has copied Rousseau's Saint-Preux so faithfully that he finds himself forced to marry a former pupil's sister whom he had seduced. Célinde returns to the more sophisticated delights of Paris, and the curtain-line comments:

> Je vous avais bien dit que ces bergeries-là ne dureraient point... Bon sang ne peut mentir.

La Fausse Conversion was not performed until 1899[21], but the same year 1846 saw the production at the Porte-Saint-Martin, in November, of *La Juive de Constantine*, 'drame anecdotique en cinq actes et six tableaux'[22]. Written as an act of homage to the acknowledged masters of 'mélodrame' such as Pixérécourt, Gautier's play shows as well as any the close affinity between this genre and some of the manifestations of Romanticism in the theatre of the 1830s and 1840s:

> En étudiant le « Shakespeare du boulevard », et en acceptant son esthétique pour ce qu'elle valait, Théo ne faisait que remonter aux sources du théâtre qui avait enchanté sa prime

jeunesse. En fait, le même élan qui avait poussé Gautier à adhérer aux formes du romantisme, l'invitait, au seuil de sa maturité, à jeter un dernier regard sur sa jeunesse, sur son passé de romantique impénitent.[23]

The style of *La Juive de Constantine* alternates between the prosaic and the emphatic, and it is not this feature of the play which lifts it above the level of melodrama. Its plot is eventful enough to satisfy any devotee of the popular boulevard theatre —though there is a distinct borrowing from *Romeo and Juliet* in the story of the heroine who is drugged in order to feign death, and who recovers consciousness in the family vault. Gautier's subject, however, is not so much feuding families as warring religions: Léa, the "belle Juive", is rejected by her father because she loves a Christian, and nearly falls victim to the fanaticism of her Mohammedan lover. While not a pure drama of ideas on this subject like Lessing's *Nathan der Weise*, nor yet a tragedy spiced with propaganda like Voltaire's *Zaïre*, Gautier's play has enough of a thesis to raise it above the banality of the popular thriller. Characterization, too, is subtler than that of melodrama, and motives are mixed: what moves the hitherto inexorable Jewish father to give his hand to his daughter's lover in the play's final tableau is not any simplistic demonstration of Christian virtues, but the example of a Mohammedan girl who gives her life in the cause of tolerance and forgiveness. Altogether, *La Juive de Constantine* shows the formula of melodrama being handled by an intelligent playwright who was obviously receptive to Romantic influences.

Another play which cannot be classed as a pure Romantic drama (always supposing that such a category exists), but which deserves a mention in any account of Romanticism in the theatre, is Auguste Vacquerie's *Tragaldabas* (Porte-Saint-Martin, July 1848). Vacquerie was very near to Hugo (his brother Charles had been the husband of Hugo's daughter Léopoldine), and the production of his play served as an occasion to rally the supporters of a style of drama with which the latter had been prominently identified. The first night has been described as a "bataille d'*Hernani* à rebours": as on the former occasion, the theatre was the scene of noisy confrontations between the author's partisans and their opponents, but now it was the Romantic 'establishment' that was under attack. Vacquerie's supporters included, besides Hugo and his sons, Gautier, Charles Meurice, Saint-Victor, Banville, Champfleury, Murger, Balzac, George Sand, Dumas, Alphonse Karr, Gozlan, Émile de Girardin and others; while prominent in the opposing camp were Musset, long since disillusioned with the extravagances of Romantic drama, and François Ponsard, who since the success of his *Lucrèce* in 1843 had been regarded as the leader of the anti-Romantic movement in the theatre[24].

Tragaldabas is a comedy. It contains a synthesis of many traits of genuine Romantic drama, together with a saving element of parody and lighthearted humour. The plot depends on an absurd bargain between the heroine, Dona Caprina, and her down-at-heel cousin Tragaldabas that in return for a modest allowance he will pretend to be married to her; this will keep her suitors at a distance, and allow her the initiative in choosing a husband. Dona Caprina and her lover Eliseo indulge in a scene of *marivaudage* not unlike that of Musset's characters in *Le Chandelier*; Tragaldabas himself is a sort of cowardly Don César de Bazan, who is finally saved from having to fight a duel by dressing in an ass's skin and going off with a troupe of strolling players; Minotoro and Grif, two *spadassins*, are caricatures of a familiar Romantic type; and at its best, Vacquerie's verse shows an inventive, comic use of language that recalls Hugo and foreshadows Rostand:

> Tu m'as — et ton tarif disputait chaque écu —
> Payé comme mari, mais non comme cocu.
> J'en conviens avec toi, ce n'est qu'une nuance;
> Les deux mots ont entre eux une étroite alliance,
> Mais, dans quelque union qu'ils aient toujours vécu,
> Mari ne veut pas dire absolument cocu.
> On peut les distinguer par extraordinaire.
> On ne lit pas encor dans le dictionnaire:
> *Mari*, voyez *cocu*. Quand nous nous promenons,
> Et qu'à te voir si belle on demande nos noms,
> Toi-même m'en voudrais si, suivant ton programme,
> Je répondais: Je suis le cocu de madame! (III, i)

Tragaldabas ran for seventeen performances, with Frédérick Lemaître in the name part. There is an evident kinship with the spirit of the latter's earlier successes, *L'Auberge des Adrets* and *Robert Macaire*; but for all the obvious elements of parody and self-conscious comedy, Vacquerie's play shows genuine Romantic affinities in its colourful, imaginative plot and its overall literary character. Moreover, its lighthearted lack of concern with the serious issues of the real world stamp it as an example of 'art for art's sake'; and at a moment when the growing opposition between 'artists' and 'bourgeois' had just been exacerbated by the 1848 Revolution, it is easy to understand how the production of such a play, in spite of its indifferent quality, could serve as a pretext for the confrontation of rival ideologies.

Though the production of *Tragaldabas* is sometimes referred to as bringing the Romantic period in the theatre to a symbolic close, there is another play, produced in 1850, which may perhaps be a rival claimant for this honour, since it marks the last contribution by a major literary figure of the Romantic generation to the type of poetic historical drama which had presented the principal challenge to traditional classical tragedy. This is Lamartine's *Toussaint Louverture* (Porte-Saint-Martin, April 1850). The sixty-year-old author had been the hero of the idealist left at the time of the 1848 Revolution; and the subject of the republican patriot, who had led the people of Haiti in their successful rising against slavery and French domination, was an excellent vehicle for the revolutionary sentiments of liberty, equality and fraternity. The play, which Lamartine called "une tragédie moderne", had been begun in 1839 and completed in 1840, with a view to production at the Théâtre-Français; but part of the manuscript was mislaid, and though fragments of the play were published in the *Revue des Deux Mondes* in 1843, the newly-written version was not ready until 1849, when Frédérick Lemaître was commissioned to help the poet to adapt it to the requirements of stage performance. When it was performed in the following year, Frédérick himself played the part of the negro hero; reviews were not very favourable, but the play was warmly received by its audiences.

Toussaint Louverture has a noble theme: it presents an idealistic challenge to militarism, to imperialism and to racial prejudice. But the means of dramatic expression are those of the melodrama: there are the same lavish use of local colour, the same reliance on sensational *jeux de théâtre* and *coups de théâtre*[25], the same attempts to arouse indignation and pathos by extremes of characterization. It is not difficult to imagine the same play written in prose by Pixérécourt; as it is, the verse, with its recognizable harmonies, confers on the play a curiously hybrid quality:

> O mornes du Limbé! vallons! anses profondes
> Où l'ombre des forêts descend auprès des ondes;
> Où la liane en fleur, tressée en verts arceaux,
> Forme des ponts sur l'air pour passer les oiseaux;
> Galets où les pieds nus, cueillant les coquillages,
> J'écoute de la mer les légers babillages;
> Bois touffus d'orangers, qui, respirant le soir,
> Parfumez mes cheveux comme un grand encensoir,
> Et qui, lorsque la main vous secoue ou vous penche,
> Nous faites en passant la tête toute blanche!
> Roseaux qui de la terre exprimez tout le miel,
> Où passent en chantant si doux les vents du ciel!
> De ces climats aimés rêveuses habitudes,
> Que j'aime à vous poursuivre au fond des solitudes! (I, ii)

There is no doubt that such passages succeed in establishing the play as 'literary drama'; but there is little coherence between the two styles. The typically Lamartinian elegies, the stirring patriotic tirades, stand out as so many purple passages, while action and characterization remain undisguisedly those of melodrama. Lamartine's poetic genius is the best possible illustration of Steiner's dictum that "the lyric mode is profoundly alien to the dramatic"[26]; and whereas Hugo at his best, in *Hernani* or *Marion de Lorme*, had succeeded in amalgamating the two aspects of Romantic drama into a coherent whole of some real originality, *Toussaint Louverture*, considered as an example of poetic drama, is a noble failure.

(ii) *Rachel, Ponsard and the classical counter-attack*

AS well as being the last notable attempt at historical drama in verse, *Toussaint Louverture* was Frédérick Lemaître's last Romantic role—and though the great actor was to live until 1876, and gave his last stage performance as late as 1875, from 1850 onwards his career marked a steady decline:

It was not that he lost any of his skill or was surpassed by another player: he remained undisputably the first actor of France. But the times had changed, and the theatre with them. The heroism and idealism, the panache and gusto of the Romantic era had been finally extinguished in the bloody repression of the June Days; mediocrity and frivolity took their place.[27]

Moreover, Lamartine's play marked the end of an era at the Porte-Saint-Martin, the theatre which, from the first triumphant success of *Antony* in 1831 onwards, had been so intimately identified with the best and worst of Romantic drama. The Porte-Saint-Martin closed its doors in the summer of 1850, and although it was to open again under new management, its repertory was henceforth to be much less distinctive in character.

If 1850 for several reasons, therefore, marks a significant terminal date in the history of Romantic drama, there had been signs long before this that the end was approaching, and that public taste was changing. Alongside what we may call the negative factors—the abandoning of the theatre by Hugo and Vigny, the adoption by both Dumas and Musset of formulas no longer expressive of their former Romantic idealism, the indifferent quality of the 'drames romantiques' that were written in the 1840s—we may set the more positive evidence of a return to favour of the classical repertory, and of the development of new kinds of play more in keeping with the spirit of the times.

At the time of *Henri III* and *Hernani* the young Romantics had exulted in a victory which, they thought, had destroyed classical tragedy for ever:

> Tout à coup des jeunes gens réunis en groupe se donnent la main, ferment une ronde, et dansent en s'écriant: Bravo! Bravo! nous en avons fini avec le classique; Melpomène est enfoncée; nous sommes délivrés des harangues de Corneille, des fadeurs de Racine, du clinquant et des jongleries de Voltaire. Bravo! bravo![28]

Their victory had never been as complete as that, of course: not only Corneille, Racine and Voltaire, but also modern authors of tragedy such as Delavigne and Lebrun had continued to be performed in the years following the writing of these lines[29], and a steady trickle, if not a stream, of new tragedies had been written, throughout the 1830s, according to the traditional classical formula. But even the masterpieces of seventeenth-century tragedy were poorly attended at the Théâtre-Français, and so mediocre were the new plays that the Académie Française instituted a prize for the best tragedy to be written. The first ten years of the period during which Romantic drama flourished did in fact correspond to the absolute nadir of traditional tragedy, both old and new; but a turning-point came in 1838, and by the early 1840s tragedy at the Théâtre-Français was in a much healthier state. This was due almost entirely, according to contemporary commentators, to the young actress Rachel. Born Rachel Félix in Switzerland in 1821 of poor Jewish parents, she had had a very brief training at the Conservatoire, before being taken in hand by the actor Samson. Her début as Camille in *Horace* attracted the enthusiastic notice of the critic Jules Janin, who was to be largely responsible for launching her, and in the course of the next four or five years she took over nearly all the most important roles in the classical repertory: Hermione, Pauline, Émilie, Roxane and particularly Phèdre. The effect on the public was quite sensational, and the genuine admiration of the connoisseurs led to the wider following of the fashionable public: classical tragedy was soon playing to full houses, and the declining fortunes of Romanticism in the theatre faced a real challenge from a reinvigorated classicism.

Rachel had the undoubted good fortune to arrive exactly at the most favourable moment. By 1838 it must have seemed clear that the inspiration behind Romantic drama was running out of steam, and this certainly favoured the return of public taste to the traditional repertory; but before she came on the scene there was a real dearth of talent at the Théâtre-Français. And not only did Rachel possess a rare talent, but the nature of her gifts was such that it helped to bridge the gulf between the old and the new in matters of taste. For although she possessed a marvellous purity of diction, her unconventional background and training had left her with a relatively natural stage presence, owing more to intuition than to the highly stylized technique inculcated by the traditional 'formation classique':

Elle était, de toutes les artistes naturellement inspirées, celle qui était la moins faite pour le métier. Ainsi, les leçons des maîtres, elle les avait oubliées, la première fois que son pied foula les sentiers d'un vrai théâtre... Ajoutez qu'elle avait en elle-même, et par un don surnaturel, la vraie et sincère image des passions qu'elle racontait à la foule.[30]

In other words, though no doubt it would be wrong to push the parallel too far, she had something of the appeal of Marie Dorval —or of Harriet Smithson, who had made such an impression on French audiences in 1827. Janin suggests, moreover, that she had something else in common with the English actress: that she accomplished for French tragedy what Miss Smithson had achieved for Shakespeare:

Avant mademoiselle Rachel, c'était le *tragédien* qui était le maître absolu de la tragédie, et la *tragédienne* ici, chez nous, jouait inévitablement le second rôle... Miss Smithson cependant... précédait, elle annonçait mademoiselle Rachel et, sans le savoir, elle lui traçait sa voie après avoir habitué le peuple français à ne pas croire uniquement aux tragédiens, mais encore aux tragédiennes.[31]

It was Racine's heroines, and certain roles of Corneille's theatre, which provided the vehicle for Rachel's extraordinary success: though she did play in new tragedies, her real achievement was to rehabilitate the masterpieces of the past. And this had already taken place by 1843—Rachel's crowning triumph, her performance as Phèdre, came in January of that year—so that *Les Burgraves* would have had to be a very much better play for it to be able to withstand the current trend at the Théâtre-Français: the ebb-tide of Romanticism began to flow there earlier and more strongly than elsewhere.

But it was not only with Rachel, and with Racine, that *Les Burgraves* had to contend. While Hugo's play was still running at the Théâtre-Français, a new play in the classical idiom was performed at the Odéon, and received with considerable enthusiasm. This was *Lucrèce*, by an unknown lawyer from Provence, François Ponsard. It was played in April 1843, with Dorval in the name-part as the celebrated symbol of chastity and fidelity, and Bocage as Brute (Junius Brutus), the patriotic idealist. *Lucrèce* is not a very distinguished play, and Ponsard fell a long way short of the genius that was attributed to him by those who were looking for another Corneille or another Racine. In any case, the success of *Lucrèce* was at least partly due to the compromises he made between the strict classical form of the seventeenth and eighteenth centuries, and the Romantic formula of the 1830s. To quote Gautier, reviewing the play:

A la représéntation, nous avons été fort surpris. Nous nous attendions à une œuvre purement classique et notre attente a été trompée assez heureusement. Le passé ne se recommence pas, et, dans les pastiches les plus résolus, la vie moderne entre toujours par quelque coin. L'unité de lieu n'est pas gardée dans *Lucrèce*, puisque l'action se promène de Collatie à Rome. Brute est un personnage de drame, s'il en fut, car la tragédie rigoureuse n'admet pas le mélange du sublime et du grotesque... L'abus de la couleur locale, tant reproché aux poètes de la nouvelle école, est poussé fort loin par M. Ponsard, et son style, souvent énergique et libre, n'a pas cette sainte horreur du mot propre, cet académique amour de la périphrase qui distingue les auteurs de l'école classique.[32]

The most interesting of these remarks is the one concerning the character of Brute: Gautier goes on to compare him to Hamlet and Lorenzaccio, "qui cachent tous deux un grand dessein sous un masque grimaçant ou stupide"[33]. But in spite of these affinities with certain features of the works of the 'nouvelle école', *Lucrèce* remains a tragedy rather than a new-style 'drame': for all the local colour, the reader is not given the impression that the events portrayed in the play are the inevitable result of specific historical contingencies. Instead, they are the outcome of a clash between characters who are no more than the moral abstractions typical of the second-rate classical tragedies of the previous century and a half; and the chaste Lucrèce and Tarquin the wicked ravisher are much more representative in this respect than the slightly subtler character of Brute.

Even more than in the case of Rachel's début—for her outstanding talent would no doubt have made its mark, if less sensationally, at any other time—Ponsard's play owed its success to a happy conjunction of circumstances, in particular the opportune timing which produced the competition with *Les Burgraves*. But its success was brief: there were 39 performances

13 'Musset en page allemand', by Devéria

14 'Hugo à l'époque des *Burgraves*', by Daumier:

Hugo lorgnant les voûtes bleues,
Au Seigneur demande tout bas
Pourquoi les astres ont des queues
Quand les Burgraves n'en ont pas

up to the annual closing of the Odéon in June, and the takings to begin with were exceptionally good; but in September, when the theatre opened its new season with *Lucrèce*, the public had already lost interest. Janin, in his biography of Rachel, speculates on what the effect might have been if the young Ponsard, instead of choosing the Odéon, had offered his play to the Théâtre-Français, where *Lucrèce* might have had the advantage of Rachel's interpretation of the leading role:

> *Lucrèce* a manqué à mademoiselle Rachel; mademoiselle Rachel est la mère de *Lucrèce*. Elle avait donné le mouvement, elle avait imposé la révolution littéraire d'où *Lucrèce* est sortie.[34]

But this could hardly have made *Lucrèce* a better play. As it was, it already enjoyed a success out of all proportion to its literary or artistic merits, and one can only assume that other, non-aesthetic factors, played a large part in determining this success. Indeed, in his choice of subject and in his treatment of it, Ponsard was responding to an increasingly widespread desire for the reassertion of moral values based on marriage and the family, and for the repudiation of the anti-social characteristics, in particular the glorifying of free love and individualism, with which the Romantic dramatists were felt to have identified themselves. So that *Lucrèce* was perhaps less important as the rallying-point for an artistic counter-offensive against Romanticism than as the first important expression of the ethical ideas that were to be associated with 'l'école du bon sens'. When Ponsard's heroine says:

> Je veux rester fidèle
> Par mon aïeule instruite, aux mœurs que je tiens d'elle.
> Les femmes de son temps mettaient tout leur souci
> A surveiller l'ouvrage, à mériter ainsi
> Qu'on lût sur leur tombeau, digne d'une Romaine:
> « Elle vécut chez elle, et fila de la laine ».
> Les doigts laborieux rendent l'esprit plus fort,
> Tandis que la vertu dans les loisirs s'endort.
> Ainsi, celle qui prend l'aiguille de Minerve,
> Minerve, applaudissant, l'appuie et la préserve.

Le travail, il est vrai, peut ternir ma beauté,
Mais rien ne ternira mon honneur respecté (I, i)

she is not only speaking as a Roman matron in a 'tragédie à
l'antique', but also as the mouthpiece of the author, offering his
public an edifying contrast to the excesses of Romanticism.

The proof that Ponsard was no doctrinaire supporter of the
classical aesthetic is to be seen in his next two plays, both of
which owe a good deal to Romantic influences—and both of
which, incidentally, are much better plays than *Lucrèce*. *Agnès
de Méranie* was played at the Odéon in December 1846, and
Ponsard again had Bocage and Marie Dorval for his leading
roles; the play was a failure, and contemporary comment suggests that indifferent staging and mediocre acting were largely
responsible. The subject is taken from mediaeval history, and
concerns the conflict between the secular and the ecclesiastical
powers in twelfth-century France: Philippe-Auguste's first
marriage has been annulled, with the agreement of the French
bishops, and he has been happily married for some years to
Agnès when the new Pope, Innocent III, revokes the divorce,
declaring Agnès's marriage invalid and her children illegitimate. On the King's refusal to accept this, France is placed
under a papal interdict; and finally Agnès takes her life, as the
only way to save her husband and her country. Considered by
classical canons (it was labelled *tragédie*), *Agnès de Méranie* is
poorly constructed: the forces represented by the King and the
papal legate are unequally matched, and the outcome is hardly
in doubt; the Queen reaches her decision quite early in the play,
and altogether there is too little action. But judged by the looser
standards appropriate to Romantic drama, Ponsard's play not
only offers individual portraits of the King and Queen whose
marriage is broken by the arbitrary power of Rome, but also
presents this moving personal drama in a historical framework
that convinces us of its authenticity. This is historical drama
rather than tragedy, because the protagonists are shown to be
victims of historical forces operating in an identifiable locality
and at a unique moment in time.

Ponsard's third play, *Charlotte Corday* (Théâtre-Français,
March 1850), was even further removed from the formula of
classical tragedy; and if we apply this same definition of his-

torical drama, there are few plays of the period which are so authentically 'historical'. The choice of subject was inspired by the publication of Lamartine's *Histoire des Girondins* in 1847, but although Ponsard has been influenced by the general tendency among mid-century historians to 'whitewash' the Girondins, the interpretation he presents does not strike the reader as one-sided: the Girondins themselves are not shown as wholly admirable, nor are their opponents wholly black, for the moderation of Danton, and the caution of Robespierre, are effectively contrasted with Marat's bloodthirstiness. Ponsard's is in fact a responsible interpretation of a historical event, supported by references to contemporary sources (particularly for the views put into the mouth of Marat); and but for the fact that the play is in alexandrines, one would be tempted to see it as continuing the tradition of the 'scènes historiques'. Its authentic treatment of historical material, indeed, is very much in the spirit of that tradition, as is its lack of focus on the central character: to quote Latreille, "cette œuvre constitue une série d'épisodes, et non un drame"[35]. What may perhaps be said to give the necessary unity to the play is the way in which Ponsard has captured the spirit animating the Revolution: all the characters, from Charlotte herself to her victim Marat, contribute to the portrayal of a historical entity larger than themselves, and we have no difficulty in believing in the historical determinism which stamps these characters as belonging to a particular time and place.

Ponsard's handling of the alexandrine in *Charlotte Corday* is at once more functional and poetically more expressive than in his earlier plays. It is sufficiently of the nineteenth century to be able to accommodate without strain the specific vocabulary of the Revolutionary era, and yet quite unlike Hugo's line, with its bizarre imagery and idiosyncratic rhyme: instead, there are pre-Romantic harmonies that Chénier would not have disowned, reminiscent both of the *Bucoliques*:

Oui, oui, Dieu soit loué! la saison sera bonne.
Les foins sont abondants, et, quand viendra l'automne,
Si l'espoir des pommiers échappe aux vents du nord,
Le cidre remplira le pressoir jusqu'au bord.
A demain. C'est assez. L'heure est trop avancée,

Faucheurs; n'aiguisez plus votre faux émoussée.
Emportez vos râteaux, faneuses, et demain
Aux premières chaleurs mettez-vous en chemin (II, i)

and of the stirring verses of the *Iambes*:

Poignard, agent du crime, agent déshonoré,
Ennoblis-toi! tu sers un intérêt sacré.
Frappe; ne tremble pas dans des mains généreuses;
Montre aux crimes hardis des vertus vigoureuses;
Et souviens-toi qu'Athène entoura d'un feston
Le fer d'Harmodius et d'Aristogiton. (IV, ii)

If the neo-classical *Lucrèce* formed the basis of Ponsard's considerable contemporary reputation (not only did he win the
Academy's prize for the best tragedy in 1843–44, but he was
himself elected to the Academy in 1856), his most distinguished
achievement in the theatre was a play that was much more
modern in flavour, in which he adopted the vehicle of Romantic
historical drama in order to give expression to a highly topical
plea for liberty and the rule of law.

(iii) 'L'école du bon sens' and the 'well-made play'

DESPITE the role usually assigned to him in the literary
histories as the spearhead of a 'classical revival', Ponsard's
allegiance was, as we have seen, neither completely nor
exclusively given to the backward-looking opponents of
Romanticism. The revival of tragedy 'à l'antique' was in any
case a minor, and ephemeral, part of the reaction against
Romantic drama, though the successful *Lucrèce* was naturally not
without its imitations, such as *Virginie*, a tragedy on a very
similar subject by Latour de Saint-Ybars, in which Rachel
played at the Théâtre-Français in April 1845. A more important
manifestation of this reaction, and one that was to be much
more durable in its effect, was the movement which came to be
known as 'l'école du bon sens': the significance of the label is
explained by Ponsard in the Preface to *Agnès de Méranie*:

Pour ma part, je n'admets que la souveraineté du bon sens;
je tiens que toute doctrine, ancienne ou moderne, doit être
continuellement soumise à l'examen de ce juge suprême.

The 'école' was a loose association of writers, particularly play-wrights, who adopted Ponsard as their leader, and who took a stand against the 'école de la fantaisie': the Romantics of the 1840s. What they objected to in Romantic literature was the cult of the mediaeval and the exotic, the extravagances of plot and characterization, and the unhealthy moral climate; to combat these, Ponsard and his colleagues upheld traditional moral values and positive commitment to a political ideal. In an article in *Le Spectateur Littéraire*, a periodical which appeared briefly in 1848 to promote the views of the group, Émile Augier attacked the Romantics for not having made a stand for political liberty, declaring that the 'école du bon sens', for its part, "se réclame du progrès et de la démocratie". Where the Romantics had upheld the individual's right to be anti-social, putting a high premium on energy and individualism, Ponsard, Augier and their followers value above all a respect for stable social institutions:

Dans la lutte de l'individu contre la collectivité, c'est pour la collectivité qu'Augier se prononce. C'est à ce point de vue de l'intérêt social qu'Augier se place toujours et uniquement.[36]

Thus Lucrèce, the symbol of honour and chastity, was joined by Virginie, killed by her father, the republican Virginius, to prevent her becoming a victim of a tyrant's lust; and subsequently by the equally exemplary heroes and heroines of modern dramas, the most influential of these being without a doubt those of Augier, whose *Gabrielle* was produced at the Théâtre-Français in December 1849.

Augier's career as a dramatist had started a few years earlier with a number of short comedies, and of *proverbes* in the manner of Musset, in one of which, *L'Habit vert* (Variétés, February 1849) he actually had the collaboration of Musset himself. But he lacked the light touch necessary to the successful *proverbe*, and was more at home with the earnest moralizing of the 'pièce à thèse'. As Dumas *fils* was to do later, he rejected the notion of 'l'art pour l'art', and had an ideal view of the theatre as a lay pulpit:

Vous dites que [le théâtre] n'a corrigé personne: je le veux bien: mais la même objection pourrait s'opposer aux livres de morale et à l'éloquence de la chaire; d'ailleurs le but n'est pas de corriger quelqu'un, c'est de corriger tout le monde: le vice universel n'est pas possible à supprimer, mais on peut en supprimer la contagion; et de tous les engins de la pensée humaine, le théâtre est le plus puissant, voilà tout.[37]

Gabrielle, written in alexandrines, is at best an uneasy compromise between conventional 'haute comédie' and the 'pièce à thèse' at which Augier was evidently aiming: its moralizing takes the form of sententious preaching, and both characterization and dialogue are lacking in subtlety. However, Julien, the husband of Gabrielle, who is momentarily tempted to leave him for the young colleague for whom she feels a passing attraction, is a forceful spokesman for the 'école du bon sens' as he replies to the idealistic challenge of his rival:

> — Les bonheurs négatifs sont faits pour les poltrons:
> Nous serons malheureux, mais du moins nous vivrons.
>
> — Voilà certes une belle et vive poésie.
> J'en sais une pourtant plus saine et mieux choisie,
> Dont plus solidement un cœur d'homme est rempli:
> C'est le contentement du devoir accompli,
> C'est le travail aride et la nuit studieuse,
> Tandis que la maison s'endort silencieuse,
> Et que pour rafraîchir son labeur échauffant
> On a tout près de soi le sommeil d'un enfant.
> Laissons aux cerveaux creux ou bien aux égoïstes
> Ces désordres au fond si vides et si tristes,
> Ces amours sans lien et dont l'impiété
> A l'égal d'un malheur craint la fécondité.
> Mais, nous autres, soyons des pères — c'est-à-dire,
> Mettons dans nos maisons, comme un chaste sourire,
> Une compagne pure en tout et d'un tel prix
> Qu'il soit bon d'en tirer les âmes de nos fils,
> Certains que d'une femme angélique et fidèle,
> Il ne peut rien sortir que de noble comme elle!
> Voilà la dignité de la vie et son but!
> Tout le reste n'est rien que prélude et début...   (V, v)

Nothing could be more unequivocal than this attack on the whole ethos that was associated with Romantic drama; and the celebrated curtain-line, however fatuous it may sound when quoted out of context, indicates no less certainly the erring Gabrielle's acknowledgement that her husband's precept and example have brought her back to the path of domestic virtue:

O père de famille! ô poète! je t'aime!

Even more than most products of the 'bon sens' movement, *Gabrielle* illustrates the truth of Gide's saying about 'beaux sentiments' and 'mauvaise littérature': at least, if 'beaux sentiments' are not an automatic guarantee of artistic mediocrity, they are by no means sufficient on their own to ensure artistic worth. After *Gabrielle*, however, Augier did succeed in adapting himself rather better to the realistic portrayal of the society of his times. A similar message, that of responsibility towards others instead of anti-social individualism, is expressed in the form of 'comédie de mœurs' in *Le Gendre de Monsieur Poirier* (Gymnase, April 1854) and in a noteworthy example of domestic tragedy in *Les Lionnes pauvres* (Vaudeville, May 1858); but in his most characteristic plays Augier avoided the extremes of comedy and tragedy, and adopted an intermediate form of domestic drama such as Diderot would have approved of. His prose plays avoid the sententious emphasis produced in *Gabrielle* by the use of the alexandrine; his characterization becomes less conventional; and the construction of his best plays owes a good deal to the formula developed in the 1820s and 1830s by Scribe.

Scribe's substantial contribution to the history of the French nineteenth-century theatre lies outside the story of Romantic drama. He never identified himself with any of the ideological attitudes or literary forms which distinguished the Romantic playwrights; yet although certain Romantics—Gautier in particular—showed a marked hostility towards what he stood for in the theatre, he did not repay this by a similar hostility towards his Romantic contemporaries. He appears to have been content to pursue his career as the most popular, as well as the most prolific, playwright of his age, quite indifferent to the debates that were carried on so vigorously for a quarter of a century between the literary *avant-garde* and their conservative opponents. If Gautier's scornful appraisal anticipates one aspect of Scribe's reputation in the eyes of posterity:

Le théâtre, tel qu'on l'entend de nos jours, n'a rien de littéraire; la pensée n'y est que pour fort peu de chose... Nous proclamerons donc que, l'art dramatique n'étant plus qu'un exercice d'adresse, l'auteur d'*Une chaîne* est l'homme le plus adroit de ce temps-ci; mais, pour ce qui nous regarde, nous avouons qu'une œuvre sans portée et sans style nous intéressera toujours fort peu[38]

—Sarcey's more objective assessment gives the other side of the coin:

Ne croyons pas l'avoir jugé en disant qu'il *n'avait pas de style*. Il écrivait mieux que beaucoup d'autres qui croient avoir du style; car il ne cherchait pas à écrire... Pour construire une pièce comme les grandes comédies de Scribe, il faut dix fois plus d'invention dramatique et de génie que pour écrire telle grande tirade qu'il est de convention d'aimer.[39]

The key word is of course 'construire': Scribe was the master craftsman, who took over from Beaumarchais's two great comedies the structural complication, the almost bewildering succession of twists and turns of the plot, and set himself to entertain his spectators by skilful manipulation of the ingredients of surprise and suspense. The term 'la pièce bien faite' was coined at this time: it was of course used literally, before being applied ironically in a pejorative sense, and one might hazard the following attempt at an objective definition: a play in which plot is constructed according to a tight logic, not according to the looser, less predictable dictates of character; in which character is subordinated to plot, and plot conceived in terms of *exposition, nœud* and *dénouement*, with a series of contrived climaxes to create suspense. As Sarcey recognized clearly enough, the formula perfectly suits the 'comédie-vaudeville', of which Scribe wrote literally hundreds[40]: the more importance the genre of a play attaches either to the realistic portrayal of everyday life, or to the plausible presentation of character, the more inappropriate are the mechanics of the well-made play, which tend to turn characters into puppets controlled by chance. Scribe's historical plays such as *Le Verre d'eau* (Théâtre-Français, November 1840), or *Adrienne Lecouvreur* (Théâtre-Français, April 1849) suffer from this defect; and among dramatists of the second half of the century, it is the authors of *vaudevilles* and farces such as Labiche and Feydeau who exploited the formula of the 'pièce bien faite' with the greatest success. Similarly with regard to Augier, the most obviously comic of his plays, *Le Gendre de Monsieur Poirier*, in which character—at any rate in the case of Poirier himself— approximates to caricature, is the one which best accommodates the formula of the well-made play.

Elsewhere, although the unravelling of the plot still intrigues the reader and holds his interest, for the most part we look in vain for those extra qualities—of ideological content, psychological penetration, or literary style—that are capable of making the well-made play into a memorable work of art. The 'drames modernes' of the Romantic playwrights, by contrast, had possessed such qualities in an immediately recognizable way: Vigny in *Chatterton*, and Dumas at any rate in *Antony* and *Kean*, made use of the theatre for the propagation of challenging, positive ideas consistent with the ethos of the young Romantics in the 1830s; and even in *Richard Darlington*, *Teresa* or *Angèle* the characterization has a dynamic quality that bears the unmistakable stamp of the age that produced them. One must assume that the homely bourgeois morality of Augier's anti-Romantic plays corresponded to a contemporary need— but now that that need is no longer spontaneously felt, it is more difficult for the reader to appreciate the ideas that inspired them. The morality of the 'école du bon sens' strikes us today as negative (based above all on the prohibition contained in the Seventh Commandment) and pedestrian; and for something more positive and dynamic in the social drama of the mid-century (and also owing more to Romantic influences), we must turn from Augier to Dumas *fils*.

(iv) Dumas fils, or the Romantic turned 'bourgeois'

ALTHOUGH the name of Dumas *fils* is generally coupled with that of Augier as representing the Second Empire reaction against Romanticism in the theatre, he was by temperament and upbringing more akin to the dramatists of his father's generation. As a writer, he was motivated by an intense involvement at first hand in the issues he chose to deal with, and rather than the cautious 'bon sens' morality of a Ponsard or an Augier, his plays illustrate the visionary quality of the crusading idealist. More fully than any other playwright of the century, Dumas *fils* exemplifies the 'drame de la pensée' adumbrated by Vigny in the Preface to *Chatterton*.

It is true that Dumas and Augier frequently coincided in their moral outlook, but the former's earliest works reveal a striking moral ambiguity. *La Dame aux camélias* (Vaudeville, February 1852), his first and most celebrated play, shows a sympathy with Romantic attitudes that is quite foreign to the playwrights of the 'école du bon sens': a recent editor of the play writes that "whatever its final implications, there can be little doubt that, in its point of departure at least, Dumas's drama is fundamentally Romantic"[41]. It is based, just like *Antony* or *Chatterton*, or like *Lorenzaccio* or any other play by Musset, on a deeply-felt personal experience. Marie Duplessis, the real-life original of Dumas's heroine, had had a meteoric career as one of the most celebrated courtesans of her age, before dying of consumption in 1847 at the age of 23. Dumas, who had been her lover for a period in 1844–45, and in whose favour she had for a time endeavoured to renounce the opulent life to which she was by then accustomed, wrote the novel *La Dame aux camélias* within a few months of her death. An idealizing Romantic biography, it created the legend of the sublimely unselfish courtesan, capable of heroic self-sacrifice. The success of the novel in 1848 inspired Dumas to adapt it for the theatre, and he wrote his play in 1849 in the hope that it would be put on at the Théâtre-Historique. But his father's theatre went bankrupt, and although other directors were interested, the subject was provocative enough to arouse the censor's interest; the play was banned, as offending against public morality, and it was only after the change of régime in December 1851 that it was able to be staged. Its success was phenomenal, the initial run of over two hundred performances being quite exceptional for the period; and within little more than a year, Verdi had made of it, in *La Traviata*, one of the great lyric operas of the century.

Dumas's subject is an updating of that of Hugo in *Marion de Lorme*: Marguerite, like Marion, makes the supreme sacrifice, in order to save her lover, of returning to her former life as a kept woman, and each thus forfeits her lover's respect; similarly, both plays end with the union of the lovers for a moment of sublime happiness before the death, in one case of Didier, in the other of Marguerite herself. To rehabilitate a seventeenth-century courtesan was one thing, however; to romanticize a notorious contemporary who had died a few years earlier, and who had been known to the whole of Paris, was quite another: hence the play's difficulties at the hands of the censor. It is true that the public morality against which the play was judged to have offended is given a powerful champion in the person of Monsieur Duval, Armand's father, who takes advantage of his son's absence to plead with Marguerite to give him up, since their liaison is not only ruining Armand's own future, but also jeopardizing his sister's chances of marrying the man she loves. The scene between Marguerite and Monsieur Duval in Act III is the pivot of the play from the structural point of view; it is also the scene in which the play's thesis is presented most clearly. Dr. Clark argues that, since "social morality emerges triumphant from *La Dame aux camélias*", therefore "in its essence, the play is profoundly anti-Romantic"[42]; Marguerite accepts the justice of the interdict pronounced by society against the woman who has broken its laws, and she submits, "not so much because she is overwhelmed by Duval's arguments, but rather because he succeeds in reawakening in her the voice of her own reason, which she has for so long been endeavouring to quiet"[43]. Nevertheless, the fourth Act brings about a considerable modification of this situation, and even Monsieur Duval's position as the upholder of the moral law is compromised, for the message that Armand brings from his father to the dying Marguerite is in effect the sanctioning of their illicit union on the grounds that their love has proved itself to be something totally exceptional. However firm Dumas's condemnation of the individualist ethic through the mouth of his *raisonneur* may have appeared in Act III, the play ends on a thoroughly Romantic note with the deathbed idealization of Marguerite; and the emotional climax of the lovers' reunion, leading to the curtain-line "Dors en paix, Marguerite! il te sera beaucoup pardonné, parce que tu as beaucoup aimé!" is a powerful challenge to the intellectual conviction with which the moral argument has earlier been presented.

La Dame aux camélias is Romantic, too, in a more fundamental

way. Jean Anouilh was to make one of his characters express the
view, a century later, that "Il y a l'amour, bien sûr. Et puis il y
a la vie, son ennemie"[44]; and overshadowing any didactic effect
that the victory of society over the individual might have in
Dumas's play, is a similarly poignant sense of the inevitable
defeat of idealism by prosaic reality. Seen in this light, *La Dame
aux camélias* is one of the great Romantic tragedies of the
century; it shares the same theme, the incompatibility between
ideal love and the demands of society, with plays like *Hernani*,
Antony, *Marion de Lorme* or *Ruy Blas*: those lyric dramas which
formed such a significant part of the Romantics' contribution
to the theatre of the 1830s. And by the same token, *La Traviata*
has taken its place alongside such works as *La Bohème*, *Tosca*,
and *Aïda* as one of the masterpieces of Romantic opera based on
the same universal theme.

By the time he published the Preface to *La Dame aux camélias*
in 1867, the Romantic in Dumas had given way to the moralist,
and he appeared less concerned to idealize the courtesan than
to carry out a sociological investigation into the conditions
which produce her. *Diane de Lys* (Gymnase, November 1853)
deserves a mention alongside *La Dame aux camélias* as another
play in which the emotional sympathy, here claimed by the pair
of adulterous lovers, is in conflict with the moral law represented
by the husband; but thereafter the moralist progressively took
charge, and Dumas's name became identified with a series of
sententious 'pièces à thèse', like those of Augier, but dealing
even more exclusively with the narrow field of sexual relations.
In the best of his later plays, however, this preoccupation with
sexual morality, which had become something of a pathological
obsession with Dumas[45], produced plays which were a good
deal more challenging than the routine didacticism of the earlier
Le Demi-monde (1855), *Le Fils naturel* (1858) or *L'Ami des femmes*
(1864). *Les Idées de Madame Aubray* (1867), for instance, is an
excellent example of what Vigny would have called 'le drame
de la pensée': the action is intimately linked to the thesis, and
the dénouement is, in the sort of terms of which Dumas was
fond of using, "la résultante mathématique, fatale, des circonstances, des passions, des caractères, présentés et développés
dans le courant de l'action"[46]. If *La Femme de Claude* (1873)
suffers by subordinating realistic characterization to a crude

kind of symbolism, nevertheless these two plays together illustrate the possibilities of a theatre created by an idealist and visionary writer, in the service of a morality at once more strict than the conventional bourgeois ethic, and remarkably forward-looking and practical in terms of proposed reforms. Such plays serve to show that even in his most didactic theatre, the Romantic in Dumas had by no means disappeared: *La Dame aux camélias* was not an isolated concession to an earlier fashion, and the playwright who became the most determined adversary of the pure aestheticism of the latter-day Romantics:

L'art pour l'art: trois mots absolument vides de sens. Toute littérature qui n'a pas en vue la perfectibilité, la moralisation..., est une littérature rachitique et malsaine[47]

also provides the clearest example in the mid-century theatre of the persisting influence of Romantic idealism.

Notes to Chapter Eleven

1. Cf. Affron, *op. cit.*, p. 62; Baldick, *op. cit.*, p. 187.
2. Published in *Le Charivari* of 31.iii.1843. See Plate 14.
3. *Les Maîtres du théâtre français*, pp. 207–208.
4. Quoted in Hugo, *Théâtre*, ed. cit., II, p. 1827.
5. See Olga W. Russell, *Étude historique et critique des Burgraves de Victor Hugo*, Paris, 1962, ch. ix, 'La Fortune des *Burgraves*'.
6. *Ibid.*, pp. 231 ff.
7. 'Note' accompanying the first edition of the play.
8. Frédérick is said to have commented: "Ils disent bien, ils ne jouent pas" (quoted by Russell, *op. cit.*, p. 234). Cf. also Descotes, *Le Drame . . .*, p. 337.
9. See *Théâtre*, II, pp. 1369 ff.
10. Preface to *La Légende des siècles*, *première série* (1857).
11. A. Robertson, 'Richard Wagner' in *The Decca Book of Opera*, London, 1956, p. 430.
12. *Les Maîtres du théâtre français*, p. 207.
13. The exact nature of the collaboration between these two authors, and the extent of the responsibility of each, being impossible to determine with precision, one can only follow publishing tradition, and be guided by the inclusion of a particular play in the

collected works of one or the other, however unsatisfactory this may be. According to J. Richer, "Ils avaient convenu de signer tour à tour les pièces écrites en collaboration. Dumas était réputé seul auteur de *Piquillo*, de l'*Alchimiste*, de *Caligula*, tandis que *Léo Burckart* revenait à Gérard" ('Nerval et ses deux *Léo Burckart*', *Mercure de France*, CCCVII, 1949, p. 646).

14. See J. Richer, *art. cit.*, *ibid.*, pp. 645–653, and a substantial fragment from the 'version inédite', *ibid.*, pp. 654–678.

15. See C. Dédéyan, *Gérard de Nerval et l'Allemagne*, 3 vols., Paris, 1957–59, II, pp. 527–547.

16. Preface to *Léo Burckart*.

17. Quoted by Richer, *art. cit.*, p. 652.

18. See Richer, *art. cit.*, p. 648; Dédéyan, *op. cit.*, II, pp. 541–543.

19. *Art. cit.*, p. 653. Nerval's play has been included, together with *Hernani* and *La Tour de Nesle*, in a volume of representative Romantic dramas edited by J. Richer, Paris, 1957; and it was in fact staged in Paris during the 1964–65 season (see F. Bassan, *Esprit Créateur*, V, 1965, p. 178).

20. See Dédéyan, *op. cit.*, II, pp. 475–526.

21. See Claude Book-Senninger, *Théophile Gautier, auteur dramatique*, Paris, 1972, pp. 215–226.

22. This play has never been republished since its original edition (Paris, 1846).

23. Book-Senninger, *op. cit.*, p. 235.

24. See G. Bertal, *Auguste Vacquerie, sa vie et son œuvre*, Paris, 1889, p. 30.

25. Cf. the close of Act III, where Toussaint, disguised as a blind beggar in order to reconnoitre the French camp, suddenly throws off his disguise and stabs to death a lieutenant of his who has come to offer his services to the enemy: "On se précipite pour saisir Toussaint; mais, à la faveur de la confusion, il s'élance en trois bonds sur la pointe du rocher qui forme le cap élevé sur la mer derrière la tente du conseil, et se lance dans les flots".

26. *Op. cit.*, p. 138.

27. Baldick, *op. cit.*, p. 210.

28. *Le Constitutionnel*, 2.iii.1829, quoted by O. E. Fellows, *French Opinion of Molière (1800–1850)*, Providence (R.I.), 1937, p. 15.

29. See A. Joannidès, *La Comédie-Française de 1680 à 1900*, Paris, 1901, which tabulates performances of every play for the years in question.

30. J. Janin, *Rachel et la tragédie*, Paris, 1859, pp. 65–66.

31. *Ibid.*, p. 69.

32. *Histoire de l'art dramatique en France depuis vingt-cinq ans*, Brussels, 1859, III, p. 48.
33. *Ibid.*
34. *Op. cit.*, p. 383.
35. C. Latreille, *La Fin du théâtre romantique et François Ponsard*, Paris, 1899, p. 201.
36. R. Doumic, *Portraits d'écrivains*, p. 81.
37. Preface to *Les Lionnes pauvres*.
38. Quoted by Sarcey, *op. cit.*, IV, pp. 128–129.
39. *Ibid.*, p. 137.
40. Cf. N. C. Arvin, *Eugène Scribe and the French Theater, 1815–1860*, Cambridge (Mass.), 1924, Appendix A.
41. *La Dame aux camélias*, ed. R. J. B. Clark, London, 1972, p. 24.
42. *Ibid.*, p. 44.
43. *Ibid.*, p. 43.
44. *Ardèle, ou la Marguerite*, in *Pièces grinçantes*, Paris, 1956, p. 14.
45. Cf. the apocalyptic tone of the Preface to *La Femme de Claude*.
46. *Théâtre complet: Théâtre des autres*, Paris, n.d., I, p. 115. Cf. "Le théâtre est aussi impitoyable que l'arithmétique", Preface to *Les Idées de Madame Aubray*.
47. Preface to *Le Fils naturel*.

12 Romantic Revival

(i) Hugo's later writings for the theatre

HUGO'S 'private' theatre consists of the historical drama *Torquemada*, written in 1869 and published for the first time in 1882; of the half-dozen titles contained in the volume *Théâtre en liberté* (1886); of two other completed plays, *Mille Francs de récompense* and *L'Intervention*, both written in 1866 but not published until this century; and of a number of fragments and plans of uncompleted works. Unlike Musset's 'armchair theatre', which provided the playwright with the means of conquering the excessive fantasy of his earliest dramatic works and of evolving a more stageworthy style, Hugo's 'théâtre en liberté' seems to have allowed him to give an increasingly freer rein to his imagination, and the latest of the plays collected under this title are the least governed by traditional theatrical considerations. In addition to its primary aesthetic meaning, the title of the collection can also, as J.-J. Thierry points out, be interpreted in another sense: the plays written in exile during the Second Empire allowed the poet to express his republican zeal with a force and directness that would have been impossible in a play destined for the stage[1]. This is so in particular of the most substantial of the plays in the volume, *Mangeront-ils?*; it is also true of *Torquemada*, the play from this period which squares most clearly with the notion of 'Romantic drama' as developed in the 1830s.

Torquemada is a formidable indictment of religious fanaticism in the person of the central character, as well as of selfish despotism on the part of rulers both temporal and spiritual. As in *Les Burgraves*, the dramatic interest centres on the fortunes of a pair of innocent young lovers, but whereas Otbert and Régina had been saved, Sanche and Rosa are put to death by the Inquisition. Structurally, *Torquemada* resembles Hugo's earliest plays; indeed, the plot shows even less of a linear progression, and the static, 'operatic' solos and duets are even more pronounced. But in spite of a genuine lyrical freshness attaching to the lovers, their death fails to produce the tragic impact of the end of *Hernani* or of *Marion de Lorme*: for the first time, the lovers are a totally passive couple, and their fate is inflicted on them by the agency of others. The metaphysical dimension we look for in tragedy is quite lacking: chance, rather than fate, determines the dénouement, and *Torquemada* is a historical drama rather than a Romantic tragedy. Its powerful satire stamps it as the sort of historical drama one would expect from its author at this period—the period of *Les Châtiments* and *La Légende des siècles*—even if the attack on religious intolerance is a little subtler and more *nuancé* than the invective directed against Napoleon III. The self-seeking King Ferdinand of Aragon and the depraved Pope Alexander Borgia are conventional enough portraits of evil rulers, whose self-portrayal borders on caricature; but the character of Torquemada himself, although perhaps too static to be entirely successful dramatically, has a surprising credibility as a psychological study: we can understand, even though we are revolted by, this fanatic whose warped sense of Christian charity consigns men's bodies to the fire of the Inquisition in order to save their souls. There is an effective contrast in Part I, Act II, with another form of Christianity equally of its time, the humble asceticism of Saint Francis of Paul; but the thematic climax of the play occurs at the end of Part II, Act II, a climax which comes over in powerfully operatic terms in a long soliloquy by Torquemada exulting, against the spectacular background of the fires of an autodafé, in the spiritual redemption of his victims:

> O fête, ô gloire, ô joie!
> La clémence terrible et superbe flamboie!
> Délivrance à jamais! Damnés, soyez absous!
> Le bûcher sur la terre éteint l'enfer dessous.
> Sois béni, toi par qui l'âme au bonheur remonte,
> Bûcher, gloire du feu dont l'enfer est la honte,
> Issue aboutissant au radieux chemin,
> Porte du paradis rouverte au genre humain,
> Miséricorde ardente aux caresses sans nombre,
> Mystérieux rachat, des esclaves de l'ombre,

Autodafé! pardon, bonté, lumière, feu,
Vie! éblouissement de la face de Dieu!
Oh! quel départ splendide et que d'âmes sauvées!
Juifs, mécréants, pécheurs, ô mes chères couvées,
Un court tourment vous paie un bonheur infini,
L'homme n'est plus maudit, l'homme n'est plus banni;
Le salut s'ouvre au fond des cieux. L'amour s'éveille,
Et voici son triomphe, et voici sa merveille!
Quelle extase! entrer droit au ciel! ne pas languir!

Berret, while appreciating the "visions épiques" of such
scenes, wrote in 1927 that "un pareil drame fait horreur, plus
qu'il n'émeut; il fait crier nos nerfs, et notre raison, qui se
rebelle, est hors de prise"[2]. We today, living as we do in an age
of violence produced by ideological fanaticism, are perhaps
better able to accept Torquemada as one of Hugo's most
impressive characters; though the play, however powerful its
message, relies too much on the formula of melodrama. A crude
black-and-white opposition between groups of characters has
taken the place of the *grotesque/sublime* antithesis within the
single character, and one feels that this is the result of the playwright being too much influenced by the polemicist.

Mangeront-ils?, the only play of Hugo's later years so far to be
admitted to the repertoire of the Comédie-Française (in 1919),
is a much freer sort of composition, and Professor Affron is right
in seeing here the strongest Shakespearean influence on Hugo[3].
The play has something of the general tone of Shakespearean
comedy; its imagery is less forced, less heavy, than is often the
case with Hugo, and possesses some of the lightness and spontaneity of Shakespeare's; and in particular there is the spirit-
like Aïrolo, a benign *meneur du jeu* who watches over the good
fortunes of the lovers and defeats the plans of the evil King.
Here again we have a couple of young lovers, as innocent as
those of *Les Burgraves* and as passive as the pair in *Torquemada*
were shortly to be; but the reader is never unduly anxious about
their fate, for the King is a singularly inept tyrant, and indeed
there is a distinct element of comic self-parody here on Hugo's
part. The lovers, Aïrolo, and the centenarian Zineb all act out
a hymn to Nature, in a sort of dramatized version of the
Pathetic Fallacy; and the King, the enemy of the life-force, is
soon defeated. The whole makes a highly successful blend of

lyricism, fantasy and parody: a blend which was as new in Hugo's theatre as it was out of tune with the realist, positivist attitudes to drama prevailing in the theatre of the mid-century.

Comic invention and parody are surely the key to *Mille Francs de récompense*, despite the play's very different idiom; and it seems mistaken to write, as Thierry does, of its "réalisme très nouveau"[4]. Though it is set in Paris in the 1820s, a setting which does offer some resemblance to the milieu of *Les Misérables*, its highly-contrived plot, with such a wealth of complications and coincidences, makes it a self-conscious parody of traditional melodrama; while there is a very large element of comic fantasy in the figure of Glapieu, the convict with the heart of gold who controls and comments on the action, promoting the interests of the young lovers and defeating the scheming of the wealthy capitalist who fills the role of 'traître de mélodrame'. Such rhetoric as there is is tongue-in-cheek, and it is difficult to see in *Mille Francs de récompense* the preoccupation with problems of justice and social equality that Thierry claims to find[5]. If such topics are introduced, they are there as conventional plot-devices; and the handling of the plot is saved from banality by the imaginative creation of Glapieu, whose role on the one hand foreshadows that of Aïrolo, and on the other looks back to that of Tragaldabas and Robert Macaire.

Of Hugo's other completed plays from this period, *La Grand'mère* (from the *Théâtre en Liberté*) and *L'Intervention* are thoroughly conventional trifles, as regards both characterization and plot: they are sentimental plays with a predictable outcome, and reveal little sign of Romantic inspiration. The other pieces, both completed and uncompleted, show more evidence of Romantic fantasy, but are too slight to be taken very seriously. The three plays discussed above, however, form a substantial addition to Hugo's dramatic output. *Torquemada* represents a most interesting combination of historical drama and 'pièce à thèse': with its powerful denunciation of fanaticism, it is very much the sort of historical play towards which Voltaire had been moving a century earlier, but freed of the limiting conventions of pre-Romantic tragedy. *Mangeront-ils?* and *Mille Francs de récompense* break new ground, and Hugo shows himself capable in both plays of an altogether lighter touch. What the three plays have in common is a critical attitude towards authority: where *Torquemada* uses the rhetorical broadsides of Voltairian philosophical drama, the subversive effect of the other two plays is produced more discreetly through the medium of Aïrolo the nature-spirit and symbol of liberty, and of Glapieu the convict-philanthropist, representing downtrodden humanity. Even if Hugo had not already been discouraged from writing for the theatre after the failure of *Les Burgraves*, his 'private' dramas of the 1860s show that in any case the sort of play he was interested in would have been unlikely to find a theatre. For these are all in their way examples of a 'théâtre engagé', and it is here that Romantic drama finally fulfils itself as a drama of ideas—not according to the safe, cautious programme of the 'école du bon sens', but as a radical challenge to the authoritarian institutions of church and state.

(ii) *From Hugo to Rostand*

HUGO'S 'private theatre', particularly if we consider his more tentative, experimental pieces, reveals a tendency towards a kind of fantasy that had been almost entirely absent from the Romantic drama of the 1830s and 1840s. But the nature of Hugo's poetic genius prevented him from going very far along the road from Romanticism to Symbolism: his imagination was too robust and sensual, his writing altogether too explicit to have much in common with the vague mysticism cultivated by the Symbolist poets:

> Si Victor Hugo est souvent, dans ses poèmes, un admirable visionnaire, rien de moins chimérique que son œuvre dramatique, d'une brutalité qui semble presque étrangère à notre génie.[6]

The explicitness of French Romantic drama (indeed, of nearly all French Romantic literature) is one of its principal distinguishing features, contrasting strongly not only with the deliberate ambiguity characteristic of Symbolist writing, but also with the dreamy, mystic idealism found in much of German Romantic literature. Verlaine's aspirations towards suggestiveness and ambiguity:

> Il faut aussi que tu n'ailles point
> Choisir tes mots sans quelque méprise:

Rien de plus cher que la chanson grise
Où l'Indécis au Précis se joint[7]

and Mallarmé's injunction to avoid the explicit—"peindre, non
la chose, mais l'effet qu'elle produit"[8]—were, indeed, reactions
against the explicit literalness of their predecessors, and the
French Symbolists had few antecedents in the Romantic
literature of their own country.

Such prescriptions not only reject certain characteristics of
French Romantic literature which had nowhere been illustrated more regularly than in the drama of the period, they also
constitute a fundamental challenge to the very nature of all
truly dramatic writing, which depends on action and conflict
realizable in flesh-and-blood terms. Nevertheless, the second
half of the century was to produce numerous attempts at a
poetic drama either anticipating, or else deliberately based
on, the Symbolist aesthetic—an aesthetic which H. M. Block
formulates as follows from an analysis of Mallarmé's theoretical
writings:

1. Drama is the expression of inner life, the revelation of
   an *état d'âme*;
2. Drama is the expression of mystery, the revelation of the
   hidden wonder of the universe;
3. The language of drama is poetry rather than prose,
   evocative rather than descriptive, and relying upon suggestion as opposed to statement;
4. The stage is detheatricalized, reduced to the barest and
   simplest elements of histrionic performance;
5. The theatre brings into play all of the arts, interrelated
   within a poetic structure.[9]

Mallarmé's own attempts to reconcile the claims of poetry and
the theatre were abortive: although *Hérodiade* was conceived as
a tragedy, and the *Après-midi d'un faune* as an *intermède* "exigeant
le théâtre"[10], the reception given to the latter when it was read
at the Comédie-Française in 1865 definitively discouraged the
poet from further writing with the theatre in mind:

Les vers de mon *Faune* ont plu infiniment, mais Banville et
Coquelin n'y ont pas rencontré l'anecdote nécessaire que

demande le public, et m'ont affirmé que cela n'intéresserait
que les poètes... J'abandonne mon sujet... et je commence
Hérodiade, non plus tragédie, mais poème... Je gagne ainsi
toute l'attitude, les vêtements, le décor et l'ameublement,
sans parler du mystère.[11]

Nevertheless, it is quite clear that Mallarmé had started out
with the ambition to create a viable poetic drama in emulation
of Banville, whose work he much admired, and whose *Diane au
bois* greatly influenced the conception of his own *Après-midi
d'un faune*. *Diane au bois*, however, was less hermetic in expression,
and had more regard for conventional dramatic form, than
Mallarmé's poem: in fact, it is not unlike one or two of the
shorter pieces of Hugo's *Théâtre en liberté*: *La Forêt mouillée* or *Sur
la lisière d'un bois*. Performed at the Odéon in 1863, it embodies
not so much the intellectual challenge of Symbolism as Parnassian elegance and charm.

Even so, *Diane au bois* is hardly typical of Banville's theatre;
much more representative is a kind of anecdotal comedy, rather
closer to the formula of Romantic historical drama, of which he
composed several successful examples:

Notre poésie dramatique, d'où peu à peu s'était enfui le
souvenir de l'Ode, était tombée au dernier degré d'appau-
vrissement et de misère, quand Hugo parut, et dans ses
puissants creusets, ressuscitant Shakespeare, mélangea si
intimement la poésie tragique et la poésie lyrique, pour en
faire un seul et même métal, qu'il semble impossible de les
séparer désormais. Ce qu'il a fait pour la Tragédie, dans mon
petit coin, avec mes humbles forces, et sans en rien dire, j'ai
tenté de chercher comment on pourrait le faire pour la
Comédie.[12]

Banville's is a self-consciously literary theatre, catering for a
public of connoisseurs. His most original plays are no doubt
those in which he dramatizes an episode from the life of a
literary figure: Socrates in *La Femme de Socrate*; two seventeenth-
century dramatists: Hardy in *Florise* and Dufresny in *Le Cousin
du Roi*; poets in *Gringoire* and *Ésope*; while in others he introduces the gods and legendary figures of antiquity (*Deïdamia,
Diane au bois, La Pomme*) or uses characters created by other

dramatists (*Le Beau Léandre* is a pastiche of Marivaux, and *Les Fourberies de Nérine* a sequel to Molière's *Fourberies de Scapin*). Many of these plays were performed with success at the Théâtre-Français or the Odéon, and while Charpentier's estimate of Banville's theatre as "un des points culminants de notre art dramatique"[13] is surely over-indulgent towards the work of a poet who was content to aim at agreeable entertainment rather than at anything more profound or disturbing, the peculiar charm of a play like *Florise* (published in 1870) does give it a place apart in the nineteenth-century theatre. While set in a precise locality and historical setting, this and the other anecdotal plays do not aim at precision or plausibility in characterization, and they have none of the 'literalness' which marks the Romantics' treatment of historical subjects:

> Nulle intention chez Banville de peindre les caractères, de reconstituer une époque ou un milieu, de faire « vrai », au sens où l'entendent les réalistes, c'est-à-dire de se soumettre à l'observation des apparences mouvantes et trompeuses.[14]

Instead, Banville's characters are poetically-conceived types, allegorical or symbolic figures; and this is nowhere better seen than in the heroine of *Florise*, the gifted actress who represents the poet's inspiration and the spectator's ideal of beauty.

If this is a feature of Banville's theatre which forms a contrast with Romantic drama, there is another feature which indicates a much closer affinity with Hugo as a dramatic poet; for Banville shares the same inventive approach to vocabulary and rhyme, and creates the same rich, colourful effects. The following passage from *Le Cousin du Roi* reproduces a style found in *Cromwell* and in *Marion de Lorme*:

> Avant-hier, j'allai tout seul au Cours-la-Reine,
> Vers midi; la journée était chaude et sereine,
> J'écoutais les propos des buveurs de soleil,
> Entretien toujours neuf, quoique toujours pareil!
> « Que fait-on? — La princesse a quitté la Savoie,
> Et certaine Philis brûle encor pour Cavoye...
> Qui gèle! — Cossé boit! — Madame de Conti
> Joue à la Niobé, car Clermont est parti. —

Fagon purge. — Boufflers pour le camp de Compiègne
Arme ses cuisiniers. — Et la Maintenon? — Règne
A jamais! » J'écoutais, je glosais, comme aux temps,
Beaux temps perdus, où, dans mes salons éclatants
De jets d'eau, de lumière et de fleurs indiennes,
J'hébergeais chaque soir trente comédiennes! (sc. iii)

—while the whole dialogue of *Les Fourberies de Nérine* is a masterpiece of comic writing. Compared with Hugo's, or even Musset's,
the range of Banville's dramatic writing is of course very
limited; but his poetic gifts kept alive the tradition of a particular kind of Romantic drama during the period between
Hugo and Rostand.

Banville is the most notable representative of a certain kind
of post-Romantic poetic drama, distinguished by its strong
Parnassian flavour. Like much Parnassian literature, his plays
are a serene, cultured expression of the joys and pleasures of
life; their subject-matter is thoroughly of this world, and such
supernatural references as they contain are allegorical evoca-
tions of the anthropomorphic gods of the Greek pantheon.
When we turn to Villiers de l'Isle-Adam, however, we encounter a very different sort of link between Romanticism and
Symbolism: a cosmopolitan intellectual current which drew on
the occult writings of various sects, Christian and non-Christian,
and which found expression more readily in German than in
French Romantic literature. In non-dramatic works of the
Romantic period, it is true, one can find exceptions such as
Balzac's *Séraphita* or *Louis Lambert*, but works in dramatic form
showing a similar inspiration had been rare indeed: for instance,
Musset's early dramatic poem *La Coupe et les lèvres* and Nerval's
L'Imagier de Harlem both suggest the influence of *Faust*, *Part II*,
but it is noticeable that in the latter's *Léo Burckart* the borrow-
ings have been confined to the more traditional *Part I* of
Goethe's drama[15].

The first two Acts of Villiers's *Axël*, entitled 'Le Monde
religieux' and 'Le Monde tragique', reproduce an atmosphere
not too far removed from that of *Torquemada* or of *Les Burgraves*:
but as the other two Acts, 'Le Monde occulte' and 'Le Monde
passionnel', follow in their turn, all resemblance even to Hugo's
'epic drama' is left behind: material setting becomes steadily

less important, and the behaviour of hero and heroine becomes increasingly gratuitous—a process which would no doubt have continued into the projected fifth Act, 'Le Monde astral', if this had been written. It is not that the play is lacking in dramatic action: indeed, the plot, involving the renunciation of power, knowledge, and even life itself by Axël, in spite of his ideal love for Sara, follows a fairly conventional line of development; but the psychological motivation of the two characters is so arbitrary that they soon cease to have any valid point of reference in normal human experience. In fact, as has been pointed out, the forces controlling the characters are "forces éternelles" heavy with symbolic meaning: "L'Or, d'abord, et la Forêt, et l'Orage, et la Descente aux enfers, et le Voyage"[16]. With *Axël*, drama has replaced the sort of imaginative creation that can be related to recognizable individual experience by the 'complexe inné' of the Jungian archetype, which is no longer meaningful in individual terms[17]; and by the same token, it has ceased to be drama suitable for public presentation. *Axël* was in fact given a public performance at the Théâtre de la Rive Gauche in 1894, but the incongruity of this undertaking was commented on by an anonymous critic:

C'est là un poème philosophique dramatisé et dialogué qui perd à se voir réalisé par des moyens scéniques, les imaginations de l'auteur s'adressant à l'imagination du lecteur.[18]

Although *Axël* is consistent with the programme of the new Symbolist drama as defined by Mallarmé, this was not Villiers's only attempt at dramatic writing, and in *Le Prétendant* (1875), he produced a historical drama much more squarely in the tradition established during the Romantic period. His early play *Morgane* had been published in a limited edition of 25 copies in 1866, in the hope that it would be produced at the Gaîté; it was in fact accepted, but the production was shelved. *Le Prétendant*, which was a revised version of the earlier play, also failed to achieve production in 1875, and it was long thought that the text had been lost; however, it was discovered and published in 1965, and had its première in a French Television production in the same year[19]. A historical drama in prose, set in Italy at the time of the Napoleonic wars, it lacks the lyrical expansion of Hugo's verse dramas, though Villiers's conception of his subject is much nearer to Hugo's than to the prosaic, melodramatic formula of Dumas *père*. In fact, the intrigue and conspiracy, and the themes of patriotism and politics, provide a backcloth for a tragedy thoroughly Romantic in mood. The heroine, Morgane, having engineered a successful *coup d'état*, throws victory away because she is tricked into believing that Sergius, the pretender, whose Queen she is to become, does not reciprocate her love; however, although her rival, Lady Hamilton, restores the political status quo, she ultimately fails to separate the lovers, whose serene exaltation in their final duet as they face the firing-squad captures something very like the tone of the last scene of *Hernani*:

> — Va! C'était notre fatalité!... Aussi bien nous étions fatigués de ce monde, de ses aurores banales, de son midi brûlant et de ses misérables nuits!... Puisque la pourpre royale nous est refusée par le sort, que ce soit notre sang qui nous en couvre. Nous étions trop grands pour la vie!

> — Un dernier baiser, Sergius! Notre âme est comme un beau soir d'exil!... Je meurs avec toi, sans regrets.

The scene makes an interesting comparison with the wholly voluntary death of the lovers at the end of *Axël*; whereas Axël's celebrated line "Vivre? les serviteurs feront cela pour nous" (IV, ii) seems to be the gratuitous expression of an over-fastidious aestheticism, the death-wish expressed by Sergius and Morgane, however similar it may appear at first sight, is wholly credible in the context of Romantic idealism.

The dramatist who most successfully reconciled the aesthetic aims of the new poetic drama and the more down-to-earth requirements of stage production was the Belgian Maeterlinck. Maeterlinck, who enjoyed an almost unprecedented international reputation throughout the first half of his long career as a writer, up to the beginning of the Great War, made his name as a dramatist with a series of plays written during the 1890s and 1900s, of which the best known are probably *Pelléas et Mélisande* (Bouffes-Parisiens, 1893) and *L'Oiseau bleu* (Arts Theatre, Moscow, 1908). The distinctive quality of Maeterlinck's Symbolist dramas was, to quote the citation which

accompanied the award of the Nobel Prize for Literature in
1910:

> their richness of imagination and poetic realism; sometimes
> in the dim form of the play of legend [they] display a deep
> intimacy of feeling, and also in a mysterious way appeal to
> the reader's sentiment and sense of foreboding.[20]

Like Banville's, Maeterlinck's characters are allegorical repre-
sentations rather than individuals with a documentary *état
civil*; but the sombre tones of his gothic settings contrast strongly
with the sun-drenched landscape of the former's world. However, in spite of this predilection for the gothic, there is little in
common between Romantic drama and for instance plays like
L'Intruse or *Les Aveugles* (both produced at Paul Fort's Théâtre
d'Art in 1891). The essential meaning of the plays—the apprehension caused by the presence of Death—is conveyed not
explicitly, but by suggestion; the dramatis personae are given
only the most rudimentary identification (L'Aïeul, Le Père,
L'Oncle; Trois Aveugles-nés, Une Jeune Aveugle, Une
Aveugle folle . . .); and in place of the vigorous, emphatic
rhetoric of Romantic drama Maeterlinck uses understatement,
and incantatory rhythms based on the repetition of simple
phrases. Similarly, in referring to his first play, *La Princesse
Maleine* (published in 1889), the author himself talks of "ces
répétitions étonnées qui donnent aux personnages l'apparence
de somnambules un peu sourds constamment arrachés à un
songe pénible"[21].

However, the same feature receives severe criticism at the
hands of the rationalist Sarcey, in a review of *Pelléas et Mélisande*
which blends malicious amusement with the expression of a
serious critical standpoint. Asking "pourquoi chaque personnage répète toujours deux fois le même membre de phrase ou
le même mot", Sarcey puts this reply into the mouth of an
admirer of Maeterlinck:

> Ce qui serait tic ou procédé chez tout autre, est une beauté
> de plus chez Maeterlinck. Maeterlinck veut vous donner une
> impression de naïveté; ses personnages flottent dans l'irréel;
> ils ne parlent pas; c'est une sorte de balbutiement enfantin.
> Vous allez voir tout à l'heure Mélisande; elle, c'est une autre

affaire: elle répète trois fois chaque mot. Elle ne dit pas, comme vous ou moi, qui vivons dans le réel: « Je me suis enfuie », mais bien: « Je me suis enfuie, enfuie, enfuie ». Cela est très beau; il faut l'admirer.

The most serious charge brought by Sarcey against this sort of theatre, set in an "au-delà maeterlinquois", is its lack of psychological substance:

La scène est assez joliment faite; mais comme toute cette psychologie est sommaire! Je sais bien ce que me diront les admirateurs de Maeterlinck: c'est intentionnellement qu'elle est sommaire. Eh! bien, je le regrette! Je préférerais à ces silhouettes qui projettent sur le rideau d'une lanterne magique des gestes soi-disant suggestifs une étude de caractère ou de passion.

Sarcey's attack is not purely destructive: still less is it the destructive attack of a philistine unable to appreciate poetry. It is a sincere exposé of the inherent weakness of this kind of poetic drama: "qu'au théâtre les êtres symboliques sont représentés par des acteurs en chair et en os et que l'on est obligé de donner une forme à l'irréel". And his final paragraph, while appreciating the virtues of Symbolist poetry, points to the difficulty, if not the impossibility, of effectively expressing that poetry through the medium of Symbolist drama:

Vous trouverez plus de plaisir à la lecture que nous n'en avons goûté à la représentation. Au théâtre, on est agacé de cette fausse naïveté, qui paraît concertée et voulue; ce qu'il y a de banal et de puéril dans ces inventions et dans ce langage saute aux yeux. Le livre met en branle l'imagination, qui achève ce que l'auteur indique. Il s'en dégage un subtil parfum de poésie.[22]

Maeterlinck had himself been ready to agree at the time of his first play, *La Princesse Maleine*, that the new Symbolist drama should ideally be read, not staged: indeed, he went beyond merely proclaiming this as a theoretical basis for his own drama, and explicitly annexed the masterpieces of the past, particularly those of Shakespeare, as evidence in support of his thesis:

La plupart des grands poèmes de l'humanité ne sont pas scéniques. *Lear, Hamlet, Othello, Macbeth, Antoine et Cléopâtre* ne peuvent être représentés et il est dangereux de les voir sur la scène. Quelque chose d'Hamlet est mort pour nous le jour où nous l'avons vu mourir sur la scène. Le spectre d'un acteur l'a détrôné et nous ne pouvons plus écarter l'usurpateur de nos rêves.

La représentation d'un chef-d'œuvre à l'aide d'éléments accidentels et humains est antinomique. Tout chef-d'œuvre est un symbole et le symbole ne supporte jamais la présence active de l'homme... L'absence de l'homme me semble indispensable.[23]

However, the publication of *La Princesse Maleine* inspired the laudatory review by Octave Mirbeau in *Le Figaro* which 'launched' Maeterlinck on the literary world; and though this first play was never performed, the playwright's ensuing association with Paul Fort and Lugné-Poë succeeded in overcoming for a time his reservations about stage performance of Symbolist drama: indeed, during the 1890s, productions of his plays at the Théâtre d'Art and Théâtre de l'Œuvre helped to make of these ventures the most important attempt at this period to establish a serious literary theatre. But there were few unqualified successes, and it is significant that the most successful plays of Maeterlinck's Symbolist period were those in which his text became the libretto for a musical drama: *Pelléas et Mélisande* (with Debussy's music) in 1902, and *Ariane et Barbebleue* (with music by Dukas) in 1907.

In the end, Maeterlinck himself seems to have recognized the inadequacy of his concept of Symbolist drama, writing in 1902:

Il est temps que les poètes le reconnaissent: le symbole suffit à représenter provisoirement une vérité admise ou une vérité qu'on ne peut ou qu'on ne veut pas encore regarder; mais quand vient le moment où l'on veut voir la vérité même, il est bon que le symbole disparaisse.[24]

And in *Monna Vanna*, performed in the same year at the Théâtre de l'Œuvre, he adopts something much nearer to the formula of Romantic drama. This play has a precise historical setting: the siege of Pisa at the end of the fifteenth century by Florentine mercenaries; its style is very different from the "balbutiement enfantin" lampooned by Sarcey: it is much more direct and forceful; and instead of a vague transcendental metaphysic, the play is based on the sort of moral dilemma favoured by writers of tragedy from Corneille onwards. Prinzivalle, general of the besieging forces, sends an ultimatum to the starving inhabitants of Pisa: he will relieve the siege and spare the city if Vanna, the wife of the Pisan commander, will give herself to him for one night. Guido, the commander, is revolted and rejects the offer, but Vanna herself, inspired by love of her fellow-men, accepts. When she visits Prinzivalle, he respects her and allows her to return unviolated, for he has loved her secretly since childhood; to repay his generosity, she takes Prinzivalle back to Pisa with her, since he has incurred the displeasure of his Florentine masters. Guido refuses to believe she has not been violated, and proposes to exact a cruel vengeance on Prinzivalle; outraged by this, and moved by admiration for Prinzivalle, Vanna now returns his love, and the play ends with her resolving to free him so that they can escape together. If the heroine's dilemma— personal chastity versus the saving of thousands of innocent lives—is a thoroughly classical device, the dénouement betrays a Romantic ethic: Vanna regards herself as freed from the marriage-bond by her husband's inhumanity, and chooses a higher ideal in the form of the love of Prinzivalle.

While the Symbolist drama pioneered by such writers as Villiers and Maeterlinck, inspired by Mallarmé's precept and Wagner's example, was to provide the most striking reaction against the realist 'drame moderne' which predominated in the theatre of the last third of the century under the twin influences of the 'well-made play' formula inherited from Scribe and the 'pièce à thèse' of Augier and Dumas *fils*, ventures into historical drama with Romantic affinities, such as we have examined in *Le Prétendant* and *Monna Vanna*, were by no means isolated. Even Sardou, whose name is more closely linked than any other with the banal social drama of the period, was versatile enough to be able to write plays of a very different kind. In plays like *Patrie* (1869), *La Tosca* (1887) or *Thermidor* (1889), he tackled historical drama with a Romantic flavour, just as readily as he adopted Scribe's formula for historical comedy in *Madame Sans-gêne* (1893) or set himself to write a serious thesis-play, in imitation of Dumas's *Madame Aubray*, in *Daniel Rochat* (1880). One hallmark of a Sardou play, whether on a modern or a historical subject, was a punctilious attention to detailed realism of setting—an inheritance from the 'couleur locale' which had so preoccupied Dumas *père*, for instance, in his historical dramas, just as much as from the realist theatre of the Second Empire. In Sardou's case, there is a tendency for such stage 'business' at times to conceal a certain absence of more weighty or more memorable qualities. Not invariably, by any means: the subject of *Thermidor*, for instance, was capable of provoking a near-riot in the Comédie-Française by left-wing students objecting to Sardou's condemnation of Robespierre and the Terror; the banning of the play by the Minister of the Interior was upheld by Clemenceau after a stormy Cabinet meeting.

La Tosca is perhaps a more representative illustration of the shortcomings of Sardou's historical drama. The subject-matter is that of Puccini's opera, and the details of the plot are very largely the same as in the libretto by Giacosa and Illica; the theme is an inspiring one: the fight of Italian patriots to throw off the harsh tyranny of a reactionary régime; and there is the same interplay of political intrigue, passion and jealousy. But whereas Hugo's dramas, as we have seen, already possess an operatic quality of their own, even before being adapted to the lyric stage, Sardou's *La Tosca* on the other hand reads as an exciting melodrama and little more. The lyrical idealism which makes *Tosca* such a brilliant—and moving—opera, is the creation of Puccini's music, not of Sardou's prose; and for all its theatrical efficiency, the drama of 1887 is nearer in its inspiration to the historical romances written by Dumas *père* for the Théâtre-Historique than to the masterpieces of Romantic drama.

For Sardou, like Scribe before him, was the servant of the theatrical public, ready to exploit whatever dramatic form seemed assured of a popular success. The Romantic dramatists had had nobler aspirations than this: their ambition had been to create new forms; not to follow public taste, but to guide and direct it. Towards the end of the century this role was taken over, on the one hand by the poetic drama of the Théâtre d'Art and Théâtre de l'Œuvre, and on the other by the Théâtre-Libre of André Antoine. The Théâtre-Libre is often thought of as being exclusively devoted to furthering the cause of Naturalism in the theatre, and indeed many of Antoine's most notable productions were in this vein; but his programme was in fact remarkably eclectic, and alongside the notorious 'comédies rosses' and the documentary 'tranches de vie' that were characteristic of the Naturalist aesthetic, he staged the works of poets like Banville and Catulle Mendès, and made several ventures into historical drama on traditional subjects. The season 1888–89, indeed, counted two such plays among its most distinguished productions: Hennique's *La Mort du duc d'Enghien* in December 1888, and *La Patrie en danger* by the Goncourt brothers in the following March. These two works by authors identified with the move towards Naturalism in the novel—the Goncourts' play had been written in 1867, within two years of their most celebrated novel *Germinie Lacerteux*, while Hennique was one of Zola's young disciples who formed the 'groupe de Médan'—are an interesting illustration of the evolution of the historical drama under the influence of documentary realism, away from the poetic idealization of Hugo's theatre, and in the direction of the 'scène historique' favoured in the 1820s by Stendhal and others. *La Mort du duc d'Enghien*, for instance, is described by the historian of Antoine's theatre in these terms:

> It is one of the most exaggerated examples in contemporary French drama of a loosely constructed play . . . it justifies, more than any other play of the Théâtre-Libre, the characterization of free drama.[25]

Though when the same writer goes on to say that "it has nothing whatever in common with the ultra-realist or so-called naturalist drama", he surely fails to acknowledge the search for documentary accuracy—the published version of Hennique's play contained a list of his sources—as well as the episodic construction of such plays, as factors relating them to the Naturalist aesthetic[26]. A great many Naturalist plays were adaptations of contemporary novels—those of the Goncourts or Zola, for instance—in which the original was cut up into a series of more or less independent 'tableaux': here, the history of the Napoleonic Era is treated in the same way, and the result is a documentary historical drama very much of its time.

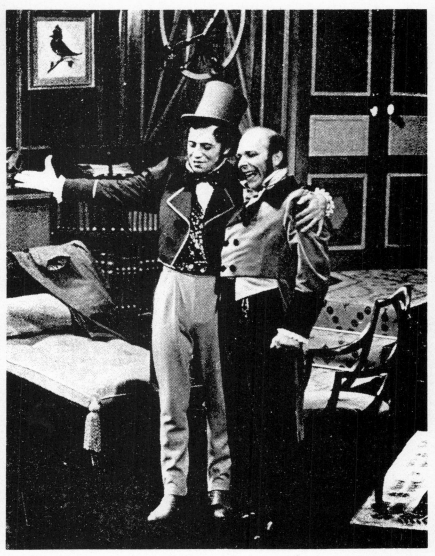

15   Scene from *Le Faiseur* (Comédie de l'Est, 1965)

16 Scene from Cyrano de Bergerac (Comédie-Française, 1964)

La Patrie en danger, similarly, looks back to those eighteenth-century aspirations towards a 'national theatre' which had preceded the attempts to create such a theatre with 'scènes historiques' drawn from French national history: Edmond de Goncourt writes in the Preface to the play, published in 1873, of his hopes that one day

> cette œuvre mort-née sera jugée digne d'être la voix avec laquelle un théâtre national fouettera le patriotisme de la France.

It is hardly surprising that *La Patrie en danger*, like *La Mort du duc d'Enghien* and Sardou's *Thermidor*, should deal with an episode from the Revolutionary period. On the one hand, this period was now distant enough for historical perspectives to be clearer, while as a source of republican and patriotic themes it gained new topicality with the Franco-Prussian War and the Commune of 1870–71; so that it now held the same sort of attraction for dramatists as the Wars of Religion had had at the end of the *ancien régime*.

The Goncourts' play has the same episodic structure as Hennique's: its five acts span the years 1789 to 1794. However, there is not quite the same impression of sober, unadorned document; the authors have imposed on their historical material something at least of the stylization that is necessary to turn a factual chronicle into a work of dramatic art. Thus, the long arm of coincidence is evident in the way in which the members of the Valjuzon family keep meeting Perrin, the son of one of their servants, who becomes a general in the revolutionary armies, but who retains his loyalty to the family in which he was brought up; there is a touch of caricature in the portrayal of the Chanoinesse, the uncompromising representative of the *ancien régime*, and her brother, the Comte de Valjuzon, too, is slightly larger than life in his role as a Scarlet Pimpernel type of adventurer; while the scene between the lovers, Blanche de Valjuzon and Perrin, in prison as they await the tumbril, captures something of the lyrical exaltation of true Romantic drama in spite of its prosaic idiom:

> — Blanche, je vous aime!... Blanche, nous allons mourir; Blanche, je suis heureux!

— Je serai brave, allez! Mais comme on ne peut pas savoir...
si j'avais sur la charrette un moment de faiblesse... Eh bien,
vous me laisserez m'appuyer un peu... comme cela, sur
votre épaule... n'est-ce pas?... comme si j'étais votre
femme!...

— Oui, comme si vous étiez ma femme!... (V, iii)

Nevertheless, if less obviously a 'slice of life' than Hennique's
play, *La Patrie en danger* is very much in keeping with the move
away from the tightly organized structure of the well-made
play, and both works represent a significant departure from the
treatment of historical material as a subject for development in
traditional terms of 'character' and conflict between characters[27], towards the Brechtian conception of a looser, more
objective 'epic theatre'. For the time being, however, the
historical plays performed at the Théâtre-Libre were addressed
to a minority public of connoisseurs; the mainstay of the literary
drama of the period, as well as its more frankly commercial
output, remained the social comedies, social dramas, problem-
plays and thesis-plays which dealt, more or less realistically,
with subjects taken from contemporary life. There was nothing
to suggest a revival of popular interest in the sort of Romantic
historical drama that had had such a wide appeal in the 1830s.
Yet the century was to close with the unprecedented success of
just such a play: Rostand's *Cyrano de Bergerac*, produced at the
Porte-Saint-Martin in December 1897, a pure, vintage Romantic drama according to the formula of the *Préface de Cromwell*,
and a play which made its appeal not to an *avant-garde* coterie,
but to the whole theatregoing public of Paris.

(*iii*) '*Cyrano de Bergerac*', *or the triumph of Romantic drama*

NOTHING in Rostand's previous career as a dramatist can
have suggested that he was capable of writing the most successful play of the century. A native of Marseille, he had completed
his schooling in Paris, and had begun to write for the theatre
while still a law-student. *Les Romanesques*, a charming comedy
which combines the manner of Marivaux with the inconsequential gaiety of Anouilh's *Bal des voleurs*, was performed at the
Théâtre-Français in 1894; and this was followed by two plays
written for Sarah Bernhardt at her Théâtre de la Renaissance:

La Princesse lointaine (1895) and *La Samaritaine* (1897). The first
of these was a dramatization of the mediaeval legend of the
troubadour prince Joffroy Rudel's love for Mélissinde, Queen
of Tripoli; while the latter, called an "évangile en trois tableaux", was based on the biblical account of the encounter
between Christ and the Samaritan woman. Critical opinion
was most favourable towards *Les Romanesques*: the character of
Mélissinde was found too enigmatic, and it was judged by some
critics that Rostand had not entirely solved the problems
inherent in the presentation of the figure of Christ on stage. All
three plays aroused serious critical interest, and Rostand was
recognized as a versatile poet with a talent for pleasing rhymes;
Sarcey wrote of *Les Romanesques*:

> L'auteur manie le vers d'une main preste et aisée; il parle
> une langue franche et alerte, qui tient de Scarron, de Regnard
> et de Banville, la langue que Vacquerie avait retrouvée pour
> *Tragaldabas*. Les rimes y sonnent des fanfares imprévues et
> joyeuses; c'est un enchantement. [28]

But there was a feeling that his was perhaps a lightweight talent,
and that as a playwright his ability was best seen in the construction of single scenes or tableaux, rather than on the level
of a full-scale work. Sarcey, for instance, hoped that Act I of
Les Romanesques would survive as a one-act play, while in the
case of *La Princesse lointaine* he found that the two middle acts
"ont fatigué par leur longueur et leur subtilité"[29]. In short, this
was a respectable début for a minor playwright, but with very
little indication of the peculiar qualities of *Cyrano de Bergerac*;
to quote Joseph Bédier, who was to succeed the playwright as
a member of the Académie Française, on the eve of *Cyrano* even
the most generous of Rostand's colleagues must have thought of
him as a "fils de Théodore de Banville ... [qui] ne saurait
jamais séduire qu'une élite, raffinée et même un peu blasée, de
délicats"[30].

For *Cyrano*, Rostand accepted the offer of Constant Coquelin,
probably the greatest actor of his day, who had been so impressed by the script of *La Princesse lointaine* that he had written
to the author: "Faites-moi un rôle et je le jouerai où vous
voudrez, quand vous voudrez"[31]; and the Porte-Saint-Martin

was chosen because the Théâtre-Français could not accept the play for immediate production. Author and cast were apprehensive before the first night: the central character was a bizarre, little-known figure; the play was a long one; the production was spectacular and costly; and there was competition with other plays of distinction that were being performed at the same time—all factors militating against the likelihood of success. But the notices were unanimously favourable, many being quite extravagant in their enthusiasm; and right from the start it was clear that this was no ordinary success. "Heureux serons-nous", one critic exclaimed, "quand nous serons bien vieux, de pouvoir dire: J'y étais!"[32]. As Faguet was to write, it was "le succès le plus grand par toute l'Europe et dans les deux mondes que l'on eût vu depuis *Le Cid*"[33]—a success all the more remarkable because, as Bédier remarks, "ce fut le succès du *Cid*, mais sans la querelle du *Cid*, le succès d'*Hernani*, mais sans la bataille d'*Hernani*"[34].

The quality of *Cyrano de Bergerac* that probably first strikes the spectator or reader is its astonishing verbal virtuosity: the surprising rhymes, the contrived puns and plays on words, the picturesque vocabulary, the colourful technical terms, the variety of rhythms, all of which communicate such a feeling of movement and vigour. Not only the celebrated *tirades*: Cyrano's extravaganza on the qualities of his enormous nose, his 'profession de foi' in the speech beginning "Moi, c'est moralement que j'ai mes élégances", the *ballade* composed while duelling (all in Act I, scene iv), the fierce declaration of independence built on the repeated refrain "Non, merci!" (II, viii), the fantasy describing his imaginary journey to the moon (III, xiii)—not only each well-known set piece, but indeed the rich verbal fabric of the whole play, gives constant proof of Rostand's mastery in manipulating the resources of the language and the technique of the Romantic alexandrine. Sarcey, as we have seen, had suggested seventeenth-century analogues: Scarron with his burlesque wit, and the imaginative fantasy of Regnard's rhyming; and nearer to Rostand's own time, the technical skill of a Vacquerie or a Banville. And of course there is one debt that overshadows all of these inheritances from the past: *Cyrano*, as the work of a poet, is unmistakably in the tradition of *Cromwell* and of *Ruy Blas*, a marvellous illustration of the rich possibilities of Romantic drama as Hugo had conceived it—and a play which one would like to think Hugo himself, had he still been alive, would have been generous enough to salute as a masterpiece.

But *Cyrano de Bergerac* is not merely the work of a skilled literary craftsman; and perhaps it is misleading to describe the outstanding virtuoso passages as 'set pieces'. For they strike us less as set pieces by the author than as virtuoso performances on the part of his hero. These exhibitionist *tirades* are not obtrusive 'purple passages': they belong in their context, as an integral part of the portrayal of a consistent dramatic personality; and Rostand's conception of his hero's character, as not only an extrovert, swaggering, swashbuckling Gascon but also as a highly-skilled juggler with words, is surely the essential foundation of his success. Nowhere else in the whole of nineteenth-century Romantic drama can be found such a perfect fusion of character and style, for Cyrano epitomizes the Poet as Hero, the hero *par excellence* in an art form which depends above all on the act of poetic creation; a poetic drama which exploits to the full the spirit of the French language: concrete, colourful, but also witty and satirical; lending itself equally well to exalted flights of poetic fancy, to spirited invective, and to the understatement of neat repartee. In the gallery of Hugo's characters, Don César—a minor, episodic figure—and Aïrolo had best conveyed this impression of the creative genius with words; the same quality is apparent in several of Musset's heroes—Fantasio in particular—but it is totally lacking in Chatterton, Vigny's poet-hero whose distinctive quality we are asked to take on trust. Tragaldabas had displayed it, in a grotesque, somewhat ignoble manner; but perhaps the character before Cyrano most convincingly endowed by his creator with this sort of genius is Dumas's Kean.

Rostand's hero, like Dumas's, is several sizes larger than life; but both are credible, as realizations of the type of creative genius which in real life transcends the cramping conditions of ordinary, prosaic existence. They are successful embodiments of genius because their starting-point was in each case a historical figure who left behind a rich stock of anecdotes testifying to a life lived on the grand scale—and just as much, perhaps, because the historical setting in which each lived was one in which we

can readily believe such excess to have flourished: in the case of
Kean, the flamboyant social life of Regency London, and for
Cyrano the France of Richelieu with its superficial gaiety and its
underlying tensions. Rostand's own earlier plays can be seen
by comparison to have lacked this essential *rapport* between the
subject chosen and the playwright's natural bent: in *La
Princesse lointaine* the dying troubadour Joffroy Rudel was a
subject altogether too elegiac for Rostand's robust manner, and
the deliberate archaisms of language, as part of the conscientious
attempt at a mediaeval setting, give this play a somewhat
academic flavour; and a not too dissimilar criticism could be
made, *mutatis mutandis*, of *La Samaritaine*—though Rostand was in
fact blamed by some contemporaries for the worldly nature of
some of the passages put into the mouth of Christ[35]. But with
Cyrano de Bergerac, the concordance between the poet-hero and
his age, on the one hand, and the dramatist's mode of expression
on the other, was complete, and no other Romantic drama
started with the advantage of such an inspired choice of subject.

Pedantic scholars were not slow, on the appearance of
Rostand's play, to examine it from the point of view of detailed
historical accuracy, and to find it wanting[36]; while more recent
research has established the fact that Cyrano was not a native
of Gascony, but of Paris, and that the name Bergerac came not
from the town of Périgord, but from a small family property
in the Ile-de-France. But Rostand was faithful in this latter
respect to the state of knowledge current at the time when he
wrote the play; and more generally, without making a fetish of
fidelity to trivial detail, he has squarely based his principal
character, and most of his subsidiary characters as well, on
seventeenth-century source-material. In particular, quotations
from, and allusions to, Cyrano's writings, and references to his
celebrated exploits, make this a very well authenticated
portrait; and altogether, the play is remarkable for the accuracy
of its portrayal of a clearly defined time and place[37].

It is largely, of course, a humorous portrayal; and scenes like
the silencing of Montfleury and the deflating of the pompous
Vicomte in Act I, or the defeat of Guiche's plans by the account
of the visit to the moon in Act III, combine a genuine documentary flavour with a highly successful kind of comic writing.
The characterization of minor figures like Raguenau, and

scenes such as the first encounter between Cyrano and Christian, are inspired by the same comic spirit, and even the scene at the siege of Arras in Act IV, which culminates in the death of Christian and most of Cyrano's other comrades, has as its centre-piece the comic episode of the arrival of Roxane in a carriage laden with food and drink. Much of the comic atmosphere of the play derives from the characterization of Cyrano and his companions as Gascons, with their tall stories, ready wit, extravagant exploits and boisterous good spirits; but there is another sort of verbal comedy which also has considerable prominence in the play: a kind of writing based on the poetic conceits, the *vers galants*, and the sophisticated word-play of *précieux* usage. A set piece like the *ballade* brings the two styles together: if we add the choreographic element of the duel itself, the result is imaginative comic writing of a very high order:

> Je jette avec grâce mon feutre,
> Je fais lentement l'abandon
> Du grand manteau qui me calfeutre,
> Et je tire mon espadon;
> Élégant comme Céladon,
> Agile comme Scaramouche,
> Je vous préviens, cher Myrmidon,
> Qu'à la fin de l'envoi je touche!
>
> Vous auriez bien dû rester neutre;
> Où vais-je vous larder, dindon?...
> Dans le flanc, sous votre maheutre?...
> Au cœur, sous votre bleu cordon?...
> — Les coquilles tintent, ding-don!
> Ma pointe voltige: une mouche!
> Décidément... c'est au bedon,
> Qu'à la fin de l'envoi, je touche.
>
> Il me manque une rime en eutre...
> Vous rompez, plus blanc qu'amidon?
> C'est pour me fournir le mot pleutre!
> — Tac! je pare la pointe dont
> Vous espériez me faire don. —
> J'ouvre la ligne, — je la bouche...
> Tiens bien ta broche, Laridon!
> A la fin de l'envoi, je touche.

Prince, demande à Dieu pardon!
Je quarte du pied, j'escarmouche,
Je coupe, je feinte...
　　　　　　　(*Se fendant.*) Hé! là, donc!
(*Le vicomte chancelle; Cyrano salue.*)
À la fin de l'envoi, je touche.

But *Cyrano de Bergerac* is not just a burlesque comedy. Like
those masterpieces of Romantic opera, *La Traviata* or *La
Bohème*[38], it juxtaposes scenes which present a humorous picture
of a lively milieu with scenes of genuine pathos, and the
successful 'mélange des genres' is not the least striking way in
which Rostand has obeyed the spirit of the *Préface de Cromwell*.
Cyrano himself illustrates perhaps better than any other
Romantic hero Hugo's aesthetic based on the antithesis between
grotesque and *sublime*. His enormous nose may not, like Triboulet's
deformity, symbolize moral turpitude, but it does represent in a
vivid, visual form the earthbound physical reality which, according to the Romantic metaphysic, constantly frustrates and
defeats the human spirit in its aspirations towards the ideal;
Cyrano's grotesque appearance is enough to destroy all the
dreams of an exalted love for which his romanesque imagination
longs. For although he is the terror of all who wear a sword, and
can himself take on a hundred opponents single-handed, he
subscribes to the conventional *précieux* conceit of the swooning
lover at the thought of the unapproachable Roxane:

Et je m'évanouis de peur quand je vous vois. (II, iv)

For a moment, he is encouraged to think that the celebrated
beauty might possibly love him in spite of his ugliness; but
once the misunderstanding has been resolved, and Roxane has
confessed her love for the handsome Christian, he unhesitatingly
sacrifices himself to bring about the lovers' happiness. For the
rest of Act II and throughout Act III, the tone of comedy persists even in the scenes with Christian: the bargain is struck, and
Cyrano's assertion that he will derive an aesthetic pleasure from
wooing Roxane by proxy is evidently not entirely a pretence:

Cela m'amuserait!
C'est une expérience à tenter un poète.

Veux-tu me compléter et que je te complète?
Tu marcheras, j'irai dans l'ombre à ton côté:
Je serai ton esprit, tu seras ma beauté. (II, x)

However, at the siege of Arras, in the face of probable death, the mask finally drops. Christian guesses at Cyrano's own love for Roxane, and the latter admits at last that she loves in Christian not the handsome exterior, which is his own, but the poetic imagination and eloquence which—though she does not know it—are Cyrano's. Christian nobly stands down, and Cyrano's hopes rise again, when Christian's death makes it impossible ever to tell Roxane the truth. Cyrano's heroic lie to his dying friend:

...J'ai tout dit. C'est toi qu'elle aime encor! (IV, x)

binds him for the rest of his life, according to his quixotic ethic, and for fifteen years, Roxane mourns the husband who never was.

The pathos of Christian's death, and of Cyrano's ultimate sacrifice, are absorbed into the movement and excitement of the battle-scenes, so that the overall impression created by Act IV is one of rich spectacle rather than of emotion. But the death of Cyrano in Act V must count as one of the most moving scenes in all Romantic drama: the scene may be muted in tone compared with the lyrical exaltation of the closing scenes of *Hernani* or *Marion de Lorme*, for instance, but in the union of two lovers, kept apart by fate, at the very moment at which death is about to separate them for ever, we can easily recognize the theme common to all the great Romantic tragedies.

Rostand's effects are no doubt somewhat contrived; for instance, the device by which Cyrano involuntarily discloses his love to Roxane—she allows him to read Christian's last letter, and as dusk falls, he continues to read the letter he knows by heart until she finally recognizes the voice that had serenaded her on Christian's behalf fifteen years earlier (V, v)—hardly stands up to a coldly rational analysis. But how effective this *coup de théâtre* is in theatrical terms; and how artistically right it is—even if implausible from the point of view of strict psychological realism—that Roxane should become aware of Cyrano's love for her at the very moment that she realizes that he is dying. Similarly, the simplicity of the dialogue at this climax:

> — Ces pleurs étaient de vous?
>> — Ce sang était le sien (*ibid.*)

may be criticized as lacking in subtlety. But how fitting it is that this elegiac finale should be simple and direct in its appeal, and not depend on the artifices of *précieux* imagery. In any case, in the last 'movement' of the closing scene, Cyrano the imaginative poet comes into his own again. He has remarked ruefully on the absurd anticlimax of his end; instead of dying a hero's death, he has been killed in a cowardly ambush:

> ...J'aurai tout manqué, même ma mort.

But the impression we are left with is not one of failure, but of serene accomplishment:

> — Le Bret, je vais monter dans la lune opaline,
> Sans qu'il faille inventer, aujourd'hui, de machine...
>
> — Que dites-vous?
>
>> — Mais oui, c'est là, je vous le dis,
> Que l'on va m'envoyer faire mon paradis.
> Plus d'une âme que j'aime y doit être exilée,
> Et je retrouverai Socrate et Galilée!

—and, as the dying man improvises his final dialogue with Death, of heroic achievement:

> Je sais bien qu'à la fin vous me mettrez à bas;
> N'importe: je me bats! je me bats! je me bats!
> Oui, vous m'arrachez tout, le laurier et la rose!
> Arrachez! Il y a malgré vous quelque chose
> Que j'emporte, et ce soir, quand j'entrerai chez Dieu,
> Mon salut balaiera largement le seuil bleu,
> Quelque chose que sans un pli, sans une tache,
> J'emporte malgré vous, et c'est...
>
>> — C'est?...
>>> — Mon panache.

It would be wrong to dismiss Cyrano's 'panache' as empty bombast. A part of the play's success was no doubt due to the sort of jingoistic bravado that was welcome to French ears at a time when national pride needed some sort of a boost; but the true appeal of Rostand's hero is less parochial, and less superficial, than this. Despite his extravagance, Cyrano is a human character with whom most readers and spectators find it possible to achieve the necessary degree of sympathetic identification; this is not so much because in our wishful thinking we aspire to the same sort of heroic action, as because he gives expression to a Romantic idealism, a nostalgia for absolute values, that is latent in most of us. It does not matter that he is not a successful lover; indeed, it is essential that his ideal should remain unfulfilled: Roxane is Cyrano's 'princesse lointaine', and the swashbuckling Gascon, like the pale troubadour, dies at the very moment when his dream is about to become reality, in order to preserve the purity of the dream. It is the steadfast pursuit of the ideal, the unwavering belief in the dream, that counts; and Rostand's hero is a positive embodiment of Romantic aspirations which strike a responsive note in us all.

If, as we have suggested earlier, one of the distinctive marks of Romantic literature is its explicitness, its avoidance of the nebulous and suggestive, then *Cyrano de Bergerac* can properly be called a masterpiece of Romantic drama. Like Hugo's, Rostand's imagery is picturesque and predominantly visual in its nature; and *Cyrano de Bergerac* marks a triumphant return to the Romantic notion of a kind of literature in which the first priority is placed on communication with the reader or spectator, away from the Symbolist view of literature as a medium for the expression of the author's private dream-world. And not the least eloquent tribute to Rostand's success in *Cyrano* is the hostile criticism directed against the play by the Symbolist writers and their partisans:

On dira qu'au bout de près d'un demi-siècle *Cyrano*, pris comme symbole, est toujours applaudi et même lu. Soit. Mais il faut des chansons légères, des romans-feuilletons voire policiers, des vaudevilles et même de la poésie à la Rostand pour contenter les éléments les moins exigeants du public. Il reste une clientèle qui a des satisfactions d'un ordre plus relevé, clientèle plus restreinte parce qu'elle possède une sensibilité plus délicate et une curiosité d'esprit plus affinée. A cette clientèle-là le symbolisme a prodigué des joies moins grossières.[39]

At the beginning of the century Constant in his *Réflexions sur Wallstein*, followed by Stendhal in *Racine et Shakespeare* and then by Hugo in the *Préface de Cromwell*, had argued for a new form of drama to replace classical tragedy, precisely because the latter had become a minority art-form appealing to an élite with a certain cultural background. And the Romantic dramatists of the 1830s, whatever their differences, had been united in their aim to produce a popular drama with the widest possible appeal. *Cyrano de Bergerac* may be said to have fulfilled this aim more successfully than any other play of the century: it was a thoroughly popular success, without the need to read into that term any pejorative implications. As such, it was destined to remain unique in Rostand's theatre: neither in *L'Aiglon* nor in *Chantecler* did he manage to reproduce the same appeal to a wide public. The six hundred performances of *Cyrano de Bergerac*, however, stand as the ultimate vindication of the formula proposed in the *Préface de Cromwell*; and Rostand's election to the Academy in 1901, just over three years after the première of *Cyrano*, not only marks the official recognition of its author as one of the great dramatists of the century, but may also be seen as the belated consecration of Romantic drama.

Notes to Chapter Twelve

1. Hugo, *Théâtre complet, ed. cit.*, II, p. 1903.
2. *Op. cit.*, p. 323.
3. *Op. cit.*, pp. 97ff.
4. Hugo, *Théâtre complet*, II, p. 1907. Professor Affron talks of *Mille Francs* . . . as an example of 'pseudo-realistic' theatre (*op. cit.*, p. 83).
5. *Op. cit.*, p. 1908.
6. J. Charpentier, *Théodore de Banville*, Paris, 1925, p. 189.
7. 'Art poétique', *Jadis et naguère*, Paris, 1884.
8. *Correspondance, 1862–1871*, ed. H. Mondor and J. P. Richard, Paris, 1956, p. 137.

9. *Mallarmé and the Symbolist Drama*, Detroit, 1963, pp. 102–103.
10. Quoted by Block, *ibid.*, p. 21.
11. Quoted in G. Michaud, *Mallarmé, l'homme et l'œuvre*, Paris, 1953, p. 43.
12. 'Avant-propos' to *Comédies*, Paris, 1908.
13. *Op. cit.*, p. 254.
14. *Ibid.*, p. 162.
15. The appeal of the occult on an intellectually less demanding level had of course been abundantly illustrated in the predilection of writers like Gautier for what Cassagne calls "le bric-à-brac fantastique du moyen âge, les sorcières, les diverses diableries, les incubes, les succubes, les vampires, tous les démons de la nuit et du jour, les philtres, la magie noire ou blanche" (*op. cit.*, p. 314). One play which catered for the same taste was *Le Vampire*, a 'drame fantastique' by Dumas *père* and Maquet (Ambigu-Comique, December 1851), whose accumulation of gothic horrors nevertheless manages to suggest something of the atmosphere of the more sensational among Balzac's 'études philosophiques'.
16. *Axël*, ed. P. Mariel, Paris, 1960, p. 29.
17. *Ibid.*
18. Quoted by P. Mariel, *op. cit.*, p. 23. On the other hand, for evidence of the success of this production with a certain public, see J. A. Henderson, *The First Avant-Garde (1887–1894): Sources of the Modern French Theatre*, London, 1971, pp. 106–107.
19. See the edition by P. G. Castex and A. W. Raitt, Paris, 1965.
20. Quoted in W. D. Halls, *Maurice Maeterlinck: A Study of his Life and Thought*, Oxford, 1960, p. 103.
21. Preface to *Théâtre*, I, Brussels, 1911.
22. *Op. cit.*, VIII, pp. 408–423.
23. Quoted in J. Robichez, *Le Symbolisme au théâtre*, Paris, 1957, p. 83. Elsewhere, Maeterlinck proposed having his plays performed by marionettes, as a means of overcoming the objection expressed by Sarcey above. See Henderson, *op. cit.*, p. 156.
24. *Le Temple enseveli*, Paris, 1902, p. 131; quoted in Halls, *op. cit.*, pp. 72–73.
25. Waxman, *op. cit.*, p. 101.
26. Compare the comments of J. A. Henderson, for whom Hennique's play represents "an attempt to apply so-called 'scientific' naturalism to historical drama" (*op. cit.*, p. 54).
27. Compare Sarcey's comment on *La Mort du duc d'Enghien*: "On ne me fait connaître à fond aucun des personnages qui ont joué un rôle dans ce drame sanglant, on ne me donne pas la moindre

idée de l'époque où il s'est passé, et l'on appelle ça du théâtre;
mais c'est le contraire du théâtre, c'est la négation du théâtre"
(*op. cit.*, VIII, p. 276).

28. *Ibid.*, p. 204.

29. *Ibid.*, pp. 204, 206, 212.

30. *Discours de réception à l'Académie Française, prononcé le 3 novembre 1921 par Joseph Bédier*, Paris, 1921, p. 24.

31. Quoted by E. Ripert, *Edmond Rostand, sa vie et son œuvre*, Paris, 1968, pp. 83–84.

32. Quoted by Bédier, *op.cit.*, p. 24.

33. Quoted by J. W. Grieve, *L'Œuvre dramatique d'Edmond Rostand*, Paris, 1931, p. 49.

34. *Op. cit.*, p. 25.

35. Cf. Ripert, *op. cit.*, pp. 71–72.

36. Cf. E. Magne, *Le Cyrano de l'histoire: les erreurs de documentation de 'Cyrano de Bergerac'*, Paris, 1903.

37. Cf. Ripert, *op. cit.*, pp. 85ff.

38. Murger's *Scènes de la vie de Bohème* had been published serially in 1848, and in book form in 1851. In its dramatized form, as a 'pièce mêlée de chants', it was staged at the Variétés in November 1849. Puccini's opera was not produced until 1896.

39. A. Dinar, *La Croisade symboliste*, Paris, 1943, p. 184.

13 Conclusion

(i) Romantic drama, history and tragedy

THE more closely one examines the writings for the theatre that have traditionally gone under the name of Romantic drama, the more one may be tempted to wonder whether any real critical value attaches to this label. What have works like *Le Roi s'amuse* and *On ne badine pas avec l'amour*, *Chatterton* and *Napoléon Bonaparte* in common other than the fact that they were all written within the space of four or five years? Is 'Romantic drama' a convenient chronological label and no more? It is true that the highest common factor possessed by these plays, which are fairly characteristic examples of the spread of form and content to be found in the work of the four major dramatists of the period—representing as they do prose and verse, historical and domestic subject-matter, realism and fantasy, structure ranging from classical concentration to the open form of 'epic' drama—does seem to be their chronological coincidence. Yet in saying that, we are of course acknowledging something more: 'Romantic drama' is a more significant label than 'drama of the 1830s'. For although chronological coincidence must always imply in some measure the reflection of the literary climate of a particular age, this can seldom have been more so than in a period remarkable for the solidarity and enthusiasm with which young writers and artists banded themselves together into an intellectual and cultural *avant-garde*. This does not mean that the plays of the period all express an identical ideological or moral outlook, or that they are based on an identical aesthetic; but rather, that in their diverse ways they reflect that sensibility which was characteristic of the Romantic generation.

This may take the form, most obviously, of the cult of the individual at the expense of the collective values of the

community: the resigned self-absorption of Didier or André del
Sarto at one extreme, and the ruthless individualism of Richard
Darlington or Kean at the other, are equally products of the
age of *René* and *Manfred*. It may find expression in the awareness
of the struggle for political freedom which united the intel-
lectuals of most European countries in this post-Napoleonic era:
a theme to which it was impossible to give direct expression in
an age of strict censorship, but which surely underlies the
portraits of tyrants and corrupt rulers in plays like *Marion de
Lorme*, *Lorenzaccio* or *Ruy Blas*. We may recognize it in those
thesis-plays which examine contemporary social issues, *Antony*
and *Chatterton*; and conversely in the escapist flights of fancy
which characterize some of Musset's comedies like *Fantasio* or
Le Chandelier. There is no uniform manifestation of the Romantic
sensibility, but the drama of the 1830s gives expression to a
variety of contemporary attitudes, of which the most important
common denominator is perhaps the primacy accorded to
feeling over the rational faculty. Not that this was a new
phenomenon: the eighteenth century may be said to have seen
the transition from the Age of Reason to the Age of Feeling at
the point at which the generation of Voltaire gave way to that
of Rousseau. We have attempted to analyse, in an early chapter,
those features of eighteenth-century dramatic writing which
anticipated Romantic drama in this respect; and have suggested that the "Plus je sens vivement, plus je sens que je suis"
of La Chaussée's D'Arviane (a proposition to which we can
imagine Diderot's Dorval, as well as certain heroes of eighteenth-
century tragedy, subscribing just as readily) makes him a clear
precursor of Hernani, Antony and Chatterton. Indeed, what
we call the Romantic sensibility is the bringing together of
features of the intellectual climate that were widespread before
the Revolution; the Revolution itself, and the Napoleonic Wars,
acted as a catalyst, breaking down the accepted view of an
ordered society, and Romantic works with heroes like Werther,
Obermann and René were already exerting a powerful influence round the turn of the century.

But Romantic drama cannot be defined merely as the expression of Romantic attitudes through the medium of a Romantic
sensibility: this could not be effective in the theatre until there
had been a linguistic and stylistic revolution, and for such a

revolution the precept of the *Préface de Cromwell* and the practical example of *Hernani* and Hugo's other verse plays were almost entirely responsible. It was this which enabled 'Romantic' subject-matter to be put across to an audience in a challenging literary and dramatic form. And it was not only a question of sweeping away the restricting conventions and the tired taboos of the previous century; Hugo's most important achievement was a positive one: the creation of a new, dynamic art-form that would enable Romantic dramatists to rival the old forms they were supplanting. For the literary quality of the new drama remains a factor of the highest importance: Hugo, Vigny, Musset, and Dumas at any rate in his early years, were all conscious of the gulf that separated at least their aspirations, if not always their achievements, from the popular offerings of *boulevard* drama; and we have already quoted Gautier on this same subject:

> Le théâtre, tel qu'on l'entend de nos jours, n'a rien de littéraire; la pensée n'y est que pour fort peu de chose ...mais, pour ce qui nous regarde, nous avouons qu'une œuvre sans portée et sans style nous intéressera toujours fort peu.[1]

If we accept this premise, we must acknowledge, I think, that the Romantic dramatists were much more successful in verse than in prose. Hugo's verse dramas stand out as the most memorable examples of the genre, and alongside them we may include those prose plays such as *Lorenzaccio* and Musset's early *comédies*, in which the playwright has achieved a truly poetic manner. Indeed, a Romantic play in the prosaic idiom of bourgeois domestic drama is something of a contradiction in terms, and of the cases in which these dramatists did choose a modern setting, the most successful, like *Antony*, *Chatterton* or *Kean*, seem to have been those in which the stylistic resources of Romantic rhetoric enabled them to overcome the restrictions of a purely naturalistic dialogue.

Of the variety of dramatic forms within which the Romantic dramatists practised, the one which best suited their aspirations, at the same time as enabling them to transcend the limitations of ordinary domestic subject-matter, was the historical drama in verse; and indeed, it is the group of Hugo's plays comprising *Cromwell*, *Hernani*, *Marion de Lorme*, *Le Roi s'amuse*, *Ruy Blas*, *Les Burgraves* and *Torquemada* which in the minds of most readers constitutes the really essential corpus of Romantic drama. This is where the real test lay: to challenge the prestige of tragedy 'à l'antique' by revitalizing the formula for a tragedy based on modern historical subjects, which had been inherited from Voltaire. For this was the formula that Hugo adopted, and one which had little difficulty in prevailing over the alternative of the 'scène historique'. Despite the brief vogue of the latter in the 1820s, due to the appeal that its fidelity to historical fact made to the scholarly reader, the 'scène historique' could never have been a viable proposition from a theatrical point of view; instead, Hugo followed Voltaire in choosing subjects 'en marge de l'histoire', and indeed went beyond Voltaire in writing 'historical' plays whose only genuinely historical feature was the imaginative use of a vague 'couleur des temps'. In his plays on modern subjects, Voltaire had already broken with the classical practice of taking the major figures of history for his heroes: instead of dealing with the fortunes of great empires, in the persons of Corneille's Augustus Caesar and Julius Caesar, or Racine's Nero and Titus, plays like *Adélaïde du Guesclin* and *Tancrède* are based on the fortunes of *private* individuals. *Cromwell* is the only one of Hugo's verse tragedies (if we leave *Les Burgraves* on one side as a venture into a quite different epic style) unequivocally to present a major historical figure as its hero: elsewhere, the rulers and statesmen—Louis XIII and Richelieu, François I, the Emperor Charles V—are relegated to a subsidiary place, while the principal interest is reserved for the misfortunes of a private individual or individuals. In *Ruy Blas*, the King of Spain does not himself appear; while *Torquemada* makes an exact parallel with Voltaire's practice in *Mahomet*: Hugo uses the figure of his religious fanatic, as Voltaire had used his impostor, to put across the didactic message of his play, but the foreground of the plot, and the reader's sympathy, are claimed by the young lovers who are in each case their victims. Even the prose plays which may appear to follow a contrary practice, by presenting Marie Tudor and Lucrèce Borgia as principal characters, are hardly exceptions in fact, since it can be said that both of these heroines are treated very much as private individuals, and the importance of state affairs is considerably played down.

In other words, Hugo is not writing historical drama in the sense in which Shakespeare's 'Histories' are historical plays, or in which Brecht's *Galileo* has a truly historical character. And if *Lorenzaccio* may at first sight seem to correspond more nearly to Shakespearean practice in this respect, such an impression is surely deceptive: for although Musset's respect for historical accuracy is of quite a different order from Hugo's, it is after all really left to the ancillary characters of *Lorenzaccio* to convey the sense of the period, as it is in *Marion de Lorme* or *Ruy Blas*. Rather than embodying the existential, contingent characteristics of a specific period, the central character himself, just like Hugo's heroes and heroines, expresses the essential Romantic attitudes: the boredom, the fatalism and the death-wish that we encounter in so many other products of the Romantic attitude to life. In the final analysis, the Romantic dramatists who chose to treat subjects from history were less concerned to write genuine historical drama than to use a selected period from the past in order to provide an imaginative analogy with the present.

And also, of course, in order to create a suitably dignified and elevated setting for their own kind of lyrical tragedy. The qualification: '*lyrical* tragedy' is important, for although the capacity of the poetic dramas of Hugo, Rostand and others to move an audience is not in doubt, the nature of their emotional appeal remains a matter for controversy, and there are many who would not accept our reaction to Romantic drama (or to opera) as a valid tragic emotion. George Steiner is the most forthright of such critics: for him, tragedy is incompatible not only with the Romantic sensibility, but with the positivist values of the modern world at large:

> In the nineteenth century, Laplace announced that God was a hypothesis of which the rational mind had no further need; God took the great astronomer at his word. But tragedy is that form of art which requires the intolerable burden of God's presence. It is now dead because His shadow no longer falls upon us as it fell on Agamemnon or Macbeth or Athalie.[2]

This is an argument of some weight: on the whole, Romantic drama often strikes us as lacking the metaphysical dimension provided by the traditional systems of religious thought, such as had been present in Greek tragedy as well as in Shakespeare's and Racine's. There are exceptions, of course; and one of the functions of the soliloquies in *Lorenzaccio* is to establish this extra dimension that is lacking from most of the drama of the period. At the other end of the spectrum Antony and Adèle, Chatterton and Kitty Bell are the victims of social conventions and the prejudices of their fellow-men, not of the arbitrary injustice of the gods; and the same is true, *mutatis mutandis*, of the historical forces at work in such plays as *Christine*, *La Maréchale d'Ancre* or *Toussaint Louverture*. The heroes of the most typical Romantic dramas—Hernani, Didier, Triboulet, Ruy Blas, Cyrano—fall between these two extremes: they are men who do seem at times to be at grips with intangible forces larger than themselves, and not merely with the self-interest or malevolence of their fellows. But while Hugo's heroes are ready enough to see themselves as the victims of an impersonal fate, it is only too easy, in this sort of drama in which the contingencies of time and place count for so much, for the noble concept of tragic fate to be brought down to the level of mechanical chance. It was perhaps only in *Lorenzaccio* that the full potential of the philosophical scheme of things outlined in the *Préface de Cromwell* was to be realized; only in the person of Lorenzo does the poignant antithesis between man's highest aspirations and the frustrations of his earthbound condition suggest a battle for a human soul between metaphysical forces of good and evil.

For Hugo himself was more interested in the aesthetic possibilities than in the metaphysical implications of the *sublime/grotesque* dualism: this emphasis is clear from the *Préface*, and it is borne out equally clearly in the plays. We have had occasion to remark on the absence of any real spiritual dimension from *Hernani*, and the remark would be valid for the rest of Hugo's lyrical dramas: indeed, one feature distinguishing *Les Burgraves* from the earlier plays is that it expresses, in however crude a form, something of the visionary theodicy that was to be embodied in such works as 'Ce que dit la bouche d'ombre' and the *Légende des siècles*. However, there can be no doubt of the ability of the purely human characters of the earlier plays to move us in a way that is quite impossible with the shadowy symbols of *Les Burgraves*. Indeed, the closing scenes of *Hernani* and *Marion de Lorme* are written with a directness and simplicity which makes the deaths of Didier, and of Hernani and Doña Sol, more moving than the profounder, but more reflective, working-out of the tragedy of *Lorenzaccio*.

But the lack of a spiritual dimension is accompanied in Hugo's lyric dramas, as it is in *Cyrano de Bergerac*, by a very obvious theatricality; so that while the dénouements of these plays are excellent displays of emotion—and while they have no difficulty in producing an emotional response on the spectator's part—there is a sense in which they remain self-conscious displays of *simulated* emotion. We are moved by the death of Hernani and Doña Sol, or the death of Cyrano, in the same way that we are moved by the death of Mimi or La Traviata: these are all highly successful examples of a sort of set piece: the Romantic death-scene. They readily move us to tears, but compared with our reaction to the greatest masterpieces of tragedy, it is an emotion felt from the outside. In all great tragedy—and perhaps, as Helen Gardner suggests, "tragedy that is not 'great' is not tragedy, but 'failed tragedy' "[3]—we are forced to participate in the hero's sufferings. We suffer with Phèdre, or Lear, to the point at which we welcome their death as a release not only from their sufferings but from our own anguish. I think we begin to feel something approaching this tragic identification in the cases of Musset's Lorenzo and of Hugo's Marion, but generally speaking, the emotion aroused by these Romantic tragedies falls short of Aristotle's "purging of the passions"; in Shakespearean terms the proper analogue would be *Romeo and Juliet*, not *Hamlet* or *King Lear*.

(ii) Romantic drama and the evolution of the French theatre

BY the time Romanticism in the theatre had come and gone, the long-standing conventions governing dramatic literature, the hierarchical attitudes towards genres and styles, had been swept away. Even the exclusive prestige of tragedy itself had been seriously challenged, and in the so-called 'classical revival' of the 1840s there had been more than a hint of compromise with the style of the new drama. In this respect, 1830 had been a point of no return, and there can be little doubt that this date was the most important division between old and new in the French theatre since the end of the Middle Ages.

Since the Romantic writers demanded complete freedom for the artist:

Que le poète se garde de copier qui que ce soit, pas plus Shakespeare que Molière, pas plus Schiller que Corneille[4]

they did not try to replace one orthodoxy by another. In the second half of the century, as we have seen, the Romantic formula was virtually abandoned; the intellectual and cultural climate had not remained static, and as a pure Romantic drama, *Cyrano de Bergerac* already represents something of an anachronism. However, since the time of *Cyrano*, there have continued to be vigorous challenges to the realist or naturalist idiom which has predominated in the theatre over the last hundred years; and there is a sense in which the writers with creative imagination responsible for these challenges can legitimately be seen as the successors of the Romantic dramatists.

Claudel's poetic drama may seem most obviously to carry on from the Symbolist theatre of Villiers and Maeterlinck; but his historical plays in particular are recognizably in the mainstream of a tradition going back to the 1830s. Montherlant's historical dramas such as *La Reine morte*, *Le Maître de Santiago* or *Port-Royal* illustrate even more clearly a Romantic approach to history in the theatre; and though Cocteau's theatre, throughout a long career, showed him to be most eclectic in his inspiration, his *L'Aigle à deux têtes* is a vintage Romantic drama, faithful to the spirit as well as to the form of its nineteenth-century models. Vigny's more philosophical version of historical drama finds a modern analogue in Camus's *Caligula* or *Les Justes*, and in Sartre's *Le Diable et le bon Dieu*; Giraudoux's romantic idealism, and his fantasy, have much in common with the spirit of Musset's *comédies*; while the fertile genius of Anouilh, of all the twentieth-century French dramatists the most consummate man of the theatre, has a real affinity with the genius of Dumas *père*. None of these analogies ought to be pushed too far, of course; and it would be foolish to look for anything so tangible as specific influences. It seems pertinent to remark, however, that for all the differences between them, such twentieth-century dramatists have this in common, not only among themselves but also with their predecessors of the Romantic generation: they seek to transcend the banality of ordinary existence by the creation of a fictional world—in the cases considered, usually based on the idealized reproduction of a scene from the past—in which characters who are theatrically larger than life, in that they represent a poetic condensation of our everyday experience, act out a fable that instructs, uplifts or moves us. To achieve this, they all rely on the traditional concept of the coherence and unity of the dramatic character; and on the power of the literary language to make their heightened transcription of reality significant and memorable. In other words, the mainstream of twentieth-century drama has remained a *literary* drama, and these writers have seen the playwright's function as consisting in communication with the widest possible literate and cultured public. The Romantic dramatists had constituted the *avant-garde* of the writers and artists of their day, in the sense in which J. A. Henderson defines the term:

> The attitude to which we may apply the label of avantgardism . . . depends on a concept of art which sees the creative act as the cult of originality and novelty, a process of renewal of artistic genres—or a kind of progress—depending essentially on a rejection of the past. It is thus a characteristically Romantic attitude. In literature it stems from the Romantic revolt which burst upon France in the first decades of the nineteenth century, and which, it may be argued, is still its central force in the mid-twentieth.[5]

But they were not an *avant-garde* in the sense in which this term is increasingly used in our own day, of artists who seek to communicate with a highbrow minority in ever more esoteric ways. It is abundantly clear from all their writings about the theatre, as well as from the plays themselves, that they wanted to broaden, not to restrict, the appeal of the theatre as a cultured art-form; and with the possible exception of Claudel, whom the general public will no doubt always find a difficult dramatist, that is equally true of the twentieth-century playwrights mentioned so far.

The traditional concept of a literary theatre has been under serious attack during the twentieth century. The Surrealist cult of the subconscious has helped to undermine the traditional notions of coherent characterization and dialogue, substituting the arbitrary incoherence of random experience for the ordered logic of a work of art; while the determined efforts of Artaud and other influential theorists to play down the role of language in the theatre and to stress the importance of gesture, mime and spectacle have had the effect, when put into practice, of devaluing the role of the creative writer vis-à-vis that of the producer, and of radically altering the relationship between the spectator and what he sees on the stage.

Considered in the light of some of the more extravagant developments in the post-war theatre, the programme of the *Préface de Cromwell* now looks almost as conservative as that of Boileau's *Art poétique*: Romantic drama and the classical tragedy it replaced seem to have an equally old-fashioned look by the side of Mnouchkine's *1789* or *1793*, the 'happenings', the 'street theatre' and other spectacles favoured by the contemporary *avant-garde*. Yet we must not forget the very real emancipation effected in its time by the *Préface*, the new lease of life given by the Romantic dramatists to a serious theatre that had become choked by convention and was virtually moribund. Not only French, but Western drama as a whole, benefited from this new injection of vitality, and the important critical debate on the relationship between art and nature, realism and convention, as well as the wide range of experimentation that was carried out within the extended limits of serious theatre, surely helped to pave the way, if indirectly, for such works as Brecht's *Galileo*, Shaw's *Saint Joan* or Arthur Miller's *Crucible*.

If Hugo and his contemporaries had been able to survey the drama of our own age, there are some plays—*Le Maître de Santiago*, *Caligula*, *Le Diable et le bon Dieu*—that they would have had no difficulty in recognizing as the products of an aesthetic close to their own. In the work of dramatists like Brecht or Anouilh, perhaps, they would have acknowledged a fundamentally similar outlook, despite the techniques that mark their plays as products of the twentieth century. But the inconsequentiality, the self-indulgence, the lack of rigorous artistic control, that characterize much of the *avant-garde* theatre of today: these they would reject as utterly foreign to their notion of literary drama as an art-form. There is no lack of stimulating new ideas in today's theatre, but one thing remains in short supply: the well-written play. The opposite of the 'well-made play' is all too often, today, a play that is badly thrown together; and the best examples of Romantic drama can still provide a useful lesson in effective dramatic craftsmanship, in the imaginative use of language, and in the means of moving or arousing the spectator without being subject to the vagaries of ephemeral fashion.

Notes to Chapter Thirteen

1. See p. 360.
2. *Op. cit.*, p. 353.
3. "To the question 'What is a Tragedy?' a preliminary answer can at once be given, on the model of W. P. Ker's answer to the question 'What is a ballad?': 'A Tragedy is *Œdipus Rex*, *Antigone*, *Hamlet*, *King Lear* or *Phèdre*'. And at once we can add that such a list shows that 'Tragedy' is a term of honour and more than a description of a certain literary 'kind'. In giving such a list we are naming masterpieces of art. To speak of 'great tragedy' is really a tautology. Tragedy that is not 'great' is not tragedy, but 'failed tragedy' ", *Religion and Tragedy*, London, 1971, p. 17.
4. *Préface de Cromwell*, ed. cit., p. 255.
5. *Op. cit.*, p. 10.

Appendix

(i) A chronological list of plays, 1827–52

COMPLETE with regard to Hugo, Vigny and Musset, this list includes that part of Dumas's output during the period which falls within a fairly broad definition of 'Romantic drama', except for a few plays written in collaboration, and which are not included in the playwright's collected works. Other plays identifiable as Romantic dramas are included, but as a general rule, plays belonging to the genres of *tragédie*, *comédie* (including *comédie-vaudeville*, etc.), *mélodrame*, *opéra*, *opéra-comique* and *ballet* have been omitted, unless they have been discussed in this volume. The date given in each instance is that of first performance, in the case of plays performed; otherwise, that of publication or of composition.

The following abbreviations have been used: a. = act; j. = *journée*; p. = prose; perf. = performed; prol. = prologue; pub. = published; trans. = translated; v. = verse; AC = Ambigu-Comique; FD = Folies-Dramatiques; Gai = Gaîté; Gym = Gymnase; Nou = Nouveautés; OC = Opéra-Comique; Od = Odéon; Op = Opéra; Pan = Panthéon; PSM = Porte-Saint-Martin; Ren = Renaissance; TF = Théâtre-Français; TH = Théâtre-Historique; TN = Théâtre-National; Var = Variétés; Vau = Vaudeville; Ven = Ventadour.

1. 1827 (pub.) *Cromwell.* Hugo. 5a, v. Not perf.
2. 1828, Feb. *Amy Robsart.* (Hugo and) Foucher. 5a, p. Od.
3. 1828, Apr. *Roméo et Juliette.* Vigny and Deschamps (trans. from Shakespeare). 5a, v. Accepted TF, not perf.
4. 1828 *Christine.* Dumas. Accepted TF, not perf.
5. 1829, Feb. *Henri III et sa cour.* Dumas. 5a, p. TF.
6. 1829, May *Marino Faliero.* Delavigne. 5a, v. PSM.
7. 1829, Jun. *Le Carrosse du Saint-Sacrement.* Mérimée. 1a, p.
    (pub.) (Perf. TF Mar. 1850.)
8. 1829, Jul. *Marion de Lorme.* Hugo. Accepted TF, not perf.
9. 1829, Oct. *Le More de Venise.* Vigny (trans. from Shakespeare). 5a, v. TF.

10. 1830, Feb.   *Hernani.* Hugo. 5a, v. TF.
— 1830, Mar.   *Christine.* Dumas. 5a, v. Od. (See no. 4 above.)
11. 1830   *La Quittance du diable.* Musset. 1a, p. Accepted Nou, not perf.
12. 1830, Dec.   *La Nuit vénitienne.* Musset. 1a, p. Od.
13. 1831, Jan.   *Napoléon Bonaparte.* Dumas. 6a, p. Od.
14. 1831, May   *Antony.* Dumas. 5a, p. PSM.
15. 1831, Jun.   *La Maréchale d'Ancre.* Vigny. 5a, p. Od.
— 1831, Aug.   *Marion de Lorme.* Hugo. 5a, v. PSM (See no. 8 above.)
16. 1831, Oct.   *Charles VII chez ses grands vassaux.* Dumas. 5a, v. Od.
17. 1831, Nov.   *La Reine d'Espagne.* Latouche. 5a, p. TF.
18. 1831, Dec.   *Richard Darlington.* Dumas. 3a + prol., p. PSM.
19. 1832, Feb.   *Teresa.* Dumas. 5a, p. Ven.
20. 1832, Apr.   *Le Mari de la veuve.* Dumas. 1a, p. TF.
21. 1832, May   *La Tour de Nesle.* Dumas (and Gaillardet). 5a, p. PSM.
22. 1832, Nov.   *Le Roi s'amuse.* Hugo. 5a, v. TF.
23. 1833, Feb.   *Lucrèce Borgia.* Hugo. 3a, p. PSM.
24. 1833, Apr.   *André del Sarto.* Musset. 3a, p. (Perf. TF Nov.
    (pub.)   1848.)
25. 1833, May   *Quitte pour la peur.* Vigny. 1a, p. Op.
26. 1833, May   *Les Caprices de Marianne.* Musset. 2a, p. (Perf. TF
    (pub.)   Jun. 1851.)
27. 1833, Oct.   *Struensée.* Gaillardet. 5a, p. Gai.
28. 1833, Nov.   *Marie Tudor.* Hugo. 3j, p. PSM.
29. 1833, Dec.   *Angèle.* Dumas. 5a, p. PSM.
30. 1834, Jan.   *Catherine Howard.* Dumas. 5a, p. PSM.
31. 1834, Jan.   *Fantasio.* Musset. 2a, p. (Not perf. until 1866.)
    (pub.)
32. 1834, Jun.   *Robert Macaire.* Lemaître (and others). 4a, p. FD.
33. 1834, Jul.   *On ne badine pas avec l'amour.* Musset. 3a, p. (Not
    (pub.)   perf. until 1861.)
34. 1834 (pub.)   *Lorenzaccio.* Musset. 5a, p. (Not perf. until 1896).
35. 1835, Jan.   *Chatterton.* Vigny. 3a, p. TF.
36. 1835, Apr.   *Angelo.* Hugo. 3j, p. TF.
37. 1835, Aug.   *La Quenouille de Barberine.* Musset. 2a, p. (Not
    (pub.)   perf. until 1882.)
38. 1835, Nov.   *Le Chandelier.* Musset. 3a, p. (Perf. TH Aug.
    (pub.)   1848.)

39. 1836, Apr.   *Don Juan de Marana.* Dumas. 5a, p. PSM.
40. 1836, Jul.   *Il ne faut jurer de rien.* Musset. 3a, p. (Perf. TF
        (pub.)   Jun. 1848.)
41. 1836, Aug.   *Kean.* Dumas. 5a, p. Var.
42. 1837, Jun.   *Un Caprice.* Musset. 1a, p. (Perf. TF Nov. 1847.)
        (pub.)
43. 1837 (pub.)   *Faire sans dire.* Musset. 1a, p. Not perf.
44. 1837, Oct.   *Piquillo.* Dumas (and Nerval). 3a, p. and v. OC.
45. 1837, Dec.   *Caligula.* Dumas. 5a + prol., v. TF.
46. 1838, Oct.   *Paul Jones.* Dumas. 5a, p. Pan.
47. 1838, Nov.   *Ruy Blas.* Hugo. 5a, v. Ren.
48. 1839, Apr.   *L'Alchimiste.* Dumas (and Nerval). 5a, v. Ren.
49. 1839, Apr.   *Mademoiselle de Belle-Isle.* Dumas. 5a, p. TF.
50. 1839, Apr.   *Léo Burckart.* Nerval. 5a, p. PSM.
51. 1839   *L'École des ménages.* Balzac. 5a, p. (Pub. 1907;
                   not perf. until 1910.)
52. 1840, Mar.   *Vautrin.* Balzac. 5a, p. PSM.
53. 1840, Nov.   *Le Verre d'eau.* Scribe. 5a, p. TF.
54. 1841, Jun.   *Un Mariage sous Louis XV.* Dumas. 5a, p. TF.
55. 1842, Feb.   *Lorenzino.* Dumas. 5a, p. TF.
56. 1842, Mar.   *Les Ressources de Quinola.* Balzac. 5a, p. Od.
57. 1843, Mar.   *Les Burgraves.* Hugo. 'Trilogie en vers'. TF.
58. 1843, Apr.   *Lucrèce.* Ponsard. 5a, v. Od.
59. 1843, Jul.   *Les Demoiselles de Saint-Cyr.* Dumas. 5a, p. TF.
60. 1843, Sep.   *Paméla Giraud.* Balzac. 5a, p. Gai.
61. 1843, Nov.   *Louise Bernard.* Dumas. 5a, p. PSM.
62. 1843, Dec.   *Le Laird de Dumbiky.* Dumas. 5a, p. Od.
63. 1845, Apr.   *Virginie.* Latour de Saint-Ybars. 5a, v. TF.
64. 1845, Oct.   *Les Mousquetaires.* Dumas (and Maquet). 5a, p.
                   AC.
65. 1845, Nov.   *Il faut qu'une porte soit ouverte ou fermée.* Musset. 1a,
        (pub.)   p. (Perf. TF Apr. 1848.)
66. 1846, Apr.   *Une Fille du Régent.* Dumas. 4a, p. TF.
67. 1846, Nov.   *La Juive de Constantine.* Gautier. 5a, p. PSM.
68. 1846, Dec.   *Agnès de Méranie.* Ponsard. 5a, v. Od.
69. 1846 (pub.)   *La Fausse Conversion.* Gautier. 1a, p. (Not perf.
                   until 1899.)
70. 1847, Feb.   *La Reine Margot.* Dumas (and Maquet). 5a, p.
                   TH.
71. 1847, Jun.   *Intrigue et amour.* Dumas (trans. from Schiller).
                   5a, p. TH.
72. 1847, Aug.   *Le Chevalier de Maison-Rouge.* Dumas (and
                   Maquet). 5a, p. TH.

73. 1847, Dec. *Hamlet.* Dumas (adapted from Shakespeare). 5a, v. TH.
74. 1848, Feb. *Monte-Cristo.* Dumas (and Maquet). 10a, p. (2 evenings). TH.
75. 1848, Apr. *Les Girondins.* Dumas (and Maquet). 5a, p. TH.
76. 1848, May *La Marâtre.* Balzac. 5a, p. TH.
77. 1848, Jul. *Tragaldabas.* Vacquerie. 5a, v. PSM.
78. 1848, Aug. *Le Faiseur.* Balzac. 5a, p. Accepted TF, not perf.
79. 1848, Oct. *Catilina.* Dumas (and Maquet), 5a, p. TH.
80. 1849, Feb. *Louison.* Musset. 2a, v. TF.
81. 1849, Feb. *L'Habit vert.* Augier (and Musset). 1a, p. Var.
82. 1849, Feb. *La Jeunesse des Mousquetaires.* Dumas (and Maquet). 5a, p. TH.
83. 1849, Apr. *Adrienne Lecouvreur.* Scribe. 5a, p. TF.
84. 1849, May *On ne saurait penser à tout.* Musset. 1a, p. TF.
85. 1849, Jul. *Le Chevalier d'Harmental.* Dumas (and Maquet). 5a, p. TH.
86. 1849, Sep. *La Guerre des femmes.* Dumas (and Maquet). 5a, p. TH.
87. 1849, Nov. *La Vie de Bohème.* Murger (and Barrière). 5a, p. and v. Var.
88. 1849, Nov. *Le Comte Hermann.* Dumas. 5a, p. TH.
89. 1849, Dec. *Gabrielle.* Augier. 5a, v. TF.
90. 1850, Mar. *Charlotte Corday.* Ponsard. 5a, v. TF.
91. 1850, Mar. *Le Vingt-quatre février.* Dumas (adapted from Werner). 1a, p. Gai.
92. 1850, Mar. *Urbain Grandier.* Dumas (and Maquet). 5a, p. TH.
93. 1850, Apr. *Toussaint Louverture.* Lamartine. 5a, v. PSM.
94. 1850, Oct. (pub.) *Carmosine.* Musset. 3a, p. (Not perf. until 1865.)
95. 1851, Apr. *Le Comte de Morcerf* (*Monte-Cristo,* Part III). Dumas (and Maquet). 5a, p. AC.
96. 1851, Apr. *La Barrière de Clichy.* Dumas. 5a, p. TN.
97. 1851, May *Villefort* (*Monte-Cristo,* Part IV). Dumas (and Maquet). 5a, p. AC.
98. 1851, Aug. *Mercadet.* Dennery (adapted from Balzac, no. 78). 3a, p. Gym.
99. 1851, Oct. *Bettine.* Musset. 1a, p. Gym.
100. 1851, Dec. *L'Imagier de Harlem.* Nerval. 5a, p. and v. PSM.
101. 1851, Dec. *Le Vampire.* Dumas (and Maquet). 5a, p. AC.
102. 1852, Feb. *La Dame aux camélias.* Dumas *fils.* 5a, p. Vau.

(ii) Roles created by the leading actors, 1827–52
(The numbers indicate the titles of plays according to the *Chronological List*, above.)

(a) *Men*
Arnault: Monte-Cristo (95, 97); Lord Ruthwen (101).
Auguste: Sir Hugh Robsart (2); Nangis (8); Jeune Vénitien (12); Marquis da Silva (18); Orsini *and* Marigny (21); Oloferno (23); Lord Clinton (28); Sir John Scott (30); Don Sanchez (39); Claudius (45).
Barré: Godard (76).
Beauvallet: Saltabadil (22); Angelo (36); Aquila (45); Lorenzino (55); Job (57).
Bocage: Didier (8); Antony (14); Delaunay (19); Buridan (21); Le Duc (25); Alfred (29); Don Juan (39); Junius Brutus (58); Philippe-Auguste (68).
Boileau: D'Alençon (70); Premier Fossoyeur (73); Jacopo (74); Un Juge d'instruction (76); Caton (79); Lord de Winter (82); Brigand (85); Lenet (86); Napoléon (96).
Brindeau: Clavaroche (38); Valentin (40); Chavigny (42); Le Comte (65); Le Duc (80).
Chéri: Saverny (8); Eugène d'Hervilly (14); Maffio (23); Le Podestat (48); Le Président (71).
Chilly: Comte Magnus (4); Montglat (15); Secrétaire d'État (18); Louis X (21); Jeppo (23); Un Juif (28); Jules Raymond (29); Don Luis de Sandoval (39); Mordaunt (64); Villefort (97).
Delafosse: Descartes (4); Bussy d'Amboise (5); Razetta (12); Fiesque (15); Charles VII (16); Mawbray (18); Philippe d'Aulnay (21); Alphonse d'Este (23); Fabiani (28); Henri VIII (30); Don José (39).
Delaistre: Oxenstiern (4); Grimm (12); Vitry (15); Énéas Dulverton (28); Sussex (30).
Delannoy: Georges Duval (102).
Delaunay: Fortunio (38).
Doligny: Flibbertigibbet (2); Luynes (15); Tompson (18).
Édouard: Olivier Delaunay (14).
Fechter: Comte de Montlouis (66); César (79); Armand Duval (102).
Firmin: Saint-Mégrin (5); Hernani (10); Chéréa (45); Duc de Richelieu (49); Comte de Candale (54); Duc Alexandre (55); Roger (59).
Geffroy: Ludovico (9); Don Garcie *and* Don Pèdre (10); M. de Pienne (22); André del Sarto (24); Chatterton (35); Rodolfo

(36); Philippe Strozzi (55); Otbert (57); Le Régent (66); Marat (90); Stéfani (99).

Geoffroy: Mercadet (98).

Got: Guillaume (38); L'Abbé (40); Germain (84).

Grailly: Henri de Verneuil (61); Mohammed ben Aïssa (67).

Guiaud: Père Teutemberg (17); John Bell (35).

Guyon: Fra Léonardo (55); Magnus (57).

Jemma: Montsorel (52); Salvador (93).

Joanny: Duc de Guise (5); Othello (9); Don Ruy Gomez (10); Almeido (17); Saint-Vallier (22); Le Quaker (35).

Lacressonnière: Charles I (64); La Mole (70); Chevalier de Maison-Rouge (72); Villefort (74); Ferdinand Marcandal (76); Clinias (79).

Laferrière: Arthur (19); Maurice (72); Buckingham (82); Chevalier d'Harmental (85); Karl de Florsheim (88); Victor (96).

Lafontaine: Baron de Steinberg (99).

Lemaître (Frédérick): Napoléon (13); Concini (15); Richard Darlington (18); Gennaro (23); Robert Macaire (32); Kean (41); Ruy Blas (47); Fasio (48); Vautrin (52); Tragaldabas (77); Toussaint Louverture (93).

Ligier: Sentinelli (4); Borgia (15); Savoisy (16); Triboulet (22); Caligula (45); Michèle (55); Barberousse (57).

Lockroy: Dudley (2); Monaldeschi (4); D'Eysenach (12); L'Espion (13); Yaqoub (16); Gaultier d'Aulnoy (21); Gilbert (28); Henri Müller (29); Ethelwood (30); Chevalier d'Aubigny (49).

Lyonnet: Comte de Morcerf (95); D'Avrigny (97).

Maillart: Cordiani (24); Le Marquis (84); Stéphane (89).

Marius: Le Père Antoine (93).

Mauzin: Don Salluste (47); Chiffinch (62).

Mélingue: Le Mauvais Ange (39); Léo Burckart (50); D'Artagnan (64, 82); Henri de Navarre (70); Ferdinand (71); Lorin (72); Edmond Dantès (74); Catilina (79); Baron de Canolles (86); Comte Hermann (88); Urbain Grandier (92); Satan (100).

Menjaud: Roderigo (9); Medina-Sidonia (17); Léon (20); Caius Lepidus (45); Commandeur de Valclos (54).

Michelot: Henri III (5); Don Carlos (10).

Monrose: Charles II (17); Vertpré (20); Quinola (56); Macallan (62).

Monval: Pierquin (98).

Périer: Iago (9); Chevalier de Monville (17); François I (22).

Provost: Varney (2); L'Angely (8); Savoisy (21); Gubetta (23); Tronchin (25); Simon Renard (28); Exécuteur (30); Homodei (36); Van Buck (40).

Raucourt: François Cadet (52); Antoine Bernard (61); Nathan (67).
Régnier: Berthaud (80); Julien (89).
Rouvière: Hamlet (73); Dr. Fritz Sturler (88); Maurizio (92).
Saint-Firmin: Don César (47).
Samson: Don Ricardo (10); Clément Marot (22); Maître André (38); Tamponet (89).
Villot: Paul Jones (46).
Volnys: Le Baron (84).
Walter: Duc de Bellegarde (8); Colonel d'Hervey (14); Dr. Grey (18).

(b) *Women*

Allan-Despréaux (Mme): Jacqueline (38); Mme de Léry (42); La Marquise (65); La Comtesse (84); Adrienne (89).
Anaïs (Mlle): Amy Robsart (2); Doña Paquita (17); Pauline (20); Blanche (22); Marton (54); Lisette [Louison] (80).
Beauchêne (Atala): Anna Damby (41); La Reine (47); La Maddalena (48); Mme de Sauve (70); Geneviève (72); Anne d'Autriche (82); Duchesse du Maine (85).
Béranger (Mme): Laurette (12).
Brohan (Augustine): La Périchole (7).
Brohan (Madeleine): Marianne (26).
Chéri (Anna): Virginie (98).
Chéri (Rose): Bettine (99).
Colon (Jenny): Silvia (44).
Doche (Eugénie): Marguerite Gautier (102).
Dorval (Marie): Éléna (6); Marion (8); Adèle (14); La Duchesse (25); Kitty Bell (35); Catarina (36); Lucrèce (58); Agnès (68).
Doze (Mlle): Luisa (55).
Drouet (Juliette): Princesse Negroni (23); Jane (28).
Essler (Jane): Hélène (101).
Félix (Lia): Adrienne (93).
Ferrier (Ida): Amélie (19); [Jane (28)]; Angèle (29); Catherine Howard (30); Le Bon Ange *and* Sœur Marthe (39); Stella (45); Francesca (48); Duchesse de Montsorel (52).
George (Mlle): Christine (4); La Maréchale d'Ancre (15); Bérengère (16); Marguerite (21); Lucrèce Borgia (23); Marie Tudor (28).
Grave (Mlle): Herminie (61); Léa (67).
Guyon (Mme): Henriette de France (64).
Jouve (Hortense): Madeleine Turquenne (64); Artémise (72); Gringole (74); Fulvie (79); Ravanne (85); Daniel (92).
Judith (Mlle): Mathilde (52); La Duchesse (80); Charlotte Corday (90).

Lacressonnière (Mme): Mercédès (74); Comtesse de Grandchamp (76); Marcia (79).

Luther (Amédine): Cécile (40).

Maillet (Mlle): Pauline (76).

Mante (Mlle): Baronne de Mantes (40).

Mars (Mlle): Catherine de Guise (5); Desdémona (9); Doña Sol (10); Mme de Vertpré (20); La Tisbe (36); Mlle de Belle-Isle (49).

Mélanie (Mlle): Mme de Camps (14); Ernestine (29); Mme Mercadet (98).

Mélingue (Mme): Guanhumara (57); Hélène (66); La Maréchale (80).

Moreau-Sainti (Mme): Teresa (19).

Nathalie (Mme): Gabrielle (89).

Noblet (Louise): Paula (4); Isabella (15); Agnès Sorel (16); Jenny (18); Messaline (45).

Paul (Zélie): Mme de Lacy (14); Carolina da Silva (18).

Pauline (Mlle): Éléna de Koefeld (41).

Périer (Mme): Marguerite (70).

Person (Mme): Catherine de Médicis (70); Louise Miller (71); Ophélie (73); La Carconte (74); Aurélia (79); Milady de Winter (82); Vicomtesse de Cambes (86); Marie de Stauffenbach (88); Jeanne de Laubardemont (92).

Plessey (Mlle): Comtesse de Candale (54); Charlotte (59).

Rachel (Mlle): Virginie (63).

Rey (Mme): Mme de Nevers (70); Charinus (79); Mme Bonacieux (82); Clarisse *and* Bathilde (85); Nanon (86); Ursule de Sablé (92).

Volnais (Mlle): Isaac, fils de Toussaint (93).

Bibliography

(The publisher's name is given only in those cases in which a publication is undated.

The following abbreviations are used in referring to periodicals cited more than once: *E.C.* = *Esprit Créateur; Eur.* = *Europe; F.S.* = *French Studies; M.L.R.* = *Modern Language Review; R.H.L.F.* = *Revue d'Histoire Littéraire de la France; S.V.E.C.* = *Studies on Voltaire and the Eighteenth Century.*)

A. *Modern Editions of eighteenth- and nineteenth-century texts*
  (*i*) *The Pre-Romantic Period*
D'Argenson, *Notices sur les œuvres de théâtre*, ed. H. Lagrave (*S.V.E.C.*, XLII–XLIII, Geneva, 1966).
Beaumarchais, *Théâtre; lettres relatives à son théâtre*, ed. M. Allem, Paris, 1934.
Constant, *Wallstein, tragédie en cinq actes et en vers, précédée de quelques réflexions sur le théâtre allemand*, ed. J. R. Derré, Paris, 1965.
Crébillon *père*, *Théâtre complet*, ed. A. Vitu, Paris (Garnier), n.d.
Diderot, *Le Fils naturel*, ed. V. Tasca, Bordeaux, 1965.
Diderot, *Writings on the Theatre*, ed. F. C. Green, Cambridge, 1936.
La Chaussée, *Mélanide*, ed. W. D. Howarth, Brighton, 1973.
Mercier, *Le Déserteur*, ed. S. Davies, Exeter, 1974.
Pixérécourt, *Cœlina*, ed. N. Perry, Exeter, 1972.
Sedaine, *Le Philosophe sans le savoir*, ed. E. Feuillâtre, Paris (Larousse), n.d.
Staël, Mme de, *De la littérature considérée dans ses rapports avec les institutions sociales*, ed. P. Van Tieghem, 2 vols., Paris, 1959.
Staël, Mme de, *De l'Allemagne*, ed. H. W. Eve, Oxford, 1906.
Voltaire, *Lettres philosophiques*, ed. G. Lanson, 2 vols., Paris, 1924.
Voltaire, *La Mort de César*, ed. A. M. Rousseau, Paris, 1964.
Voltaire, *Zaïre*, ed. J. Guntzberger, Paris (Larousse), n.d.

  (*ii*) *The Romantic Period*
Balzac, *Lettres à Madame Hanska*, ed. R. Pierrot, Paris, 1967–.
Balzac, *Théâtre*, ed. R. Guise, 3 vols., Paris, 1969–71.
Dumas *père*, *Mes Mémoires*, ed. P. Josserand, 5 vols., Paris, 1954–68.

Dumas *père*, *Antony*, ed. M. Baudin, New York, 1929.

Dumas *père*, *Kean* in Sartre, *Kean*, ed. D. Bradby, London, 1973.

Gautier, *Histoire du romantisme*, Paris (Librairie des Bibliophiles), n.d.

Gautier, *Les Maîtres du théâtre français*, ed. A. Britsch, Paris, 1929.

Hugo, *Théâtre complet*, ed. J. J. Thierry and J. Mélèse, 2 vols., Paris, 1963.

Hugo, *Préface de Cromwell*, ed. M. Souriau, Paris, 1897.
ed. E. Wahl, Oxford, 1909.

Hugo, *Cromwell*, ed. A. Ubersfeld, Paris, 1968.

Hugo, *Hernani*, ed. H. F. Collins, London, 1968.

Hugo, *Marie Tudor*, ed. R. E. Palmer, London, 1961.

Hugo, *Ruy Blas*, ed. H. F. Collins, London, 1966.
ed. A. Ubersfeld, Vol. I, Besançon and Paris, 1971.

Lamartine, *Toussaint Louverture* in *Œuvres poétiques complètes*, ed. M. F. Guyard, Paris, 1963.

Latouche, *La Reine d'Espagne*, ed. F. Ségu, Paris, 1928.

Lemaître (and others), *L'Auberge des Adrets* and *Robert Macaire*, ed. C. Cœuré, Grenoble, 1966.

Mérimée, *Théâtre de Clara Gazul*, ed. P. Martino, Paris, 1929.

Mérimée, *La Jaquerie, suivie de La Famille de Carvajal*, ed. P. Jourda, Paris, 1931.

Musset, *Théâtre complet*, ed. P. Van Tieghem and J. Sarment, Paris, 1948.

Musset, *Théâtre*, ed. M. Allem, Paris, 1958.

Musset, *Lorenzaccio* in *La Genèse de Lorenzaccio*, ed. P. Dimoff, Paris, 1936.

Musset, *Lorenzaccio* and *Un Caprice*, ed. Marjorie Shaw, London, 1963.

Musset, *Correspondance*, ed. L. Séché, Paris, 1907.

Nerval, *Poésie et théâtre*, ed. H. Clouard, Paris, 1928.

Nerval, *Léo Burckart* in *Le Drame romantique*, ed. J. Richer, Paris, 1957.

Stendhal, *Racine et Shakespeare*, ed. H. Martineau, Paris, 1928.

Vigny, *Théâtre complet*, ed. A. Dorchain, 2 vols., Paris, 1929.

Vigny, *Chatterton*, ed. E. Lauvrière, Oxford, 1908.
ed. L. Petroni, Bologna, 1962.

Vigny, *Stello* in *Le More de Venise, Journal d'un poète, Morceaux divers*, Paris (Nelson), n.d.

(iii) *The Post-Romantic Period*

Augier, *Théâtre complet*, 7 vols., Paris, 1929.

Dumas *fils*, *La Dame aux camélias*, ed. R. J. B. Clark, London, 1972.

Rostand, *Œuvres complètes*, 6 vols., Paris, 1910–25.

Rostand, *Cyrano de Bergerac*, ed. H. Ashton, Oxford, 1942.
Sardou, *Théâtre complet*, 15 vols., Paris, 1934–61.
Villiers, *Axël*, ed. P. Mariel, Paris, 1960.
Villiers, *Le Prétendant*, ed. P. G. Castex and A. W. Raitt, Paris, 1965.

B. *Historical and Critical Works*
   (i) *The Pre-Romantic Period*
Ault, H. C., 'Charles IX ou l'École des rois, tragédie nationale', *M.L.R.*, XLVIII, 1953, pp. 398–406.
Besterman, T., *Voltaire on Shakespeare (S.V.E.C.*, LIV), Geneva, 1967.
Bochner, J., 'Shakespeare en France, 1733–1830', *Revue de Littérature Comparée*, XXXIX, 1965, pp. 44–65.
Borgerhoff, J. L., *Le Théâtre anglais à Paris sous la Restauration*, Paris, 1912.
Bray, R., *Chronologie du romantisme, 1804–30*, Paris, 1932.
Breitholtz, L., *Le Théâtre historique en France jusqu'à la Révolution*, Uppsala, 1952.
Brenner, C. D., *Le Développement du proverbe dramatique en France et sa vogue au xviiie siècle*, Berkeley, 1937.
Brenner, C. D., *L'Histoire nationale dans la tragédie française du xviiie siècle*, Berkeley, 1929.
Brun, A., 'Aux origines de la prose dramatique: le style haletant', *Mélanges de linguistique française offerts à Ch.Bruneau*, Geneva, 1954, pp. 41–47.
Carlson, M. *The Theatre of the French Revolution*, Ithaca (N.Y.), 1966.
Collins, H. F., *Talma: A Biography of an actor*, London, 1964.
Des Granges, C. M., *Geoffroy et la critique dramatique*, Paris, 1897.
Donnard, J. H., *Le Théâtre de Carmontelle*, Paris, 1967.
Duchet, C., 'La Saint-Barthélemy: de la 'scène historique' au 'drame romantique', *R.H.L.F.*, LXXIII, 1973, pp. 845–851.
Fontaine, L., *Le Théâtre et la philosophie au xviiie siècle*, Versailles, 1878.
Gaiffe, F., *Le Drame en France au xviiie siècle*, Paris, 1910.
Gaudon, J., 'Talma et ses auteurs', *Modern Miscellany presented to E. Vinaver*, Manchester, 1969, pp. 85–96.
Ginisty, P., *Le Mélodrame*, Paris, 1910.
Green, F. C., *Minuet: A Critical Survey of French and English literary ideas in the eighteenth century*, London, 1935.
Guex, J., *Le Théâtre et la société française de 1815 à 1848*, Vevey, 1900.
Hartog, W. G., *Guilbert de Pixérécourt, sa vie, son mélodrame, sa technique et son influence*, Paris, 1913.
Hérissay, J., *Le Monde des théâtres pendant la Révolution, 1789–1800*, Paris, 1922.

Lacey, A., *Guilbert de Pixérécourt and the French Romantic Drama*, Toronto, 1928.

Lancaster, H. C., *French Tragedy in the time of Louis XV and Voltaire*, *1715–1774*, Baltimore, 1950.

Lanson, G., *Nivelle de La Chaussée et la comédie larmoyante*, Paris, 1887.

Lieby, A., *Étude sur le théâtre de M.-J. Chénier*, Paris, 1901.

Lunel, E., *Le Théâtre et la Révolution*, Paris, 1910.

Marsan, J., 'Le Mélodrame et Guilbert de Pixérécourt', *R.H.L.F.*, VII, 1900, pp. 196–220.

Marsan, J., 'Le Théâtre historique et le romantisme', *R.H.L.F.*, XVII, 1910, pp. 1–33.

Pikulik, L., *Bürgerliches Trauerspiel und Empfindsamkeit*, Cologne, 1966.

Pitou, A., 'Les Origines du mélodrame français à la fin du xviiie siècle', *R.H.L.F.*, XVIII, 1911, pp. 256–296.

Pougin, A., *La Comédie-Française et la Révolution*, Paris, 1902.

Pugh, A. R., 'Beaumarchais, the *drame bourgeois* and the *pièce bien faite*', *M.L.R.*, LXI, 1966, pp. 416–421.

Ridgway, R. S., *La Propagande philosophique dans les tragédies de Voltaire* (*S.V.E.C.*, XV), Geneva, 1961.

Rivoire, J. A., *Le Patriotisme dans le théâtre sérieux de la Révolution*, Paris, 1950.

Trahard, P., *Les Maîtres de la sensibilité française au xviiie siècle*, 4 vols., Paris, 1931–33.

Trahard, P., *La Sensibilité révolutionnaire* (*1789–94*), Paris, 1936.

Treille, M., *Le Conflit dramatique en France de 1823 à 1830, d'après les journaux et les revues du temps*, Paris, 1929.

Trotain, M., *Les Scènes historiques : étude du théâtre livresque à la veille du drame romantique*, Paris, 1923.

Vauthier, G., *Essai sur la vie et les œuvres de N. Lemercier*, Toulouse, 1886.

Wierlacher, A., *Das bürgerliche Drama, seine theoretische Begründung im achtzehnten Jahrhundert*, Munich, 1968.

Williams, M. A., 'A Precursor of Hernani', *F.S.*, XIII, 1959, pp. 18–25.

(ii) *The Romantic Period*

Affron, C., *A Stage for poets : Studies in the theatre of Hugo and Musset*, Princeton (N.J.), 1971.

Allevy, M. A., *La Mise en scène en France dans la première moitié du xixe siècle*, Paris, 1938.

Baldick, R. A. E., *The Life and times of Frédérick Lemaître*, London, 1959.

Baschet, R., *Du Romantisme au Second Empire: Mérimée (1803–70)*, Paris, 1958.

Bassan, F., 'Dumas père et le drame romantique', *E.C.*, V, 1965, pp. 174–178.

Bellessort, A., *Victor Hugo: essai sur son œuvre*, Paris, 1951.

Berret, P., *Victor Hugo*, Paris (Garnier), n.d.

Bertal, G., *Auguste Vacquerie, sa vie et son œuvre*, Paris, 1889.

Biré, E., *Victor Hugo après 1830*, 2 vols., Paris, 1891.

Biré, E., *Victor Hugo avant 1830*, Paris, 1902.

Book-Senninger, C., *Théophile Gautier, auteur dramatique*, Paris, 1972.

Bowman, F. P., 'Notes towards the definition of Romantic theatre', *E.C.*, V, 1965, pp. 121–130.

Braun, S. D., *The 'Courtisane' in the French Theatre from Hugo to Becque, 1831–1885*, Baltimore, 1947.

Bromfield, J., *De Lorenzino de Médicis à Lorenzaccio*, Paris, 1972.

Brun, A., *Deux Proses de théâtre*, Gap, 1954.

Butor, M., 'Le Théâtre de V. Hugo', *Nouvelle Revue Française*, XXIV, 1964, pp. 862–878; 1073–1081; XXV, 1965, 105–113.

Callen, A., 'The Place of *Lorenzaccio* in Musset's theatre', *Forum for Modern Language Studies*, V, 1969, pp. 225–231.

Carlson, M., *The French Stage in the Nineteenth Century*, Metuchen (N.J.), 1972.

Cassagne, A., *La Théorie de l'art pour l'art en France*, Paris, 1906.

Chahine, S., *La Dramaturgie de V. Hugo (1816–1843)*, Paris, 1971.

Chevalley, S., 'Dumas et la Comédie-Française', *Eur.*, 490–491, 1970, pp. 101–107.

Chevalley, S. and Bassan, F., *Alexandre Dumas père et la Comédie-Française*, Paris, 1972.

Dale, R. C., '*Chatterton* is the essential Romantic drama', *E.C.*, V, 1965, pp. 131–137.

Dédéyan, C., *Gérard de Nerval et l'Allemagne*, 3 vols., Paris, 1957–59.

Denommé, R. T., 'The Motif of the *poète maudit* in Musset's *Lorenzaccio*', *E.C.*, V, 1965, pp. 138–146.

Descotes, M., *Le Drame romantique et ses grands créateurs*, Paris (P.U.F.), n.d.

Doumic, R., 'L'Œuvre du romantisme au théâtre', *Revue des Deux Mondes*, VIII, 1902, pp. 923–935.

Draper, F. W. M., *The Rise and Fall of French Romantic Drama, with special reference to the influence of Shakespeare, Scott and Byron*, London, 1923.

El Nouty, H., 'Théâtre et anti-théâtre au xixe siècle', *Publications of the Modern Language Association of America*, LXXIX, 1964, pp. 604–612.

England, S. L., 'The Characteristics of French comedy during the period 1815–48', *R.H.L.F.*, XLI, 1934, pp. 185–197, 362–374.

England, S. L., 'Bibliographie de pièces de théâtre parues en France de 1815 à 1848. Avec indication des pièces ayant un caractère social ou une tendance sociale', *R.H.L.F.*, XLI, 1934, pp. 573–604; XLII, 1935, pp. 117–126, 251–262, 408–415, 569–592.

Estève, E., *Alfred de Vigny, sa pensée et son art*, Paris, 1923.

Evans, D. O., *Le Drame moderne à l'époque romantique, 1827–1850*, Paris, 1923.

Evans, D. O., *Social Romanticism in France, 1830–1848*, Oxford, 1951.

Evans, D. O., *Le Théâtre pendant la période romantique (1827–48)*, Paris, 1925.

Fargher, R., 'Victor Hugo's First Melodrama', *Balzac and the Nineteenth Century: Studies presented to H. J. Hunt*, Leicester, 1972, pp. 297–310.

Gaudon, J., *Victor Hugo dramaturge*, Paris, 1955.

Ginisty, P., *Le Théâtre romantique*, Paris, 1922.

Glachant, P. and Glachant, V., *Le Théâtre de V. Hugo: les drames en prose*, Paris, 1903.

Glachant, P. and Glachant, V., *Le Théâtre de V. Hugo: les drames en vers*, Paris, 1902.

Gochberg, H. S., *Stage of Dreams: the dramatic art of A. de Musset*, Geneva, 1967.

Grimsley, R., 'The Character of Lorenzaccio', *F.S.*, XI, 1957, pp. 16–27.

Haig, S., 'Vigny and *Othello*', *Yale French Studies*, XXXIII, 1964, pp. 53–64.

Hunt, H. J., *Le Socialisme et le romantisme en France*, Oxford, 1935.

Janin, J., *Rachel et la tragédie*, Paris, 1859.

Kushner, E., 'Histoire et théâtre chez Vigny', *E.C.*, V, 1965, pp. 147–161.

Lacretelle, J. de (and others), *Victor Hugo*, Paris, 1967.

Lafoscade, L., *Le Théâtre d'A. de Musset*, Paris, 1901.

Lancaster, H. C., 'The Genesis of *Ruy Blas*', *Modern Philology*, XIV, 1917, pp. 129–134.

Lanson, G., 'Victor Hugo et Angélica Kauffman', *R.H.L.F.*, XXII, 1915, pp. 392–401.

Latreille, C., *La Fin du théâtre romantique et François Ponsard*, Paris, 1899.

Lebois, A., *Vues sur le théâtre de Musset*, Paris, 1966.

Lefebvre, H., *Alfred de Musset dramaturge*, Paris, 1955.

Lote, G., *En préface à Hernani*, Paris, 1930.

Maigron, L., *Le Romantisme et les mœurs*, Paris, 1910.

Masson, B., *Musset et le théâtre intérieur: nouvelles recherches sur 'Lorenzaccio'*, Paris, 1974.

Milatchitch, D. Z., *Le Théâtre de Honoré de Balzac*, Paris, 1930.

Milatchitch, D. Z., *Le Théâtre inédit de Honoré de Balzac*, Paris, 1930.

Nebout, P., *Le Drame romantique*, Paris, 1895.

Oliver, A. R., 'Romanticism and Opera', *Symposium*, XXIII, 1969, pp. 325–332.

Parigot, H., *Le Drame d'Alexandre Dumas: étude dramatique, sociale et littéraire*, Paris, 1899.

Paterson, H. T., *Poetic Genesis: Sébastien Mercier into Victor Hugo (S.V.E.C., XI)*, Geneva, 1960.

Raitt, A. W., *Prosper Mérimée*, London, 1970.

Richer, J., 'Nerval et ses deux *Léo Burckart*', *Mercure de France*, CCCVII, 1949, pp. 645–678.

Riffaterre, M., 'Un Exemple de comédie symboliste chez V. Hugo', *E.C.*, V, 1965, pp. 162–173.

Rigal, E., 'La Genèse d'un drame romantique: *Ruy Blas*', *R.H.L.F.*, XX, 1913, pp. 753–788.

Rudler, G., 'La Source de la scène des portraits dans *Hernani*'. *M.L.R.*, XIII, 1918, pp. 329–332.

Russell, O. W., *Étude historique et critique des Burgraves de V. Hugo*, Paris, 1962.

Sakellaridès, E., *Alfred de Vigny auteur dramatique*, Paris, 1902.

Schenck, E. M., *La Part de Charles Nodier dans la formation des idées romantiques de V. Hugo jusqu'à la Préface de Cromwell*, Paris, 1914.

Séché, A. and Bertaut, J., *La Passion romantique: Antony, Marion Delorme, Chatterton*, Paris, 1927.

Sessely, A., *L'Influence de Shakespeare sur A. de Vigny*, Berne, 1928.

Shaw, M., 'Les Proverbes dramatiques de Carmontelle, Leclercq et Alfred de Musset', *Revue des Sciences Humaines*, XIII, 1959, pp. 56–76.

Simon, G. M. S. C., *Histoire d'une collaboration: A. Dumas et A. Maquet*, Paris, 1919.

Sleumer, A., *Die Dramen Victor Hugos*, Berlin, 1901.

Smet, R. de, *Le Théâtre romantique*, Paris, 1929.

Tonge, F., *L'Art du dialogue dans les comédies en prose d'A. de Musset: étude de stylistique dramatique*, Paris, 1967.

Ubersfeld, A., 'Désordre et génie', *Eur.*, 490–491, 1970, pp. 107–118.

Ubersfeld, A., 'D'un Commandeur à l'autre, ou la Chanson de Gubetta', *Littérature*, IX, 1973, pp. 74–85.

Van Tieghem, P., *Musset, l'homme et l'œuvre*, Paris, 1944.

Wicks, C. B., ed., *The Parisian Stage, Part II (1816–30)*, Alabama, 1953.

Wicks, C. B. and Schweitzer, J. W., ed., *The Parisian Stage, Part III* (*1831–50*), Alabama, 1960.

(*iii*) *The Post-Romantic Period*

Antoine, A., *Mes Souvenirs sur le Théâtre-Libre*, Paris, 1922.

Bédier, J., *Discours de réception à l'Académie Française*, Paris, 1921.

Block, H. M., *Mallarmé and the Symbolist Drama*, Detroit, 1963.

Charpentier, J., *Théodore de Banville*, Paris, 1925.

Grieve, J. W., *L'Œuvre dramatique d'Edmond Rostand*, Paris, 1931.

Halls, W. D., *Maurice Maeterlinck: A Study of his Life and Thought*, Oxford, 1960.

Henderson, J. A., *The First Avant-garde (1887–1894): Sources of the Modern French Theatre*, London, 1971.

Knowles, D., *La Réaction idéaliste au théâtre depuis 1890*, Geneva, 1934.

Lamm, M., *Modern Drama*, Eng. trans., Oxford, 1952.

Magne, E., *Les Erreurs de documentation de Cyrano de Bergerac*, Paris, 1899.

Ripert, E., *Edmond Rostand, sa vie et son œuvre*, Paris, 1968.

Robichez, J., *Le Symbolisme au théâtre*, Paris, 1957.

Seillière, E., *La Morale de Dumas fils*, Paris, 1921.

Taylor, F. A., *The Theatre of A. Dumas fils*, Oxford, 1937.

Waxman, S. A., *Antoine and the Théâtre-Libre*, Cambridge (Mass.), 1926.

(*iv*) *General*

Auerbach, E., *Mimesis: the Representation of Reality in Western Literature*, Eng. trans., Princeton (N.J.), 1953.

Bailey, H. P., *Hamlet in France*, Geneva, 1964.

Brereton, G., *Principles of Tragedy*, London, 1968.

Camus, A., 'Sur l'avenir de la tragédie', *Théâtre, récits, nouvelles*, Paris, 1962, pp. 1699–1709.

Decugis, N. and Reymond, S., *Le Décor de théâtre en France du moyen âge à 1925*, Paris, 1953.

Descotes, M., *Le Public de théâtre et son histoire*, Paris, 1964.

Gardner, H., *Religion and Tragedy*, London, 1971.

Gide, A., *L'Évolution du théâtre*, ed. C. Wildman, Manchester, 1939.

Gouhier, H., 'Remarques sur le "théâtre historique"', *Revue d'Esthétique*, XIII, 1960, pp. 16–24.

Howarth, W. D., 'History in the theatre: the French and English traditions', *Trivium*, I, 1966, pp. 151–168.

Joannidès, A., *La Comédie-Française de 1680 à 1900*, Paris, 1921.

Leech, C., *Tragedy*, London, 1969.

Levitt, P. M., *A Structural Approach to the Analysis of Drama*, The Hague, 1971.

Lioure, M., *Le Drame de Diderot à Ionesco*, Paris, 1973.

Petit de Juleville, L., *Le Théâtre en France*, Paris, 1927.

Rahill, F., *The World of Melodrama*, University Park (Pa.), 1967.

Sarcey, F., *Quarante Ans de théâtre*, 8 vols., Paris, 1900–02.

Smith, J. L., *Melodrama*, London, 1973.

Steiner, G., *The Death of Tragedy*, London, 1963.

Thomson, P., *The Grotesque*, London, 1972.

Index

ELEPHANT BILL